About the Authors

DR. RALPH EARLE is president of the American Association for Marriage and Family Therapy, as well as Psychological Counseling Services, Ltd., and is an affiliate of Scottsdale Memorial, Scottsdale Camelback, St. Luke's, and Mesa Lutheran hospitals in Arizona. He is also a certified sex educator and therapist for the American Association of Sex Educators, Counselors and Therapists, and a diplomate in Marital and Sex Therapy—The American Board of Family Psychology.

DR. GREGORY CROW is a psychologist in private practice in Scottsdale, Arizona. He is affiliated with Scottsdale Memorial and Scottsdale Camelback hospitals, and is former program director at the Treatment Centers of America in Scottsdale, and of the intensive outpatient chemical dependency program of Psychological Counseling Services, Ltd.

"Psychologists Earle and Crow argue convincingly that sex addiction is a recognizable—and treatable—psychological disease. . . . *LONELY ALL THE TIME* is a compassionate, thorough book."

—*Kirkus Reviews*

"This excellent, jargon-free volume stands out for its clarity and comprehensiveness."

—*Publishers Weekly*

LONELY
ALL
THE
TIME

Recognizing,
Understanding
and
Overcoming
Sex Addiction,
for Addicts
and
Co-Dependents

Dr. Ralph Earle
AND
Dr. Gregory Crow
WITH
Kevin Osborn

This Book Is Produced by
The Philip Lief Group, Inc.

POCKET BOOKS
New York   London   Toronto   Sydney   Tokyo   Singapore

The Twelve Steps on pages 229–31 are reprinted and adapted with
permission of Alcoholics Anonymous World Services, Inc.

POCKET BOOKS, a division of Simon & Schuster Inc.
1230 Avenue of the Americas, New York, NY 10020

Library of Congress Cataloging in Publication Number 89-165379

ISBN: 0-671-66999-0

First Pocket Books trade paperback printing June 1990

10 9 8 7 6 5 4 3 2 1

POCKET and colophon are registered trademarks of
Simon & Schuster Inc.

Printed in the U.S.A.

To our parents,
for their unconditional love,
and to our family,
especially our spouses,
who refuse to be co-dependents.

The authors would like to acknowledge the following people for their generous contributions to this book: our patients; the staff of PCS, our professional family; Dr. Henry Reuss and Dr. Robert Hamilton; Philip Lief, Nancy Kalish and Cathy Hemming of The Philip Lief Group; and Susan Meltsner.

Contents

    The Deadly Potential of the Disease

    II   Sex Addiction Is a Family
         Disease
                                                       127

6   IS THERE A STRANGER IN THE HOUSE?   129
    Living with a Sex Addict

7   ADDICTED TO THE ADDICT: 149
    The Co-Dependent Personality

8   STUCK ON THE MERRY-GO-ROUND: 171
    Co-Dependent Roles and Reactions

9   NEW VICTIMS, NEW PLAYERS: 187
    The Children of Sex Addicts

    III   Recovering from Sex
          Addiction
                                                       205

    RST STEP: 207
    Out for Help

    E STEPS: 229
    iving for Both Sex Addicts and

    CT: 251
    Road to Recovery

    T: 271

CONTENTS

LONELY
ALL
THE
TIME

INTRODUCTION
How This Book
Can Help You

everal months ago, an attractive couple in their
fifties, tormented with concern for their adult son,
came into our offices seeking help. Tall, broad-
shouldered, and still handsome at fifty-three, Fred is a recovering alcoholic who now plays an active role in Arizona politics; his wife, Ginger, a
striking redhead and a devout Catholic, had raised their children almost
entirely on her own, because her husband's alcoholism had made him an
unreliable parent. Embarrassed, hurt, and confused, they found it impossible to comprehend how their son Matthew, who apparently shared their
deeply held religious convictions, could have been arrested for exhibitionism—not just once, but three times. "He's such a nice guy," Ginger
protested. "I just don't understand it."

At first, they both insisted, "Nothing like this had ever happened
before." However, when we questioned them, they remembered that
more than ten years earlier, their neighbors had accused Matthew, then
sixteen years old, of exposing himself. At the time, they had asked their
son about it, but when Matthew denied it, they immediately believed him
and never brought the subject up again. In the wake of his arrests,
however, Matthew had recently confessed to this and other teenage
episodes of exhibitionism.

A week later, we met Matthew for the first time. With his bronzed

1

skin, thick, curly black hair, and height—just over six feet—Matthew looked as if he belonged in a *GQ* or *Esquire* fashion layout. Although only twenty-seven years old, he had already used his good looks and surface charm to his advantage, becoming district sales manager for a high-tech corporation. To an outsider, Matthew had always appeared to embody an American success story. Yet his ability to concentrate on the job had deteriorated as he had found himself focusing on his exhibitionistic sexual obsession for from six to ten hours a day.

That was when Matthew, perhaps because of the fear of being identified by adult victims, had begun exhibiting himself to children. His wife, who had earlier shut her eyes to his compulsive sexual behavior, felt she could no longer expose their children to this risk. After his third arrest for exhibitionism, she had taken their three children and left him, moving out of state.

Finally forced to face the consequences of his sexual behavior—the loss of his family, alienation from his parents and siblings, the deterioration of his career, and the possibility of imprisonment—Matthew desperately wanted to change his life. Although his exhibitionism had caused him a great deal of hidden personal pain for years, Matthew had denied his problem and its destructive effects on himself and those around him until his entire world began to crumble.

Addicted to Sex?

Throughout our professional lives, we have worked with patients like Matthew, people who repeatedly engaged in sexual behavior that they felt totally powerless to control. But when we joined our areas of expertise—one of us specializes in marital, family, and sex therapy, the other in chemical dependency and the family—and formed our first therapy group for sex addicts just over six years ago, we had no idea how pervasive a problem it really is.

Today, the treatment of family addictions in general, and especially sex addiction, is the major focus of our work. We see both sex addicts and family members of sex addicts on an individual basis, as well as in couples and family therapy. In addition, we encourage these patients to join one of our ongoing therapy groups—one for sex addicts and a separate group for family members, especially spouses and partners. Our practice with these patients forms the basis for all of the material included in this book.

Who are sex addicts and what are they hoping to find—or escape— through their compulsive sexual behavior? Sex addicts are people who, desperately afraid of any truly intimate relationship, repeatedly and compulsively try to connect with others through highly impersonal, nonintimate behaviors: masturbation, empty affairs, frequent visits to prostitutes, voyeurism, and the like. Sex addicts—numbering in the millions, both men and women, young and old, of all races and religions— become mesmerized with the thrill and rush of adrenaline that they can

2

achieve only through their obsessive, highly ritualized patterns of sexual behavior.

Some sex addicts are straight, others gay. Some of those who are gay have repressed their homosexuality. For these people, recognizing and getting help for their sex addiction also means coming to terms with their true sexual orientation, and it can be quite painful. You will meet some of those people in the pages that follow. Through this book and the numerous case studies within, we want to reach out to the sex addict, whether gay or straight, and his and her family. For just as sex addiction cuts across ethnic and economic lines, so it cuts across sexual ones. All the information you will find in this book applies to *all* sex addicts, no matter what their sexual orientation.

Anyone who has ever had an orgasm recognizes the enormous power of sex. The incredible rush of sexual pleasure a person feels during orgasm is indeed intoxicating—and not just for the addict. But a person who is not addicted to sex, no matter how much or how often he or she enjoys sex, can have fun doing other things as well, while the sex addict frequently finds little gratification in anything else. For the sex addict, the quest to duplicate this sexual euphoria over and over becomes an obsession. Neglecting or sacrificing jobs, spouse and family, friends, and personal well-being, a sex addict ritualistically sets out to recapture a sexual high again and again.

How Much Is Too Much?

When talking about sexually criminal behavior—like Matthew's compulsive exhibitionism—most people would readily admit that anyone who behaves that way has a serious problem, even if they might balk at calling it an addiction. Indeed, not all exhibitionists are sex addicts. Like Matthew, however, some do feel *compelled* by their sexual ritual to exhibit themselves—no matter how much it betrays their own values and standards of acceptable behavior. And these exhibitionists can rightly be called sex addicts.

When talking about noncriminal sexuality, on the other hand— masturbation, say, or one-night stands, or pornography—it becomes much more difficult to single out problematic behavior. Because they define masturbation as a sin, for example, some people maintain that any masturbation at all poses a problem, while others just as vehemently maintain that no matter how much a person masturbates, it represents a problem only when people try to repress it. Confronted with this gray area, many of our patients want to know where to draw the line. "How much sex is too much sex?" they ask.

We answer that sex addiction does not depend so much on the amount of sexual activity involved, but on the attitude of the addict. Just as some people can have two or three drinks a night, yet still not have a problem with alcoholism, some people can have several affairs, or masturbate several times in a day, or pick up a series of prostitutes, without being addicted to any of these behaviors. No one can say, for example,

"Okay, masturbate more than three times in a day and that's it, you're addicted!" But for sex addicts who masturbate, masturbation has become the focus of their lives. These sex addicts obsessively think about sex almost all the time and compulsively masturbate whenever they get the chance.

Uncontrolled lust alters the behavior, thoughts, and feelings of sex addicts, gradually dominating every aspect of their lives. But the strength of their sexual obsession makes it impossible for sex addicts like Matthew to stop their self-destructive sexual behavior, despite the threat it represents to their families, their vocations, their physical and emotional health, and even their freedom. Indeed, their obsession with immediate sexual gratification effectively blinds them to the consequences of their actions, causing them to deny that their sexual behavior has any lasting effect on themselves or others.

What's in a Name?

If you have difficulty accepting the fact that some people can become addicted to certain sexual behaviors in the same way others can become addicted to alcohol or drugs, you are not alone. Many of our professional colleagues avoid using the term sex addiction, preferring to identify the disease as compulsive sexual behavior or to compartmentalize sex addicts according to their specific behaviors: exhibitionists, masturbators, voyeurs, and others. In fact, although both of us have dealt with patients' compulsive sexual behavior for as long as we have practiced as family psychologists, we only began treating these patients as sex addicts—specifically thinking of the disease in those terms ourselves—after learning of the work of Patrick Carnes. Following the lead of Sex Addicts Anonymous, a self-help group founded in Minneapolis by some Alcoholics Anonymous (AA) members who also suffered from sexual compulsiveness, Carnes had opened the first treatment center for sexual dependency in the late 1970s. On hearing of Carnes's findings on sex addiction, which would later become the basis for his ground-breaking study, *Out of the Shadows,* we began our own practice with sex addicts and their families.

Although we believe that the terms sex addiction and compulsive sexual behavior can be used interchangeably, at that time, we chose to use the term "sex addicts" to describe these patients, the term we still prefer to use today. The phrase directly points to the parallels between sex addiction and other addictions, especially the destructive impact not only on the addict but on his or her family as well. Even more important though, explicitly stating the addictive nature of the disease helps indicate the most effective course of treatment for sex addicts and their families.

Parallels Between Sex Addiction and Other Addictions

Sex addiction does mirror other addictions. Sex addicts use sex just as alcoholics use alcohol: as an anesthetizing drug that allows them to

4

escape from their lives, if only temporarily. Sex addicts fall into a pattern of turning to their self-destructive rituals whenever they feel any kind of stress. As dependence on ritualized sexual behavior increases, sex addicts lose all sense of self-esteem and life becomes a personal hell. Matthew described the emotional ramifications of his sex addiction, using words that recovering alcoholics and drug addicts would immediately grasp: despair, loneliness, frustration, guilt, anger, and self-hatred. Matthew himself felt that his sexual behavior involved horrible, weird, disgusting actions that made him loathe himself. Yet, despite these feelings, Matthew—in the grip of his own sexual compulsion—could not stop his behavior without help.

Like other addictions, sex addiction also exercises a powerful impact on those closest to the addict. Sex addiction is a family disease. Family members become as sick as the sex addict, denying the reality of the disease as vehemently as—or more vehemently than—the addict. Family life becomes centered around the sex addict's behavior, as spouse or partner, parents and siblings—and even children—become involved in the effort to protect the sex addict from the consequences of his or her disease, to keep the family secret hidden. And, we have discovered, if the family successfully keeps the disease underground, sex addiction—like other addictions—may be passed down from generation to generation, establishing a painful legacy for the sex addict's children and grandchildren.

This Book Can Help

Fortunately, the cycle of sex addiction can be halted. But first the problem must be recognized for what it is. Because the problem has only recently been identified, millions of Americans who suffer from sex addiction—and the millions more whose lives they touch—know little or nothing about the nature of the problem. And although the years lost to obsession and the families ruined by sexual compulsion have always been tragic, even more is at stake today. With the devastating epidemic of AIDS transforming every casual sexual encounter into a potentially fatal one, people will certainly die as a direct consequence of sex addiction.

With this book, we hope to alert readers to the signs, symptoms, and psychology of sex addiction—in themselves and/or in those they love. Because a sex addict's sexual behavior is more easily concealed from loved ones than, say, an alcoholic's drinking, family members often need expert help in order to recognize the disease. With this in mind, we will identify the ways in which sex addiction affects both the addict and his or her family: not just a spouse or partner, but parents, siblings, and children as well.

Using case studies from our own practice that draw on both sides of relationships between sex addicts and family members, we will illustrate the destructive consequences of sex addiction to both addicts and those close to them. In PART I, we outline the behavior patterns and family histories typical of the sex addicts we have treated. In PART II, we describe the various methods of coping developed by family members, especially spouses and partners, in reacting to the sex addict. In this way, we hope to help those readers suffering from sex addiction in themselves or in their families to identify and begin to comprehend this family disease, so that they can seek the help they need. If you are addicted yourself or involved with a sex addict, we believe this book can help you emerge more accepting and understanding of yourself, as well as the other person.

This book not only provides a way of recognizing and understanding the disease of sex addiction, though. It also offers a way out, recommending in PART III healing strategies that will help both sex addicts and their loved ones, especially spouses or partners, recover from sex addiction. It suggests ways of confronting, withstanding, and working through the traumatic and lingering effects of sex addiction. By providing concrete advice and recommending courses of action that have already proved successful in helping our patients recover from the family disease of sex addiction, we hope to guide readers, both addicts and family members, to their own recovery. And we offer strategies that will allow sex addicts and their loved ones to continue their personal growth through their recovery and that of their children.

In many ways, recovery programs for other addictions—especially alcoholism—have paved the road for the course of treatment we recommend. We believe mutual support groups that use AA's Twelve Steps lie at the heart of recovery from any family addiction, including sex addiction. Through our experience, we know that both sex addicts and those close to them can draw comfort, support, and strength from people who have gone through similar experiences. Especially when combined with other forms of therapy, the success of self-help groups in arresting addictions and compulsive behaviors—from alcoholism and drug addiction to gambling and eating disorders—offers new hope to sex addicts and their families.

Although this book is addressed primarily to the millions of sex addicts and their family members, readers with a more general interest may find it intriguing and useful as well. In making general readers—even those attracted to this book solely by their curiosity about the sexual exploits of addicts—aware of the challenges faced by sex addicts and members of their families, we hope to foster a greater public understanding of this disease. When it strikes our ministers, politicians, and yes, even our therapists, perhaps we can cut through the sensationalism and scandal to get these sex addicts the help they need.

Finally, we hope to familiarize more professionals in the mental health field with the symptoms and manifestations of sex addiction as well. With all the attention currently focused on adult children of dysfunctional families (affected by alcoholism, divorce, incest, and other disturbing conditions), sex addiction—so often an outgrowth of these childhood situations—merits a closer look. As professionals, we need to lead a reasonable, open, and informed discussion about the controversial disease of sex addiction. Now that we have entered a new age of recovery from all addictions and compulsive behaviors, a more widespread acceptance of this disease, among professionals as well as the public, will result in better, more informed treatment programs administered by qualified professionals. And with this progress, we will offer much-needed help to those millions of sex addicts and their family members who turn to us for treatment.

Transforming Yourself

If you or someone you love is a sex addict, you don't have to give up hope. No matter how much your efforts to keep the disease secret have alienated and isolated you from others, you can get better if you allow yourself to ask for help. Alone, you will remain powerless and helpless to defeat the illness of sex addiction. But if you can reach out and join with others—self-help groups as well as professionals experienced in treating sex addiction as a family disease—you will gain their strength and power, and increase your own. With the help of others, you will learn not only to survive, but to cope and heal. You will embrace a new way of living that will transform your sexuality from a shameful, painful burden to a joyful, shared pleasure. This book will help you explore how to do just that.

What Is
Sex
Addiction?

I

1

OUT OF CONTROL:
The Nature of Sex Addiction

As usual, the men and women in our Thursday night therapy group look as though they would rather be someplace else. Some fidget like young boys forced to sit in church on a sunny day. They keep looking at the door as if they'd just love to bolt through it. Others, legs crossed, arms folded across their chests, eyes staring at a spot in the middle of the floor, sit as still and expressionless as stone statues.

One member of the group, a ruggedly handsome man with broad shoulders and barrel chest of the college all-star football player he once was, is clearly more anxious than the others. It is his turn to talk. He crosses and recrosses his legs several times before clearing his throat and beginning to speak.

"My name is Hank," he says, "and I'm an addict." In a voice barely above a whisper, he rushes through the last three words, running them together into a reluctant one-word confession. Tugging at his shirt collar, he chuckles nervously. "Man, that's still a killer to say out loud. Took me fifteen years to say it the first time. Yeah, fifteen years I had this problem, but I kept telling myself I could handle it. I could stop any time I wanted to. I was in control. You know what I mean?"

He grins sheepishly and glances around the room, his blue eyes darting from face to face, looking for reassurance. He gets none. Yet, every man in the room, like any man or woman who has ever struggled to overcome an addiction, knows exactly what Hank means. That first step—acknowledging that that individual is *not* in control, is in fact powerless when it comes to the addiction, and that his or her entire life is out of control because of it—is, as Hank put it, "a killer." It is particularly difficult for Hank and the other members of our therapy groups to admit their particular addiction, one that is accompanied by even more shame and self-disgust than alcoholism, drug addiction, or compulsive overeating, spending, or gambling.

Hank and the men and women you will read about in this book are addicted to sex. They depend on specific, ritualized, frequently repeated sexual acts to make them feel good when they are feeling bad and to make them feel even better if they are already feeling good.

"I guess I began to figure out I had a problem fifteen years ago," Hank explains. "Before that, I just thought I was one of those guys with an especially high sex drive. I didn't think having affairs and one-night stands now and then was any big deal. Hey, when I was in college, sleeping with as many women as possible, as often as possible, was the thing to do. I just never stopped, not even after I got married.

"But, a couple of years back, I started cruising around a lot, looking for a hitchhiker to pick up, someone I could come on to. You would not believe the time and energy I spent just looking, and when I wasn't looking, I was thinking about looking, and thinking about what I would do once I found what I was looking for.

"The fantasy was the thing. It only takes so much time to *have* sex, but to look for women and think about having sex . . . well, that was what got me to the point where I'd be at work but my mind wouldn't be there at all. I'd count the minutes until I got off work, so I could drive around, hoping some wild thing would happen. Even when I knew that my wife expected me home in half an hour, it would still take me three hours to get there. I'd see a woman, any woman, and I'd have to follow her. It was like I had no choice, and before I knew it, I'd have driven twenty miles in the wrong direction and have to race home, the whole time trying to come up with the excuse I'd give my wife this time. And that was *if* I had the sheer force of will to snap out of it at all."

Hank's addiction took him far beyond merely cruising in his car and fantasizing about picking up hitchhikers. Throughout the twelve years of his marriage, he carried on several extramarital affairs and had numerous one-night stands. He was obsessed with pornography and could spend hours on end masturbating when he was on a sexual binge. Eventually, Hank began frequenting adult bookstores, knowing he would connect with men who would masturbate him.

When Hank first came to us for treatment eighteen months ago, he referred to himself as a sex fiend, a pervert, and a weirdo. But is that what he is? It certainly is tempting to attach such labels to him and millions of other men and women who partake in the sorts of sexual behavior that Hank did, as often as he did. Yet Hank does not fit most of our preconceived notions about sex fiends or perverts, who steal away in

WHAT IS SEX ADDICTION?

the middle of the day to slink into porno movies and massage parlors or lurk in the bushes waiting to expose themselves to unsuspecting victims.

At thirty-eight, Hank is a successful insurance salesman and respected member of his community. Bright, personable, and always quick to tell a joke or share a bit of sports trivia, Hank makes a good impression at large parties, bars and clubs. Certainly, his gift of gab and winning smile were what kept him afloat at work long after his obsessive pursuit of sex cut into the time and energy he devoted to selling insurance. Married and the father of two sons, seven and ten, Hank says he values his family, and calls himself a family man, even though his addiction has all but destroyed any relationship he ever had with his wife and children. But Hank, like all sex addicts, is quite adept at fooling himself and keeping up a nearly flawless front for the benefit of others.

"I've been an elder in my church for years," Hank states. "What a joke. All these people looking up to me. I loved it, but it was a huge lie. My whole life was a lie."

For more than a decade, Hank lived the lie—presenting himself as the community-minded businessman, upstanding citizen, natural leader and family man—all the while indulging his every sexual fantasy and descending deeper and deeper into his sex addiction.

Hank's story is not unusual. In our practice as clinical psychologists and family therapists in Scottsdale, Arizona, we treat men and women of all ages, religions and ethnic groups, members of the clergy, blue-collar workers, lawyers, doctors, entrepreneurs. Some come to us under court order after being arrested for their sexual exploits; some come begrudgingly at the insistence of their spouses or partners. Chances are, if sex addicts contact us on their own, their lives have become so unmanageable that even they can no longer deny the problem. Reality has finally caught up with them, and their carefully orchestrated double lives have collapsed for one reason or another. In Hank's case, his wife finally left him—something she had been threatening to do for years.

All of our sexually addicted patients get from sex the same things drug addicts get from drugs and alcoholics get from drinking: an intensely pleasurable high, comparable to nothing else in their lives; a means to anesthetize painful feelings such as sadness, anger, anxiety or fear; and a way to escape the pressures and problems of daily living. The urge to escape and repeatedly recapture the high is extremely powerful, so powerful, in fact, that sex addicts, like alcoholics and other addicts, are virtually helpless to resist it. They *want* to stop. Time and again, they *promise* to stop. They even *try* to stop, but they cannot.

"Sure, there were plenty of times I thought that what I wanted was so bizarre, that what I was doing wasn't normal," Hank recalls. "But that didn't stop me, because what I wanted, I *really* wanted, and I wanted it all the time—anonymous, spontaneous sex with anybody. The urge was so strong. I just had to hook up with someone—anyone—and have it happen. All I wanted was the sex. It sounds crazy now, but I was driven. It felt so good while I was doing it, and afterward, when I was feeling bad, I'd find myself thinking about doing it all again, so I could feel good again.''

Inevitably, the sex addict's euphoria lasts only as long as the sexual ritual itself. While alcoholics or drug addicts come down slowly as the drug of choice leaves the system, sex addicts feel that dazed, dismal, guilt-ridden, morning-after effect almost instantaneously. Sexual hang-overs set in immediately after orgasm, plunging sex addicts into depression and self-hatred. The shame and disgust they feel about the sex that thrilled them only moments before makes the aftershock all the more devastating. Each and every time they indulge their intense, irresistible sexual urges, sex addicts come face to face with the lie they are living. As Hank did, they feel like frauds and cowards, but that is not enough to make them stop. Indeed, the pressure created by their negative thoughts about themselves and their feelings of remorse, shame, and self-hatred build to the point where relief is absolutely necessary. Like alcoholics who treat a hangover by having a drink, sex addicts seek relief through more sex and the high that sex gives them—setting off the vicious cycle of a progressive disease that will ultimately render their lives unmanageable.

WHAT IS SEX ADDICTION?

George is a short, dark-haired dynamo, an organized, efficient, achievement-oriented young man who, at twenty-six, has already risen through the management ranks to become regional staff supervisor for a large hotel chain. But despite his outward appearance of success, George feels miserable. He hates the job he worked so hard to get. Even though he performs exceedingly well at work and has been commended by his superiors on numerous occasions, he frequently feels incompetent and constantly tells himself that he is not working hard enough or up to his potential, not distinguishing himself often enough or getting ahead fast enough.

Raised in a Catholic family, George had a workaholic father who was rarely at home, and his mother ruled with an iron fist, setting impossibly high standards for her children and harshly criticizing them when they failed to live up to those standards. Consequently, George grew up trying desperately to do everything right, but believing nearly everything he did was wrong. He became a perfectionist, frantically seeking other people's approval and always on the lookout for his own mistakes.

As an adult, the pressure George places upon himself is enormous, and at times his feelings of not measuring up are unbearable. George's misery is compounded by his sense of isolation. He wants close friends and longs for a normal intimate relationship with a woman. He has neither, and when not working, spends his time alone, blocking out his pain by masturbating repeatedly while reading pornographic magazines, watching X-rated movies, or listening to anonymous women deliver erotic messages over the telephone as part of a phone sex service.

"The way I look at it now," explains George, who came to us for help one year ago, "I used sex as an anesthetic, so I wouldn't have to face my feelings or the reality of my life. You have a headache, you take an aspirin. You hate your life, you take something stronger. Some guys drink, take cocaine, shoot heroin. Sex was my drug. I took it to kill the pain, only it became a worse problem and caused more pain than what I was trying to escape originally."

Sex: Using It as a Drug

How can George, or anyone else for that matter, think of sex as a drug? Isn't sex, a natural and wonderful part of life, a gift to be enjoyed and shared with a trusted partner, helping us feel close to others and bringing out the best in us? Many people view sex this way. Sex addicts almost never do. Indeed, the various, generally negative connotations George and other sex addicts associate with sex are an integral part of their disease and will be discussed in detail throughout this book.

However, to begin understanding sex addiction, it helps to think of sex as a drug—the sex addict's drug of choice. George uses sex as an anesthetic—to numb his pain. For other sex addicts, sex is a tranquilizer that helps them relax and relieve the stresses of their lives. Still others use sex as a mood elevator—to make them feel better when they are feeling depressed—or as a mind-altering substance that allows them to escape reality. And all use sex as an intoxicant—a means of getting high.

For example, sex gives Janet a feeling of euphoria and intense pleasure she knows no other way of achieving. While fantasizing about sex and engaged in sexual activity, Janet is dizzy with joy, literally intoxicated with the feelings that take hold of her mind and body. Her sexual high is all the more powerful because it stands in such dramatic contrast to the rest of her life.

A slender, impeccably dressed, forty-seven-year-old accountant, Janet became aware of her sexual addiction after seeking treatment for depression and marital woes. Feeling trapped in an unhappy marriage, Janet had sought solace in an equally miserable affair—one that lacked warmth, intimacy, and any kind of real human connection. Although it satisfies nothing but her enormous sexual needs, and even those only briefly, Janet has stayed in the same affair for the past five years. She feels powerless to change the situation, although she frequently expresses how fervently she wishes she could and how little she thinks of herself because of her behavior. She bitterly calls herself the other man's whore. "What else would you call me?" she asks. "Sex is all there is to the relationship."

Despite the misery she feels, Janet returns to her shallow, emotionally barren affair time and time again. Drawn like a moth to a flame, she cannot resist the pull of the one thing in which she can lose herself totally, if only temporarily—sex.

Just as one alcoholic drinks only beer, while another prefers straight whiskey, and still another sticks with wine, the activities sex addicts choose also vary. Some choose voyeurism, while others masturbate.

15

Some are turned on by pornographic pictures, while others get high on erotic messages they hear over the telephone. Some have an endless stream of affairs, a mind-boggling number of one-night stands, or they regularly visit prostitutes. And some commit sex crimes like rape or child molesting, exhibitionism or obscene phone calling.

However, none of these pursuits, in and of itself, indicates sex addiction. The sex act itself is less telling than

- the overwhelming urge to partake in it,
- the utter disregard for the consequences that inevitably occur,
- and the inability to stop—no matter how sincerely the addict wants to stop or how desperately he or she tries.

Sex: An Obsession

"I think about sex all the time," Janet reveals. "Sometimes I can't think of anything else. It interferes with everything I should be doing."

The last statement says a great deal about the nature of sex addiction. As the disease progresses, the overwhelming desire for sex and the constant thoughts about it interfere with family relationships, friendships, work, other responsibilities and everything else the addict once held dear.

Many a compulsive overeater wakes up thinking about what he or she will have for dinner that night. Thoughts of having a drink rarely leave the mind of many an alcoholic, who may actually count the minutes until he or she can leave work and get to the nearest bar. Likewise, sex addicts' waking hours are consumed with thoughts of their next sexual high.

Of course, most of us fantasize about sex from time to time. We respond to stimuli that excite us—the sight of a pretty girl in a skimpy bikini, a steamy sex scene on TV, or the scent of a lover's cologne on someone else. However, our sexual thoughts are rarely more than fleeting images or urges, even when they occur several times during the course of the day or interrupt the other things we are doing.

On the other hand, many sex addicts have told us that they spend fifty percent or more of their time thinking about sex, and only sex. A sex addict's fantasies can continue for hours on end, and he or she sees the realities of daily living as intrusions. The fantasies take control, and the addict's life revolves around the ability to get the next fix: the specific, ritualized sexual acts that he or she *knows* will produce a high. And the high is all that really matters.

For sex addicts, sex is the focal point of their entire lives. Sex is an obsession, a strong and uncontrollable preoccupation. Sex addicts are haunted by persistent, repetitive sexual thoughts that they rarely can ignore and often can stop only by engaging in the sexual activity with which they are obsessed. The obsessive thoughts influence the addicts' actions and relationships and give them a distorted view of reality. The addiction, not the addict, is in control.

16

Sex: A Compulsion

Just as an obsession is a persistent repetitive thought, a compulsion is a persistent repetitive behavior. The two almost always go hand in hand and are particularly powerful if they come into play as a result of an individual's need to relieve stress or escape unpleasant feelings.

Your own experiences can give you an idea of what a compulsion is like. For instance, have you ever turned off the TV, locked the door, crawled into bed, turned out the light, shut your eyes, and then suddenly wondered whether you really *did* lock the door? You may shake your head and think that, of course, you locked the door, that you always lock it before you walk to your bed. Still, the idea that, maybe this time, you didn't lock the door will not leave your mind. No matter how many times you push the thought out of your mind, it keeps returning. And so, to stop worrying and relax enough to go to sleep, you get up and check the door.

Whether we worry about having locked our doors, having left water running or cigarettes burning, or having put the correct address on an envelope, most of us are occasionally plagued by nagging thoughts that won't leave our minds until we *do* something about them. If you can imagine such an experience being many, many times stronger, you can get a general idea of how sex addicts' obsessions compel them to participate in their sexual rituals over and over again.

The compulsion, this virtually irresistible urge to repeat a behavior again and again—regardless of the immediate harm it can cause or its long-range consequences—overrides a sex addict's logical thinking, moral judgment, and even the strongest desire *not* to do the compulsive behavior. First, the obsession takes possession of the addict's mind, and then it compels him to act accordingly.

Thus, in later chapters, when we say a sex addict is feeling stressed and therefore begins to be obsessed with sex and to proceed to obtain the high fantasized about, we rarely, if ever, mean he or she *consciously decides* to go out and get a quick fix for unpleasant feelings. Instead, those feelings—which the sex addict may not recognize or be the least bit aware of—automatically trigger the obsession/compulsion mechanism. Once that mechanism is running at full steam, the addict is out of control—driven to satisfy the overpowering need for the sexual high.

This does not excuse the addict or mean he or she will never be able to control sexual urges or should not bother to get help in order to change. It does partly explain, however, why an addict can really want to stop compulsive behavior but be unable to do so independently—which is the essence of addiction.

THE SEEDS OF SEX ADDICTION

Why do some people who drink become alcoholics while others do not, some drug users develop addictions while others do not? What separates a compulsive overeater from someone who is simply overweight, or a compulsive spender from someone who merely likes to shop? How does sex become an obsession, a compulsion, and finally an addiction for some people but not for others?

Although we are more aware than ever before that people suffer from addictions, and new, effective treatment programs are being developed every day, there still exists no one definitive answer to those questions. We do know that a great many addicts, including most of the sex addicts we have treated, grew up in homes where one or both parents were emotionally, physically, or sexually abusive, were addicted or demonstrated compulsive behaviors, a fact we will explore in great detail in Chapter 3. But whether addiction is hereditary, learned through example, or a combination of the two has not been proven conclusively.

Fortunately, even without clearly knowing why one person becomes an addict while another does not, we do know that all addicts have several common attributes, including:

- a tendency to hold low opinions of themselves and to constantly remind themselves of their deficiencies;
- distorted or unrealistic beliefs about themselves, their behavior, other people, and the events that occur in the world around them;
- a desire to escape from or to suppress unpleasant emotions;
- difficulty coping with stress;
- at least one powerful memory of an intense high experienced at a crucial time in their lives and an ever-present desire to recapture that euphoric feeling;
- an uncanny ability to deny that they have a problem.

These commonalities are the seeds of any addiction. Those seeds grow particularly well when the potential addict learned coping skills from addicted or compulsive parents and isolates himself or herself from close relationships because of lack of confidence in social skills. To better understand how addictions develop and to explain what we, as therapists, look for when we want to find out if someone is indeed a sex addict, let's look at each of these factors in detail.

Seed No. 1: Negative "Self-Talk"

Self-talk is a term that we and our patients find helpful for describing what we say, think, and *feel* about ourselves and about the world in which we live. Addicts are generally plagued by negative self-talk.

Few people—and almost no addicts—take the time on a daily basis to thoroughly examine their thoughts and feelings. Consequently, we are not always consciously aware of the self-talk—and the assumptions we make about other people based on it—going on in our minds. Even so, it significantly influences the way all of us interact with the world in which we live.

What does a sex addict's self-talk sound like? Well, most addicts we've treated, sexual or otherwise, are plagued by low self-esteem. They feel inadequate and unlovable, so their self-talk most often says "I'm a horrible person" or "I can't do anything right." Their poor self-image also colors their view of the rest of the world, leading them to feel "Other people are better than me" or "Nobody really cares." Addicts who believe this sort of self-talk have a ready-made justification for compulsive behavior. For one thing, the sexual acts they themselves find repugnant after the fact fit right into their view of themselves as horrible people.

But more important, focusing on their sexual fantasies and pursuits silences negative self-talk and provides temporary relief from the painful feelings that come with it. For instance, Janet's self-talk constantly reminds her that she deserves her unfulfilling marriage and that she is too weak to end her abusive affair. George's self-talk rarely lets him escape the fact that he hates his job and is so socially inept that he has no close friends or intimate relationships. The constant misery created by their negative self-talk propels both Janet and George toward the only thing they know will definitely make them feel better—in her case, an empty sexual affair; in his, chronic masturbation.

CORE BELIEFS

In his ground-breaking book, *Out of the Shadows,* which first brought sex addiction to public attention, Dr. Patrick Carnes organized the many variations of sex addicts' negative self-talk into four core beliefs. Those beliefs are central to sex addicts' self-image and influence their view of the world. Carnes, whose book has helped many of our patients to understand their problem, asserts that, although few addicts are consciously aware of these beliefs and may recognize them for the first time only after they are well on their way to recovery, they nonetheless operate on a daily basis as if the following were irrefutable and unchangeable truths:

- "I am basically a bad, unworthy person."
- "No one would love me as I am."
- "My needs are never going to be met if I have to depend on others."
- "Sex is my most important need."

In our work with sex addicts, we have discovered that they also hold a fifth core belief: "If I have to depend on my social skills to get close to anyone, it will never happen." Nearly all of sex addicts' self-talk can be traced back to these core beliefs, and most compulsive sexual behaviors either compensate for or reinforce these beliefs.

Core beliefs, the foundation of addicts' version of reality and negative self-talk—how addicts think and feel about themselves as well as interpret everything around them—are a perpetual presence and part of all other seeds of sex addiction. To help you identify negative self-talk in yourself or others, we have underlined typical addict self-talk each time it appears in the text.

Seed No. 2: "Diseased" Thinking

Sex addiction, like all other addictions, is a disease of the body, mind, and spirit—affecting how addicts behave, feel, and think. The last is more clearly seen in the myths, self-talk, and irrational ideas that increase the addiction's power and make it easier for addicts to rationalize their own behavior.

DISEASED THINKING ABOUT THE ADDICTION

Whether it's thinking "Everybody does it, why shouldn't I?" or blaming other people for not satisfying their sexual appetites, sex addicts latch onto any excuse to justify their behavior. Their pat answers or elaborate rationalizations become almost automatic responses to any situation.

"How can I tell you what it's like?" George struggles to explain the state of mind that is as much a part of his addiction as his repeated masturbation, frequent calls to phone sex services, and liaisons with prostitutes. "This madness just takes over. It's like a fog, and when I'm in it, I can rationalize *anything*."

Like recovering alcoholics, recovering sex addicts call this type of thinking insanity. While possessed by their particular brand of insanity, sex addicts' decisions and actions are not based on sound judgment. Although they are able to think clearly and rationally during those times that they are not in the grip of the addiction, when they are, their thoughts run far afield of what the rest of us call reality. Indeed, in recovery, when the fog has begun to lift, addicts themselves can barely believe the extremes they went to in order to justify their compulsive behavior, the lies they told, or the ways they fooled themselves and tried to fool everyone around them.

DISEASED THINKING ABOUT THEMSELVES

Already victimized by their own low self-esteem, sex addicts invariably reinforce their negative self-images with negative self-talk. For instance, Janet sees her miserable marriage and her compulsion to continue her equally unhappy affair as evidence of her own moral failure and unworthiness. She takes her self-criticism several steps further, persistently telling herself "I don't deserve a normal life" or "I'm completely unlovable"—assessments certainly outside the bounds of reality.

Generally, we find that the first signs of this kind of self-talk are rooted in real events that occurred years earlier: acts of abandonment, neglect, or abuse that left the sex addict feeling unloved or unwanted. In Janet's case, she felt neglected during her father's chronic illness and felt abandoned following his death when she was nine years old. Because of this, she felt utterly powerless to shape or even adjust to her world.

As often happens, Janet made a natural, if illogical, leap from recognizing that "Something bad is happening to me" to concluding that "I'm an intrinsically bad person." Although such a conclusion is perfectly understandable when drawn by a vulnerable and impressionable child, and even though it was reinforced by a domineering mother who abused Janet emotionally, regularly informing her that she was indeed a bad girl, it was still irrational. The resulting poor self-image became the cornerstone of the diseased thinking that goes hand in hand with Janet's sex addiction.

Generally, sex addicts' beliefs about themselves are all built on this foundation of unworthiness. No matter how much we encourage her, Janet finds it next to impossible to say anything good about herself. Yet she is relentless in cataloging her faults. She could easily list a hundred things that she considers wrong with her. And these "flaws" only further erode her poor self-image.

DISEASED THINKING ABOUT OTHER PEOPLE

Bill, a forty-year-old Health Department inspector, is small and drab with a receding hairline and a neatly trimmed moustache, which he pulls at habitually whenever anyone else in the therapy group is talking. Like Janet, he experienced the death of a parent at an early age. His sexual addiction began during adolescence, and it ultimately brought about the end of his marriage and nearly cost him his job. Bill has been in treatment with us for more than two years and has curtailed his addictive behaviors, which included voyeurism, exhibitionism—for which he was arrested on several occasions—and countless visits to prostitutes, sometimes several times in a single day. However, he continues to struggle with his diseased thinking.

"I know that it's really sick," Bill confesses. "But still, sometimes when I see some woman on the street, I can't help thinking that she's out there for me. She's been put there for my pleasure, and she's just waiting for me to make my move."

Bill, like other sex addicts, does not limit his warped view of reality just to himself and his compulsive sexual behavior. He sees other people solely in terms of his own addictive needs. Bill has viewed women as a means to an end, that end being the high he achieved while peeping at them through windows or exposing himself to them. He has yet to learn to see women in any other light. Men have fared no better. Bill saw his Health Department supervisors and the managers of the restaurants he inspected only as obstacles.

"They were keeping me from more important matters," Bill explains. "Actually, from the only thing that mattered—sex. So I conned them and lied to them, said I was doing one thing when I was really doing another. They were nothing but a hassle."

If other people can't be used sexually, sex addicts seldom have patience for them. They see their spouses or partners, a prostitute, or a stranger in a bar—or on the street for that matter—as sex objects designed to satisfy their own desires. Employers, co-workers, customers, other members of their family—and everyone else who does not fall into the category of sex object—are considered intruders who can't help them and may even stand in their way.

SEEING SEXUAL STIMULI EVERYWHERE

If someone the addict views as a sex object responds in any way, by making eye contact, for instance, the sex addict jumps to what he or she thinks is a logical conclusion—that interest has been expressed, a connection has been made, or a tacit agreement to have sex has been forged. Seen through the addiction's veil of insanity, *any* reaction is interpreted as attention and consent. Sometimes the irrational perception is merely wishful thinking, attributing sexual connotations to another person's perfectly innocent and nonsexual actions. But at other times, the addict is so intent on fulfilling sexual fantasies and completing sexual rituals that he or she picks up sexual signals when no such signs exist at all. A sex addict eventually sees sexual stimuli everywhere.

Several years ago, we treated a thirty-one-year-old restaurateur and compulsive voyeur named Steve. Steve told us about a time when he was driving and saw a vague, shadowy form three blocks ahead of him. Certain he was looking at a woman, he stared intently at his sex object, quickly convincing himself she was someone waiting just for him. He drove slowly, becoming more and more excited with each block. But when he finally caught up to her, Steve discovered that the object he'd turned into an exquisite, sexual-fantasy playmate was, in fact, a telephone pole.

Not only do sex addicts fabricate details and attribute sexual meaning to nonsexual objects, they often miss real details that would be obvious if they were thinking rationally.

"About three years ago," Bill painfully remembers, "I was out picking up women every day, hookers mostly. But this one day, I picked up a transvestite. At first I didn't know, I really thought he was a woman. If I had been thinking clearly, hell, if I had been thinking at all, I would have realized that this person was a man.

"But I was really crazed for sex, and when I'm like that I might as well be blind, deaf and dumb. I actually went to a motel room with this person before I finally figured it out. I know it sounds totally insane. But my head was so out of it that somebody could have hit me with a two-by-four and I wouldn't have felt it."

The state of mind Bill describes is typical of sex addicts in the grip of powerful sexual fantasies. Numb—blind, deaf and dumb, as Bill put it—to all rational thoughts, reality gives way to altered perceptions and does not return until orgasm is reached.

Seed No. 3: Unrealistic Attitudes: All You Need Is Sex, Sex Is All You Need

All of us, addicted or not, see in sex exactly what we want to see. We all attach certain personal, emotional meanings to our sexual behavior. From young children who marvel at the pleasurable sensations created by touching certain parts of their bodies, to the adolescent who sees losing his or her virginity as a rite of passage into adulthood, to couples whose lovemaking is the ultimate expression of trust, commitment and intimacy, sex is nearly always viewed as more than purely a physical experience or simply a biological function. Indeed, thoughts, feelings and value judgments associated with sexual behavior separate human beings from animals—and in this respect, sex addicts are no different from anyone else. However, the intensity of their attitude toward it, their total dependence upon it, and their ability to attribute inappropriate meaning or significance to sexual behavior when there is no evidence to support their contention definitely separates sex addicts from the rest of the population.

To begin with, sex addicts attach supreme significance to sex. It represents the fulfillment of every need, the answer to every question, the solution to every problem.

Whether they decide that sex is love, power, their special talent, or desired by their partners in the way it is by them, sex addicts believe in their interpretations, unwaveringly and wholeheartedly. It never crosses their minds, for instance, that the sex objects they have selected may not feel the way they want and need those objects to feel—even when those individuals express disgust or actively resist their advances. The sex addict merely projects his or her own desires onto the other person— even when that person is a complete stranger, a prostitute, a model in a magazine layout, or a disembodied voice over the phone. In the sex addict's mind, the fantasy *is* reality. For the most part, the sex objects need not exist at all, for in the sex addict's head they are alive and meeting the addict's every need.

SEX IS LOVE

Believe it or not, the driving force behind most sex addicts' compulsions is a desperate need for love. In fact, sex addicts tend to interpret sexual interest and sex of any kind, with anyone, as an act of love, rarely recognizing their mistake until they are well into their recovery.

Like most sex addicts, Janet, the forty-seven-year-old accountant, felt deprived of love as a child. In her case, she felt abandoned when her father died and felt unloved each time her abusive mother told her she was a bad girl. Searching for the affection and validation of her self-worth she had missed out on during childhood, Janet discovered that sex offered her at least the illusion of being loved and appreciated. When her husband seemed unable to love her enough or keep up with her sexual appetites, Janet, once again feeling empty and abandoned, began an affair. Her lover is inattentive and abusive, but sex—and the mistaken impression that she is loved during it—keeps her tied to her lover.

Similarly, George, the perfectionist hotel staff supervisor, reaches out for love from behind closed doors and believes he has found it each time he listens to an anonymous voice "talk dirty" over the telephone. And Bill, the reformed voyeur and exhibitionist, felt an intimate connection between himself and the victims he peeped at through bedroom windows—even though they did not know he was outside watching them.

In each instance, the addict's intense *need* for love is real. It is the belief that the sexual compulsions are acts of love that is irrational.

Nonaddicts know the difference between sex and love. Oh, they may confuse the two occasionally, but never as often or as completely as the sex addict. And once they wise up, they rarely make the same mistake again and again and again.

"I'd feel really dirty after peeping through windows or exhibiting myself," admits Bill. "I'd wash all my clothing right away, but that still left the dirtiness of *me*. I'd try to clean myself up and get a good night's sleep, hoping I'd wake up with a clear head the next morning. But I never did. I just woke up wanting to do it all over again."

To abruptly sobering sex addicts, what seemed profound just seconds earlier suddenly feels silly or, even worse, filthy. Yet in no time flat, they are fantasizing again, deluding themselves into believing that the love they crave is out there and that their sexual rituals can make it happen.

Janet is a prime example. Five or six times in less than thirty minutes of her therapy session, she wavers back and forth between the delusion that the man she is having an affair with "really cares for me" and the more sober recognition that "it's a dead-end affair, he really doesn't have any desire to be with me except for the sex."

The truth of the matter is that the sex that sex addicts do have is rarely, if ever, part of a balanced, intimate relationship. Sex addicts may call what they do making love, but they really love only the event and the high they get from it. Although it is extremely difficult for even those sex addicts in recovery programs to accept, it really is the high, not the love, that they go back for time and again.

SEX IS POWER

Perhaps because their lives are chaotic and unmanageable in general, sex addicts tend to see nearly every aspect of daily living as being controlled by other people. Their employers call the shots at work. Their spouses manipulate and shame them into toeing the line at home. Their parents are able, after all these years, to stir up feelings that addicts also see as being beyond their control. Everywhere they look, sex addicts see someone else in the driver's seat or someone else's rules and expectations frustrating or confusing them. Sex is the one area in which sex addicts believe they can reclaim some of their power.

Surprisingly, most of the addicts we've treated describe the sexual act itself as something controlled by the sex object—who ultimately can either satisfy or thwart their sexual desires. Yet, such a belief adds to the power trip. You see, each time addicts do achieve a sexual high, getting the sex object to do what they want, they believe they have wrested away the sex object's control and scored another point in the ultimate power game.

According to the sex addict's belief system, sex is not an experience to be shared, but rather a prize to be won. Consequently, the hunt and the conquest become as intriguing as the sex act itself.

Todd, thirty-five, an investment analyst and father of three, who only recently began his recovery, claims to have had hundreds of one-night stands, at least fifty of them during the last year of his marriage. Like

Bill, he is divorced and, like George, is a perfectionist. Driven to outproduce the other analysts in his investment firm, he is almost as obsessed with his financial status as he is with sex. A fanatic about his appearance, Todd runs three miles daily and works out several times each week. With his fashionably cut blond hair and trendy semicasual clothes, he looks as though he has just stepped out of a men's magazine or the latest hit television show. It comes as no surprise that Todd prides himself on his power to entice women.

"The trick is to get a woman to have sex, or want to have sex, with me without her knowing how much I want it," Todd claims. "If I let her know how much I want her, she'll play games with me, she'll toy with me, she'll jerk me around.

"I work in an office where half the people are women, and I know just how to get them to do what I want them to do every time. I work hard developing these subtle kinds of relationships with them. It's like a little dance I do—listening to them, asking them about little details they wouldn't think I would remember, talking about my kids so they'll think I'm sensitive, you know, just building a little at a time. I make sure that I don't act chauvinistic like the other guys. I have ulterior motives, of course. I'm manipulating all the time. But it works."

Todd can't help grinning as he relates his foolproof methods for getting what he wants from women. The heady rush of power and sense of complete control Todd feels whenever he makes sex happen is so exciting that sex itself often seems anticlimactic.

Sex addicts feel that they must manipulate other people, play on their sex objects' desires and weaknesses, or in the most severe cases violate them sexually, thinking all the while that "If I do the right things, I can make it happen."

This self-talk goes hand in hand with the diseased thinking we described earlier. By constantly looking for, and even inventing, signs that their sexual objects want contact as badly as they do and will give them what they need, sex addicts believe they have a basis for doing what they have learned will make sex happen.

SEX IS PROOF OF ADEQUACY

In addition to priding themselves on their ability to snare the sex objects of their choice, sex addicts like Todd usually feel that sex is something they do particularly well. Falling short of perfection in other areas of their lives and constantly feeling inadequate since perfection is the only standard they find acceptable, sex addicts confirm and reconfirm their adequacy with sex. Like alcoholics who pride themselves on their ability to drink others under the table, sex addicts often believe that sexual performance is the one special talent they have.

Certainly Robin, a thirty-year-old, dark-haired, green-eyed pediatrician, believes the only thing she does well is have sex. In all other areas of her life, she judges herself harshly, minimizing her accomplishments and setting impossibly high standards for herself. Although she concedes that her colleagues think she does a good job in her pediatrics practice, their praise has no meaning for her. A compulsive overeater who none-theless could not bear the thought of having a less than perfect body, Robin became a bulimic, bingeing and then purging what she had eaten to control her weight. Even as a child, Robin drove herself to be perfect, thinking that the slightest mistake on her part would destroy what little sanity there was in a family made up of an alcoholic father, a mother with a life-threatening heart ailment, and a sickly sister. The ultimate "good little girl," Robin neither masturbated nor had sex until she left home at age twenty-two, but when she did, Robin made a life-changing discovery.

"Sex comes naturally to me, I don't have to work as hard at it as I do with everything else," Robin explains. "Honestly, I'm not really good at much else. I'm a washout at parties, and I'm uncomfortable in almost any kind of group. It's hard for me to be around lots of people. And I'm not good at going out on dates because I can't figure men out. I don't know what they want me to be."

It is clear to see from Robin's critique of her social skills that she does not think very highly of herself or her ability to get along with other people in nonsexual situations. During nearly every minute of every day, Robin is plagued with self-doubt. Nothing she does is good enough to meet her exacting standards. The only exception is sex. Alone in the dark, masturbating—which Robin does at least once and as many as a dozen times a day—or in bed with a man she barely knows, Robin stops judging herself. During sex, she is finally okay.

Like other sex addicts, Robin's self-esteem is all wrapped up in her ability to attract sexual partners and achieve orgasms. She believes that "If I can excite someone else's interest, I must be okay." Her tremen-dous need to prove she is indeed okay sends her in pursuit of one sexual high after another.

SEX MAKES YOU SPECIAL

Keith, a forty-six-year-old real estate broker, came to us for treat-ment because of his obsessive sexual fantasies involving young girls. The father of two teenage daughters, he was terrified that he might soon be unable to control his urge to have sex with girls their age, including some of their friends. His fear was understandable, considering that he had acted on almost every other sexual impulse he had ever had. He soon revealed a long list of addictive sexual activities, which he had once merely thought about and now seemed unable to live without. These included making obscene telephone calls, having anonymous encounters with men in adult bookstores, and having extramarital affairs in spite of the threat they presented to his marriage.

In talking to Keith, we discovered that his sexual encounters, like Robin's, were futile attempts to overcome feelings of social inadequacy. But he did not simply want to feel okay. He needed to prove he was special, unique, a cut above the average man.

"I felt it was the ultimate approval for a girl to go to bed with me," he recalls. "If I could get some woman into bed, then I felt like I must be somebody, like I still had it, that magic, that special something that turns them on.

"I was raised with this idea that girls didn't give in easily, that they knew it was bad to go to bed with just anybody. So if they gave in and had sex with *me,* actually wanted to do it with me, then I knew I really must be someone special, out of the ordinary.

"I liked that idea, even if it wasn't true. I think it's why I had such a hard time giving up the affairs, you know. Without sex, what am I? Just a big, fat nobody."

THE GRAND DELUSION

Whether they call what they are looking for love, power, a sense of adequacy or uniqueness, what sex addicts want is for others to confirm that they are really wonderful people. They want this so much that they frequently *feel* that it is happening, regardless of the way others actually react. *Sex addicts see any sexual connection, even the ones they imagine, as much deeper and more meaningful than they are.* What's more, they misconstrue the temporary euphoria they feel as they lead up to and reach orgasm as proof that their sex objects think they're great and that their needs, whatever they might be, are being met. This grand delusion fuels the addiction, prompting sex addicts to return to their fantasies and repeat their actions in order to feel loved, in control, adequate, or special. Nowhere else can sex addicts validate their sense of self-worth. Yet, on some level or some of the time, they do know that the validation is imaginary.

As Bill, the Health Department inspector recovering from an addiction to voyeurism, exhibitionism, and frequent sex with prostitutes, puts it, "I really craved the attention I got from prostitutes. It's not like I really didn't know they were only with me because I paid them to be. But still I felt like they accepted me, maybe even liked me. I didn't get that from other people, not my wife, certainly not my boss or the people I worked with. It was like we spoke different languages. But my fantasy women, the women of the streets, they understood me. And I needed that understanding. I really did."

And so Bill created and believed the grand delusion that his sexual high fulfilled his emotional needs.

Seed No. 4: Stress

Sex addicts are most susceptible to acting on their addictive urges when under stress. Whether they experience stress because they hate their jobs as George does, want to outproduce their colleagues as Todd does, fear they will make mistakes as Robin does, or see their marriages falling apart as Hank did, sex addicts handle stress in a specific way: by escaping into compulsive sexual behavior. Of course, after the sexual high itself ends, nothing has really changed except for the additional stress that rushes into their lives as they berate themselves about the sex in which they have just indulged.

THE ART (AND STRESS) OF DECEPTION

To make matters worse, addicts—and sex addicts in particular—experience a higher level of stress than most other people do, precisely because of the way they live their lives. As much as they try to deny it or hide it behind sexual posturing, all sex addicts feel tremendously guilty about their sexual behavior. They view it as being out of control, and they want to cover up that shameful behavior. The pressure involved in leading a double life is enormous and constant.

"It takes a lot of time, a lot of planning," explains Hank, the insurance agent. "Sometimes I'd call my wife in advance and tell her some story, like I was having car trouble or something, just so I could go and meet somebody. Mostly I stuck to things I actually might do, like meeting a client at his house to discuss his policy or going to see a friend to talk about his problems. My wife would believe me. But there was always the chance she wouldn't or that I'd be so out of it when I got home that I'd forget which lie I had told her. I could always get caught. Every day was a disaster waiting to happen."

Coming up with excuses for sudden disappearances and chronic lateness, keeping various stories straight, and projecting a false image only adds to the strain in the sex addict's life. This added stress, often so powerful that it blocks out the original source of pain and anxiety, keeps the vicious cycle of sex addiction in motion. The original stress leads to sex, which leads to more stress, more sex, more stress.

MORE STRESS: KEEPING OTHERS FROM GETTING TOO CLOSE

Like Bill, who distanced himself from people in the real world, sex addicts often complain that they have few friends, yet they won't allow themselves to make any new ones or maintain the friendships they do have. For example, Mitch, a forty-eight-year-old auto mechanic who now owns and manages his own garage, functions perfectly well when supervising his staff or working on a car with another mechanic, but he does not feel close to these men.

"For a long time I built walls around me," he says. "I isolated myself, just so people wouldn't find out who I was or about the sexual things I did. I was afraid to let anyone get close to me emotionally."

Mitch's only relationships were either strictly for business or strictly for sex. And even the sex he was obsessed with was almost always anonymous, taking place daily in the darkened booths of adult bookstores. Similarly, George, who deals with people daily in his job as a hotel staff supervisor but feels totally inadequate in social situations, isolates himself from people—and the pressure to get them to like him—by holding up in his apartment and consoling himself with masturbation, pornography, and phone sex.

Nearly every sex addict we have ever treated has, in one way or another, expressed the core belief that "If I have to depend on my social skills to get close to anyone, it will never happen." Mitch and George choose isolation while Robin and Keith compensate for their insecurity in social situations by turning nearly every encounter into a sexual opportunity.

Yet, no matter how distasteful it may be for sex addicts to interact with people, all of them do it in one way or another. As much as George may wish to lock himself away from the outside world with a telephone and a large supply of porno magazines, in reality he deals with people all day long as part of his job. Interaction is required when Keith sells real estate or Hank sells insurance and serves as an elder in his church. Robin must relate to patients and their parents, nurses, and other doctors. Paul, a fifty-six-year-old history professor, not only contends with students and colleagues, but also is an active participant in local charity drives and community causes. No addict lives in a vacuum, and each social situation dredges up old inadequacy demons, creating stress that is compounded by the ever-present demand to keep sexual exploits secret.

Because they must keep a major area of their lives hidden, sex addicts generally make it all but impossible to get close to them. They turn away from conversations that involve anything deeper or more personal than sports or the weather. While Paul can be downright gregarious at times and gets along well in superficial settings, he rarely shares his true feelings, and the mere thought of letting anyone see below the surface horrifies him. He works hard to project himself as an extrovert, always trying to be the life of the party. No one suspects the deep, dark secrets he hides, although the fear remains that other people will discover who he really is.

Like Paul, many sex addicts are quite proficient at making extremely superficial small talk and sharing facts about everything but themselves, which is why they often do well in education, business, and at many other occupations, as well as make a positive first impression.

"I always had a joke or a story to tell," says Hank, who used his social skills to sell insurance as well as maintain the deception that he was an upstanding citizen, devoted family man, and all-around nice guy. "I was a whiz at trivia and determined to make a great first impression. I would say things that would make me seem neater and smarter and deeper, little stories I made up to impress people. I was never actually honest with anybody."

Honesty is definitely not any addict's strong suit, and we have yet to meet a sex addict who didn't have a major problem opening up to other people. Because sex addicts fear discovery, the last thing they want to do is talk about themselves candidly. At home, at work, and especially in social situations, they dare not forget that "If I start opening up about myself, it will be impossible to prevent people from knowing that I have this problem. And if they know that, they're sure to reject me. They'll think I'm some kind of a pervert." Besides, if other people knew about their secret lives, the addicts themselves might have to break down the wall of denial and face up to their addiction. Making sure such a travesty does not occur only multiplies the stress in sex addicts' pressure-cooker lives.

Isolated, even from their spouses and children, with no one to trust or talk to, sex addicts bottle up their feelings and bury them—in sex. Refusing to open up to anyone, they have no way to measure their core beliefs against reality, so they perpetuate their grand delusions. Their negative self-talk stays alive and powerful, leaving them in a near constant state of emotional distress, one they have learned can only be relieved by indulging the sexual compulsions that caused it in the first place.

PULLED IN OPPOSITE DIRECTIONS

Each of us responds to stress, pain, loneliness, loss, and discomfort in his or her own way. Some people identify the sources of their discomfort and change what they can or take advantage of a constructive outlet such as counseling, meditation, or exercise. Others neurotically blame themselves for any misfortune. And we all have seen those people who blame anyone but themselves for their problems and try to beat the competition to the punch. But addicts always respond to pain and anxiety in the same way—by finding something that will anesthetize them and allow them to forget about the pressure they feel.

The sex addicts we've treated—once they stop denying their problems and making excuses for them—attribute much of their anxiety to acute loneliness and strong fears of abandonment and rejection, fears that actually increase their loneliness as they distance themselves from others. Hank and Janet, for example, rebuff their spouses' attempts to get close, repeatedly pushing them away in order to thwart the threat of rejection, which they see as inevitable. Then, all three turn around and literally demand that their spouses show them affection or attention by doing their sexual bidding. This is one of the many seesaw aspects of sexual addiction.

Bouncing back and forth between contradictory needs and finding that what they do to fulfill one automatically takes away from another keeps the addiction on its course. Although Janet and her husband hardly talk to each other and rarely get close physically, she desperately wants someone to love her. At the same time, she is compulsively drawn to the fleeting state of euphoria she gets from sex with her longtime lover—as abusive and uncaring as he has repeatedly proven to be. Her sex-only affair leaves her all the more desperate for love, while making her feel all the more undeserving of it. Her inability to find love or believe she ever will once again triggers her compulsion to have sex, trapping her in the paradox that drives sex addiction. The same can be said for Todd who has hundreds of one-night stands, while deep down he really wants intimacy. George is yet another example.

"I never liked the girls who liked me," says George. "I always wanted the ones who didn't like me at all." The paradox here is that if George tries to relate to the women he is attracted to—who he already knows are not interested in him—he will get what he fears most: rejection. Consequently, he has never had an intimate relationship with any woman.

Seed No. 5: In Search of the Ultimate High

Many alcoholics can remember the very first time they got drunk. It was a real discovery—as if they had found the secret of life. "Wow, this is great! <u>What a tremendous feeling</u>," they thought, and sought it out again and again, only to discover that the longer they went on pursuing that original feeling, the more they had to drink to achieve it. The sex addict follows the same pattern, constantly searching for the fantastic high he or she once felt during a particular sexual episode, although not necessarily the first one. It is often the best feeling the addict has ever experienced.

All addicts associate an incomparable sense of euphoria with their drug of choice, whether it is alcohol, cocaine, gambling, or sex. That the addict links this mind-numbing high with a sexual experience rather than, say, a drinking experience, plays the single biggest role in drawing him or her toward sex addiction instead of alcoholism or other compulsive behaviors. Naturally, the addict wants to feel it again and eventually the drive to recapture that glorious sexual high will take precedence over all else.

THE FIXATION

Addicts and nonaddicts alike have had highly exciting and pleasurable past sexual encounters. But, perhaps because of the timing of an incident, its intensity, the risk involved, or the mixed emotions associated with it, sex addicts—unlike nonaddicts—store up those memories, latch on to them, and refuse to let them go. George, the hotel staff supervisor, vividly recalls the high he felt the first time he masturbated. Ever since, his life—to varying degrees at various times—has revolved around attempts to re-create that ultimate high or to find new sexual highs that would match or surpass it. The memory of his original euphoric feeling almost never leaves his mind.

Of course, many of us hang on to memories of good sex and even think about sex when we should be thinking about other things, like work or what to cook for dinner. That does not make us sex addicts. The addicts we treat report that they spend more than fifty percent of their waking hours pointedly thinking about sex. Those whose jobs allow them a certain degree of freedom and a significant amount of unstructured time—traveling salespeople, real estate brokers, truck drivers, ministers, and entrepreneurs—devote an even greater portion of their days to indulging freely in fantasy, as well as acting out those fantasies.

Another difference between sex addicts and the rest of the population is that once the fantasy begins, prompted by almost any real or imagined cue, a sex addict will seldom bring it to a halt unless absolutely forced to do so.

"I would blow up at my wife for no reason except that she interrupted my fantasy," admits Keith, the forty-six-year-old real estate broker. "To her, it came out of nowhere. She'd come into the room just wanting to do something or say something, and I'd jump all over her. She was infringing on *my* freedom and *my* time, so I got angry. I wanted her out of my way, so I could stay in my head where the sex was."

For sex addicts, staying in their heads, focusing on the fantasies found there, is much more interesting and exciting than real life. At least

31

some of the time, they do not want to stop fantasizing. But more importantly, once sex addicts fix their minds on the object or idea that initially turned them on, they find it virtually *impossible* to shift their attention to anything else.

"I'm jealous of other guys who see some girl, whistle at her, and then forget about it," admits Don, a fifty-year-old federal parole officer. "They've got it easy. I saw this one girl the other day. She was about fifteen, wearing a short skirt, showing off her long legs. It was impossible not to notice her, and I know some of the other guys did, but I couldn't get her out of my mind. I just kept thinking about her. I didn't want to, but four or five hours later, she was still there in my head. I finally had to masturbate just to make her go away."

Don, a tall, powerfully built man whose blank stare is no doubt the result of years of appearing to pay attention to one thing while thinking about another, had both an alcoholic father and stepfather and is himself an alcoholic as well as a sex addict. Sexually molested at age six and in turn molesting his niece eight years later, Don began masturbating several times a day while serving in the armed forces almost thirty years ago. Although he describes affairs and one-night stands as too much work, he is also a compulsive womanizer. When chasing skirts threatened to cost him his job, and he was masturbating so often that his penis was often left raw and bleeding, Don finally recognized that his little problem was out of control and checked himself into a hospital. Although his behavior has changed during treatment, he still finds himself consumed by sexual thoughts. He wants to switch off his brain, but cannot.

A sex addict's fantasy is like a hypnotic trance that takes over the addict's mind. He or she may even "lose time," the way some of us do when driving a familiar route to work, for instance. We go off on some mental tangent, then discover we've arrived at our destination in no time at all and without paying conscious attention to how we got there. Sex addicts spend much of their time in this trance state, fixated on their fantasies, but at the same time trying to function in the world outside their heads.

Perhaps once or twice in a lifetime, a nonaddict might experience "love at first sight," the feeling of being instantly turned on sexually, physically, or emotionally to someone else at a first meeting. A sex addict, on the other hand, regularly and repeatedly experiences "lust at first sight." Over and over again, sex addicts will feel an irresistible sexual attraction to colleagues, friends, complete strangers, or any other sexual stimuli, without any emotional attraction at all.

A nonaddict, having a meeting over lunch with an attractive business associate, might notice how attractive that person is, wonder what the colleague might be like in bed, and even briefly imagine seducing him or her before going back to the office. But such thoughts would be fleeting, and the nonaddict would rarely allow them to interfere with the business to be conducted. A sex addict, on the other hand, would not be able to turn off sexual thinking and generally would not want to. From start of the meal to finish, the addict would focus on his or her sexual fantasies.

Needless to say, little business would be conducted during this business lunch, and the sex addict might very well feel compelled to come on to the other person—regardless of the consequences.

Our sexually addicted patients repeatedly tell us that their obsession with sex prevents them from living the way they would prefer to live. Try as they may to conduct business, carry on a conversation, or play Parcheesi with their children, sexual fantasies keep distracting them.

Hank, the insurance agent who is driven to have sex with "as many women as possible, as often as possible," would really like to be the devoted family man most people already think he is. Yet, he rarely comes out of his fantasy world long enough to achieve this goal.

"When I'm in my fantasy mode," he says, "I'm basically living inside my head. I'm living in the house with my family, but I'm not all there. Even if I'm not fantasizing, I wish I was. I'd be playing ball with my boys and hoping they'd lose interest so I could go inside to my den and fantasize, or I'd be out at a restaurant with my wife and the waitress would be this hot number in shorts, and I'd want to rush through dinner so I could get home to think about her—and masturbate.

"The thing was that I could never just fantasize. I had to finish it. I would wake up in the morning and decide I'd want to go cruising, and I'd just do that all day. Sometime during that day I would have to find a place to masturbate or find somebody to have sex with. Something would have to happen, or I thought I'd go nuts. It was that intense."

Hank, like other sex addicts, feels as if he is drowning in confusion as he desperately tries to concentrate on nonsexual matters while being pulled by the magnet of his sexual thoughts. He may try to pay attention to his wife or his kids or his work, but Hank cannot squelch the fantasies galloping through his mind. It is the nature of obsessions that the harder one tries to get rid of them, the stronger they become.

When Hank or anyone else with a sexual addiction begins to fantasize, lust takes over, and the adrenaline begins to flow, almost always setting off the compulsion to have sex. On the one hand, the fantasy itself produces a high that little else in the addict's life can match, so there are few things to persuade him or her to stop the sexual thinking. On the other hand, the strength of the fantasy compels the addict to actually have sex—regardless of the effect doing so may have on other areas of his or her life. In the fantasy mode, Hank's desire to be a good husband and father evaporates, as does Janet's need for love, or George's half-hearted hopes of having a normal relationship. Concerns about keeping a job, getting arrested, contracting diseases—all disappear. The fixation on achieving the ultimate high simply renders all consequences meaningless. Nothing matters except completing the cycle that began with that first sexual thought.

RITUALS

Sex addicts use rituals to re-create the euphoria of past orgasms or intensify the pleasure of new sexual adventures. Once something triggers the overpowering need for sexual gratification, sex addicts feverishly begin the specific behaviors that they know will excite them further.

For instance, Bill, the Health Department inspector, repeats a certain ritual each time he picks up a prostitute. Soon after Bill feels himself getting turned on, whether he was stimulated by a secretary walking past his desk or a television commercial, Bill finds the nearest mirror, fusses with his thinning hair, changes to one of his lucky ties, and splashes on a specific brand of cologne. He goes to his car, locks himself in, and, savoring the explicit sexual images playing in his imagination, waits a full ten minutes before starting the engine. He drives the same route to the pickup strip he has chosen on this day, then circles the area repeatedly, his excitement building with each circuit and honing in on the prostitute he wants on the third pass. He circles a few more times, and when the tension reaches a peak, he approaches the hooker of his choice and procures her—using virtually the same words each and every time. The ritual continues right up until orgasm as he dictates exactly what he wants the prostitute to do and repeats exactly his part of the ritual.

Rituals extend and intensify the fantasy, prolong the high and heighten the orgasm, enabling addicts to literally lose themselves in sex and have the all-consuming pleasure last as long as possible. Often, sex addicts accidentally stumble upon the actions that will later become essential elements of their rituals. Bill, for example, first went through most of the steps in his driving ritual by chance, while returning from one of his restaurant inspections. But he found the experience so arousing that he systematically and obsessively sought to recapture that first euphoria. In this way, sex addicts fixate on a particular routine and repeat it again and again.

Many addicts rely on far more intricate rituals than Bill's. For many addicts, especially those like George whose pleasure does not require another person's participation, each sexual experience is an elaborate performance. They write the script, give themselves the starring role, and direct the ritualistic drama most likely to bring on the ultimate high.

Even when the ritual fails to usher in as intoxicating a sexual high as the addict desires, he or she will repeat it anyway, hoping that it will work better the next time. If sexual experiences disappoint them or leave them feeling depressed—as is the case more and more often as the disease progresses—sex addicts simply attend more carefully to the details of their ceremonial rites the next time around. If the old routine ceases to get them as high as it once did, they add new twists, different cues, fresh sex objects, or new types of sex, making the rituals ever more elaborate, in hopes of creating an even better high. When sex is good, they want more. When it isn't, they still want more. Like the baseball pitcher who thinks he's more likely to win a game by wearing his lucky shirt or a student who thinks she does better on tests when she uses her lucky pencil, sex addicts believe their rituals will get them what they want.

Of course, most people use certain rituals to enhance their sex lives. Lighting a candle as a signal that one partner would like to have sex, wearing sexy lingerie, giving each other massages before going upstairs to make love—little rituals like these often lead up to relaxed, pleasurable sex. In fact, such rituals can strengthen a relationship and give lovers a way to keep their sex lives interesting and satisfying.

Unlike the harmless, even healthy rituals used by nonaddicted consenting adults, compulsive rituals, the kind in which the sex addict indulges, are rarely healthy. They are motivated in part by fear, the way superstitions are. Hearing addicts talk about their rituals, we often get the impression that they believe they must do every part of a ritual in just the right way and in the exact same sequence every time or they will not achieve the high they desire. Of course, failing to complete the ritual or achieve the high gives them yet another excuse to try again.

For sex addicts, rituals are vain attempts to control every facet of their sexual experiences. But as usual, the addict is not really in control at all. For example, when George gets aroused by the idea of being dominated by a woman, it is a foregone conclusion that he will pick up the telephone and dial the phone sex service. He will then listen to one erotic recorded message after another until he masturbates to climax— while sitting in a particular chair in a room that is lit in a particular way, and so on. Once the first step of the ritual has been taken, all others will be taken too.

THE POINT OF NO RETURN

Like the alcoholic whose decision to take that first drink is sure to lead to a binge, when the sex addict begins the ritual by fantasizing, he or she sets the addiction in motion. As soon as he walks over to the mirror to fuss with his hair or change his tie, Bill, whose ritual begins with these actions, has really already given himself permission to go the whole route to orgasm. Because he feels guilty about his past sexual escapades, Bill may delude himself by thinking, "I'll just go see if I can drive through that neighborhood to test myself." But no matter how much he denies the fact that he has lost control, the results of that test have been fixed in advance.

Sex addicts prove this to themselves each time they:

- decide to drive to a particular street where prostitutes can be found (but *not* pick up one);
- decide to go to an adult bookstore (but *not* exchange sexual favors with a stranger);
- decide to steal some articles of underwear from a friend's dresser (but *not* masturbate in them);
- decide to go to an XXX-rated movie (but *not* connect with a stranger to provide oral sex);
- decide to go to a singles bar (but *not* take anyone home to have sex);
- decide to start cruising (but *not* masturbate while trying to catch the eye of someone passing by);
- decide to go to a neighborhood where the addict has engaged in voyeurism before (but *not* peep through any windows this time).

In taking the first step of the ritual, even in thinking the first thought about the ultimate high, the sex addict, throwing caution to the wind, has already turned any maybes into certainties, passing the point of no return. Thus, the entire ritual is one extended act of foreplay that builds up to orgasm—no matter what the addict previously decided to do or not to do.

INSTANT HANGOVER

Failing to pass the tests they give themselves, when sex addicts come down from the intoxication of sex, guilt and shame hit them like a cold shower, often only seconds after they have reached the heights of pleasure. As if riding on a vicious roller coaster, the addict drops in an instant from the highest high to the lowest low.

Depressed, unhappy, agitated, guilty, ashamed, inadequate, scared, stupid, horrible, sad—these are the words that the addicts we treat use to describe their emotional states when they are not thinking about or acting upon their sexual urges. Their obsessions and compulsions relieve such feelings, but only temporarily. When the sexual ritual has been completed, the same feelings wash over them, often leaving them worse off than they were before. Typically, they want to get away from the sex object and out of the situation as quickly as possible.

"I would have these affairs, how many I don't remember," says Don, the parole officer. "They were one-nighters mostly: the kind of things where you really don't know what to say at the woman's house. You're trying to be nice, but inside, you're screaming, 'Hurry up and get to bed!' Afterward, you don't want to talk to her, and you're screaming inside, 'Goddammit, leave me alone!' At that point, you're just trying to get out the door."

As soon as the euphoria evaporates, the need to keep their exploits secret also hits sex addicts with full force. Suddenly, they are consumed by anxiety over "getting out of here before I get caught," or diseases they might have picked up, or the money they have been spending on prostitutes or phone sex services. "I must be crazy doing this," the addict thinks—and swears it will never happen again.

Furthermore, to cover up any trace of a secret life, the addict often goes beyond mere deception to outright hypocrisy, loudly proclaiming traditional moral values about the right things to do. In the aftermath of compulsive sex, overcome with shame and disgust, the addict sees his or her actions all too clearly. "If other people knew what I was doing, they would be disgusted too. They'd know that I'm really just a fraud," the addict believes, and finds the thought unbearable.

Consciously or unconsciously setting out to make themselves feel better, sex addicts end up feeling worse, often losing all hope of *ever* feeling better. "If I told anyone I was really hurting in this affair," says Janet, "I just know they'd answer, 'Well, what do you expect?' It's so obvious that I'm getting what I deserve. I don't do anything to change the situation, just keep going back for more. But what *can* I do? It's really hopeless."

Each time she looks at her life realistically, Janet feels a despair that she can relieve only by returning to her lover and satisfying her sexual desire. Afterward plagued with guilt and shame, she feels even more hopeless, at times even suicidal.

Janet is typical of other sex addicts who frantically try to escape their pain by pursuing the ultimate high. When they are not doing that, sex addicts stew in their own hopelessness. Eventually, they can stand it no longer and are driven once again to begin the vicious cycle of their addiction.

Seed No. 6: Denial

The endless repetition of compulsive behavior makes the addict's life completely unmanageable. Although most sex addicts who seek treatment eventually describe their lives and their behavior as "out of control," "done in spite of consequences," or "beyond help," many—especially those patients referred to us through the courts or those coerced by a family member to consult us—initially take a defiant attitude, denying that their obsession with sex presents a problem or really matters at all.

Like all addictions, sex addiction is a *disease of denial*. Addicts use denial to protect and maintain the addiction. They would have to give up the pursuit of the high if they recognized it as a problem. Without the high, there would be nothing but misery, they think, and to protect themselves from the misery, they deny the problem.

Some addicts admit their actions but deny the impact. Mitch, the auto mechanic and garage owner who interacted with other people for business or sex and for nothing else, was arrested for masturbating in a public toilet and picked up several times in police sweeps of adult bookstores. He could not deny that these things happened, and like all sex addicts he felt guilty about his sexual behavior. But he buried this guilt for years, telling himself things like, "Screw it," "Who cares?" and "Go for it, you only go around once."

Other sex addicts argue that they have their behavior under control, often pointing to the one area of their lives—such as work, children, or home life—that they have thus far managed to protect from the effects of the disease. For instance, even though Janet's home life was falling apart, she still functioned at work. Other addicts we've seen have had run-ins with the law, but believe their behavior cannot be all that bad since the home seems to run smoothly. As long as an addict has one manageable area of life to point to, he or she will use it to bolster the denial. Indeed, it is often seeing that last bastion of sanity crumble that finally convinces the addict to stop denying that a problem exists and to think more seriously about getting help.

During lucid moments, addicts may temporarily break through the wall of denial. Unfortunately, when they can clearly see their compulsive behavior and shamefully judge it as stupid or insane, addicts who already suffer from low self-esteem feel even more certain that "I really must be worthless to keep doing these stupid things" or "I must be really screwed

37

up.'' Of course, these are the thoughts that caused the pain that set off the addiction. As always, the addicts do not want to feel the pain. Some simply accept that they are "weak-willed and beyond help.'' The utter hopelessness of the situation is all the more reason not to change.

Of course, addicts can always point to other people to confirm that their problem is not so bad. Other people engage in more inappropriate sexual acts or have lost more as a result of their behavior, they say. The argument is well supported by the addict's experiences. As Mitch crawled deeper into his addiction, his close contacts became more and more limited to other people who frequented adult bookstores, people willing to participate in his ritual of impersonal mutual masturbation or fellatio. As a result, Mitch confirmed his idea that the world really was screwed up, especially sexually, and saw many people he believed sicker than he was.

When Hank said earlier that admitting his addiction to sex was "a killer,'' he was referring to the struggle all addicts go through when they peel away the layers of denial. Denial is what keeps addiction alive. It is the one seed that must flourish for the addiction to grow, and we will tell you a great deal more about it in later chapters.

WHAT SEXUAL ADDICTION IS NOT

In writing this book, we do not intend to raise unnecessary alarm. Certain sexual behaviors of your own or attitudes you've observed in your spouse or lover may concern you, but just because you want to make love more often than your partner, or vice versa, does not mean one of you has a sex addiction. Likewise, finding out that your partner masturbates or knowing that he or she has sexual fantasies about other people does not indicate sex addiction—or even a sexual problem. Even if you or your partner experience sexual problems at times, if, for the most part, your sex is a controlled, balanced behavior, you have little cause for concern.

Some of our patients worry about their teenagers' sexual behavior. Rest assured that most adolescent sexual experimentation is perfectly normal. A teenager just discovering sex may sometimes resemble the proverbial kid in the candy store. But if you have provided your child with a good, basic sex education, including instruction in responsibility and disease prevention, you probably shouldn't worry too much about his or her appetite for sex, even if it seems especially robust. Similarly, you probably have little cause for concern when considering certain periods in your own or your spouse's past when either of you freely indulged in your sexual appetites or explored new avenues of sexuality.

Many couples also come to us for counseling after one of the partners has had one or more affairs. Certainly a partner's infidelity causes pain, puts strain on the relationship, and is a good reason to get counseling. But one or several affairs during the course of a long-term relationship seldom point to the problem of sex addiction. Affairs *do* generally signal a problem—even a crisis—in a relationship, and if your partner has had an affair, you have every right to be angry, hurt, confused—in short, to feel all the emotions you feel. But unless your partner has had multiple affairs throughout most of your relationship, and *is unable to stop when she or he wants to stop,* the problem is probably not sex addiction.

If you, your partner, or both of you experiment with exotic or unusual sexual practices, or even express a desire to, that alone does not indicate sex addiction. If your partner, for example, suggests bondage or something that strikes you as repugnant, simply say no. Don't automatically label anyone a sex addict for suggesting or even indulging in sexual activities that you find distasteful or just plain silly. It may not be true— and it certainly will not help your relationship.

Just as getting drunk once or twice doesn't make you an alcoholic, or several homosexual experiences do not necessarily mean you are a homosexual, one or two sexual experiences that you feel embarrassed or even ashamed about do not mean you are a sex addict.

Without the element of compulsion, sex addiction does not exist. Sex addiction is more than just sexual behavior. It's a progressive disease that affects mind, body and spirit. The key to identifying it lies in your inability to stop obsessive sexual behavior even when it is ruining your life.

After reading the rest of this book, you still should be cautious about judging yourself or someone else to be a sex addict. We have tried to paint the clearest possible picture of what sex addiction is, why it occurs, and how it creates chaos for addicts and their loved ones. We also offer help and hope for recovery. Yet, the first step toward recovery will almost always be to seek a professional's evaluation and help. We encourage you to take that step if you recognize yourself or someone you know on the pages that follow.

2

GOING TO EXTREMES:
The Acts of Sex Addiction

ill, the forty-year-old Health Department inspector introduced in Chapter 1, has been in treatment with us for over two years. For the past four months, he has not indulged his compulsions to watch women through windows, expose himself, or have sex with prostitutes. Yet, he still gets a certain gleam in his eye when he talks about these pursuits. He has learned to control his impulses, but the memories of past sexual exploits remain fresh and powerful in his mind.

"I started masturbating when I was, I don't know, twelve or thirteen, I guess," he tells us, warily eyeing the tape recorder we are using to capture his sexual history for this book. He sips black coffee from a styrofoam cup and—after reconfirming that we will not use his real name or reveal where he lives—decides it is safe to continue. "In the beginning, I only did it at home, in the dark, maybe watching TV. The beach movies turned me on and shows like 'Gilligan's Island,' anything that had girls with big breasts bouncing around in their bikinis. Sometimes, I would get my hands on a *Playboy*, but bathing suit ads in any magazine did the trick. I'd take the magazine into the bathroom when no one was around, look at the pictures and masturbate."

Countless adolescent boys have experimented with masturbation and been stimulated by the sight of partially exposed female bodies on

41

television or photo layouts in magazines. And so far, Bill's sexual history is no different from theirs. However, as all sex addicts do, Bill soon crossed the line that separates experimentation from abuse, curiosity from obsession, and the enjoyment of the pleasurable sensations his body can produce from the compulsion to have more and better orgasms. He began looking for ever more thrilling ways to achieve a sexual high.

"By the time I was in high school, I was standing by the window watching girls walk home from school and exposing myself," Bill recalls. "I'd be masturbating and the lights would be on to make sure they would see me. I guess around that same time, I was getting high on marijuana and masturbating in my car too. I got arrested for that once."

Bill gets up from his chair and begins to pace. The memory of the arrest is painful, humiliating. As he always does when he feels nervous, Bill fiddles with his moustache, pulling at the hairs, fluffing them out, smoothing them down, no doubt thinking that he has not yet touched on those behaviors that really dredge up his guilt and self-disgust.

"When I started dating my wife, I got into weirder and weirder things," he reports, still pacing. "For one thing, I started stealing women's underwear out of the laundry room at college. Then I started peeping into windows. The first time, it just sort of happened. One day, I passed this open window and I looked in and saw a girl wearing nothing but a towel, combing out her hair and, well, this wave of desire hit me, and I couldn't look away. I got so turned on watching her that I had to go right back to my room and masturbate. It was really intense. *Really* intense. After that, I would go out looking for windows to peep in.

"I know now that I did the most peeping when something was bothering me, like grades or screwy phone calls from my mother, things like that. But at the time, I just knew I needed to do it. I *had* to. I just couldn't stop peeping. I got married, thinking that would change things, but my sex life at home just came to a halt. I was more interested in peeping."

Like other addictions, sex addiction is a progressive disease. It gets worse over time. As the time and energy consumed by the addiction increases, the ability to think, act, and relate to other people in a healthy manner decreases. Meanwhile, the feelings of humiliation and self-hatred get stronger, and obsessive sexual thoughts become more powerful and longer lasting.

Like alcoholics who must consume progressively more alcohol to achieve the effect they desire, sex addicts, endlessly searching for that intense, all-consuming sexual high, act out sexually more often, increase the risk involved and/or add new twists to their rituals and routines. Many, although not all, will add new sexual activities to their repertoire, hoping to reach new highs. Often, this experimentation with the forbidden involves more and more sexual taboos, adding to the illicit power of the ritual.

"I got a job where I had to travel a lot, driving in my car," Bill continues. "I would spend a lot of drive time fantasizing about picking up girls on the street. Then one day it happened. I picked up a hitchhiker, and she asked if I wanted to have sex for money. She looked really scuzzy, but I got really excited about it and just went ahead and did it without a second thought. I started picking up hitchhikers whenever I could. Not all of them had sex with me, but just thinking that *maybe* they would . . . well, it made the job a lot more interesting anyway.

"Then I had to do a few restaurant inspections near where the prostitutes hang out, and the next thing I knew, I was down there every day. During my lunch hour, either I'd drive around looking and masturbating or pick up hookers. One hour turned into two hours, then three. I was exhausted, hardly working at all. My life was a mess, but I couldn't stop."

As we pointed out in Chapter 1, sex addicts each have their own preferences when it comes to sexual activities and the rituals that go with them. Thus, while the progression of Bill's addiction and certain aspects of his story—especially his evaluation that each new sexual experience that he later made part of his ritual "just sort of happened" the first time—are similar to those of other addicts, his actual means of achieving sexual highs may not be.

As we also pointed out in Chapter 1 and will stress throughout this chapter, the sex acts themselves do not necessarily tell us that a person is sexually addicted. In fact, although some people might still call them perversions, many of the sexual behaviors favored by sex addicts can, and often do, occur in normal relationships. What differentiates sex addicts from others is their repeated, persistent, uncontrollable thoughts about the sexual activity; their repeated, persistent, uncontrollable behavior; and their inability to stop. In addition, a sex addict's sexual encounters always remain highly impersonal, sometimes giving an illusion of closeness and intimacy, but in reality entailing none at all.

Ideally, two lovers should have what philosopher Martin Buber would call an "I/Thou" relationship, one that brings out and affirms the very best in both of them and adds to their value as individuals. However, the sex that gets addicts high involves an "I/It" relationship, one that impersonalizes sex, turning lovers entirely into sex objects and devaluing everyone involved, including the addicts themselves. This is clearly seen in Bill's account of his sexual history. For example, the sexual partners who excited his desire and stimulated orgasms were nearly always anonymous: pictures in magazines, electronic images of bikini-clad actresses on his TV set, *any* schoolgirl who happened to spot him in the window masturbating, *any* college coed he happened to see through a window, and *any* prostitute he chose to procure on a given day.

Many sex addicts further impersonalize sex by viewing others as sexual body parts instead of as whole people. Andy, a twenty-seven-year-old elementary school teacher who gets high on pornography, masturbating, and prostitutes, admits that he has a hang-up about women's breasts, finding it impossible to see beyond them. For him, the only part of a woman that has any value is her breasts. Obsessed with their own and other people's body parts, addicts like Andy seldom really care about another person's thoughts, feelings, or desires.

Of course, our culture, through virtually all popular media, encourages a fascination with breasts, chests, legs, shoulders, genitals, and buttocks. But sex addicts carry this fascination to an extreme. Extremes are what sex addiction is all about.

Sex addicts' need for love, power, affirmation, control, and instant gratification is extreme. The lengths they go to in order to escape or anesthetize painful feelings are extreme. And, as this chapter will reveal, any sexual behavior sex addicts use to achieve a high is also taken to extremes.

All sex addicts indulge in some of the following activities, while many more fantasize about the ones they do not partake in. Keith, for example, a real estate broker with two daughters of his own, has thus far confined his activities to extramarital affairs, anonymous encounters with men in adult bookstores, and obscene phone calls, although he has tried several other behaviors. However, he does persistently fantasize about having sex with young girls, fantasies he has not yet acted upon, but fears he will. And the truth is, he might—if his addiction were to progress much further.

Whether or not the sex addict eventually acts out his or her fantasies, knowing the range of sexual behavior in which sex addicts indulge, even if only in fantasy, often helps addicts and nonaddicts alike understand the disease.

"VICTIMLESS" BEHAVIORS

All addictive sexual behavior claims a victim: the addict. But certain sex acts—from voyeurism to rape—also directly claim other victims. We feel this distinction is important, and therefore we have separated sex acts into two categories, depending on whether or not they sexually victimize others as well as the addict. In the section on victimless sexual behavior we include:

AFFAIRS: sexual liaisons outside of a marriage or monogamous relationship, nearly always putting that relationship in jeopardy and causing a great deal of emotional pain. In a sense, the betrayed spouse is surely a victim. But, because the spouse is not physically a victim of the sexual act in question (because, indeed, the spouse is usually not even physically present or in any way directly involved in the act in question), he or she is not a victim in the sense that we are here using the word. Hence, we are covering this material as part of the "victimless" section.

Our references to affairs include both many sexual liaisons with one person over an extended period of time and a series of single sexual encounters with different partners over the course of many one-night stands. The latter can also be the source of sexual highs for addicts not involved in other long-term relationships, such as marriage.

MASTURBATION: attaining sexual pleasure from self-stimulation; manipulating one's own genitals in order to achieve orgasms.

PORNOGRAPHY: erotic, explicit, sexually stimulating pictures, magazines, movies, and books indulged in at home or in adult bookstores and movie theaters, with or without masturbation. More "innocent" stimuli, such as magazine advertisements and TV shows, can also serve as pornography for the sex addict.

PHONE SEX SERVICES: These services involve time-limited, tape-recorded erotic messages or actual people, usually women, who answer calls and talk dirty, based on prepared scripts or in response to what the caller says he or she desires.

FETISHISM: attaching sexual significance to objects (such as underwear, leather goods, or spike-heeled shoes) and incorporating them into sex acts to stimulate desire and enhance pleasure.

PROSTITUTION: sex for money; procuring and paying someone to perform sexual acts. Prostitutes can be picked up on the street, procured at massage parlors, found working in bars or hotels, or delivered by calling a service that furnishes them.

BESTIALITY: having sex with animals.

SADOMASOCHISM: sex acts in which one partner voluntarily submits to being tied up, spanked, or otherwise punished while the other inflicts the punishment. Bodily harm and pain sometimes, but not always, result from the practice. The sex addict might act out either the punished or punishing role in this situation.

Also, sex addicts, because their highs almost always involve rituals, may prefer certain sexual positions over others or favor oral or anal sex, for instance. Variety in these areas is part of most couples' sex lives. However, a sex addict may demand one exclusively or insist upon it in spite of his or her partner's objections.

Although some people might call the activities described in this section sinful, most people can and do engage in at least one of them at some point in their lives. The sex addict, however, takes each behavior to its limit and beyond, looking for more from it and often doing more of it than the rest of the population. For the sex addict, these activities offer a high he or she knows no way of matching, and so repeats them compulsively.

Sex addicts also distort and devalue the relationships in which sex occurs and repeatedly act in ways that go against their own moral codes. Both these facets of sex addiction are worth looking at a bit more closely before beginning our discussion of sexual behavior itself.

Distorting Relationships and Contradicting One's Own Ethical Beliefs

Wayne, an advertising copywriter in his mid-forties, came to us for treatment after being discharged from a drug rehabilitation program.

Upon learning that Wayne had had "at least one woman on the side" throughout the twenty-two years of his marriage and "couldn't resist" having one-night stands each and every time he went away overnight on business trips, the counselors who treated his addiction to cocaine suspected he might be addicted to sex as well.

A fast-talking man prone to wearing western-cut polyester suits, cowboy boots, and cologne, Wayne only agreed to enter therapy with us because he hoped to reconcile with his wife from whom he had been separated for a little over a year. He doubted he was a sex addict, but the fact that he had used the separation from his wife as an excuse to go on a prolonged sexual binge suggested to us that he was indeed sexually addicted. We became even more certain of it as Wayne told us about his sexual relationship with his wife.

"I can't think of a single time when I didn't fantasize about someone else while having sex with my wife," Wayne admits. "I always fantasized about somebody else or some other situation that would help me reach orgasm. I couldn't just be there with my wife and think, 'Well this feels good; this turns me on.' The truth is, nothing we did actually turned me on unless my mind was off somewhere else, thinking about doing something else, with someone else. A lot of times I had to think that way if I wanted to have an orgasm. Hell, I always had to."

For sex addicts, and Wayne most certainly is one, sex is an egocentric experience instead of a sharing, caring, and sensitive interaction. Sex, even with someone with whom the addict has a long-term relationship, provides nothing more than the physical contact necessary to stimulate an orgasm. The other person is merely a convenient object used by the addict to achieve the sexual high.

For sex addicts, sex *always* means more than their long-term relationships and is *completely* impersonal nearly all the time. These extremes differentiate sex addicts from the many people who occasionally, or even frequently, have liaisons for which sex is the primary purpose and that *do not* mean more than the relationship. Sex can be joyful, exhilarating, and just plain fun.

As therapists, our personal beliefs about the morality of certain sexual behaviors are entirely irrelevant to our identification of sex addiction. Individuals must resolve questions of sexual ethics on their own.

Yet, ethical issues constantly come into play where sex addiction is concerned because the sex addict's behavior often does not jibe with his or her own beliefs about sexual morality. This is one of the most fundamental characteristics of sex addiction, which in many ways is an illness of hypocrisy. Sex addicts, often raised in strict religious families and believing in the values they were taught as children, are incapable of meeting their own moral standards. The addiction renders them powerless to live the way they would like to live or conform to their own moral code and the image they are desperately trying to project to the outside world.

The obsessive fantasies, compulsive behaviors, and loss of control that are the hallmarks of sex addiction place addicts in one ethical dilemma after another. They do what they do, in spite of what they believe.

Of course, some addicts manage to uphold their beliefs—in the sanctity of marriage, for instance—and still maintain their addiction. You see, the sex addict does not always have to go outside a monogamous relationship to meet his or her needs. Just as rape can take place within a monogamous relationship, so can sex addiction. An addict can chronically masturbate, indulge in pornography, or use phone sex services without technically being unfaithful.

In addition, some sex addicts act on their addiction only within the context of their marriage or relationship, putting tremendous pressure on their lovers to have sex several times a day every day or to participate in sexual rituals that excite the addict but not the other person.

"It seems like I always want more sex than the men I go out with," complains Robin, the pediatrician, who often masturbates a half-dozen times a day to appease the sexual desires the current man in her life does not. "I can feel this incredible energy all the time. I feel horny all the time. I mean it. I could have sex four times a day easy. The more I do it, the better I like it. I want to do it all the time. So I get really mad if the guy I'm going out with doesn't want to do it at *least* once a day. I say, 'What's the matter with you? Isn't this what you've been waiting for?' I thought that's what men were supposed to want."

Very often, in long-term relationships, the sex addict's partner—male or female—ends up feeling used, reduced to the status of a prostitute expected to supply sex upon demand. Several couples have come to us for counseling primarily because one partner complains to the other: "All you ever think about is sex." When the accused partner is a sex addict, that assessment is pretty accurate. That gets us back to the original premise—regardless of their moral beliefs, sex addicts distort and devalue relationships, turning sexual partners into sexual objects, viewing them almost entirely as an impersonal means to an end.

Several sex addicts have told us that they got married or involved in long-term relationships because they hoped to solve their problem. But relationships entered into for this reason seldom work out. A sex addict's focus on sex and body parts puts an incredible strain on a relationship in which both partners are expected to share not only their bodies, but also their responsibilities—to wash dishes together, keep a home running, and take care of the kids. For the most part, however, sex addicts find it easier to treat strangers, rather than spouses or lovers, as sex objects. So, rather than expecting one person to service their extreme needs, they go outside the relationship, either sticking with one new sex partner for a length of time or seeking out brief contacts with many sex objects. Their demand for a totally sexual exchange drives them to other channels—prostitutes, affairs, phone sex—where they can create and maintain their own little fantasy worlds. But while this strategy may allow them to keep sexually addictive behavior out of their marriage beds, it nevertheless eats away at the foundation of sex addicts' relationships.

Affairs (and One-Night Stands)

Because in this world no one is perfect, many people end up cheating on their spouses or partners, and often feel guilty and regretful. As with any sexual behavior, when considering the issue of affairs, it's impossible to identify with certainty the exact point of no return when infidelity becomes addiction. But it is pretty safe to say that a person who has been married for thirty years and has had one affair or even several affairs is probably not a sex addict unless there are other signs of sexual addiction. On the other hand, Wayne, the advertising copywriter and recovering cocaine addict who is also addicted to sex, claims that throughout his twenty-two-year marriage, he has *always* had at least one affair going, and counting one-night stands, has had sex with more than 200 women so far. It is the great frequency of affairs over an extended period of time and the apparently constant need to cheat that leads us to suspect sex addiction.

Another clue, perhaps the most important one, is Wayne's inability to change his behavior on his own. Wayne, although balking at the term addiction, did view his repeated infidelity as a problem, found it painful, and wanted to quit, but felt powerless to stop. When Wayne tried to stop, he—as sex addicts almost always do—went through the same patterns that follow the discovery of any other addiction. He felt *initial remorse, promised* to quit, did indeed quit for a while but then, after *a period of "sobriety,"* began having compulsive affairs again.

This kind of repetitive behavior, despite awareness of the potentially disastrous consequences, is one of the most clear-cut signs of addiction. For instance, Wayne's wife found out about his affairs, threatening the marriage, which Wayne claimed he wanted to preserve. Yet, even knowing that his wife would make good her promise to leave him if he strayed again, Wayne continued to have affairs. His behavior had definitely gotten out of control.

Similarly, Janet stays in her five-year-old affair even though it is destroying both her marriage and her self-respect. "I feel an intense physical and sexual need to be with a man other than my husband," she explains. "I know the affair I've been having is just an affair, and nothing's going to come of it. I know this man only wants to be with me when he wants sex, that he doesn't have any desire to be with me, you know, just to be with me. It hurts. But then I keep coming back for the sex too. Every once in a while, he'll ask me if I want to do something else, go to lunch instead, or something, but I always say no, let's go to bed. I need that physical closeness, but later I think there's something wrong with that.

"I probably should have broken the relationship off long ago," Janet continues miserably. "It doesn't make any sense to be in a situation that always ends up hurting me and not do anything about it." But Janet does not do anything about it.

Janet sticks with her affair in order to attain the sexual highs she craves but sees few other ways to get. Although some female sex addicts do have multiple affairs and countless one-night stands, nearly all of the ones we've treated are much more likely than men to confine their addiction to masturbation and/or one or two long-term affairs.

That may be explained by the fact that sex addicts in general tend to exaggerate our culture's sexual mores, including the cultural double standard that frowns on promiscuous women while excusing or even praising men's varied and frequent sexual adventures. Robin and Janet, already feeling shame and confusion about their powerful sex drives, are also concerned about breaking society's rules about what is acceptable for a woman to do. They therefore channel their sexual obsessions and compulsions into behaviors they can get away with—masturbation and affairs.

Because society and their own paradoxically rigid moral codes tell both female and male addicts that what they are doing is wrong or bad, they nearly always justify their affairs in some way, coming up with some rationale that they feel makes their behavior okay. For instance, women—who must contend with the taboo against female promiscuity—often insist that their lovers of the moment were first their good friends. By setting up friendship as a criterion for having an affair, they delude themselves into believing that they are actually emotionally intimate with the other person. This, however, is seldom the case.

Male sex addicts may also use the good-friends excuse, but are generally more prone to use rationales like "I have a high sex drive" or "everyone does it; I'm not really hurting anyone" or even "the affairs help my marriage; my wife doesn't like the same sexual things I do (or my husband doesn't want sex as often as I do), so the affairs take the pressure off and we get along better." Regardless of the words they use, sex addicts are nonetheless employing excuses to justify and deny the seriousness of the problem.

Masturbation

Some people may believe that masturbation is bad, a perversion or a sin, but in truth the act itself is rarely a cause for concern. In fact, most men and women masturbate at some point in their lives. If nonaddicts feel comfortable with it, masturbation often provides a much-needed sexual release and helps them understand how their own bodies respond sexually. In fact, in sex therapy, we sometimes recommend masturbation to clients—usually women who, because of societal mores, have never felt free to explore and enjoy themselves sexually. In most cases, we teach self-stimulation to allow our patients first to understand themselves and then to teach their partners what feels good and what doesn't. If the person enjoys it and wants to continue to masturbate occasionally, that's fine, too. But again, we make such suggestions to *nonaddicted* clients.

For sex addicts, masturbation can become an obsession or the only way to get the sexual pleasure they need in the same way alcoholics need a drink or heroin addicts need a fix. Soon, anything perceived as the least bit erotic or sensual leads to masturbation. Compulsive masturbators—

both male and female—usually masturbate quite frequently, as often as six, ten, or more times a day. They may even masturbate to the point of injuring their bodies.

In fact, we recently saw one patient, a twenty-eight-year-old social worker, who had admitted herself to the hospital with a nine-inch gash in her vagina. She was in a typical sex addict's state of denial, claiming to have no idea how it had happened. Don, the federal parole officer, sometimes masturbated until his penis was bleeding, yet felt powerless to stop. In addition, for a compulsive masturbator, self-stimulation becomes a ritual, something a person must do at certain times of the day or night, or must do in the same way each time in order to achieve the desired sexual high. Rather than masturbation itself, the obsession, frequency, denial, and inability to stop are what clue us in to the existence of sex addiction.

Pornography

As with masturbation, a fondness for pornography does not always indicate obsession. Because contemporary American culture—in movies, television, and advertisements—constantly elevates or debases the human body (depending on your point of view), it would be difficult to avoid exposure to erotica or pornography. In fact, as with masturbation, in our treatment of nonaddicts we have sometimes found movies that some people would call pornographic useful as sex education tools. Combining such films with books and therapy can help a couple learn how to tell each other what they like and don't like. Watching videotapes featuring couples enjoying themselves sexually or movies that teach specific sexual techniques can sometimes be more helpful than just listening to a therapist's advice. If the couple sees something they don't care to try, they don't have to; but if they see something they haven't done that they think might be enjoyable, the film encourages them to talk about it and shows them how to do it.

But again, what might help a nonaddicted couple enhance their sex life utterly consumes the sex addict. Pornographic books, magazines, films, and videos fuel sex addicts' explicit, long-lasting fantasies, becoming ends in themselves or part of other rituals. Masturbating while looking at pornography gets to be the preferred, sometimes exclusively preferred, route to a sexual high. Pornography is habit-forming for the addiction-prone individual. If a magazine becomes the only option for sexual stimulation that a person will consider, when watching an X-rated movie is repeatedly chosen over going out and getting to know people or is more important than work or family, when a person views pornography as "the only way to get through the night," then that person has a problem.

Phone Sex Services

"Those 976 numbers are really addictive," Don comments on those services that offer recorded erotic messages. "Just when you start to get excited, it's over. So you call again. It's a different recording this time and you get even more excited. So you call five or six times in a row to hear the whole sequence. The whole time the excitement is building up to what you just know is going to be an unbelievable orgasm. While you listen, you masturbate. And then when you're done masturbating, well then, that's it.''

Other phone sex services offer addicts live telephone playmates. Working from a script or tailoring sex talk to individual callers, the voice talks dirty for as long as callers want, charging their credit cards by the minute.

Phone sex appeals to sex addicts because, like pornography, it provides sexual stimulation without requiring any real personal contact. For example, when George gets home from the hotel where he works and calls such a service, asking the voice on the other end of the line to talk about the kind of sex that excites him, he is able to follow his rituals and have his orgasms without having to reveal anything about himself to another person. Indeed, some sex addicts, because they find that even the minimal amount of socialization it takes to pick up a prostitute is too stressful for them, use the phone services regularly—an expensive practice, as it turns out.

"Those phone services were the thing that really got to me,'' George admits. "I was calling two or three times a night, racking up $350 phone bills every month. If I had just stuck with the hookers, I wouldn't have gotten into so much trouble, because the hookers get paid in cash. But between the phone bills and the cash for the hookers, my paycheck was spent before I even got it.''

When the monthly phone bill arrives, the financial cost of the addiction really hits home. Later, the addict may become aware that there are emotional costs as well.

Fetishism

Although sex addicts take their fetishes to bizarre extremes, almost everyone finds certain objects sexually stimulating, usually because they have previously been associated with pleasurable sex. A fetish is the attachment of sexual significance to nonsexual objects and can heighten sexual arousal for both partners.

For example, stores and catalogs selling sexy lingerie flourish because of the widespread and accepted fetish for silky or revealing undergarments that generally arouse both partners in the sexual relationship. Scented oils, silk sheets, and spike heels worn with lacy stockings and garter belts are also nonsexual objects that can be sexually stimulating. Even things like those that might seem kinky or even silly are used occasionally during sex and are seen as acceptable by both partners.

Sex addicts, however, cross the line that separates enjoyment from obsession. They go from periodic use of an object to enhance sexual pleasure to exclusive use, needing the object to be part of their sexual ritual if they are to become aroused at all and achieve an orgasm. The sex

51

partner and the relationship are meaningless in comparison to the object, which in the addict's mind has almost magical powers to get him high.

Male sex addicts, for example, frequently develop compulsive fetishes for women's underwear. One former patient habitually stole panties from his girlfriend and masturbated in them. Afterward, he stored them away in a sack, amassing a small collection that he kept hidden in his garage.

What's more, extreme fetishes are rarely shared. Indeed, they often are a turn-off to the other person, who rightly feels devalued when coerced by the addict to participate in them.

Prostitution

Once again, frequenting prostitutes does not necessarily indicate addiction. Some clients of prostitutes are sexually addicted, but many are not. Even though people who use prostitutes risk damaging their monogamous relationships—and in the age of AIDS risk their lives and their partners' lives as well—for the nonaddicted, having sex with prostitutes is a matter of choice. You may be opposed to prostitution in general and hold a low opinion of even those people who pick up prostitutes two or three times in a lifetime, but in all probability, such people are not sex addicts.

Although we do not employ sexual surrogates in our own counseling practice and would discourage our patients from looking for surrogates among street hookers, we concede that a therapeutic angle to prostitution may exist. We have seen nonaddicted patients, for instance, who care so much for their spouses or partners that they feel anxiety about their ability to perform sexually, worrying that their sexual failure might destroy the relationship. It is possible for such a person, by having sex with a surrogate, to gain new confidence that can sometimes be transferred into his or her marriage or ongoing relationship.

Unfortunately, finding an effective sexual surrogate who also happens to turn tricks is extremely rare. So, although the possibility of benefits does exist, more often, especially in unsupervised situations, such encounters with prostitutes turn out disastrously.

Like pornography and phone sex services, prostitution appeals to sex addicts because it satisfies their sexual hunger without demanding any relationship more profound than that between a buyer and a seller.

After he had picked up prostitutes only five or six times, Andy, the young elementary school teacher, already obsessed with pornography and masturbation, suspected he could easily get hooked on hookers as well. His suspicion was confirmed when he went out and hooked up with a prostitute each night for a week before his wedding. During that week—and the months that followed—he repeated the same pattern over and over again, using the afternoon hours that schoolteachers have free to pick up street hookers or procure them at various massage parlors, spending money he did not have to spare, and going against his own values. His behavior was out of control.

Because people never feel good about betraying their values, it takes something very powerful to push them in that direction over and over again. The battle between beliefs and behavior, with behavior winning constantly, nearly always points to sex addiction. Andy also showed another clear-cut sign of addiction—he sincerely wanted to stop using prostitutes, but could not bring himself to do so. It is not prostitution, but the addict's compulsion to follow the same patterns over and over again, despite the desire to stop, that is the true problem.

Bestiality

Bestiality is more common than many people think, especially among those who grow up on a farm or around animals. Often, these experiences occur before adulthood, as part of youthful sexual exploration. And although most people view bestiality in itself as a perversion, like other behaviors seen in a negative light, it does not always indicate sex addiction. For instance, Chuck, a construction worker in his early thirties whose sex addiction revolved around prostitutes and pornography, experimented with bestiality but he never fully incorporated it into his compulsive rituals.

"A few times while I was masturbating, I let a dog lick me," whispers Chuck, clearly embarrassed by the memory. "I was just experimenting, just trying to find out what stimulated me the most. I guess that's why you go through all these things—to find out what works."

If having his dog lick him *had* worked, Chuck might have gotten the dog to do it on a regular basis, making it part of the sexual ritual. Then bestiality would have become part of his sex addiction. Of course, even though he had only experimented with his dog, Chuck was still a sex addict. He simply was not addicted to bestiality.

It is worth noting at this point that experimenting with a wide range of sexual behaviors *for the express purpose of finding ways to get a higher high* is a common practice among sex addicts, and it sometimes tips us off to look for other clues.

Like the other avenues of sexual excitement to which sex addicts turn, bestiality obviously allows the person to avoid any emotional involvement with an equal. Although unappealing and perhaps downright disgusting to many people, unlike human relationships, which most sex addicts feel ill equipped to handle, interacting with animals requires little effort on the part of the addict. In addition, most animals offer the unconditional affection that the addict so desperately craves.

Sadomasochism

Although often thought of as kinky, when both partners view sadomasochistic play as an exciting sexual adventure, when they avoid doing anything truly cruel or physically violent, and when they don't rigidly cling to roles that satisfy neurotic needs to punish or be punished, the practice can add variety to a couple's sex life. If both are willing partners, kinky sex does not necessarily point to a problem.

However, engaging in sex where partners playfully tie each other up, spank each other lightly, or take on dominant and passive roles differs sharply from the actions of truly sadistic and masochistic people. Whether or not the participants are sexually addicted, when sadomasochism gets out of hand and involves real physical torture, it clearly reveals personality problems and a need for professional help. However, those problems lie in the aggressive impulses and violent temper of the sadistic partner and the self-destructive martyrdom of the masochist, rather than in sex addiction.

In sex addiction, incessant fantasizing and compulsive behavior are focused on the sexual turn-on of sadomasochism, not on aggression or violence. However, because aggression and violence are part of the sex acts in which the addict indulges, they do become necessary for achieving the desired high and put the sex addict in danger of receiving or inflicting serious physical harm.

VICTIMIZING BEHAVIORS

Many sex addicts compulsively act out behaviors that are accurately classified as sex crimes, causing direct physical and emotional damage to other people as well as to themselves. The sex acts we categorize as victimizing behaviors are:

OBSCENE PHONE CALLS: telephoning randomly chosen victims or personal acquaintances, hoping either to get a shocked response from them or to engage them in conversation during which the caller can masturbate to climax.

INAPPROPRIATE TOUCH (FROTTEURISM): pinching, grabbing, or rubbing with or up against another's genitals, breasts, buttocks, or other sensitive areas—without the other person's consent.

VOYEURISM: watching unsuspecting victims, usually through windows, often while the victim is fully or partially undressed.

EXHIBITIONISM: exposing one's genitals to strangers in order to elicit a response (which the exhibitionist interprets differently than the victim).

CHILD MOLESTATION: performing any sexual act—from inappropriate fondling to intercourse—with a child or teenager, using force, fear, or deception to manipulate the victim.

INCEST: carrying out the above behavior with one's own children or with trusting and easily controlled sisters, brothers, cousins, or other family members.

RAPE: using violence or the threat of violence to have sex with an unwilling partner.

Although they differ in the degree of personal violence involved, each of these activities seriously victimizes another person in addition to victimizing the addict. The voyeurs, for example, violate their victims' privacy, whether the victims are aware of the voyeurs or not. Exhibitionists and obscene phone callers may not physically assault their victims, yet they do violate and threaten their peace of mind and their rights to privacy. And finally, rapists, child molesters, and incesters violently attack every aspect of the victims' lives, inflicting deep emotional wounds that may never completely heal.

Through our work with sex offenders, we have found both that sex addiction does not always involve sexually criminal behavior and that committing sex crimes does not always indicate sex addiction. Many sex crimes are acts of aggression rather than sexual desire, and many people who commit them are not compulsive but sociopathic—viewing people as objects all of the time, acting without regard to the consequences on any impulse they feel at any given moment, and showing little or no remorse for the harm they cause to others (who are meaningless to them in the first place).

Unlike the "victimless" behaviors described earlier, when explaining victimizing behaviors, we will make no attempt to explore their possible benefits. There are none. These crimes of victimization can never be condoned. Whether or not sex addiction causes the offender to commit them, *all* of the behaviors we will describe here are criminal offenses. They *always* indicate a deep-seated psychological problem that demands both professional help and punishment to the full extent of the law.

Obscene Phone Calls

Nick was referred to us through the courts after he was convicted for making obscene phone calls. Nick did not know how to deal with anger. He blew up at his employers or at strangers and regularly got into fights at bars, parties, and sporting events. And still he had more anger to get out of his system, so he released it by making threatening phone calls, and his threats were sometimes of a sexual nature. When caught and confronted by the law, Nick proved able to control his behavior and had stopped making those calls even before his first session with us. Nick was *not* a sex addict.

Sexually addicted callers cannot stop their behavior on their own. They are not venting anger. They are indulging their sexual desires and partaking in their sexual rituals.

Keith, the sexually addicted real estate broker we have referred to earlier, has been making obscene phone calls since he was a teenager, and he used them as the main vehicle for his sexual satisfaction for many years before adding extramarital affairs and anonymous encounters with men in adult bookstores to his repertoire of behaviors. By the time he was thirty-two, Keith had an elaborate ritual built around his calls. It began when he picked up a phone book. Riffling through it, his excitement grew rapidly, and when it reached its first peak, he would let his finger come to rest on a randomly chosen listing. The first time he dialed the number, when a woman answered, he said nothing. He simply listened to several repetitions of the word hello and, if he was lucky, got to hear the woman ask "who is this?" or "is anyone there?" and so on. Then he hung up and for several minutes conjured up fantasies about the woman whose voice he had just heard—imagining that he had gotten her out of the shower, that she was naked or dressed in a tight leather miniskirt and spike-heeled boots. He also told himself that his first call had excited her and that she was breathlessly waiting for him to call back. Now, extremely stimulated, Keith dialed again, this time adopting a fake accent and attempting to carry on a sexually explicit conversation while he masturbated.

Like other sex addicts, those who make obscene phone calls bury themselves in sexual fantasies for hours at a time, often unable to concentrate on anything other than what's going on inside their heads. Few sex addicts *only* make obscene phone calls, however. Their sexual compulsions usually play themselves out in at least one or two other behaviors, such as masturbation or dependence on prostitution.

Inappropriate Touch

Some sex addicts subtly victimize other people by touching them where and when they do not want to be touched, overstepping appropriate boundaries. Certainly, some would argue that what is appropriate is a matter of opinion, but those on the receiving end of these sexual advances generally know they've been victimized. Their shocked or angry reaction is usually as sexually stimulating to the offender as the physical contact itself.

These addicts either brush their own genitals or breasts against another person or brush up against their victim's breasts, genitals, or buttocks. Often they place themselves in situations, such as getting on a crowded bus or squeezing through a doorway, in which they can disguise their behavior as accidental.

Like several of the other sexual behaviors that give a sex addict a high, overstepping the boundaries of touch *can* take place entirely within the context of a monogamous relationship. In a long-term relationship, in fact, a sex addict can indulge more overtly in this behavior, pinching buttocks, grabbing breasts or crotches, rubbing up against their partners at inopportune or embarrassing moments, and so on—all without the other person's consent. Spouses and lovers may feel used, but, because this behavior seems so mild, they often treat it as nothing more than an irritation.

Like those addicted to obscene phone calls, these sex addicts seldom depend on touch as their only sexual outlet. Addicts who give themselves permission to touch other people in this way frequently give themselves permission to act out in other ways as well.

Voyeurism

At one time or another, many people have sneaked a peek at another person undressing. The opportunity presented itself and the casual, nonaddicted voyeur thought, What the heck, I've already seen this much, why look away now? On the other hand, the sex addict who uses voyeurism to get a sexual high repeatedly *seeks out* such opportunities, even to the point of breaking into another person's house and hiding in a bedroom closet.

Obsessed with peeping, voyeurs will spend hours on end standing outside a window waiting for a victim to appear or driving around looking for victims. In fact, for many voyeurs, the hunt itself is as exciting—sometimes even more so—than actually catching a glimpse of the victim. These addicts devote an enormous amount of time and energy to searching for a sexual turn-on that may last no more than a few seconds. Yet they consistently tell us that nothing compares with the euphoria they feel during those brief moments. Bill, whose addiction progressed from masturbation to voyeurism and beyond, explains it this way: "It made me feel so up, I wanted to do it all the time."

Bill, who for years peeped at least two or three nights a week, spent up to three hours cruising a neighborhood, choosing a window to peep through, scouting a location, and waiting for his victim to appear—all to catch a thirty-second glimpse of a disrobing woman. The fact that Bill and other compulsive voyeurs devote such a huge slice of their lives to the pursuit of a quick flash of sexual excitement clearly demonstrates the way any sex addiction consumes the addict.

Voyeurism offers Bill the opportunity to gratify his sexual urges and his distorted need for closeness without demanding anything more than the patience to watch and wait. After getting their kicks, voyeurs either masturbate on the spot or, stimulated by what they have seen, go somewhere else to masturbate. When they get back to the car or back home, or wherever they are the next time they get the chance to masturbate, they merely conjure up the image of what they earlier glimpsed secretly. They may return to the same window again and again or hunt for a new stimulus every time. Regardless, sexually addicted voyeurs will spend night after night attempting to satisfy their compulsive urges to peep.

Exhibitionism

Contrary to what you might think, sex is not on the minds of all exhibitionists. Some act more out of rage and an urge to terrorize rather than from sexual urges. In contrast, exhibitionists who are sex addicts are obsessed with sex in general and are driven to act out the obsession in this particular way.

In many ways, we live in a narcissistic culture, that encourages us to look at our own as well as others' bodies with a meat-market mentality. Yet, narcissism (an extreme absorption with one's self that some might call egomania) is not the same as exhibitionism. Narcissists tend to think that they have great bodies. Exhibitionists, especially sexually addicted ones, focus mainly on their genitals.

Also, nudity itself does not necessarily excite the exhibitionist. For example, because of cultural differences concerning the acceptability of nudity, Europe has many more nude beaches than the United States, but the nudity there is seen as normal and lacks the genital focus that would excite a sex addict. Indeed, most exhibitionistic sex addicts would probably feel uncomfortable in such an environment. If everyone else were also naked, they would neither get the sexual attention they crave nor be in control of the situation.

Cultural norms also partially explain why male sex addicts are more likely to be exhibitionists than female sex addicts. Although some women do get sexually excited by exhibiting themselves—"accidentally" leaving their shirts unbuttoned or bending over to reveal their breasts, letting their skirts ride up or sitting with their legs spread open—our cultural fascination with women's bodies makes such exposure seem socially acceptable, even mundane. In addition, because men have been raised in a culture that freely displays women's bodies on beaches, billboards, movie screens, and the pages of magazines, many of them are numbed by this overexposure and don't react dramatically to a flash of thigh or breast. Still, some women do compulsively expose themselves to men and are no less addicted to their behavior than men who expose themselves to women.

Stuart, a computer technician, recently divorced after four years of marriage, had initially limited his compulsive sexual behavior to frequenting prostitutes and occasional voyeurism. Gradually, however, he escalated to more frequent voyeurism and then to exhibitionism, continually building on his ritual, making it more daring, more risky, and therefore more exciting.

At first, Stuart only peeked through windows. But after several months, he also gave himself permission to break into houses in order to watch his victims from a closer vantage point while masturbating furiously. From there, it didn't take much to allow himself to burst out of the closet at the moment of ejaculation, then quickly run away, leaving behind a terrorized victim.

In addition, Stuart began flashing random passers-by in public places. "I really only flashed a couple of times, but I can see how a person could get hooked," he told us during one of his first therapy sessions. A small, nondescript young man, Stuart, with his horn-rimmed glasses, white shirt with a pocketful of pens, and sensible shoes, would be unlikely to draw a second look from most people—which may be why he finds exposing himself so satisfying. "The woman would gasp," Stuart recalls vividly. "Her eyes would open wide, and I would be thinking, Wow, I really got to her. Man, did I give her a thrill or what?

"By then I would have high-tailed it out of there, ducked behind a building, gotten away in my car or whatever, but my mind was still going a mile a minute. I'd tell myself—She must think I'm really exciting. I bet she's thinking about me right now. I bet she wants me so bad.—And all the time, I'd be going over the whole flash in my mind, every step, especially the look on her face. Then I'd think, Man, I'm so high. This is so great. I got to do it again."

Sometimes Stuart *would* do it again (many exhibitionists flash repeatedly, trying to get as many reactions as they can in a given amount of time). Other times, Stuart would complete his ritual by masturbating or visiting a prostitute. But like the voyeur, it was actually that moment, that instant—sometimes no longer than a blink of an eye—when the victim saw his genitals, that truly got Stuart high.

Like other sexually addicted exhibitionists, it took Stuart quite some time in therapy before he finally realized and admitted that his thinking about the victim's reaction to him was delusional. The victim did not feel excited at all; she felt violated.

Child Molestation

Whether addicted or not, most child molesters find it difficult to communicate or socialize with other adults. They also often have drastic, unresolved problems in their relationships with one or both parents that date back to their own childhoods.

Nonaddicted molesters turn to children in an attempt to develop a "special" relationship, one which provides the offender primarily with enormous control and what they fantasize is affection. The satisfaction of their sexual needs is secondary.

In contrast, the need to develop a special, personal relationship does not carry as much weight with sex addicts, who see their first and foremost need to be sex itself. Seldom do they look upon their victims as special friends or as people who will look up to them. They see them only as sexual objects over whom they have power. The sexually addicted child molester's thoughts and fantasies revolve around the sexual arousal stimulated by young boys and girls who can be easily manipulated.

As we've mentioned before, Keith, the real estate broker, has repeated, prolonged fantasies about having sex with young girls. He finds these fantasies particularly frightening because he has two daughters of his own.

"Young girls are very attractive to me," he confesses. "A lot of the time when I'm doing other sexual things, I'm fantasizing about being with a girl who's like eleven or twelve, real sweet and willing. It scares the hell out of me and, to be honest, there were times when I actually did make an attempt to go through with it for real. At least so far, something always stopped me."

In a way, Keith is addicted to child molestation even though he has never actually been sexual with a child. Instead, he uses his fantasies about having sex with children to achieve his sexual highs. Since sex addiction is a progressive disease, had Keith not sought treatment when he did, chances are he would have someday acted upon his fantasies instead of merely being obsessed with them.

Child molestation, like incest and rape, deeply scars its victims. The betrayal of a child's trust, the use of the child as an object solely to satisfy the molester's sexual needs, and the inappropriate early exposure to sexual stimuli leaves the victim damaged and confused. Worse still, victimizing children creates in them the fears and negative self-talk that fuel the sex addict's addiction. Not all victims of child abuse become sex addicts themselves. But by sexually abusing children, sex addicts, by their own example and through the feelings they instill in their victims, pave the way for a new generation of sex addicts.

Incest

Although Don, the fifty-year-old parole officer, is not addicted to incest, he did, at age fourteen and again eight years later, molest his niece, who was only five at the time of the first incident.

"I didn't have intercourse with her, but I felt her up and stuff," Don explains. "I felt terrible. I still feel terrible. I can't believe that was me. I still ask myself, did I really do that?"

Don had merely taken up the legacy left by his brother who first molested Don when he was six years old. Countless times over the four years that followed, Don would wake up mornings to find his shorts pulled down to his ankles or wake up in the middle of the night because his brother was rubbing and fondling his penis.

Like child molesters, many adults who commit incest were themselves victims of incest or child molestation during their childhoods. Often people extremely needy and unskilled at socializing, those who commit incest cross acceptable boundaries with children because they feel unable to handle adult relationships. When they feel isolated and sorry for themselves, their neurotic needs for affection and sexual attention become focused on the most available outlet: children in their own families.

Although their thinking may be irrational, other sex addicts, for the most part, rationalize whether or not they will give themselves permission to perform certain sexual behaviors. Like teenage sweethearts in the back seat of Daddy's car who do everything but "the dirty deed," sex addicts generally draw the line somewhere, deciding masturbation and phone sex is okay, for instance, but prostitution is not. Or, as Keith did, they may permit themselves to fantasize about young girls, but not to act out that particular fantasy.

The addicts who do commit incest, however, rarely consider ahead of time whether or not they will give themselves permission to commit incest. With little or no thought about the immorality or the consequences, they fix their sexual needs and desires on children in their own families, the most vulnerable targets. Only after committing the crime do they attempt to rationalize this profound betrayal with diseased thoughts, trying to convince themselves, for example, that the child didn't really know what was happening, was learning about sex from them, enjoyed it, or even initiated it.

Rape

Rape invariably involves a combination of sexual and aggressive urges. Both nonaddicted and addicted rapists gratify their own needs by violently forcing their victims to have sex with them. Rapists, whose foremost need is to act out their anger and hatred, using sex as their weapon, are most likely sociopaths rather than sex addicts. A sexually addicted rapist's most important need is sexual gratification. The violence involved and the unwillingness of the victim produce the sexual high the addict desires. However, we cannot stress strongly enough that we are distinguishing between sex addicts and sociopaths only because their psychological treatment would be different. Both definitely *need* treatment—and regardless of the psychology behind them, their actions deserve legal punishment.

The number of sex addicts who rape are few in comparison to those who get high on rape fantasies. Because most sex addicts are themselves morally disgusted by rape, it takes an extremely powerful compulsion to drive them to act out those fantasies. And luckily, the majority never do, but instead channel their obsession into other compulsive sexual behaviors.

Unfortunately, even one sex addict who rapes is one too many. Far too many do not face the truth about their sex addiction until after they have actually attacked a victim. It is only then that they realize the criminality of their actions and recognize the pain they caused the victim.

ADDICTIVE BEHAVIORS REINFORCE ONE ANOTHER

As we pointed out at the beginning of this chapter, sex addiction is a progressive disease and as it develops the addicts' sexual needs escalate. This does not mean, however, that sex addicts who masturbate compulsively or depend on pornography will inevitably go on to rape. In most instances, they will just masturbate or indulge in pornography more and more often.

It is true, however, that sex addicts rarely confine themselves to a single compulsive behavior, and that if one source of sexual stimulation is cut off, addicts will simply turn to another—which is why sex addiction could never be controlled by laws or society in general. Eliminating one sexual outlet, such as prostitution—an admittedly impossible task— would not take care of the problem, only that particular form of the problem. Besides, for the sex addict, even a stranger walking down a public street can set off fantasies and rituals.

However, the various sexual activities described in this chapter *do* reinforce one another *in sex addicts*. To understand this, think about the alcoholics who at first will not drink until after dark, then move the deadline back to the end of the workday, then give themselves permission to get drunk during the lunch hour, and finally, get themselves going with a drink first thing in the morning. Sex addicts also give themselves permission to feed their addiction, and as their appetites become greater and greater as the disease progresses, they permit themselves more sex more often. For many, this escalating permission system involves simply allowing themselves to have affairs more often, or to masturbate more frequently, so that many sex addicts never become addicted to sexually criminal behavior at all.

Others, however, need to add more sexual acts to their bag of tricks in order to achieve a better high. Stuart, for instance, first gave himself permission to be a voyeur, then he gave himself the additional permission to break into a stranger's house to get a closer look, and finally allowed himself to ejaculate right there in front of a victim. Sex addicts who are comfortable violating others' privacy and safety by peeping through windows or making obscene phone calls are liable to later *get* comfortable with other violating behaviors. Having crossed the line into victimizing behaviors, the violation of others becomes easier and appealing as a new sexual outlet. In the addict's diseased thinking, his or her heightened lust *must* be appeased, and this justifies all actions, including criminal ones.

Certain sexual activities tend to be connected for sex addicts. In our own practice, we have often observed that voyeurs also indulge in exhibitionism, perhaps because both are visual activities or because looking at someone who does not know the addict is there loses its intoxicating power, and the next logical step is to get sex objects to see and react to the addict. Likewise, because the excitement created by one behavior demands release via another, the use of pornography and phone sex services is almost always accompanied by masturbation.

Many of our sexually addicted patients find it helpful to understand that these behaviors are connected. In general, knowing that other sex addicts have experienced many of the same patterns or have had similar fantasies often helps them acknowledge that their problems are real. Once they admit that the problem exists in other people's lives, sex addicts are forced to look at their own patterns of sexual behavior and face the possibility that the problem may also exist in *their* lives. This understanding is the first step on their road to recovery.

ADDICTION DOES NOT ELIMINATE ACCOUNTABILITY

Just as alcoholics arrested for driving while intoxicated are accountable for their actions, sex addicts cannot escape responsibility for the consequences of their behavior just because the behavior is a symptom of their disease. Criminal behavior is criminal behavior, period. We do not believe addiction is a viable criminal defense to get a rapist, exhibitionist, child molester, or any other sex criminal off the hook. It does point out the type of treatment needed, but it doesn't make a person less responsible for his actions.

Although their sexual behavior is out of control, addicts have a responsibility to seek help for their problem *before* it reaches the point of rape, incest, or other crime. Denial, of course, often prevents a sex addict from admitting the problem. But at some point, almost every addict does recognize the addiction, yet chooses to ignore it. Sex addicts who admit they have a problem can then choose to get the help they need by going into a recovery program.

Unfortunately, until they are arrested for their sex crimes, many sex addicts refuse help, refuse even to acknowledge their need for help. Like the alcoholic who doesn't hit bottom and pursue recovery until after a DWI arrest or an accident in which someone dies, some sex addicts keep up the denial until they have been caught.

It is a mistake to regard addicts as poor wretches who could never help themselves, or were in some way deprived of the right kind of help—until they end up hurting someone else or going to jail. The idea that an addict must hit bottom before being able to begin recovering is also misleading. The bottom line is wherever the addict decides it will be. Since all addictions develop progressively, anywhere along the line, each addict has ample opportunity to name his or her own bottom line and take the necessary steps to arrest the disease and seek the help he or she needs to recover. And, as we will see in Chapter 10, sex addicts have many avenues—from self-help groups to professional treatment—available to them for recovery.

But before getting into the ways sex addiction is treated, let's look more closely at its causes, paying particular attention to the addict's family background and early sexual experiences.

3

BACK TO THE SOURCE: Examining Family and Sexual Histories

Todd, the thirty-five-year-old investment analyst we introduced in Chapter 1, is divorced and the father of three children. He is also a sex addict whose compulsion to have one extramarital affair after another and as many one-night stands as possible ultimately destroyed his marriage.

Todd's parents were divorced too. In fact, Todd's father—the son of an alcoholic—married and divorced six times. He left Todd's mother when Todd was three, and except for birthday and Christmas cards, had no real contact with his son for the next fifteen years. Todd's mother—a compulsive overeater—remarried soon after the divorce. The new marriage was not much better than the first.

"They fought a lot," Todd reports. "They didn't have a close relationship. In my whole life, I only saw my stepdad hug my mother a couple of times. And they didn't sleep together, except in the beginning when they first got married. After a little while, he started sleeping on the couch, and then they had separate beds."

Today, Todd, who earns a substantial income and thoroughly enjoys the good life it buys him, is a high achiever, competitively driven to outproduce his business colleagues. A tall, handsome man, he keeps his body in peak condition through regular, almost obsessive exercise and pays painstaking attention to his physical appearance. Indeed, Todd projects a combination of masculine good looks and apparent sensitivity that women find irresistible—and Todd knows it. In the presence of a woman, his every word and deed is carefully calculated to get her to have sex with him, without her knowing that is all he's after. When it comes to sex, Todd is a master manipulator. His sex drive is hot-wired by his needs for the attention and affection he did not receive as a child.

"We weren't a close family to begin with," he says. "And I wasn't actually close to my stepdad, but I got along with him okay. He was a real disciplinarian, though. You didn't dare cross him. If you left your coat out, you'd get a spanking for it. If you didn't sweep the garage every day, you'd get whacked with the belt. I have to admit I was always a little afraid of him."

Todd, who today urgently strives to be the center of attention, seems to have been a virtually invisible member of his own family. He was punished for wrongdoings, but his other actions and interests were rarely acknowledged by his mother or stepfather. Indeed, Todd often felt as though the rest of the family "didn't even know I was there," and sometimes he did not want them to. Prompted, as any child might be, to avoid physical punishment for his misdeeds, Todd would "sneak around and do whatever I wanted. I just made darn sure I didn't get caught." He would continue to "do sneaky stuff" for the next twenty years, getting better and better at it as time passed. At thirty-five, he is capable of concealing or covering up anything—including his true feelings and his many infidelities.

The same lack of closeness and communication that kept Todd's parents from acknowledging or encouraging him also blinded Todd to much of what went on around him in his household.

"My sisters hated my stepdad," he reveals. "They say he molested them. And I guess, based on things I know now, there's a good chance that it really happened. But I didn't see it at the time."

Signs that his stepfather was molesting his sisters may have existed, but Todd did not see them or want to. For one thing, he was already busy "sneaking around," smoking marijuana and withdrawing into sexual fantasies. For another, even though Todd's stepfather showed Todd little warmth, he was still the only father Todd knew during most of his childhood, and Todd felt a certain loyalty to him. Completely missing the irony of his statement, Todd concludes:

"I like the guy. He never did anything to me. In fact, he helped me. He taught me a lot."

For all of us, childhood is a time for learning—learning about who we are and what we can do, learning to get along with other people, learning right from wrong as well as how to handle our feelings and needs, including sexual ones. We learn from everyone around us: from our churches or community groups, our friends, our schoolteachers, the media, and most of all from our parents and families. Unfortunately, sex addicts often learn some very specific and dangerous lessons. Todd certainly did. His mother ate compulsively, and his stepfather molested his sisters. Through the examples he was shown daily in his own home, Todd, like so many other sex addicts, came to believe that pain, anger, and stress could be reduced through compulsive behavior or chemical dependence. Todd's parents chose food and sex as escapes, while other sex addicts learned the same lesson growing up in homes where one or both parents were alcoholics, drug addicts, workaholics, or compulsive gamblers.

The sex addict's dim view of the world at large is the result of negative experiences in the smaller world of his or her family. In such environments, it is easy for addicts to develop low self-esteem, feeling that, because of their own inadequacies, they deserved the abuse, neglect, or rejection they received during childhood.

Low self-esteem and poor role models often lead to vital lessons *not* learned, as well. Most sex addicts do not develop adequate social skills, never learn to share emotions honestly, and are unable to communicate on more than a superficial level. Because sex addicts seldom acquire a proper sex education, they often have difficulty distinguishing between appropriate and inappropriate sexual behaviors.

LOOKING AT THE PAST OBJECTIVELY, PERHAPS FOR THE FIRST TIME

Whenever a patient comes to us with a sex addiction problem, we take an extensive family and sexual history, asking many pointed questions about the patient's parents, siblings, sexual experiences, and so on. We try to discover both the obvious and the hidden messages sex-addicted patients received about sexuality and intimacy from their families, their churches, their friends, and any other sources.

We ask: *Did anyone in your family discuss sexuality with you at all?* We often learn that no one did. Robin, now a pediatrician, told us that her parents answered any question about sexuality with, "You'll find out after you get married." Robin still has not married, but she has had plenty of experience with sex, none of which has made her any less anxious or confused about her own sexuality.

We ask: *What kinds of messages about sexuality did you hear through your church or synagogue?* Many religious teachings are prohibitive and we discover that sex addicts took them to heart in a particularly stifling, almost terrorizing manner. Raised as a Catholic, George is a chronic masturbator who recalls being told over and over again that masturbation was "like death. Every time I did it, I was committing a sin."

We ask: *Did your parents ever punish you for masturbation or sex play?* Many sex addicts vividly recall such incidents. Hank, for example, was five years old when a neighbor caught him and her daughter playing doctor.

"My dad screamed at me, 'You want to be naked? There, be naked!' Then he made me sit on the couch naked. The girl's mother was still there while all this was happening. So I just tried to huddle up in a ball on the couch, hoping she wouldn't see me."

We ask: *How did your parents treat each other?* Sex addicts may have learned more subtle lessons by observing how their parents related to each other or from the unwritten rules for acceptable behavior in their households. We often hear that the parents of sex addicts rarely showed affection toward one another. "I never even saw them hold hands," says George.

We ask: *Did you feel free to share your feelings?* As children, many sex addicts were discouraged from expressing independent thoughts and true feelings. "They had all these rules, you couldn't say this and you couldn't do that," complains Robin. "Every time you turned around you could blow it. It was like walking on eggshells all the time."

We ask: *Can you recall any particularly painful or traumatic events that occurred during your childhood?* Repeatedly, we are given accounts of the death of a family member, their parents' divorce, and molestation or incest that happened once or many times.

We ask: *Were there any problems in your family that lasted for a long time, perhaps the whole time you lived in your parents' home?* Often, we are told about the chronic illness of a parent or sibling, a physically or verbally abusive parent, or constant financial difficulties.

And we ask: *Is it at all possible that either or both of your parents had an addiction of any kind?* The overwhelming majority of sex addicts we have treated grew up with at least one parent who was addicted to something—sex, alcohol, drugs, food, gambling. And those who did not usually had a parent who set unattainable standards for children and constantly criticized them or had explosive tempers that would flare without warning.

Of course, many people who never become sex addicts had many of these same influences during their childhoods. Although most people *feel* the effects of troubled or traumatic childhoods for the remainder of their lives, not all of them *show* the effects by becoming sex addicts, or addicts of any other kind. Still, a great many do. However, the important point is that *nearly every sex addict we treat reveals these same past influences*.

For many of our patients, relating personal histories gives them the first opportunity they have ever had to look closely and objectively at themselves, the people in their lives, and the other forces that influenced them. Few people take a really hard, honest look at themselves, but sex addicts find self-examination particularly difficult. As Hank put it, "I've never been able to recognize patterns in my life, but then I never really looked for them. I never really wanted to."

And, when it comes time to scrutinize the addiction itself, many sex addicts, even those who voluntarily come to us for help, still desperately try to deny the disease. Because it forces them not only to recall the past but also to acknowledge their present unmanageable behavior, self-examination threatens the addiction. Many of our patients are horrified at the prospect of being honest and realistic about themselves. Getting past the denial that prevents them from recognizing the addiction is the first step toward recovery.

WHY INSIGHT MATTERS

With our assistance and the support of a self-help group, the sex addicts we treat eventually recognize that the low self-esteem, ever-present anxiety, and tendency to turn to compulsive behaviors that plague them today first took root years earlier and grew in the fertile soil of blatantly or subtly troubled families. Virtually every sex addict we've treated has been able to pinpoint specific episodes and/or ongoing influences that turned their homes upside down.

When attempting to identify the sources of thoughts, attitudes, and feelings that strengthen the addiction's hold on them, the sex addicts with whom we've worked most commonly cite

- One or more traumatic events during childhood—usually involving death, divorce, abuse, or victimization.
- Parents who were uncommunicative or frequently absent from the home.
- Families in which affection, encouragement, and trust were virtually nonexistent while criticism, harsh punishment, and rigid— though unwritten—rules were ever-present.
- Prohibitive messages about sex, primarily from parents, but also found in religious teachings.

Insight—the honest, objective perception of your inner self, what you do and why you do it—is necessary for recovery from any addiction. But insight alone never changes anybody. We've seen too many patients who gain insight into their behavior and still slip back into their old patterns to believe that. All too often, addicted patients come into our office, talk about their childhoods or problems with their families, perhaps read a few books about growing up in an alcoholic home or surviving incest or probing their life histories, and say, "Aha! That's it! Now I understand." Then, they stop seeing us and go right back to their old ways. All the knowledge in the world simply won't convince a sex addict to change.

In fact, a little knowledge can be a dangerous thing. We've seen several sex addicts, especially those cajoled or forced into seeing us and not yet ready to give up their denial, who have used the shallow insight gained through a short examination of their family and sexual histories as a justification for and an excuse to continue their compulsive behavior. If looked at as a way of blaming someone else and pitying oneself, exploring personal histories can do more harm than good. "No wonder I'm that way" gets turned around to "I'll always be that way," which is used as a reason *not* to change.

When undertaken with an open mind and a commitment to recovery, however, exploring personal histories can be enormously helpful to sex addicts. Understanding the forces that shaped their identities helps addicts make some sense of the chaos and confusion in their own minds. Seeing that there are real reasons for their behavior—and recognizing that reasons rooted in the past need not apply to the present—addicts can choose to change their attitudes, learn how to express their feelings, and *stop behaving in the same old way.*

LEARNING BY EXAMPLE

Like most other addicts, virtually all of the sex addicts we've treated grew up in families shattered by a traumatic event or tormented by a long-term problem. The addiction of at least one other family member seems to be by far the most common of these problems.

Don, to name just one, had an alcoholic father and later an alcoholic stepfather, whose chronic and progressive illnesses became the sole focus of his mother's attention, leaving her little time or emotional energy to nurture her children. George and several others had workaholic parents, who frenetically poured all of their energies into their jobs, neglecting their families. Others had a parent who compulsively gambled or a parent with an eating disorder. Their obsessions kept these parents from attending to their children's needs. Finally, several addicts, Hank and Todd among them, had parents or stepparents who were sex addicts themselves, leaving in the wake of their repeated infidelities, child molestations, or incestuous acts a literally unspeakable tension.

When examining addictions, it is oversimplifying matters to focus only on the more easily recognizable, tangible problems, such as a mother who drank too much or a father who gambled away every paycheck. It is easy to see connections when the addict's mother ate compulsively, or the father worked eighty hours a week. We feel it is essential to broaden the idea of addiction so that it includes obsessive or compulsive behaviors, such as incessant housecleaning or constant TV watching, that may not be as obvious or readily named as outright addictions. George, for one, grew up in a home ruled by a perfectionist mother, while Mitch lived in the shadow of a domineering, authoritarian father. Perfectionism and attempts to have total control are essentially compulsive behaviors, and though not traditionally called addictions, follow the same patterns as addictions and create remarkably similar problems in any family.

In addition, a great many of our sex-addicted patients had parents who could be described as religious fanatics. Their obsession with religion and extreme efforts to preserve religious values dominated every family interaction. This kind of family has rigid and restrictive rules, discourages honest communication between family members, frowns upon the free expression of feelings, and is fanatically devoted to maintaining the family image. Such a family differs from an alcoholic family, for instance, only because alcohol is not present. All the other patterns run parallel.

With the unspoken threat of imminent death constantly hanging overhead, chronic illnesses other than addictions also tear families apart. Robin's sister suffered from chronic bronchitis and her mother from a heart ailment that kept her bedridden for the better part of seven years. Janet's father, sick for as long as she could remember, died of cancer when she was nine. Bill's and Don's fathers also died when their sons were very young. The painful loss of a parent turned their households upside down, sometimes plunging their families into poverty and prompting their mothers to remarry for money rather than love. The loss of a parent through divorce can have similarly devastating effects on a household.

All parents—whatever their individual strengths and weaknesses—are role models for their children. A child's early learning has little to do with what his or her parents know. Children instead learn from what they see and how their parents behave. Sex addicts, in observing their parents, usually learn that compulsive behavior—of any kind—relieves stress and pain.

Todd's mother, for instance, was a compulsive overeater and he could not help but see that when things were not going well, instead of trying to work things out, his mother ate more. Because overeating was a compulsion, Todd's mother was probably not consciously aware that she ate instead of dealing with feelings, and she certainly did not intend to send the message Todd nonetheless received: "Members of this family do not feel or talk about emotions." Instead, they *do* something about them—and what they do need not have any logical connection to the real problem.

Similarly, by observing his father and stepfather, Don, who would later become an alcoholic himself, learned that drinking was a perfectly acceptable method of drowning one's sorrows. These misconceptions are not necessarily conscious, of course, but repeated observation imprints them on the potential sex addict's mind. As a result, sex addicts whose role models were addicted or compulsive are well equipped to one day give themselves permission to indulge in their own compulsive behaviors.

THE CHILDHOOD LESSONS THAT FORM A SEX ADDICT'S SELF-IMAGE

CHILDHOOD LESSON:
"I am not good enough the way I am."

George, who masturbated compulsively from the time he reached puberty until he was twenty-five, grew up in Highland Park, Illinois, in what to any outside observer appeared to be a normal family. His father worked extremely hard and rose rapidly to become a highly successful hotel manager, just as George himself would do twenty years later. His parents, born into poverty and both the children of alcoholics, had, through ambition and hard work, pulled themselves up to become an upper-middle-class family, prominent in their community and active in the Catholic church. They sent George to parochial schools where he received in his own estimation, "an excellent education."

But what looked like the embodiment of the American dream from the outside was, on the inside, more like a nightmare to young George. While they were neither alcoholics nor drug addicts, both of George's parents behaved compulsively. His mother was entirely focused on her children, wanting them to excel and expecting them to meet her exacting standards at all times. She tolerated not even the slightest mistake and her sharp, never-ending criticism cut deeply and left many scars. "I know she only wanted the best for us, but she made us feel like dirt," George remembers.

While his mother dominated and, from George's perspective, terrorized the family, his father was nowhere to be found. "He was gone before we got up and didn't get back until seven or eight at night, and sometimes not even then. Even when we took vacations at our summer house in Minnesota, he'd spend the entire time fixing up the place. He never came down to the lake with us. He was always too exhausted or too busy to do anything with us. Really, I hardly ever saw the guy."

As other sex addicts have, George described his childhood as "one test after another and I failed them all." He failed to attract his father's attention. He failed to get his mother's approval. He was awash with the pervasive sense that he was not good enough.

As a result, throughout his childhood and long afterward, George felt incompetent, unappreciated, and, like Todd, completely unrecognized. As they have for countless other sex addicts, these feelings wormed their way into George's self-image. By the time we met him, as far as George was concerned, he was a totally worthless, inadequate human being, incapable of ever really pleasing anyone.

CHILDHOOD LESSON:
"I must be perfect. If I make mistakes, catastrophic things will happen."

Virtually all the sex addicts we've seen feel tremendously insecure about their own abilities. George, like most sex addicts, adopted his parents' harsh judgments as his own, and with them a perfectionist attitude that makes it impossible for him ever to feel satisfied with what he does or who he is.

Robin, whose father was an alcoholic and whose mother had a chronic heart problem, calls herself "the only well one" in her family. She strived for perfection as a way of easing the tensions in her home and believed that the slightest mistake on her part could send her mother to bed for a week or her father on a drinking binge.

"I was always afraid of not doing well in school," she says. "I don't know what would have happened if I hadn't done well, but I thought it would have been something really awful. I was supposed to do well, that was the message I got and so I just did.

"My mom was always sick, and I always had to be real careful around her. If I did anything wrong, anything—if I disagreed with her, got a B instead of an A, wore some outfit she didn't like, you name it— the next thing I knew her heart condition would flare up. I'd watch her breathing get bad, she'd turn white as a sheet, and slump back in her bed, groaning and clutching her chest, and I'd be thinking I made that happen. It was my fault. I felt this horrible guilt. I spent my whole childhood in a state of panic, thinking I was always just an inch away from setting off a fatal heart attack."

Many sex addicts, especially those whose parents were sick or addicted like Robin's, grew up feeling they had a magical ability to control their parents' behavior and state of mind. In Robin's case, she practically felt responsible for whether her mother lived or died. Although few sex addicts we've seen felt they had this extreme a power, they did tend to feel responsible for their parents' actions. Those whose parents were alcoholics believed their own actions determined whether or not their parents would get drunk. Others, like George or Mitch, desperately tried to guess what their parents wanted and acted accordingly, in order to control physical abuse or verbal assaults. Unfortunately, their parents were volatile and thoroughly unpredictable, making their efforts to ward off beatings or criticism quite futile.

CHILDHOOD LESSON:
"No matter what I do, something bad happens."
"I was always very nervous around my father," concedes Mitch. Thirty-five years after the fact, he still cringes as he recounts the horrors of being physically abused by his father. "He always seemed like he was ready to explode. He had a real short fuse, and just about anything I did set him off. He picked on me all the time, and at one point, it got so bad, I would stutter whenever he was around, which of course made him get on my case even more. Dinner was the worst. He wanted us to sit down and eat together, every night. And every night at the dinner table, he would stare at me and not say anything. He just sat there waiting for me to do something wrong—and I knew it.

"I'd be all nervous and I'd do something like reach for my milk and knock it over. Then he'd beat me or send me to bed without supper. I got the beating when my sister did something wrong too. My mom never really said anything about it. What could she do? My dad would just blow up at her. Better me than her. I had to be the whipping boy, so he wouldn't hurt my mom or my sister. But the thing that really got to me was, every day it was something else. No matter what I did, he didn't like it. Anything was an excuse to hit me."

As the situations in their homes became worse instead of better, as the alcoholism or illnesses of their parents progressed or the beatings and tongue-lashings continued, potential sex addicts report that they felt more than ever like failures. No matter what they did, something bad happened. Their utter lack of control over situations they nonetheless continued trying to control would later show itself in the sex addicts' belief that everything in their lives was dictated by others as well as in their attempts to reclaim power through sexual activities.

CHILDHOOD LESSON:
"I can't do anything right."
From the repeated failure to control their parents' uncontrollable behavior and addictions, it was just a short hop from sex addicts to feel

as if they were and would always be ineffective at anything and everything they tried to do.

"My mom never congratulated me for anything," George recalls with a sigh. "But that's just the way she is. She's a pessimist about everything. She never considers how much fun you might have when you go somewhere, she just worries about what's going to go wrong. I guess my parents both thought that the only way we'd learn anything was if they harped on all our negative points, because they never said anything positive at all."

Many, many parents of sex addicts withheld praise while criticizing their children for every real or imagined flaw. Robin, whose perfectionism began early in life and would later contribute to both an eating disorder and her sex addiction, explains, "My mom and dad always said, 'What's wrong with you?' So I always thought something *was* wrong."

As a result of the constant criticism they hear from others, sex addicts learn to constantly criticize themselves with negative self-talk. "Something's wrong with me. I can't do anything right. I'm bad," they tell themselves. The negative view of themselves that is at the core of their addiction will be confirmed over and over again by their sexual behavior.

CHILDHOOD LESSON:
"Being good does not get me what I want."

Because they believed catastrophes would occur if they misbehaved, most sex addicts made an effort to at least appear to obey the rules of the household. "Even though I did a lot of sneaky stuff while I was growing up, I never questioned authority," claims Todd, who would continue to do sneaky stuff after leaving home.

Sadly though, the more successful they were in obeying or appearing to obey the rules, the more deprived of attention these potential sex addicts felt.

"I never got any attention," Robin observes. "My sister got all the attention, first because she was sick all the time, and then because she was always getting into trouble. There she was, practically flunking out of high school, and making out with any guy who gave her a second look, and my parents were bending over backward for her, helping her with her schoolwork, buying her a car and new clothes so she'd stop acting like a juvenile delinquent. And there I was, doing every little thing they wanted, killing myself to please them, and they didn't even notice."

Although Robin went right on trying to please her parents by being good, other sex addicts learned at an early age that the only way to get attention from their parents was to do something wrong. Todd, for example, finally got to see his father—for the first time in fifteen years—when he was busted for selling pot at age eighteen.

Unfortunately, many sex addicts who did receive special attention from their parents often would have preferred to be left alone. Mitch certainly would rather have been ignored than singled out as his father's whipping boy, a distinction that netted him both physical and verbal abuse. "He would say to me, 'I already had one son. When you were born, I wanted a girl, but I got stuck with you instead.' " Hearing putdowns like that throughout his childhood, Mitch naturally felt unwanted and figured he never would be wanted.

Like all the childhood lessons we have mentioned thus far, these feelings of being unwanted—and the belief that being good and playing by the rules would not get them the attention and affection they so desperately desired—were magnified in sex addicts' minds and incorporated into their identities, setting the stage for future sex addiction.

CHILDHOOD LESSON:
"If I try to get what I want or say what I think, I will lose the love and approval I need."

In some families, the addicted parent—often an alcoholic or sex addict—behaved abusively while the nonaddicted parent withdrew. Children often interpreted the passive parent's silence as tacitly condoning the abuse or addiction. In other families, the nonaddicted parent, unable to control the largely absent addict, took charge of the rest of the family with a vengeance. Even in cases where both parents were addicted or compulsive, one parent usually sat back while the other took charge, tyrannizing the rest of the family. Or the nonaddicted parent devoted all of his or her energy to the addict, worrying about, covering up for, and trying to reform the spouse.

Regardless of the form it took, in such homes, everything—any individual interests, any personal needs, any independent thoughts or feelings—took a back seat to the big problem in the family, even if that problem was never openly acknowledged. The message was clear: what little stability the family had could be destroyed at any moment, and the delicate balance had to be maintained at all costs.

When everything has to be done the way a domineering parent wants it done, when *any* disagreement is seen as a direct challenge to that parent's authority or as a threat to the entire family's stability, when independent thinking is not tolerated, children do not learn to assert themselves, at least not in a constructive way.

"I'm thirty now and even today my parents don't like anything that I think of on my own," Robin continues. "And I still think that if I do even a little thing wrong, and they find out about it, they'll kick me out of the family. And once I'm out, that's it. I'll be a nonperson to them."

Sex addicts, looking back on their childhoods, see that they received only conditional love, love bestowed upon them in exchange for obedience. They also see that the unpredictability of abusive or addicted parents convinced them that any choice they made on their own would be the wrong choice, any action they took on their own would be a mistake, and any thought they expressed would lead to disaster. Having already learned that no matter what they did, something bad happened, sex addicts—in self-defense—decided *not to have* needs or thoughts of their own and if they did, to keep other people from finding out about them.

75

CHILDHOOD LESSON:
"It is wrong to want what I want and wrong to think what I think."

"From day one, my mother was always saying, 'This is the way you're supposed to be. You may think you want to do *that,* but what you really want to do is *this,*' " George explains. "It really screwed me up. She didn't just tell me what I was supposed to do. She told me what I was supposed to *want* to do. I was completely under her control, completely unassertive. I just did what I was told. Most of the time I didn't know what I wanted. To this day, I feel all kinds of pressure whenever I have to make a decision. I usually end up doing what I think other people want me to do."

In order to grow, children have to become ever more independent, learning through trial and error to make for themselves the decisions once made by their parents. Each time children assert themselves, make choices and follow through, take the risk to try a new behavior and succeed, they learn to trust their own judgment, and they build a sense of their own adequacy. Because the overly controlling parent permitted no independent thoughts or actions, however, most sex addicts lack confidence and question their own judgment. What's more, as children, sex addicts were led to believe that independence and self-assertion betrayed the family and infuriated their parents, who responded with physical or verbal abuse. Thinking and acting independently was so dangerous that, if they were to do it at all, they would have to do it secretly.

CHILDHOOD LESSON:
"I am nothing without other people's approval."

Sex addicts learned one skill exceptionally well while growing up. They developed an uncanny ability to put on a façade, always trying to appear the way they thought others wanted them to be. At first, they hid their true selves from their parents. But later, as the façade became second nature to them, they hid from everyone else as well.

However, inside, behind the façade, most sex addicts feel quite hollow, and as if they have no identity of their own. "For a long time, I thought I had to be just like my brother to gain my parents' approval," remembers George, who is still struggling to discover his identity. "I was trying to *become* my brother, but that didn't work at all, because he's everything I'm not. He's not better or worse necessarily, I know that now, but we're totally different. So I stopped trying to be Joey. But by then, I felt like my mother was using me to take the place of my dad. Mom wouldn't talk to my dad at all. She just took everything out on me. If she told me I was just like my father once, she told me a hundred times. So, anyway, between trying to be my brother and constantly being compared to my dad, I didn't know who the hell I was and what I wanted to do with my life.

"When I went to college, I don't think I did it intentionally but I went into hotel management, which my dad is in. Looking back at it now, I guess I must have thought 'Hey, I can't meet my mom's expectations. Maybe I can meet my dad's.' And I've done a really good job of it: I have the exact same title and position he had at my age. And I think maybe my parents are proud of me now, because I'm living up to their standards, professionally anyway.''

Like George, most sex addicts never stop hoping that one day their parents will be proud of them. In most cases, having no clear-cut identity of their own, sex addicts' self-worth depends on other people's approval, recognition, and attention. In their quest for what they did not get during childhood, they push themselves unmercifully and judge themselves constantly. But most significantly, they delude themselves into thinking that their sexual encounters give them the approval and affection they so desperately need.

HOW THESE CHILDHOOD LESSONS SHAPE THE ADDICTS' VIEW OF THE WORLD AROUND THEM

Early childhood experiences not only mold the addicts' self-image, but also shape their view of the world around them and the people in it. And just as sex addicts learn to distrust themselves, they learn that other people can't be trusted either. For any developing child, the family is a microcosm of the universe as a whole, with parents and siblings standing in as representatives of all other people. The way the family interacts tells the child what to expect from others outside the family. Most sex addicts, through childhood experiences, come to believe that "other people hurt, use, humiliate, abandon, and reject me. I can't depend on anyone but myself." This feeling is one of the cornerstones of their disease.

CHILDHOOD LESSON:
"I cannot depend on people, because people are unpredictable."

In the homes in which many sex addicts grew up, homes where one or more family members indulged in addictive or compulsive behavior, children learned above all else that people change from one minute to the next, are unpredictable or even explosive, and therefore one should not depend on them.

Hank, who as an adult would follow in his father's footsteps, having his own compulsive affairs and a lifelong obsession with pornography, was always afraid of his father, an incester, child molester, and compulsive womanizer with a violent temper. "I never knew how my father would react to anything," Hank explains. "If I did something wrong, he might explode. But if I did something right, he might hit me anyway. Or maybe not.''

Inconsistency and unpredictability is confusing and stressful for anyone, but it is particularly harmful to young children who must trust their parents or another adult. For children brought up in this way, however, trusting anyone remains extremely difficult. Children can only feel safe and secure if they have some idea of what to expect from various situations and some reliable means to predict the results of their own actions. But sex addicts, growing up with abusive or perfectionist parents or addicted ones, live their early years in a state of constant anxiety, never knowing what will happen from one moment to the next. The world inside the walls of their family home is a terribly dangerous place, and so they believe the outside world must be too.

CHILDHOOD LESSON:
"People will always abandon or reject me."

Sex addiction is a disease that begins and ends in isolation and loneliness. Although addicts' compulsive behaviors may involve other people, sex addiction remains an essentially solitary, totally self-centered experience. Since sex addicts don't trust others, they shy away from getting emotionally involved, fulfilling their emotional needs through fantasies in which they can completely control all the players.

Addicts do not let other people get close to them, because they believe they know exactly what will happen if they do. Experience has taught them that anyone who gets close will almost always hurt or abandon them.

Virtually all sex addicts share this belief, and it almost always springs from their rocky childhoods. The original lesson takes many forms. In some cases, a traumatic event such as divorce or death leaves the child feeling alone and insecure. Todd, for example, who never saw his father during his childhood, suffered terribly from the finality of his parents' divorce.

For others—like Bill, Janet, and Don—the death of a parent triggered the belief that they were utterly alone and always would be. Bill, who as an adult would protect himself from abandonment by getting "involved" with almost no one but hookers and the victims of his voyeurism, recalls the effect his father's and grandfather's deaths had on him. "My father died when I was four, and my grandfather died at almost the same time. I really liked them. I always looked forward to spending time with them. But then, all of a sudden, they were gone, and they weren't coming back."

To a child, the death of a parent is always a shock. It is a traumatic event and most of the sex addicts we've treated rarely received the compassion or explanations they needed in order to cope with their grief. Their families almost never pulled together to support one another during the crisis created by the death. Even when a parent had been seriously ill for a long time, children were not prepared for their inevitable death.

"When I was ten, somebody woke me up in the middle of the night and told me my father was dead," explains Don, whose father and stepfather were both alcoholics. "I hadn't even accepted that he was as sick as he was, even though now I know that he was sick and dying for a long time. I just denied the whole thing and kept right on denying it. I just decided that somebody had made a mistake, it couldn't be true. I think I was angry at my dad for dying, but I couldn't have articulated it then. So I just tried to detach myself and pretended it wasn't true. I told myself that my dad had gone away for a while and concocted fantasies about the day he would come back. I guess my whole fantasy thing must have started then.''

Don's reaction to what he perceived as abandonment—pretending it had not happened—established the pattern he would follow in later years, when he would pretend that his compulsive masturbation, affairs, and even the molestation of his niece were not really problems.

Because one of the most important figures in Don's life had deserted him and he chose to deny the facts instead of face them, Don never expressed or resolved his feelings, allowing them to grow into an all-encompassing fear that he would be abandoned again by anyone he allowed to get close to him. Yet, he still needed closeness, so he, like so many other sex addicts, settled for the illusion of closeness he created in his own mind during sex.

CHILDHOOD LESSON:
"No one will ever really love me, no one will ever really care."

"As far back as I can remember, I never felt loved," says Janet, who at forty-seven still hasn't found love, although she continues to look for it through sex. "I was never close to my father," she says. "I remember him, but I never really knew much about him or what kind of person he was. All I knew was that he was sick and dying and that he couldn't be the kind of father my friends had or like the dads I saw on TV. I always had this feeling I was missing out on something important, missing the chance to have a father who really loved me. Even before he died, I felt like he had let me down."

Because of her mother's chronic heart ailment, Robin spent her childhood in a constant state of terror. "My biggest fear as a child was that my mom would die," she says, her voice sinking to a whisper. "I was afraid I'd get stuck with my dad, and he never really liked me. My mom was the only one on my side. So if she went away, then I would be all alone."

The actual loss or illness of a parent is not the only thing that convinces children who grow up to be sex addicts that the people who are supposed to love them somehow do not or aren't able to. Children frequently feel the same sense of rejection when their parents seem to love them only under certain conditions. George, for one, developed his drive to please other people at all costs because he feared his parents' disapproval. His parents' distance and constant criticism of his behavior felt like rejection. And like Janet or Bill, who lost a parent, and Robin, who feared losing one, George grew up feeling alone and insecure.

CHILDHOOD LESSON:
"People I love will always hurt me."

In homes where emotional, physical, and/or sexual abuse occur, children grow up in constant fear of being victimized by others. Both Hank and Mitch, who had physically abusive fathers, also felt neglected by their mothers, who did not protect them from the abuse. In their group sessions, both men have said more than once that actual abandonment would have been a relief in comparison to their daily diet of humiliation and torture.

"My father had complete control over our family," Hank recalls. "My mother couldn't protect me. She didn't stand a chance. But still I think I was angry at her for not trying. I mean, I knew she loved me, or anyway I thought she did. Maybe I would be sure if she had done more, although I really don't know if she could have done more. It's still confusing. One thing for sure, though, I resented the whole setup. It just didn't seem fair not to feel safe in your own home."

Virtually every sex addict we've treated has suffered some sort of abuse in his or her childhood home. Whether the abuse was physical or emotional, verbal or sexual, the recipients were left feeling shellshocked and with the impression that anyone who got close to them would invariably hurt them.

CHILDHOOD LESSON:
"If people can't get near me, they can't hurt me."

"My father would hit us all the time, with no warning," Hank reports. "He would yell at all of us, too, degrade us verbally, but the beatings were what got to me. I always feared being physically hurt. Growing up, I always felt like someone was about to jump me. All someone had to do was look at me and I got this sick feeling in my stomach. If I caught a quick movement out of the corner of my eye, I jumped out of my skin. And it wasn't just getting hit that I was scared of or just my dad who scared me. I was afraid of being laughed at. I remember I couldn't give speeches in front of a class. And if I was put on the spot to do anything, I'd just lose it. I would absolutely panic, thinking everything was going to collapse. I just couldn't perform in those situations. I was always afraid that I'd be inadequate or that people would laugh at me. And I still feel that way. I just assume that if I give people a chance to hurt me, they will."

Don also generalized the fears that began when his brother sexually molested him. "After what happened with my brother, I was terrified of people in general for a long time," he says. "My brother was only a couple of years older than me, but he was twice as big. He told me he would beat me up if I ever told anyone what he was doing to me, and I believed him. I knew exactly what he could do when he got mad because one time he locked me in a closet for hours. The whole thing really left a mark on me. I mean, if you can't trust your brother, who can you trust?"

Like many sex addicts, Hank and Don carried into the outside world their distrust of others and their powerful fears of abandonment, rejection, disapproval, ridicule, and abuse that had been forged in their homes. Since no one acted to protect Hank or Don, and neither knew how to protect himself, they saw just one alternative for avoiding pain in general—avoid the people who inflict it and anyone who might. As adults, in all their relationships with others, sex addicts who were abused as children live by the lesson they learned at home: it's best to keep a safe distance.

LEARNING (OR NOT LEARNING) SOCIAL SKILLS

CHILDHOOD LESSON:
"I have to obey the rules."

Whenever any family has a chronic problem, such as alcoholism, addiction, incessant conflict, incest, or physical abuse, that family creates an elaborate system of rules that all members live by. The rules are rarely spoken aloud, but children learn them nonetheless, through observation or from the consequences they suffer if they inadvertently break them. Although ostensibly adopted to preserve the family name or reputation, these rules in fact protect the addiction or pattern of abuse itself, getting the entire family involved in denying that a problem exists at all. Abused children, battered wives, incest victims, children of alcoholics—all tend to remain silent, refusing to acknowledge the problem to anyone inside or outside the home.

"We never talked much at home," remembers Hank, whose father, a physically and verbally abusive sex addict, molested his sisters. "My mother was such a nervous wreck that she never knew what to say, and I would never think of going to my dad. You didn't talk about your problems or your feelings. Anyone in my family would rather die than sit down and ask how another family member was feeling about something. It just wasn't done."

In Hank's family, denial was the watchword. All activity revolved around denying the family secret—his father's sex addiction, incest, and abuse—and keeping it a secret through silence.

Addiction becomes the *de facto* ruler of any family. Whether the family problem creates extreme chaos or leads to extreme control, the rules of both types of households are remarkably similar. In the book *It Will Never Happen to Me!*, Claudia Black defines the primary rules of alcoholic households as "Don't talk, don't feel, don't trust." Whether their parents are alcoholics or sex addicts, physically or emotionally abusive, sex addicts grow up living by these rules.

CHILDHOOD LESSON:
"Project and protect the right image to all people at all times."

"Remember Vince Lombardi, the coach of the Green Bay Packers?" asks Robin. "Well, he always had a sign up in his locker room that said, 'What goes on here stays here, what you hear here stays here.' That was our family motto, too: What goes on in this house stays in this house. Why would anybody have a rule like that if they didn't have serious family problems?"

In addictive and compulsive families, everyone is enlisted in projecting the right image to the rest of the world. "My parents are just really private people," Robin explains, "and they were always really concerned about what the neighbors would think, or the relatives. We'd all have to be really discreet. You couldn't say anything that would make anyone think there was anything wrong.

"The funny thing was, we weren't allowed to talk about anything inside the family, either," Robin adds. "You couldn't ask, Is Mom sick? You couldn't say, Everybody's fighting. We weren't allowed to show our feelings. When you're a little kid, you don't understand what's happening. Nobody ever explained what was going on, but you weren't supposed to ask."

Growing up in a family with unacknowledged chronic problems demands that a child learn to live behind a façade both outside and within the home. The many sex addicts who grew up in this kind of family invariably learned to play their parts well. "My older sister had been molested for years, pretty severely and under threats," Hank recalls with horror. "It says a lot that I had no idea that it was happening. And no one else did, either. She never said a word, never let on in any way."

By the time they reach adulthood, most sex addicts are quite adept at hiding behind a carefully constructed image. They make a good first impression and maintain it, easily convincing others that they *are* the image they project.

CHILDHOOD LESSON:
"Don't feel your feelings. Squelch them if you can, and if you can't, then keep them to yourself."

The children in Hank's family obeyed the rules, keeping their mouths shut and their feelings locked up tight, since emotional outbursts were considered just as dangerous as talking about "the problem." Because expressing emotions—particularly sadness, anger, or fear—threatened to destroy the façade and break through the wall of denial that surrounded the addiction and abuse, talking about unpleasant feelings was strictly prohibited in most sex addicts' families—preventing them from ever learning how to appropriately handle stress or pain.

"You could only say you felt sad if you had a good reason for it," remembers Robin. "Like if somebody died. I suppose we could *feel* sad if we wanted to. We just weren't supposed to say anything about it."

Along the same lines, Don says, "I never cried, not even when my father died. No one did, as far as I know. It just wasn't done—ever."

CHILDHOOD LESSON:
"I can get along with other people as long as relationships and communication stay on a safe, superficial level."

Even if there hadn't been house rules to discourage talking honestly about emotions and problems, most sex addicts would have had difficulty developing communication and relationship skills. Their role models communicated poorly and sometimes not at all.

"My mother always insisted on waiting until my dad got home before serving dinner, but I never really understood why," George remarks. "He'd just sit there. He would never say *anything*." Other sex addicts also grew up in homes where little or no real dialogue occurred. When conversation did take place, it usually stayed on a safe, superficial level.

Like George, most sex addicts saw only two types of communication in their childhood homes—no expression from the passive or frequently absent parent and inappropriate expression from the intimidating or abusive parent. "My dad is stoic, my brother is very stoic, and my mother is very depressing and very negative," George sums up the situation succinctly.

Hank also had one stoic parent, but in his case, the other was explosive. "My dad expressed himself, all right," Hank says. "With his fists. He could become violent in a flash."

Hank and George learned, as so many sex addicts do, that they were better off keeping their mouths shut.

CHILDHOOD LESSON:
"There are only two kinds of touches—painful ones and sexual ones."

Many sex addicts who learned to keep their mouths shut when it came to emotions like anger and sadness also *failed* to learn how to express warmth, caring, and affection. Needing just four words to do it, Don sums up the interactions he witnessed while growing up: "No touching. No talking."

Few sex addicts grew up in homes where their parents were happily married. Almost always, in a sex addict's childhood home, the displays of affection he or she witnessed (or received) were rare and highly conditional. Love came with a price tag—obedience and the demand to give up his or her identity and independence. In most instances, demonstrations of love, compassion, and warmth were never seen at all.

"My mother and stepfather just were not close. I don't think my mother ever felt comfortable being touched," recalls Bill, who at thirty-eight is a sex addict just beginning to learn how to touch and be touched, emotionally as well as physically. "I don't know if I ever really hugged or kissed my mother, either. As a kid, when people would try to hug me, I'd get real shaky and jittery," he admits. "I'd always want to break away."

All too often, the only physical touching that sex addicts observed or experienced during childhood was grossly inappropriate. Mitch, for example, never once saw his father kiss his mother, but *did* see him beat her brutally. And the closest thing to being touched affectionately that Don remembers was when his brother fondled his penis in the middle of the night.

Any warm caresses sex addicts did receive frequently were inappropriately seductive. "I don't remember *seeing* any touching or kissing," says Keith, the real estate broker who came to us for treatment because he feared he would act out his fantasies about having sex with young girls. Keith seldom saw his father, an alcoholic who had compulsive affairs and stayed away from home most nights. "My mother was touchy with me," he explains. "Although only on a few occasions. She would run her fingers up and down my arms, back or chest while we were watching TV, and it sent chills through me. It sort of confirmed that she loved me, but it was sort of scary, too, because the way she touched me got me excited—in a sexual way."

Keith recalls that this sensual touching was "the only closeness there ever was between us." And, as a result, for many years, Keith would believe being sexual was the same as being emotionally intimate.

Cut off from expressing both positive and negative emotions as children, sex addicts often lose touch with them entirely, rarely recognizing what they are feeling at any given moment or why, or even that they are feeling anything at all. Whenever sex addicts have experiences that other people would respond to with anger, fear, grief, or anxiety, they do not feel the emotion, try to understand it, or do anything constructive to relieve it. Like someone driving on a beltway, which goes around a city instead of through it, sex addicts automatically bypass their emotional responses; they go directly to relief.

All addicts deal with their feelings and daily problems in this manner, escaping to the mind- and emotion-numbing effect produced by getting high on alcohol or drugs, or by blotting out reality through compulsive overeating, gambling, spending, or sex. Why sex addicts fixate on sex in particular, and compulsively have sex, is linked to the lessons about sexuality that they learned during childhood.

SEX EDUCATION

Surprisingly, for people who compulsively perform sexual acts, sex addicts know very little about human sexuality. Few know more than they learned from high school textbooks, and many do not even know that much. And the more important aspects—intimacy, caring, trust, responsibility, and sharing—are not found in most textbooks anyway. Children learn these sexual *relationship* skills through open communication and through observation of role models who demonstrate appropriate and responsible physical intimacy with each other. But most sex addicts do not see these things in their own families.

What sort of lessons about sexuality did sex addicts absorb during their childhood years? As their behavior would show for years to come, sex addicts received messages representing one of two extremes. They were confronted with either no permission to be sexual *or* no restrictions on sexuality at all.

CHILDHOOD LESSON:
"Sex and sexuality are unspeakable."

Even those addicts who did receive some fundamental school instruction about genitals, the reproductive system, and sexual functioning learned it late in their adolescence or only after they had already noticed changes in their own bodies.

"When I menstruated for the first time, my mother stopped what she was doing and answered all my questions about it," Janet admits. "But we never talked about intercourse or masturbation or anything like that. And I was masturbating a lot when I was young. I petted a lot, too, although I didn't have intercourse until I was married. I never knew what normal was when it came to sex. I just kind of learned as I went."

Most sex addicts learn about sexuality solely through their own experiences and many of the sex addicts we've treated have no conception of normal sexuality. Like Robin, whose parents' stock answer to questions about sexuality was, "You'll find out when you get married," many sex addicts were left entirely on their own to discover and develop their sexuality. Several of our sex-addicted patients never even received the basics through classroom sex education. More often than not, their own sexual development came as a complete surprise to them.

"When I first masturbated, I couldn't figure out what was going on," remembers George, a Catholic who confesses he learned almost nothing about sexuality in his parochial school. "I started to do it, playing around just because it felt good, but then one day I had an orgasm and it was like 'Oh, no! Am I broken? I broke something!' I felt really guilty. I didn't know why, but I had this powerful feeling that I wasn't supposed to be doing what I was doing, and if my mom ever found out, she'd kill me. Still, it felt *terrific,* and I did it again right away, the next night."

CHILDHOOD LESSON:
"Sexual relationships are strained and stressful."
Inevitably, whether they were taught about their bodies or not, sex addicts know next to nothing about *appropriate sexual behavior.*

Children learn sexual attitudes, standards of appropriate sexual behavior, and patterns of sexual permission from a vast number of sources. The church, school, and friends play a part, but their families play the most critical role.

"I don't think my mother and stepfather had a good physical relationship," Janet says, wondering aloud about the messages she received as a child. "They only slept in the same room for maybe a year after they got married. Even at the time, I knew she only married him because she needed somebody, for economic reasons. She loved him because he helped her out financially, but I guess that wasn't enough to get her to go on having sex with him."

From their parents, many sex addicts learn that sex, especially marital sex, is a duty—executed but seldom really enjoyed by either partner. It consistently amazes us to hear how many sex addicts report that their parents slept in separate bedrooms. And children who observe that their parents don't have a physical relationship, or learn that one or both parents don't really enjoy sex, or hear a mother disdainfully say, "Men only want one thing" (as sex addicts often do), are likely to form extremely negative impressions about sexuality.

Because they felt uncomfortable with other people in general, sex addicts felt especially uncomfortable dating. "I had girls who were friends," Bill concedes, "but they never became girlfriends. I didn't date them or kiss them or anything like that. Maybe I could have, but I never knew where I stood with them. Maybe they wanted to get romantic, but I didn't know how to find out for sure. I thought if I tried to come on to one, she'd get a bad impression of me and stop being my friend. And lots of times I thought I probably wasn't good enough for a certain girl. And if I wasn't good enough, then I felt that I shouldn't be around her at all.''

George too admits that "In high school, I had a hard time making friends. I didn't even have a girlfriend until senior year, and then she dropped me because I wasn't aggressive enough. I always felt like if I tried anything sexual, she'd think I was horrible.''

Like Bill and George, a great many sex addicts have difficulty figuring out what others expect from them when it comes to sex. They have no conception of what is appropriate or inappropriate to do on a date and, not ones to communicate in the first place, they do not think to ask. Instead they guess, often guessing wrong. As a result, many of the sex addicts we've treated had almost no experience in dating until after they left home, and very little even then. Robin and George never dated at all. And those who did date occasionally report that the experiences made them miserable.

In dating or other potentially sexual situations, sex addicts perpetuate patterns ingrained during childhood. Lacking the self-confidence and self-assertion needed to say no or yes with authority, adult sex addicts find it extremely stressful and often impossible to let another person know what they need, want, or don't want. Indeed, the stress involved keeps most sex addicts from communicating at all with their spouses or lovers—thus preventing them from having healthy, satisfying, or intimate relationships.

CHILDHOOD LESSON:
"Sex is evil and/or sinful."

"My sister and I weren't allowed to be sexual in any way," Robin says, remembering the message about sexuality she received as a child. "Sex was taboo. We weren't supposed to think about it, much less do it, and talking about it was completely out of the question.''

In most sex addicts' homes, sex was viewed not as a "natural human function," as sex researcher William Masters has called it, but as something totally unnatural and entirely unacceptable. The vast majority of sex addicts we treat were brought up in strictly religious homes of various denominations, and the attitudes about sexuality passed down to them by their parents were based on conservative religious teachings. By the time these sex addicts reached adulthood, they had been thoroughly indoctrinated in extremely restrictive beliefs about sexuality.

"I didn't lose my virginity until I was twenty," George admits. "The Catholic church had really instilled the wages of sin in me. Sex was just wrong, period. The teachers in Catholic school made it sound like you'd die if you had sex with a girl, or that you deserved to die, at any rate. You can kiss, *maybe,* but that was it, up until the day you got married. I started masturbating as soon as I knew how, when I was eleven or twelve, even though I knew that was wrong, too. Every time I did it, I knew I had committed a sin.''

Other sex addicts, raised in other faiths, also came to believe that all sexual expression was sinful. However, in pointing out the connection we have observed between conservative religious teachings and the development of sex addiction, we in no way intend to disparage those religions. Indeed, one of us is an active member of a local evangelical church, while the other is an ordained minister who was brought up in an evangelical church.

Because our own faith is very important to us, we have an enormous respect for divergent religious beliefs. And we want to assure readers of all faiths that in treating sex addiction, we have never encouraged a patient to renounce his or her religious beliefs. Recovering from the disease does not require leaving one's church. Indeed, as therapists, we often work in concert with members of the clergy to help patients overcome various problems, including sex addiction. We have found that our patients' faith can often provide much-needed support during their recovery. Yet to ignore the extraordinary number of times we have witnessed the effect of conservative religious beliefs on our sex-addicted patients would paint a false picture of the disease.

In the strictly religious environment in which many sex addicts were reared, any sexual activity—from masturbation to intercourse—was usually regarded as "bad" behavior. Children who would later become sex addicts not only heard that message, but took it to extremes, assuming that their sexual development and curiosity were signs of perversion.

CHILDHOOD LESSON:
"Nothing is permitted, so I must keep all signs of my sexuality well hidden."

Whatever the source of the message, children who are taught that sex is "dirty" rarely learn how to feel good about their own developing sexuality. Since "nothing is really allowed," sex addicts learn to "keep all signs of sexuality well hidden"—thoughts that will later contribute to their addiction.

As a child or an adolescent, any sexual activity at all—kissing, masturbation, petting—became a source of tremendous guilt, and if discovered, severe punishment. But even when they were not punished, sex addicts report that they felt humiliated by their own sexual curiosity.

"My folks never taught me about sex. It was another one of those things we just didn't talk about," says Bill. "But one time, when I was thirteen, my stepfather checked my wallet and found a condom. Then he made this really embarrassing comment in front of my friend. 'I know what you've got in your wallet, young man,' he said, laughing the whole time. I felt really stupid. I was embarrassed and mad that he had snooped in my personal belongings."

Soon after suffering his stepfather's ridicule, Bill hid all signs of his sexuality more carefully. Bill's embarrassing experience is not uncommon. Most sex addicts' parents nurtured in their children a sense of paranoia, discomfort, and shame about sexual feelings and actions. "When my sister went off on dates, my mother would say, 'Now just remember, I know a lot of people, and they'll all be watching you,' " recalls Robin.

For Robin and many others, sexual behavior became a source of shame rather than joy, as if their every sexual indiscretion were somehow public knowledge. In Robin's case, the threat of a scandal that could shatter her family's carefully maintained image carried enough weight to make her suppress all of her natural sexual impulses. Unlike her sister, Robin never dated, and neither masturbated nor had sex until she left home. "They said if I ever had sex with anybody, I wouldn't be welcome in the house," and so she rigidly obeyed the strict rules her parents had handed down to her.

Children, both young ones whose sense of right and wrong is not yet fully developed and teenagers whose rebellion against authority is a natural part of finding their identities, often feel they can break a few rules here and there—as long as they don't get caught. Particularly when the restrictions make little sense to them, youngsters act to avoid punishment by covering their tracks rather than by abstaining from the prohibited behavior. This line of thinking is particularly prevalent among sex addicts, who carry with them into adulthood the belief that keeping their sexual activities secret protects them from being held accountable for their actions.

CHILDHOOD LESSON:
"If people find out what I am doing, I will lose one of the only things that makes me feel good."

Even those sex addicts who were exposed to sexual stimulation at a very early age learned to keep their sexuality secret. Don, for example, while suffering from molestation by his brother, was also exposed to stimulation outside the home. "We lived in a town near an army base, so there were lots of prostitutes there." Don relates that his two closest childhood friends had a mother and grandmother who were both prostitutes. "I didn't realize that at the time, but these guys knew all about sex—which was unusual for kids who were six, seven, and eight. And we knew this older girl whose mother was also a prostitute. The girl used to come over and drag us on top of her. We had intercourse, at least as well as you can when you're that young."

After being caught and punished by the girl's mother, their encounters continued but were kept secret. In addition, Don continued to be sexually molested by his brother. Unfortunately, this fact remained hidden until it was discovered accidentally. "One night when I was ten, my mother woke me up and asked me, 'Why are your shorts pulled down?' I told her I thought my brother must have done it, but I felt really embarrassed, like I was the one who had done something wrong. She must have said something to him at that point, because I remember he stopped messing with me around then."

Many sex addicts were explicitly forbidden sexual expression, but even for those, like Don, who were not, sex became just as much a source of shame and embarrassment. Don experienced perhaps even more shame than others, because he had felt pleasure and arousal while being molested.

When the molestation stopped, Don's only source of affection—unhealthy as it may have been—was taken away from him. Don, as well as other sex addicts whose early sexual experiences were discovered and who were punished in some way, learned that "If someone finds out what you are doing, they will make you stop," reinforcing the need for secrecy.

LEAVING HOME, BUT CARRYING THE BAGGAGE

When sex addicts leave their childhood homes, they carry many years of emotional baggage with them. They feel uncomfortable with themselves and uncomfortable with others. They don't know how to express their emotions appropriately. Having little sense of their own identities, they can relate to others on only a superficial level, if that. Although constantly lonely, they don't know how to ease their loneliness. They don't trust others and have little confidence in themselves. Seeking perfection, they feel like failures.

Burdened with secrets and practiced in denial, they are well equipped to develop their own compulsive behaviors. After all, most of them had very effective role models.

Having already learned how to successfully hide their sexual feelings and behaviors, they continue to do so. Believing that it is safe to indulge in any sexual practice as long as no one knows about it, sex addicts enter adulthood without a fully developed sense of sexual responsibility. They seem blissfully unaware that fulfilling their sexual needs can have negative consequences—including causing harm to others—for which they should be held accountable.

Ultimately, because sex addicts almost always perceive even normal sexual behavior as abnormal, they see only two choices, instead of a field of alternatives, in the world outside their childhood homes. They can either repress all sexual impulses, as many had done throughout their childhoods, or they can surrender to the irresistible attraction of their own "illicit" sexuality. And, after experiencing the overwhelming euphoria of some sexual adventure—the high that fuels sex addiction—many do give themselves carte blanche when it comes to sexual behavior.

"When I moved away from my parents, I really went wild," Hank recalls. "From then on, I tried to get into bed with any girl I could." Of course, a great many people "go wild" immediately after they leave their parents' homes and go through periods of frequent sexual activity with a number of partners. But remember, sex addicts tend to see all sexual activity as "bad" or unacceptable. When they open the door to one so-called sinful activity, they pave the way to indulge in many, many more. Once they have crossed the line that their parents and their own morals told them they should never cross, many a sex addict believes he or she has gone past the point of no return. Now that they are in the territory they were warned about as children, they might as well give themselves permission to explore it, and they do just that—often feverishly.

"I had to follow all their rules while I was living at home," says Robin. "And I didn't break any of their rules until I was twenty-two.

That's when I had sex for the first time. And that was the first of many, many sexual rules I broke.''

FAMILY HISTORY QUESTIONNAIRE

If, after reading these first three chapters, you have recognized yourself, you might find it helpful to let your mind work back through different events in your past. These questions may help guide you in your search. Because it will take a great deal of thought, time, and perhaps pain to answer all of these questions fully, we have broken down the questionnaire into sections. You may want to break it down even further. Try to answer these questions not with a simple yes or no answer, but with a more full explanation that calls upon certain memories you may have blocked out long ago. In looking at your past, remember that there are no right or wrong answers to these questions. Yet, in looking at your childhood family, you may discover certain patterns that have continued in your adult life.

Addictions and Compulsive Behavior:
• Do you now recognize any kind of addictive pattern in your family? In your parents' families (i.e., among your grandparents)? Were there alcohol problems, gambling, workaholism, or any other kind of addictive or compulsive behavior? When did you first learn of this problem? During your childhood? Or only recently?

If you don't recognize any addictive patterns, you may want to dig a little deeper:

• Did your family live by the same rules that govern an alcoholic or addictive household: "Don't trust, don't talk, don't feel"? What special rules—unique to your family—did you learn as a child?

• Was your family really normal or did you just think it was normal? If your family tried to hide family problems behind a "normal" façade, how much did this image fool you as a kid?

• Did you ever wish you had been born into another family? Did you seek out other families?

• Did you ever have any *sustained* feelings that you wished something bad would happen to somebody in your family?

• Was there a certain constant chaos in your family that other families didn't seem to have? Or was your family really overprotective and worried about everything, always worried to death about what everybody else was doing and how they were feeling?

• Do you feel your family was "too close," "not close enough," or balanced in between? Has there been a problem really being close to anyone else in your family? Do you all back off whenever you get close to one another?

• Did your parents have work-related problems? Were your parents able to keep a job, if they held jobs, or did they always end up getting fired, or did they change jobs a lot? Did you always seem to have financial problems when you were growing up?

• Did your parents have any persistent legal problems? Any arrests? How many? For what? Any pattern of trouble with the law?

• Did your parents have marital problems? Did your mom and dad have fights or arguments a lot? Were they close? Were your parents warm and affectionate with each other? Did you ever see them show any affection toward each other?

Covering Up:
• If you recognized or now recognize addictive patterns in your family, what attempts did your parents make to conceal these problems from you and your siblings?

• How successful were your parents' attempts to hide the truth from you? How long were you kept in the dark about the problem? Did you know more about what went on in the home than your parents thought you did? Were you aware that there *was* a problem, even though you may not have known the exact nature of the problem?

• Did both parents participate in this cover-up of the problem where you were concerned? Who put more energy into covering up and keeping the problem a secret from the kids? The parent with the addiction or compulsive behavior? Or the other parent?

• Did the secret problem make your family's home environment seem unsafe? Did you feel insecure as a child? Did you feel unsure of yourself and other members of your family? Do you still feel that way about yourself or other people?

• Did the secretiveness and the deceit used as a cover-up spread beyond the area of the immediate problem to other areas of family life?

Alienation:
• Did you participate in keeping the family secrets hidden from others? Did your family have other secrets besides an addiction or compulsive behavior? What were they?

• Did growing up without talking about the problem in your family make it hard to talk about other problems as a child? Do you still find it hard to talk about your problems?

• Did knowing there was a problem, but not being able to talk about it, make you feel isolated from people outside the family? Feel unique or weird or different?

• Did you ever feel uncomfortable about having friends over to your house? Did your attempts to preserve these family secrets keep others at a distance? Did you keep other people at arm's length because you were afraid they might find out something was wrong with you or your family?

• Did you ever have someone outside the home with whom you could share your feelings about what was going on inside the home? Did you feel isolated or friendless as a child?

Control:
• Did you try to control the tension you perceived in your home—whether aware of the exact nature of the problem or not? What were some of the ways in which you tried to control the tension?

• Did you ever try to be perfect or be good in an attempt to ease the tension? Did you adopt a special role in your family in an attempt to keep everything running smoothly?

• Did you take on extra responsibility to make things easier on your parents—and on yourself? Did you act up in an attempt to get some attention for yourself? Did you try to make everyone else in the family happy? Or did you just try to stay out of everyone else's way?

• Were you ever blamed for the tension in your home? Did you quietly accept this blame? Did you sometimes feel you were a bad child?

• Was independent thinking promoted in your family? Freedom of thought? Were you encouraged as a child to be your own person and to grow? Or were you admonished to toe the line? Did you feel totally unable to say no to anyone who asked you to do something as a child? Do you now?

• Did you have permission to show your feelings as a child? Or did you learn to hide emotions as a child? All emotions or just particular feelings? Which ones?

• What happened in your family when someone did express their feelings? Did you gradually learn it was safer to shut down your emotions or cut yourself off from your feelings entirely?

• Did you sometimes start wondering what exactly you *were* feeling? Did you sometimes not know what you felt?

• What impact did this discouragement of feelings have on you? Does it still have an effect today?

Fears:
• Did you have particularly strong fears while growing up? What were they? Do they still affect your life today?

• Were you afraid of trusting outsiders? Were you afraid of what might happen if someone outside the family discovered the problem in your family? If you were aware of the problem yourself, were you afraid of outsiders ridiculing you if they knew, too? If you weren't aware of the exact problem, were you still afraid that others might discover that your family image was just a fraud?

• Were you ever afraid that your parents might simply abandon you? Did you ever feel afraid that if you told your parents what you *really* thought or felt, they might reject you? Were you afraid of your parents' disapproval?

• Did you grow up afraid of angry outbursts or confrontations of any kind? Were you afraid of expressing—or hearing expressed—other feelings besides anger?

• As a child, were you ever afraid that you were going insane?

• Did sex frighten you as a child? If so, do you remember any incident that could help explain why it did? Does it still frighten you now?

• Did you feel a general anxiety all the time—a fear of something that would or might happen, without knowing exactly what that something was?

• Did you live in constant fear as a child? Do you now?

Trust:
• Did your parents—through both words and action—teach you to trust or not to trust others? Did your parents behave inconsistently? Did your parents ever break promises to you?

• Did the experiences inside your own home make it hard for you to trust others outside your home?

• Did you distrust almost everyone as a child? Do you now?

• Did you receive mixed messages from either parent? Or did one parent often contradict the other parent?

• Did your parents ever contradict you when you made a comment about the tensions in your home, saying something like: "You must be imagining things" or "Nothing like that happened"? Did contradictions like these make you doubt what you'd seen and heard?

• Did growing up in your childhood home make it hard for you to trust yourself? Did you feel inadequate to control the tensions and problems in your home? Did you feel inadequate in other ways?

• Did you feel utterly powerless as a child? Do you now?

• Did you or your parents set unrealistically high standards for your behavior? When you failed to meet these standards, did you feel you couldn't be trusted?

Self-Talk:
• What kind of things did you think about yourself as a child? Was your overall view of yourself as a child negative or positive? Did you feel worthless as a child? Do you feel worthless today?

• How would you fill in the following sentences (more than one response to each should come to mind):

"As a child, I was _____

_____."

"As a child, I was great at _____

_____."

"As a child, I was terrible at _____

_____."

• What kinds of things did you think about most other people when you were a child? Was your overall view of other people as a child positive or negative?

• How would you fill in the following sentences:

"As a child, I thought other people were _____

_____."

"As a child, I thought other people were better than me at _____

_____."

"As a child, I thought other people were worse than me at _____

_____."

• What kinds of things did you think about the world in general when you were a child? Was your overall view of the world as a child positive or negative?

• How would you fill in the following sentences:

"As a child, I thought the world was _____

_____."

"As a child, I thought the world was good for _____

_____."

"As a child, I thought the world was bad for _____

_____."

• Have your essential views of yourself, others, and the world in general changed since then? How would you fill in those sentences today—as an adult?

Sex Education:
• Recognizing that everyone gets some sort of sex education, what kind of sex education did you have during your childhood? What were the positive things you learned about human sexuality? What negative statements were made? By whom? To you directly, or did you overhear them made to someone else?

• Where, when, and from whom did you primarily get your sex education? In the home, school, from peers? What myths about sexuality or intimacy did you learn as a child?

• What were the sexual messages you received from your parents? Not only the things that they overtly told you, but also the messages you received covertly, through observation of your parents and their relationship?

• How did you view your parents' sexuality? What was their sexual relationship in the home like? Was affection shown openly in your family? Or not shown at all? Were your parents warm and affectionate with you and your siblings? Was touching one another something that never happened in the family? Were there negative statements about touching?

• Did the environment help you feel good about yourself as a sexual person? Or was it a restrictive environment, especially where sexuality was concerned?

• Did you ever talk to anyone in your family about sex? If you had wanted to talk about sex and sexuality, to whom would you have turned? Was there anyone in your family who might have answered your questions about sex?

• If you were brought up in a religious environment, did it enhance your understanding of healthy sexuality? Or did the religious environment create greater anxiety about sexuality? Was masturbation expressly forbidden by your family or your religion?

• Did any sexually traumatic things happen to you during your childhood? Incest or sexual abuse? Any traumatic or extremely humiliating incident? Were you ever caught and either punished or chewed out for masturbating? As a child, did you ever inadvertently see someone having sex?

• Was anyone else in your family the victim of any molestation? Was anybody in the family raped? Have you heard of any incident in your family history? Any inklings at all? Did you hear anything about that? Or do you suspect it now that you look back and admit that maybe something was going on?

• If there was incest in your immediate family and only one of your parents was involved in the incest, did you ever blame the other parent for not preventing it from happening? Did you blame yourself for the incest in your family? Do you now? Did you feel guilty about the incest in your family? Do you now?

4

DEEP IN DENIAL:
Maintaining the Illusion
of Control

At 2:00 A.M. on a Friday in early December, Keith sat in a leather reclining chair in the den of his suburban home. His body was bathed in a cold sweat and as tight as a rubber band about to snap. His head throbbed from thoughts that roared through his mind. He had come downstairs from his bedroom an hour earlier and had already made a half-dozen obscene phone calls, tricking sleepy women into talking to him while he masturbated, getting an extra jolt of excitement each time one realized what he was doing and hung up on him. Normally, this ritual relieves his tension and enables him to combat his insomnia. But tonight it was not working.

It had been an altogether rotten day for the forty-six-year-old real estate broker. Work was sheer hell, with deals falling through, an important sale getting fouled up, and a disturbing call from a client who accused Keith of setting too low an asking price for an east-side high-rise building because he "didn't have the guts" to wait for a higher bid. At noon, the woman he no longer wanted to have an affair with called and showered him with insults and recriminations. At four, the woman he wanted to start an affair with flatly refused his overtures. And on the way home, he found himself cruising past the porno bookstores he had sworn to avoid. Before he knew it, he had parked his car, gone inside, and connected

97

with a seedy-looking man for some anonymous mutual masturbation. Feeling like a complete failure, Keith missed dinner with his family (again), offering his wife a lame excuse for his lateness. Her silence was deafening as she begrudgingly served his warmed-over dinner.

The only bright spot in his entire day had been Megan, his older daughter's fourteen-year-old friend who had come to the house to make cookies for the pep-club bake sale and spend the night. She was a bouncy blonde with long coltish legs, budding breasts, and the vivacious personality Keith associated with every girl he had ever longed for but had not been able to attract during his own high school years. Just being in the same room with her made him tingle all over, and when she joined him at the kitchen table while the cookies were baking, he swore she was flirting with him.

By bedtime, the intermittent sexual images of Megan had turned into constant, detailed fantasies. He imagined her walking into his bedroom, slowly removing her clothing, and sliding into bed beside him. He saw her lying naked in the guest-room bed, looking at him lustfully, and breathlessly telling him she could not have waited another moment for him to arrive. He was overwhelmed with desire as he fantasized about the softness of her skin and the words she would whisper in his ear: "Just tell me what you want. I'll do anything you say." Keith knew his desire for Megan was wrong, but try as he might, he could not keep it from washing over him.

At 2:30 A.M., moving like a zombie, Keith climbed the stairs, fully intending to return to his own bed. But when he passed the room in which Megan slept, the door was slightly ajar, and he could not stop himself from looking in at her. He watched her from the hallway for a moment or two, then, in a daze, pushed the door open and began to step into the room.

Just then, the door across the hall burst open. Light from the bathroom flooded the hallway, and Keith's younger daughter appeared.

"Daddy, what are you doing out here?" she asked.

His heart pounding wildly, his head buzzing, Keith frantically grasped for an answer: "I thought I heard a noise," he stammered.

His young daughter immediately accepted his lie and smiled sweetly. "It must have been me," she suggested. Her innocence, her innate trust of him, brought Keith out of his fantasies with a thud. He was suddenly painfully aware of what he had almost done. The realization horrified him—and scared him straight into our office.

Coming to us on his own—and truly shaken by how close he had gotten to molesting his daughter's fourteen-year-old friend—Keith was more motivated to change than most of our clients. Yet, months of individual and group sessions would come and go before he finally acknowledged his addiction. During that time, Keith stalwartly insisted that his fantasies about young girls were the problem—not his obscene phone calls, extramarital affairs, or anonymous encounters with men in adult bookstores. He did not see the connection and repeatedly claimed that he could control those behaviors and stop doing them any time he wished.

Whether they are referring to drinking, drug use, compulsive over-eating, or sex, all addicts make the same claim—and sincerely believe it. Experienced at fooling themselves, addicts are convinced they are in control of their behavior. Adept at protecting themselves from painful realities, they deny the existence of a problem and its impact on them or their loved ones. Both the illusion of control and the extreme reliance on the psychological defense mechanism of denial are integral parts of the disease.

While in the grip of their addiction, the sex addicts whose words you will read in this chapter were literally blind, deaf, and dumb when it came to many of the things they can now readily relate to you. They have finally begun to recognize the patterns involved in their behavior.

Prior to admitting his addiction and thus beginning his recovery, Keith would say, "I can't figure out what triggers my fantasies or what sets off my desire for sex. I never see it coming, so I can't adjust or do things differently."

Today, Keith sees the connections between his thoughts or feelings and his actions, as well as the links between his past experiences and his present behavior. He even has some idea as to why he turns to sex more on some days than on others.

"I don't handle stress very well," Keith admits. "I don't handle it at all, actually. I just want to run, you know, whenever I'm under a lot of pressure at work, when there's lots of chaos around me, a hundred things going on at once, and I can't get a handle on any of them. I get that way any time I feel like someone is putting me on the spot—my boss, my clients, or my wife when she starts in on me about spending more time with her and the kids. It's like being back at the dinner table with my dad staring at me, waiting for me to do something wrong so he could have an excuse to beat up on me. The job, my wife, everything and everybody, can make me feel like I did when I knew my dad was about to hit me.

"I always got locked in my room after my dad beat me, and I'd be hurting physically and emotionally. I wanted to forget, so I'd fantasize and masturbate. Now, I don't even wait for the bad things to happen, I just skip the pain and go right to the sex.

"Fear really gets me going," he continues. "I'm afraid of a lot of stuff—losing my job, losing my wife, not meeting people's expectations, not being successful enough, you name it. I get this physical feeling of fear. My head starts to buzz, and I can feel it in my shoulders and my joints and my stomach. It's just like when I was a kid, and I want to run away, so I do, into my head.

"The thing is, when I start my routines, I don't really feel any different. Physically, I feel exactly the same, only when I'm going after sex, I call the feeling excitement, and that's good. That's very good, because I like being excited. The tension, the jittery feeling, doesn't mean something bad is going to happen anymore. It means I'm going to have sex, and I like that idea. It's going to be risky, but it's also going to feel good. I'm not afraid of taking risks for sex the way I am of taking other risks. With sex, I'm the one in control. It's about the only time I feel that way.''

Keith, who spent his childhood at the mercy of an explosive, abusive father and was powerless to prevent his father from inflicting physical and emotional pain, has a tremendous need for control. He wants to control his thoughts, his feelings, the people around him, and nearly every aspect of daily living. His compulsive sexual behavior—obscene phone calling, extramarital affairs, mutual masturbation with men he meets in bookstores—provides him with the sense of control he wants so badly, or at least he thinks so at the time. Whenever something triggers that jittery sensation, Keith is compelled to regulate his feelings and to transform his anxiety into excitement—through sexual fantasies and sexual activities. Every addict we have ever treated has had the same powerful need for control and harbors the same illusion of being in control when caught up in compulsive sexual behavior.

THE DRIVE TO CONTROL

To sex addicts, life is like a car driven by someone else careening at top speed down a perilous mountain road. Thinking that the car will crash and burst into flames at any moment, they will do anything in an attempt to get back in the driver's seat and jam on the brakes. Most people feel this way from time to time and know how frightening it can be to believe they are losing control of their lives or their destinies. Sex addicts find themselves in such a state of panic constantly.

So often reared in chaotic homes by parents whom they could not please and whose behavior they could rarely predict, sex addicts have grave difficulty negotiating the demands of daily living. They believe life itself to be as far beyond their control as their parents once were. They frantically try to please people but rarely have a clue as to what other people actually expect from them. They relentlessly drive themselves to be good employees, good spouses, good parents, and good citizens, yet they draw a complete blank when trying to figure out what constitutes "good" behavior. They are nearly incapable of anticipating the consequences of their actions and lack the self-confidence to handle surprises— and life is full of them. The slightest change at home, at work—or even something as routine as encountering travel delays due to road construction—spells disaster for sex addicts who cannot tolerate the stress of altering familiar routines. Consequently, sex addicts, who desperately want to be in control all of the time, feel out of control most of the time.

Yet, even though sex addicts find life intimidating and chaotic, they seldom turn to anyone for help to sort through their confusion or regain self-control. Because, based on their early experiences, they believe that "nobody cares," so they consciously or unconsciously decide that they'll take care of themselves. But the only way sex addicts know of to take care of themselves is to act out sexually. Sex is the one thing they are certain they can control.

Sex makes addicts feel all-powerful. In their fantasies, they believe themselves to be totally in charge of the situation, telling themselves that "What I want, that person (the sex object) will give me." When their climax has come and gone and they have sobered up, however, sex addicts feel even more out of control than before.

It is vital to your understanding of the addiction to recognize that the sex addict's efforts to bring order to the chaos he or she feels are almost always *unconscious*. Turning to sex is an automatic response to either day-to-day pressures or lifelong anxieties, and not a *deliberate* strategy to relieve painful emotions or escape problems, whatever they may be. Indeed, because most sex addicts have cut themselves off from their own feelings for virtually their entire lives, few even know when or why they're feeling anxious or upset.

"When things really stress me out, I still don't know it," says George, twenty-six, whose dependence on masturbation, phone sex services, and prostitutes relieved the stress resulting from his job as a hotel staff supervisor and his own perfectionism. "I'm just starting to see that the more things stress me out, the more desire I have to slip into my habit, my addiction." Until he entered a recovery program, all George recognized was the urge itself. Prior to seeking treatment and admitting that their addictive behavior was beyond their control, the sex addicts we have treated automatically turned to sex as a cure-all.

The Illusion of Control: Regulating Runaway Emotions

Sex offers all sex addicts a sense of power and control—and a means of controlling their own feelings. Some recall turning to sex for this reason at an early age.

"I remember being fourteen or fifteen and hearing that a friend of mine had died in a fire," Don relates. "I was feeling really low and just cut myself off from everybody, spending a lot of time alone in my room. I remember masturbating to sort of get my mind off things. That was the first time I recall doing it because something bad had happened. But I wasn't hooked on it then. I only masturbated sporadically until I was in the service. Then this girl I liked wrote me a dear-John letter. I guess I'd say now that I was feeling abandoned, but all I knew then was that I was really feeling bad. That's when I started masturbating regularly, I think, and using it to get away from those feelings."

For Don, masturbation became the best, and later the only, way he knew to relieve bad feelings. And like most sex addicts, Don used it frequently, whenever he felt the need to control the way he felt. Don had shut down his emotions as early as age six when his brother began molesting him. The lonely secret he was forced to keep, as well as a childhood devoid of affection, had given him no recourse for dealing with pain or disappointment except the one he discovered on his own—compulsive sexual behavior. "Almost anything could set me off," he explains. "But for me, the main feeling I tried to get away from was abandonment: this idea that I would always be alone."

Sexual fantasy, masturbation, and later picking up women allowed Don to escape the hurt and loneliness he associated with being abandoned.

The emotion most likely to trigger Keith's compulsive behavior was fear, which he renamed excitement the moment his sexual ritual began. And George regularly tried to bury his anger.

"It doesn't take much to get me going," George admits. "My mother will call and start in on me about something. Someone from the hotel will come into my office and dump all these complaints on me, or work will pile up on my desk, and it will seem like the whole job has gotten out of control. A lot of times I'll get really angry about those things, really resentful. I'll think 'Why me? Why is all this crap happening to me? Why can't people just get off my back already?' "

Members of Alcoholics Anonymous use the acronym HALT (Hungry, Angry, Lonely, Tired) to warn alcoholics about the feelings that are most likely to prompt them to reach for the bottle. For sex addicts, HALT feelings also trigger their compulsive behavior. This is often because sex addicts take everything that happens to them extremely personally, believing that *anything* bad that happens to them must be their fault.

George, for instance, switches in an instant from anger and resentment to self-doubt and self-criticism. "Anger's always just a flash for me," he says. "I feel it for an instant and then it's gone. But the next thing I know, I'm feeling insecure, thinking I deserve all the crap because somewhere along the line I screwed up. I hate feeling inadequate. I hate being reminded of what an insignificant, messed-up person I am."

And because George hates those feelings, he stifles them. Without consciously knowing he is doing it, George replaces the negative thoughts and feelings with sexual ones. He is powerless over other emotions, but he can *do* something about sexual feelings. He can masturbate, call the phone sex service, have sex with a prostitute. Unfortunately, after he has attended to the fulfillment of his sexual desires, George feels "exactly the same way I did before, maybe worse."

Silencing Negative Self-Talk

Although the turmoil sex addicts are unconsciously trying to control lies mostly within themselves, it frequently surfaces when some change or pressure is imposed upon them at home, at work, or as a result of other outside influences. As Mitch now realizes, "All it took was one customer arguing with me over the estimate I gave him to fix his car, or one letter from home telling me how great my brother was doing, or what a terrific family my sister was raising, and I'd be heading for the pornographic bookstores."

Like a chain of dominoes, work or marital strain or almost anything else sets off the sex addict's frustration or depression, which then sets off feelings of personal inadequacy and shame, which, in turn, set off the need to control those feelings by burying them in sexual release.

Wayne, for example, who like most sex addicts feels lonely almost all the time, feels even lonelier when on the road for his job. "I traveled a lot," Wayne recalls, "meeting with advertising clients. Being on the road in motel rooms really got to me. All alone with those four walls closing in on me, I felt like I was the only human being left on the planet. I just had to find somebody to be with. And if I couldn't pick up a woman to have sex with, I had to make one up in my head and masturbate."

Being alone triggers compulsive sexual behavior for most sex addicts. Solitude reinforces the addicts' alienation from others, giving them the time to think—something they prefer not to do because their thoughts seldom make them feel any better about themselves.

"Being alone at night would always get me thinking about my life and what a drag it was," George recalls. "Sometimes, I would go over everything I had done that day, counting up the mistakes I made or the things I didn't get done when I should have. It really got me worked up. Thinking about my personal life was even worse, since I actually didn't have one. Maybe I should have been thinking about ways to make my life better or things I could do to change myself for the better. But that never occurred to me."

Instead, to avoid thinking about his own life and to silence his own negative self-talk, George, like all sex addicts, escaped into his own little fantasy world. As the disease progresses, it takes less and less to send sex addicts off to those fantasy worlds or trigger their compulsive sexual behaviors.

For Stuart, a twenty-nine-year-old computer technician, *any* time alone posed a threat. Since he spent most of his workday alone in his car driving from company to company to repair computers, he was in constant danger of slipping into his sexual rituals.

"It got so bad at one point that just getting in the car was enough to get me going again," Stuart remembers. "It was hard for me to drive to the store and back, because I'd want to stop in the parking lot and masturbate. I couldn't even drive to meet people on the other side of town."

Whenever he had time alone to think about his problems or his life, Stuart was bombarded with negative self-talk and bowled over by a rush of intolerable feelings—sadness, deprivation, shame, anxiety—and the time he was most likely to think about himself was the time he spent alone in his car. At first, he would block the feelings and silence the self-talk with sexual fantasies and masturbation. But soon enough, he did not need to wait for the feelings to wash over him. Merely getting into his car triggered his overpowering desire for sexual pleasure and release. It should come as no surprise that all Stuart's sexual practices, from public masturbation to voyeurism to picking up prostitutes, involved driving or were performed in his car.

Clearly, anything painful or stressful will aggravate a sex addict's emotional state or stimulate negative self-talk. But, as Stuart experienced firsthand, sex addicts feel the urge to act out sexually even when nothing out of the ordinary has happened at all. After a while, the slightest hint that things *could* get out of control—and anything associated with feeling out of control (in Stuart's case, his car)—triggers the compulsion.

The childhood fears and anxieties of the addict, as well as the self-destructive behavior he or she learned to indulge in to escape those feelings, will not disappear on their own. They always lie in wait, ready to spring out and pounce on the addict, who knows only one way to fight them. Unless the sex addict recognizes and deals with them, the emotions, although long buried, stay alive, fueling addictive behavior.

Coping with Adult Responsibilities

In addition to free-floating anxiety (worries about anything) and separation anxiety (fears of abandonment and rejection), most sex addicts seem to suffer from performance anxiety. They constantly worry about their ability to perform successfully in adult roles: as parents, as spouses or lovers, as wage earners. They fear that their adult lives will turn out to be as out of control as their childhoods were.

"The biggest fear I have is a fear of not being successful," admits Todd, the divorced investment analyst who had more than fifty affairs during the last year of his marriage, and now jumps constantly from one one-night stand to another. "I have this tremendous fear of not being as important as I ought to be."

Perfectionists like Todd, who actually is very successful, set up grandiose expectations for themselves, feeling they ought to be able to do anything and everything. Many sex addicts are extremely driven, almost as compulsive about achieving success—whether they define it in financial terms, domestic terms, or other terms—as they are about their sexual behavior. They want complete control over their destinies and judge themselves harshly when they or forces in the world around them fail to conform to their rigid expectations.

Sexual rituals, as Keith noted earlier, enable sex addicts to transform their fears into excitement. The adrenaline rush of excitement seems far less dangerous than the exact same adrenaline rush produced by fear. Sex addicts believe they wield control over the risks that excite them and view the risks they fear as being far beyond their control.

Consequently, controlling their sexual satisfaction offers sex addicts relief from what they perceive as their failure to control the rest of their lives. "Having sex is the only time I relax," explains Robin, the pediatrician who masturbates up to twelve times a day and whose expectation that her lovers have sex with her on demand has destroyed one relationship after another. "During and after sex, I feel great for maybe five minutes. Then I'm ready to do it again. And that makes me relax, too. Never as much as the first time, but it helps."

In their drive for perfection and quest for control, sex addicts like Robin put relentless pressure on themselves. Job stress, marital strain, and loneliness only add to the enormous burden they already feel.

Each morning, when Bill arrives at his desk in the Health Department, he "makes a long list of things to get done that day, which is really stupid because Superman couldn't do everything I expect myself to do during a single day. Of course, I get really frustrated and mad at myself," Bill concedes. "Sex releases the tension that builds up inside me. But it also makes things worse. Since I do most of my cruising and pick up prostitutes when I should be working, I only get further behind with my work. And afterward, when my head is clear, I get down on myself for what I just did."

Sex addicts become impatient and frustrated with other people very easily, but even more so with themselves. As a result of their extremely unrealistic expectations of themselves and others, sex addicts are frustrated at every turn and become walking time bombs, hastening toward an inevitable explosion.

Controlling Sexual Gratification—or Being Controlled by It?

Obviously, in addition to trying to stifle emotions and silence self-talk, sex addicts also attempt to control the fulfillment of their own sexual needs. No matter what the specific behavior, sex addicts need to believe, and indeed do believe, that they are completely in control. Undeniably, many sex addicts do actually achieve a modicum of control. Sex addicts who primarily stick to masturbation, for instance, have all the control in the world, because they orchestrate their own fantasy, rule over all the people involved in the fantasy, and control the events that occur in their own minds. Sex addicts who rely on pornographic magazines, rent X-rated videos, or pay for prostitutes have almost as much power as the compulsive masturbator, since they purchase the stimulus or service of their choice. And all sex addicts who commit victimizing behaviors—from making obscene phone calls to performing exhibitionism, incest, and rape—control their victims through terrorism and violence.

Whether they victimize others or not, sex addicts always try to gratify their sexual needs on their own terms, regardless of the needs of the other person involved (if there even is one). Painfully aware that their wish to live their lives their way can rarely, if ever, be fulfilled, sex addicts do everything they can to have sex their way. Rituals, which allow addicts to choreograph every aspect of sexual satisfaction, reinforce the sense of power that accompanies every sexual high.

George explains that he would "plan every detail. I'd ask myself, 'What can go wrong here? Can I get caught? What can I do to make sure I don't get caught?' Before I even dialed the number for Strip-o-gram and had a prostitute sent over, if there was a chance my roommate would come home early, I figured out exactly, down to the tiniest detail, how I would get the girl out of the apartment without my roommate ever knowing she'd been there."

You might think that having to cover every contingency would make George a nervous wreck. On the contrary, it enhanced his high. "Sure, on the one hand, I was scared of getting caught. But I knew I'd be ecstatic if I didn't. It was such a triumph, such a rush, to know I pulled it off. I was playing God—calling all the shots, covering all the bases. I loved it." As you can see, at the height of his ritual, George believed he had total command over the entire situation and all the people in his world.

Compulsive overeaters often say they eat "like there's no tomorrow." If the food is there, the compulsive overeater feels compelled to eat it. Sex addicts share this short-term focus. "Don't miss out. Don't waste this opportunity," they tell themselves. Because they need to believe they have complete control and want instant gratification of their sexual urges, sex addicts have little tolerance for anyone or anything they view as an obstacle standing in their way.

"I had lots of affairs," Don admits, "but, to tell you the truth, I never really enjoyed them as much as masturbation. They're too much work. You have to find a woman. You have to deal with the woman to a certain extent. You might have to go out, go to dinner, and even if you do, there's never any guarantee that you'll have sex afterward."

Todd seems to agree with Don's assessment. "The women I have affairs with always end up wanting to be more emotionally involved than I do," he complains. "I would make it real clear from the beginning that I was married, and I didn't want to divorce my wife. I'd really try to keep them at arm's length, but sooner or later they all wanted to get closer, and I'd have to end the affair. Now, being divorced and all, I stick to one-night stands. At least with a one-nighter, the women play by my rules."

As Don and Todd discovered, even the bit players in their carefully orchestrated dramas can make them wait for sexual gratification or threaten their sense of omnipotent control. Impatient and consumed by their own need, sex addicts prefer not to waste time establishing intimate relationships and would rather find the most accessible outlet to satisfy their sexual appetites. Then they return to that outlet over and over again.

"Finding men in bookstores was just a matter of convenience," Mitch insists. "There you can meet somebody and you don't even need to say hi. No strings attached whatsoever. It's easy."

Truly intimate relationships are anything *but* easy for sex addicts. Indeed, because most find it impossible to trust anyone, believe they can depend on no one, and assume that anyone they allow to get close to them will turn around and hurt them, sex addicts often view getting involved in an intimate relationship as the ultimate way to *lose* control completely.

Sex Binges: Trying to Control the Uncontrollable

Despite the illusion of control, however, the addict is never really in control at all. Instead, he or she is being ruled by his or her own lust for sexual gratification. The sexual ritual ends up dominating the sex addict, instead of the other way around.

As we pointed out in Chapter 1, the instant hangover sex addicts suffer after getting their fix often leaves them feeling even worse than they felt before. As Bill explains it, when the prostitute he has just had sex with leaves, and his head clears, he experiences a tremendous mood swing. After the high dies away, many sex addicts recognize the implications of their sexual behavior. In a rush of unwelcome awareness, they momentarily understand perhaps *too* clearly that they did not control their feelings or silence their self-talk at all, but merely delayed the inevitable. Worse yet, when they return to reality, they are faced with the fact that they have engaged in what they believe to be "disgusting," "bizarre," "perverted," or "dirty" sexual behavior.

As sex addicts dive deeper and deeper into their addiction, their hangovers often trigger more compulsive sexual behavior. Like the alcoholic who needs an "eye-opener" to get going on the morning after, sex addicts frequently feel tempted to have more sex after each sexual episode. According to Bill, "You figure, What the hell? I did it once, I should do it twice." After paying a prostitute to perform oral sex, he often tells himself, I already feel bad, so I might as well do it again.

This sort of self-talk often leads to a full-blown sexual binge. Or as Don explains it, "I rarely masturbate just once. I do it two or three or five times in a row, two or three or five times a day for a week, maybe more. I get depressed and very down on myself after acting out, so I do it again to feel better. The more I do it, the worse I feel about myself. But thinking I'm a no-good son of a bitch is as good a reason to indulge myself as any."

Sexual bingeing can perpetuate itself indefinitely. Addicts feel bad enough about themselves when they act out once and ask themselves, "Why did I do that?" But they dig a deeper and deeper hole for themselves each time they repeat the behavior and are prompted to ask, "Why did I do that—again?" As the guilt and shame increase, so does the need to control those emotions, so addicts go round and round—anesthetizing their feelings with sex, feeling badly about what they have just done and doing it again in order to feel better, only to feel worse once again.

"It's a vicious circle," George accurately concludes, "but I believed that sex was the only way to get relief."

Like any other addiction, sex addiction is an out-of-control way of trying to control. The compulsion itself rules the addict. As the addiction gains power, the addict loses all freedom of choice. With his or her willpower to resist the obsessions and compulsions sapped, the addict becomes powerless, literally forced to obey the commands of his or her lust. However, even when life has become a living hell, addicts will not readily admit this fact to themselves or anyone else.

DENIAL

Like any other addiction, sex addiction is a disease of denial. In Chapter 1, we briefly mentioned the role of denial, and in the remainder of this chapter we will elaborate on how addicts use it to protect themselves from the painful realities of their addiction. But first, because it is tempting to think that addicts perversely, stubbornly, and *consciously* refuse to face facts, we'd like to take a bit of time to explain how denial works in general.

Denial is an *unconscious* psychological defense mechanism that protects us from thoughts, feelings, and even memories of real events that threaten our well-being. We *all* use denial as a buffer against realities that we are unable or unwilling to accept, although we rarely know we have been using denial until after we stop using it. People who are terminally ill frequently deny their impending deaths. Victims of violating crimes like rape or robbery and people who have been injured in frightening accidents often deny that such events have had an impact on them and go on with their lives as if nothing had happened. When relationships end, loved ones die, close friends move away from us, or something we wanted badly does not come our way, we are likely to deny the anger, grief, or disappointment we feel—at least until the dust settles and we are psychologically ready to face those feelings, talk about them, and ultimately let them go.

For most people, denial is a temporary stage that enables them to get through a crisis or painful adjustment period as normally as possible. It protects them from problems they are not yet ready to handle. But once they are ready, they move out of denial into other stages of adjustment. Instead of going through the motions of life as if nothing had happened, they move on to live their lives fully, even though something bad once happened.

Addicts, however, rarely make this transition on their own. They get stuck in denial, turning an essentially self-protective process into a self-destructive one. Denial blocks the addict's awareness of a disease that is destroying him or her. It prevents addicts from recognizing the impact of the addiction on their own lives and the lives of those around them.

Denial takes several forms including

SIMPLE DENIAL: maintaining that a problem does not exist at all, in spite of tangible evidence to the contrary.
MINIMIZING: maintaining that although a problem *may* exist, it is less serious than everyone else thinks it is.
BLAMING (also called PROJECTION): denying responsibility for the problem and maintaining that it is the fault of someone or something else. Blame is frequently placed on factors that cannot change, such as unhappy childhoods, critical parents, or stressful jobs.
RATIONALIZING: using a limitless number of excuses, alibis, and explanations to justify behavior.
INTELLECTUALIZING: denying the emotional impact of events or behavior by focusing on intellectual theories and generalizations to explain them.
DIVERSION: changing the subject, burying oneself in other activities.
HOSTILITY: becoming angry, uncommunicative, and even verbally

or physically abusive when caught or confronted with problem
behavior.

All addicts use at least one of these forms of denial to lie to
themselves, to their families, to their employers, and to everyone else
around them. As we discussed in Chapter 3, sex addicts usually begin
relying on denial at a very early age. Since hiding tensions and problems
such as addiction or abuse was one of the unwritten rules in their
childhood homes, they easily learned to deny their own problems as well.
From the outset, denial accompanies compulsive behavior. For example,
by the time he was sixteen, Bill was already promising to reform and then
coming up with excuses not to.

"I'd wake up in the morning feeling all right, believing that today
was the day that I would stop masturbating," he says. "I would go to
school thinking, I'm going to get a girlfriend today. But I never did, and
seeing that I didn't attract the girls I liked—or even know what to say to
them—just reminded me that I wasn't as good as the other guys. It
frustrated the hell out of me. By the end of the day, I was so wound up
and depressed that all I wanted to do was get home and relieve myself."

Bill discovered at an early age that he could rationalize his own
behavior. Every morning, Bill swore he would stop isolating himself and
masturbating, sincerely believing he would keep the promise he had made
to himself. But every afternoon, he convinced himself that he deserved
to feel good once in a while, that he needed to relieve his frustration, that
all things considered, masturbation wasn't really such an awful way to
take care of himself. Because he could make convincing excuses for his
behavior and thus deny the problem, Bill, like most other sex addicts,
avoided making any real effort to change himself.

Also, as many sex addicts do, Bill persuaded himself that change for
the better would come spontaneously, as a result of events he did not
personally control. Bill sincerely believed that finding a girlfriend would
magically and instantaneously take care of the problem, without requiring
him to do anything about it. What's more, he believed that until he did
have a girlfriend, there was nothing he could do about the problem
anyway; he simply had to go on masturbating because he had no girlfriend.

Many, many addicts use this form of denial. They wait for some
magical condition to be met and spontaneously fix everything. Many an
addict has told himself that he will stop cruising for prostitutes when
things settle down at work, or never peep in a window again once he is
married. A sex addict honestly believes she will stop having one-night
stands as soon as she meets the right man, or end her abusive affair when
her relationship with her husband improves. Denial also keeps addicts
from figuring out that their own compulsive sexual behavior actually
prevents the magical condition from being met. Bill was not going to find
a girlfriend while locked in his room masturbating (and hating himself for
doing it). Similarly, things will never settle down at work for someone
who spends three hours in the middle of the day cruising for prostitutes,

and the marital relationship will not improve for a woman who runs away from her problems by having an extramarital affair.

The most universal characteristic of addictive denial, however, is the refusal to acknowledge that the addictive behavior itself is out of control, that the addicts themselves are utterly powerless to alter or stop it. For instance, Wayne, the advertising copywriter, who had been using cocaine heavily for several years in addition to having lifelong sexual compulsions, in his first session with us said, "Whenever I've been snorting a lot of coke for a couple of weeks, I'll just stop. I just won't freebase or buy any coke for the next month. So I *do* have willpower. I can control the cocaine use, and I can do the same thing with sex. I can stop whenever I want."

The truth of the matter was that, although Wayne could curtail his cocaine use for short periods of time, he always picked it up again. After a period of abstinence, he invariably snorted more coke for more days in a row at an even higher monetary and emotional cost. He actually had no more control over his cocaine habit than he had over his sex addiction—a fact that was painful to admit, so he denied it. Nearly every addict of any kind insists, "I can stop any time I want." They even set up various willpower tests to prove the point.

As an adult, Bill would sometimes test himself by driving past prostitutes to see if he could look at them but not pick one up and pay for sex. He did this to prove to himself that he was in control of his behavior. When he failed the test, as he usually did, Bill was still able to convince himself he was in control, explaining away his compulsion by saying, "Well, I changed my mind." As you can see, Bill's thinking has changed very little since adolescence, when he promised himself to stop masturbating and then "changed his mind."

Indeed, having honed their skills since childhood, sex addicts demonstrate a remarkable ability to fool themselves. Frequently, they are so adept at lying to themselves that they even deny the guilt and shame that come with their sexual hangovers.

"I didn't feel bad about my affairs and one-nighters," Hank says. "I even felt a little self-righteous. The fact that I would try to make it with as many people as I could didn't strike me as strange. In fact, I think for a little while there I was actually proud of it. After all, I could attract any woman I wanted. I assumed it made other guys think I was really neat, too, until my best friend started teasing me about it. Telling me that I wasn't choosy. Then it occurred to me that maybe people were thinking I would go to bed with anybody."

Unless confronted, most sex addicts can keep up their self-righteous denial for decades. And, frequently, it leads to the development of a twisted sort of positive self-talk. For instance, when Robin first came to us for treatment, she insisted that "The sex itself is great: great for him, great for me, great for all of us."

Sex addicts often find that sex offers them the only sense of greatness they have ever felt. Yet, in telling themselves that "Sex is the only thing

I do really well," as Robin did, addicts are in fact denying the more painful feeling that "I can't do anything else right."

In general, positive self-talk is very healthy and helps build self-confidence. But sex addicts' positive self-talk, concentrating solely on sexual abilities and the feelings they produce, does not increase confidence in other areas of life and thus maintains the *negative* self-talk that, in turn, maintains the addiction. This form of denial enables the addict to say and believe, "Really, I'm fine. I don't need any help. Sex is the last thing that's wrong with me. In fact, it's the only thing right about me."

Sex addicts frequently take turning negatives into positives several steps further, using their diseased thinking to justify their actions. Bill, for example, constantly excused his dependence on prostitutes by claiming, "I was helping these women with rent and child support, helping put food on their tables." His old way of thinking now makes Bill laugh, "I thought they scratched my back and I scratched theirs. You know, they were helping me, and I honestly believed I was helping them. I practically had myself convinced that they would go hungry and have no place to live if it wasn't for me." Because denial allows sex addicts to ignore the reality of what they are doing, any behavior whatsoever is simply reinterpreted as an okay thing to do. Many sex addicts make this transition by comparing what they do to the "really bad" sexual behaviors they do not do. Like the alcoholic who defends himself by insisting, "I only drink beer," or the cocaine addict who believes he has the problem under control because "I only snort it; I'd never shoot the stuff," sex addicts point to sicker behaviors, or people who are worse off than they are, in order to minimize and deny their own problem.

As the disease progresses, denial frequently spreads beyond the addiction itself. Addicts simply dismiss all problems. Denial becomes a way of life. After six months of therapy, for instance, Janet still refused to acknowledge any problem in her life other than her inability to end her five-year affair. "My husband and I have a good relationship," she insisted, "as long as we don't have to talk to each other and we have no physical contact."

Although she eventually admitted, "It's really not a good relationship. It's not good for him, not good for me. I don't think he's happy, and I know I'm not," upon entering a recovery program she simply could not break through the denial.

Getting deeper and deeper into their addiction and their denial, sex addicts lie to themselves about anything and everything—even their own identities. "I always went out with lots of different women," Mitch confides, "to make sure everybody knew that there were no homosexual tendencies in me. I had to prove that point to myself, too, even though by the time I was twenty-six or so, I knew darn well that I liked guys as well as girls." Like most sex addicts, Mitch's lifelong pattern of denial prevented him from ever knowing or feeling comfortable with who he was.

Denial has always played its part in addicts' lives, allowing them to skirt all bad feelings, at least temporarily. Yet, in blocking out their negative feelings, sex addicts frequently cut themselves off from *all* emotions, alienating themselves from every aspect of their personalities, and thus becoming strangers even to themselves. All too often, they buy lock, stock, and barrel the very same façade they present to the outside world. Mitch, the bisexual auto mechanic, truly saw himself as a tough, no-nonsense, macho guy and, in that role, made many cruel, degrading remarks about homosexuals. Hank believed himself to be a devoted family man, a dedicated community member, a man of faith and humility who selflessly served as a church elder. And Todd envisioned himself as the warm, sensitive guy who stood apart from other men because he cared enough to listen to women's troubles.

Yet, Todd did not actually care. He was manipulating the women who cried on his shoulder, seducing them with his kindness. And Hank was devoted to his sexual fantasies and sexual rituals—not to his family, which was actually torn apart by his addiction. And for all his verbal bashing of homosexuals, Mitch's most coveted sexual highs almost always involved sex with men. In each instance, the addict's real behavior contradicted the image that he had created to hide his behavior in the first place. The only way to maintain the image was to go on denying the behavior. All three men were trapped in the tangled web of denial.

Lying to Others

Sex addicts almost always lie to others as much and perhaps more than they lie to themselves. They work overtime to hide their problem from family, friends, and employers. Hardly a day passes without addicts considering the question of what to tell and what not to tell, what to hide and what to do if what they've hidden is discovered.

Hank remembers, "When I decided to get married, I wondered: Should I tell her about the things that have gone on? I decided I didn't really need to tell her anything, because I wasn't doing those things any-more. I was a new person." His choice was a good example of addictive denial. Because sex addicts wholeheartedly believe their self-deception— in Hank's case, that he was a new person who no longer needed to have sex as often and with as many women as possible—the truths they hide from themselves become the secrets they keep from others. Or as Hank recalls, "At the time, I thought that was the absolute truth. But as time went on, my addiction began to gnaw at me. After six months, I started masturbating again. I began to look with lust at other women. And eventually I did go after somebody." He did not, however, tell his wife about his past or present sexual adventures.

Like Hank, many sex addicts justify covering up the truth of their addiction with their certainty that they have the problem under control.

Most addicts go beyond simply not telling the truth, however. To protect themselves and the addiction, they concoct out-and-out lies. An alcoholic once told us he must have owned the worst automobile in history, because he ended up having "car trouble" four or five times a week. Sex addicts, too, seem to have more car trouble than most other people. They constantly invent stories about getting stuck in traffic jams, taking trips to the store, going on jogging expeditions, having to work late, meeting an old friend on the street—anything they can think of that might explain their erratic behavior.

"When I first started going to the sex addiction self-help group, I didn't always go, although I always said I did," Don now admits. "I used those Sunday-night meetings as my cover. I pretended to go, but actually went out to a bar to meet a woman."

Similarly, if their obsession with sex begins to interfere with their work, sex addicts simply lie to their employers. "Since I work on my own most of the time," Bill confesses, "I used to do a lot of my acting out during the workday. We have to fill out these computerized forms, detailing the restaurants we've checked for health code violations, and send them in to the office. I forged forms like mad, tons of them. I'd work four hours a day, but turn in forms that made it look like I worked all eight hours. Twenty hours a week of forged forms. I'd rush through any inspections I did do and plan out my route carefully so it would take the least amount of driving. Then I'd list my stops so it looked like I was crisscrossing the county all day long. That way, I could put eighty or ninety miles on the Health Department's car when only thirty or forty of those miles were for work. I was lying all the time."

Many addicts, using boldfaced lies, ingenious stories, and elaborate deceptions, successfully hide their addiction from others for years. Because their addictive behavior produces few observable signs or symptoms, sex addicts tend to be far more successful than other addicts in concealing their addictions for extended periods of time. When alcoholics stagger home or to the office, those with whom they live or work can usually tell immediately that they've been drinking. Similarly, compulsive gamblers can often be found out through their financial losses, and those with eating disorders can be discovered by their weight gains or losses. But there are few reliable ways to tell when sex addicts have been on sex binges. Their moodiness, depression, remoteness, and silence can be attributed to anything from a rough day at the office to the onset of a cold or denied completely by their claiming, "I'm fine. You're imagining things."

Even when directly confronted with either evidence or suspicions of their sexual episodes, most sex addicts feel compelled to lie their way out of the situation. "I felt terrible when my wife asked me whether I was having an affair," remembers Todd, who actually had many affairs, often simultaneously. "But I knew I couldn't show any emotion. I had to act completely innocent, you know, play the right part. 'Of course not, honey. That's ridiculous,' I said. I knew she knew it wasn't ridiculous. She had all the proof right there, but I just couldn't tell her the truth. I didn't really resent her accusation, but I sure acted like I did. You never saw anyone as indignant or hurt as I pretended to be."

Most sex addicts relentlessly deny their sexual obsession, even in the face of incontrovertible evidence. Like Todd, they almost always react to any suggestion that threatens their addictive behavior with indignant protests or verbal abuse.

Despite the fact that their addictive behavior and their denial actually make all sex addicts untrustworthy, they take it as a personal insult when other people don't trust them. "I have a friend who's anorexic, and she does the same thing," says Robin, who has not only her sex addiction, but also her bulimia to hide. "We laugh about it. Here we are lying, but we get mad when people don't believe us. We're indignant that they don't believe our lies."

This indignation is *not* just an act. Through the strength of their own denial, sex addicts believe their own lies, and truly do not understand why anyone else should question them. As incredible as it may seem, Janet, who has been having an affair for years, is absolutely sincere when she says, "My husband doesn't trust me. I find that hard, because I'm not going to hurt him. I'm just about as honest as they come, and I'm very loyal."

Sex addicts *always* keep their addiction hidden from others, but not all sex addicts feel compelled to lie. They keep their secret by isolating themselves. "I don't have to explain anything to anyone," insists Mitch, who lives alone, as Robin does.

Don suggests, "No sex addict, like no alcoholic, has any close friends when he's not sober. I know with me, once my obsession got going, I stayed as far away from my friends and family as I could." In fact, sex addicts let others see their addiction even less than alcoholics, who sometimes find drinking buddies—fellow alcoholics who share and support their addictive behavior. The same cannot be said for sex addicts.

Secrecy and isolation perpetuate the addiction. Because sex addicts believe they can control their compulsive behavior, they steadfastly refuse to call on others for help. Even after they begin their recovery, sex addicts continue to find it difficult to open up about their addiction. "My two best friends and my wife know what's going on," Hank explained recently. "With them, I can be as honest as I want to be. I think it might help me to talk to them, but I don't. My first reaction is always to isolate, hoping I'll get it all cleaned up by myself, and then I'll talk to people."

In this and other ways, the secret itself proves to be a powerful force in sex addicts' lives. They are almost always terrified that discovery will destroy them. Like children who try to keep their parents from finding out they broke a window or failed biology, sex addicts can never truly escape the thought that one day they will get caught. So, they constantly wait for the ax to drop. The longer they lie and hide from reality, the stronger their fear becomes. They run from the fear, escaping to more sex, which necessitates more lies, deception, and denial. Thus, the denial becomes ever more powerful and urgent, plunging them deeper and deeper into the abyss from which willpower alone will never extract them. Their compulsive behavior continues in spite of the many dangerous consequences or devastating risks involved.

5

RISKING EVERYTHING:
The Deadly Potential of
the Disease

"Being a sex addict is like playing Russian rou-
lette," Don says, many months after seeking
treatment for his addiction. "There's only so
many times you can pull the trigger before you get a bullet. Going into a
recovery program probably saved my life."

Yet Don, who had masturbated compulsively since adolescence and
spent much of his adulthood picking up women for one-time sexual
liaisons, did not check himself into a hospital for treatment until he was
fifty years old. By then, he had already contracted and been treated for
several sexually transmitted diseases, had his life threatened by the
husband of one woman he slept with, lost his job, his wife, and his home,
and was contemplating suicide. Like most sex addicts, Don waited until
he had hit bottom before voluntarily seeking the help he had so desperately needed all along.

Such has been the case with every sex addict we have ever known.
During one Thursday-night therapy group session, we asked the group
members to try to explain how they could be so oblivious to the risks and
consequences of their own behavior.

"I know it's dangerous," says Mitch, who readily engaged in various
sexual acts with men he encountered in adult bookstores, total strangers
who easily could have been violently mentally ill, undercover vice cops,

or carriers of sexually transmitted diseases. "Sure, I could get some sort of disease. But before this AIDS thing, I thought that was no big deal. Most of the other diseases are curable. Besides, when I was going into a bookstore, the last thing on my mind was catching something. I just didn't consider the dangers at all."

Neither did Bill, even though he was arrested several times for voyeurism and exhibitionism, which destroyed his marriage, and, on at least one occasion, came close to losing him his job. Any fears or consideration of consequences invariably evaporated into the fog that enveloped Bill each time sexual thoughts entered his mind. He explains that "One minute I'd be thinking something like 'I'd better watch it. There are cops out here who know me on sight because I've been arrested so many times.' But the next minute, I just didn't care. I wanted the sex so much that nothing else mattered."

For other sex addicts, like Todd, who picked up venereal diseases more than once and eventually got divorced as a result of his constant extramarital affairs and one-night stands, the dangers are almost always on their minds but rarely taken seriously.

"I'm a lot more cautious than I used to be," Todd reports. "But I'm not as cautious as I *ought* to be. Really, I never was. When I was married, I always thought that I *could* get caught, but I never actually believed I *would*. And the times my wife did catch me—right up until the last time— I always talked my way out of it. I just thought I could get away with anything, anything at all."

Because of the illusion of control they create in their own minds, many sex addicts feel they are powerful and special enough to beat the odds or, as Todd put it, "get away with anything" without paying a price. Like Todd, they laugh off the dangers and go right on indulging their sexual obsessions.

And for some, the risk is an integral part of the high itself. "It's like hang gliding or skiing down the most advanced slope on a mountain," says Hank, who, interestingly enough, would never try such a high-risk sport or for that matter take risks of any kind at work or in his personal relationships. Like most sex addicts, Hank always goes for the sure bet and the path of least resistance in every aspect of his life—except sex.

"There's danger there," Hank continues. "But when that guy is up there ready to let go, he doesn't think about how he could fall or ski into a tree or crash-land and break every bone in his body. He doesn't think it could happen to him. Or maybe thinking about the danger makes things more exciting, more of a challenge. That's how I felt about sex. Every time was a chance to prove I could pull it off without blowing it. And I always thought I could do it. Always."

As the words of the sex addicts we treat reflect, the risks and consequences of sex addiction—from venereal disease to violence, arrest to divorce—are considerable. And yet, through their delusions about control and their denial, sex addicts ignore the risks or minimize their seriousness, shrugging off reality, and succumbing again and again to the seductive powers of their addiction. Indeed, as Hank revealed, the element of risk actually enhances arousal for some sex addicts, and they may even revamp their rituals to include more and greater danger.

Whether sex addicts simply deny the dangers or actively court the excitement of risky behavior, disastrous consequences occur, not just once, but regularly and repeatedly. Some lose their spouses, lovers, or jobs, get arrested, contract sexually transmitted diseases, even get beaten by an abusive lover or an unstable sexual partner, and still refuse to recognize the potential destructiveness of the disease, or that they even *have* a disease.

WHY ADDICTS RISK EVERYTHING FOR A SEXUAL HIGH

We have often wondered if sex addicts view the obvious risks and dangers of their sexual behavior with such a cavalier attitude because sex itself seems incredibly perilous to them. When having sex is the first family rule the addict breaks, as it was for Robin, will anything else ever seem as threatening? After all, Robin grew up believing that violating *any* family rule would get her kicked out of the family altogether and make her a nonperson. Having risked the ultimate in dire consequences, the danger of contracting a disease or picking up a violent sexual partner in a bar seems tame in comparison. Nearly all sex addicts, including Don, who was never prohibited from exploring his sexuality, share this perception that sex is the most dangerous—and exciting—act of all.

We have repeatedly observed several factors that explain why the obvious risks and inevitable consequences of sex addiction rarely persuade the addict to change or even want to change.

Denying the Existence or Seriousness of the Risk

Of all the aspects of the disease that sex addicts refuse to acknowledge, the denial of the detrimental effects of their sexual behavior does the most damage to themselves and others. This denial, more than anything else, allows the addiction to go unchecked. Their conviction that everything is under control, and that their behavior does not endanger them or anyone else, encourages sex addicts to shrug off the risks and potential consequences that might otherwise convince them to alter or altogether abandon their destructive sexual activities.

Bill lost his marriage and almost lost his job because of his addiction, but his denial persisted even in the face of the many other risks he took. He claims, "If I was in a sane mood in the first place, of course I would think about the possibility of picking up a disease, getting arrested, being robbed, or being seen by someone who knows me. I'd be able to stop myself. But once the arousal starts, I'm not sane, and I don't think about the consequences—until afterward."

The potential risks associated with their behavior seem very small, practically meaningless to sex addicts who weigh them against the intense pleasure they know they can get from the sexual high. For sex addicts, potential dangers remain merely potential—unlike the high itself, which they know they can make happen. They do not know with such certainty that the negative consequences will occur and, as long as sex addicts can convince themselves that they just might get away with their sexual acting out, the risks and potential dangers will not deter them.

Interestingly enough, like Hank, most sex addicts rarely take risks in other areas of their lives. By and large, at work and at home, they prefer to take the safe course, whenever possible. For example, Bill as a teenager and young adult took no chances while dating. He says, "I always felt more comfortable with women if I heard they were 'easy' sexually. Then I didn't have much of a risk of failing."

Their deep sense of insecurity makes it impossible for most sex addicts to take the kinds of chances other people take every day. They will not make themselves vulnerable to other people by expressing their emotions openly and honestly. Or they find it extremely difficult, if not impossible, to ask for a raise, disagree with a co-worker, or take a stand about an issue being discussed in a staff meeting because they fear they will lose their jobs. Yet, either because they don't consider the consequences or minimize them, sex addicts risk that same job by engaging in their compulsive sexual behaviors during work hours or by being obsessed with sex rather than concentrating on their work.

Believing They Are Immune to the Dangers

When not wrapped up in their sexual fantasies, most sex addicts feel insignificant and out of control. But under the influence of their fantasies and rituals, they frequently feel superior to all others. They feel like gods: omniscient and omnipotent. Sex addicts sincerely believe that "Other people might get caught doing what I'm doing, but I won't. I can't get caught."

"I have this idea that somehow I ought to be able to do whatever I want; that the rules should apply for other people, but that I should be able to bend those rules," admits Hank. "I know it's wrong. But I still find myself living as if that were true."

Even when not acting out their obsessions, sex addicts tend to view themselves as the center of the universe. For addicts who grew up feeling invisible or insignificant, there is a perverse pleasure in believing they are the focus of other people's attention. In their fantasies, sex addicts often take this overblown sense of importance even further, believing themselves undetectable, untouchable, and unstoppable.

For some sex addicts, incorporating additional risks into their sexual rituals makes them feel even more godlike. "You try and build the excitement," Wayne maintains. "Each time that you have sex, you take more chances, more risks. Sometimes, I get bored or tired with what I've been doing, so I try something more adventurous like coming on to a client, or one time I connected with a hooker in a hotel bar while my boss was sitting right across the room, and it made me feel great! Really powerful and in complete control."

Those words say it all. Illusions of power and control not only confirm sex addicts' imagined superiority, but also persuade them that they are magically protected from ruining their marriages, losing their jobs, getting arrested, contracting diseases, or suffering any other consequences of their behavior. This strategy works well until reality finally catches up with them, and even then they still have a few tricks up their sleeves.

"Stop Me If You Can": Refusing to Accept Responsibility for Addictive Behavior

Because the possibility of contracting AIDS certainly represents the most frightening and deadly danger they face, most sex addicts, if they consider the risks at all, focus on that disease and others. But sex addicts also risk their families, their jobs, and their own emotional and psychological well-being. Because attaining the sexual high is the most important need they feel, in fulfilling it they neglect the other aspects of their lives. "My affair caused me so much anxiety that I wasn't dealing with work," Janet admits. "Things weren't going well at home. I had so much anxiety I just couldn't concentrate."

Although Janet seems to be aware of the effects of her behavior, most sex addicts are not conscious that they're risking their jobs and their families by devoting almost all of their energies to the quest for sexual euphoria. Indeed, their behavior is often so blatant and so careless that an outside observer might think they were actively courting disaster. Although they go to great lengths *not* to admit their problem to themselves or others, we often think that deep down many of the sex addicts we treat know that they don't have the addiction under control and unconsciously *want* to get caught. Perhaps on some level they hope that their families or their employers will be able to force them to do what they cannot bring themselves to do—shape up and finally make the changes they need to make in their lives. Some of the addicts we work with agree with this opinion.

"There were days when I was just waiting to get caught," Bill, the Health Department inspector, tells us. "I didn't care anymore. If I lost my job, I figured that would make me get my act together."

But because putting the burden of bringing about change on someone else allows sex addicts to go right on shrugging off responsibility for their own recovery, getting caught seldom changes them.

"I did get caught once," Bill explains. "It was right after my divorce, and of course I was acting out more than ever. My supervisor found out that I had forged a bunch of inspection forms. But I'm one of their better workers, and because of the divorce, I got out of it. I had to report in more often, and it was sort of messy for a while, but in the end it was all straightened out."

Once discovered, the addict's defense mechanism of denial clicks in and prevents the consequences from bringing about a change. Bill rationalized that since the one indiscretion for which he was caught did not cost him his job, he could get away with continuing his behavior. He decided he would never actually get fired because he was one of the Board of Health's better workers. He believed this fallacy in spite of the fact that, by his own admission, he spent at least half of his work week picking up prostitutes. Clearly, the worst had happened and it had not been all that bad, removing the threat of unemployment as an impetus for change. Furthermore, he used a previously negative consequence to his advantage, justifying his form forging to his supervisor by claiming he was distraught over his divorce.

Turning Negative Consequences into Positive Opportunities

As you can see, even when sex addicts like Bill do suffer one or more losses, they still may not be motivated to reflect on their lives and recognize the damage created by their addiction. "I lost a job a few years back, although it wasn't really due to sexual acting out," Hank explains. "The economy was just really bad. I genuinely struggled, trying to make money, but my mind was eaten up by the desire to be out there cruising around. I spent most of my time at porno movies. I'd have no money, but I'd still stop in."

Like the compulsive gambler who loses big at the tables, but quickly returns to the casino, many sex addicts persist with their destructive activities, seemingly oblivious to the fact that they are only heading further down, toward their own destruction. And the further down they go, the more risks they take.

Indeed, after risking and losing their jobs or their marriages or their reputations, sex addicts frequently use their losses as just another excuse for continuing their self-demolition. As Bill did, they can use the loss to their advantage, thinking that "I'm really suffering right now. I need to take care of myself. I need to do this to feel better." Some see a loss as an opportunity, so that a divorce or the breakup of a relationship may lead the addict to say, "Well, here's my chance to really go wild." After suffering one significant loss after another, many addicts simply respond with, "I might as well go ahead and do this. What else have I got to lose?"

Hitting Bottom

Many sex addicts keep on taking risks until they really do lose everything. They suffer a slow death, killing themselves emotionally and psychologically, sinking into an ever-growing depression. They may even sink so low that they attempt suicide.

Don, an alcoholic as well as a sex addict, contemplated suicide after losing his marriage and family. Fortunately, Don ultimately used his despair over those losses to finally take steps to turn his life around. At rock bottom, he found a reason and the courage to enter a recovery program.

"There are lots of ways you can die when you have an addiction," he says. "I know an alcoholic who got shot walking into a neighbor's house because he was acting so weird. Another guy shot himself in the head. If a guy exposes himself to a kid, the kid's father might be close by and have a gun handy. He'll kill you. You could get killed by one of the weirdos who hangs out on the pickup strip. Catch AIDS. It really is a life-or-death kind of thing.''

Although Don's anxieties about the violence others might inflict upon him were so intense they bordered on paranoia, his fears were not unfounded. Sex addicts do expose themselves to physical violence by picking up one random stranger after another in bars or on the street—and to physical harm or death in many other ways.

Medical Risks

Not all sex addicts acquire sexually transmitted diseases (STDs). Those who masturbate or engage in voyeurism, for example, don't make contact with another person. But those addicts whose sexual rituals involve multiple partners are constantly in danger of contracting a wide variety of STDs and other infectious diseases. They increase the risk because, believing they are invulnerable, most sex addicts ignore the two most fundamental rules of safe sex: know your partner and take precautions to prevent STDs.

"I worried about AIDS," admits Don. "And it did slow me down some, although I got reckless a couple of times because I wanted it too bad. I got gonorrhea from a woman I worked with, even though I knew at the time that I should have said, Wait a second, I don't have a rubber. But I didn't want to miss out on the opportunity, you know, or wait until I could go find one.''

We know of no sex addict who is successful in taking adequate precautions to prevent getting or spreading STDs while practicing his or her addiction. Perhaps because they feel it would take away from their sexual euphoria, very few male sex addicts use condoms. And, by disregarding safety measures, sex addicts end up among the highest-risk populations for picking up these diseases. Because some STDs are deadly—especially AIDS, which is *always* fatal—we feel it is our responsibility to alert sex addicts as well as their partners about the real dangers they face.

Sex addicts reading the following material may be tempted to think that because they now know what to look for, they either won't pick up a disease or will be able to cure it in time to prevent discovery by their spouses or lovers. But in going over some of the symptoms and treatments for these diseases, we are in no way offering a means to justify further addictive sexual behavior. Instead, it is our sincere wish that this knowledge will spur them to seek help through any of the self-help groups and/or psychological services we will discuss in Chapter 10.

Our position is clear and leaves no room for doubt: Sex addicts should take steps to overcome their addiction *before* they contract one of these diseases—and transmit it to all of their sexual partners.

Dr. Henry Reuss, a Scottsdale obstetrician/gynecologist whose expertise proved invaluable in preparing this section of the book, urges all sex addicts, as well as their sexual partners, to be regularly screened for all of the following sexually transmitted diseases. Unfortunately, as Dr. Reuss points out, when testing active sex addicts for these diseases, "you run into the same difficulty that you do when you screen prostitutes for venereal disease: you check them and they're fine, but their next partner might be infected."

Dr. Reuss has found that most female prostitutes test positive for chlamydia, herpes, Trichomonas, and genital warts, in particular. Of course, he has seen others who tested positive for other venereal diseases as well. Obviously, sex addicts who depend on prostitutes run an especially high risk of contracting these diseases. But anyone who has any type of sex with multiple partners is also putting his or her life on the line.

Sex addicts—and the spouses or partners of sex addicts—have an extremely high risk of developing one or more of the following:

Chlamydia: A rapidly spreading infection, chlamydia can cause nonspecific urethritis (an inflammation of the urethra) in men and pelvic inflammatory disease in women. If untreated, it can cause infertility in both. As with all other STDs, pregnant women can pass chlamydia on to their unborn babies, causing them to be born with serious eye, ear, and lung infections. By law, all pregnant women are now tested for it.

Some men and women apparently develop no symptoms from chlamydia, simply carrying the organism and transmitting it to their sexual partners. Men who do have symptoms frequently experience genital pain, especially when urinating, and excrete a cloudy discharge from the penis. Women who have chlamydia often notice an abnormal vaginal discharge and the frequent need to urinate, often accompanied by severe abdominal pain.

If discovered, chlamydia can be treated with various antibiotics, and the use of condoms can provide protection against it, saving a lot of pain and misery.

Genital Warts (Condyloma): Genital warts—a virus, like AIDS and herpes—has no known cure. This STD has reached epidemic proportions in the United States. In his Scottsdale, Arizona, office, at least 25 percent of all the patients Dr. Reuss examines have these warts, and because researchers have identified a strong link between genital warts in women and cancer of the cervix, the infection is considered extremely dangerous. Pregnant women should also be alerted that babies can become infected during delivery.

Because only two of the eight viral strains that afflict humans can be seen by the naked eye, urological or gynecological examinations are often necessary to diagnose genital warts. The two visible strains, identified by flat or bumpy growths around the genitals or anus, although messy, do not cause further complications. The more dangerous microscopic strains, however, cause *no* symptoms in most men and some women, and therefore can be easily transmitted unknowingly. In addition, the warts often take several months to appear after infection, furthering the spread of the virus. Symptoms, when they do appear, may include localized genital itching, burning pain, and irritation.

Because genital warts are spread through skin contact rather than an exchange of fluids, condoms, although helpful, are less effective than they are against other STDs. Although not permanently curable, genital warts can be treated and controlled, if caught soon enough. However, they frequently reappear, especially during times of stress.

Herpes: Tens of millions of people have contracted either genital or oral herpes, although Dr. Reuss informs us that the number of new cases of herpes is now in decline. Like genital warts, herpes has been linked to cervical cancer in women and poses a life-threatening risk to babies who contract the virus. When spread to the eye (by touching a sore and then your eye), herpes can cause blindness.

Most people now know the later symptoms that accompany herpes: genital or oral blisters that form painful sores and tenderness when they burst, then scab over, and disappear. Early symptoms of herpes, which typically appear within three weeks of the initial infection, include pain and aching throughout the body as well as a tingling or burning sensation, itching, and intense pain in the infected area. After the first outbreak, which is usually the most painful and dramatic, recurring symptoms tend to be milder.

Between outbreaks of herpes blisters, condoms may help reduce the chances of contracting or spreading the disease, but from the time the first tingling or itching symptoms of an outbreak appear until the sores have completely healed, any physical contact at all with the affected areas might spread the disease. Doctors can now prescribe oral suppressants that will reduce the number or severity of outbreaks, but like genital warts, herpes has no cure.

Gonorrhea and Syphilis: The most well-known venereal diseases, gonorrhea and syphilis, carry serious repercussions if not recognized and treated quickly. Gonorrhea can cause sterility in both men and women and pelvic inflammatory disease in women. Syphilis can produce brain damage or weaken the heart and blood vessels. Both can infect babies during birth.

Men who contract gonorrhea experience a discharge from the penis and genital pain, especially when urinating. Women who have the disease sometimes develop no early symptoms or notice only a vaginal discharge until they get pelvic inflammatory disease, when they experience a high fever and localized pain. Both men and women with syphilis first develop a painless sore in the infected area: genitals, anus, or mouth. Several weeks after the sore disappears, they develop a rash and often experience a high fever.

Condoms can play an important role in helping to prevent the spread of gonorrhea and syphilis. If detected early, both venereal diseases can be completely cured with the use of antibiotics.

Vaginitis: Although the three major types of vaginal infections can all be transmitted sexually, they can be picked up in other ways as well. Trichomonas and Gardnerella are often transmitted through sexual intercourse; yeast infections, almost never. None carry serious complications for either women or men, but all can be extremely irritating.

Although men will occasionally experience a discharge or feel some discomfort due to Trichomonas, in most cases they develop no symptoms. Women with vaginitis usually notice an abnormal vaginal discharge: yellow-green for Trichomonas, watery gray or white for Gardnerella, and thick white for yeast infections. Often these discharges are accompanied by a strong odor. Both Trichomonas and yeast infections usually produce a severe itching and a burning sensation.

Use of condoms can reduce the risk of contracting vaginal infections through sexual transmission; these three can be treated with various medications.

AIDS: AIDS—Acquired Immune Deficiency Syndrome—is, of course, the most deadly STD, one that everyone is rightly concerned about. Although we have thankfully not yet seen a sex-addicted patient who has contracted AIDS, we sadly realize that it's just a matter of time. Because sex addicts who have multiple partners take protective measures only sporadically, if at all, it seems inevitable that a large number of them will develop this incurable, deadly disease.

In the earliest stages, AIDS has no observable symptoms. Because their immune systems begin to break down, AIDS patients suffer from only the symptoms of secondary infections—generalized weakness, persistent fatigue, malaise, weight loss, swollen glands, and fever. Instead of going away as most infections do, even without treatment, these get progressively worse.

AIDS has no cure, and although researchers are constantly testing new treatments, none has yet shown itself to be universally effective in controlling the disease. Sex addicts, who seldom know their sexual partners well and almost never take the initiative to use, or insist their partners use, condoms—and may even scoff at the very idea of using a condom—leave themselves wide open to being infected with this deadly disease.

Other Medical Risks: In addition to STDs, sex addicts who have sex compulsively with many different partners also run a higher risk of contracting a wide variety of other diseases, due to the frequency of their physical contact. Dr. Robert Hamilton, a Scottsdale family physician with whom we've worked on a number of occasions, stresses that sex addicts have a much greater chance of picking up infectious diseases, especially viral and bacterial infections of the upper respiratory tract, often transmitted through kissing.

According to Dr. Hamilton, just a few of the many diseases that sex addicts can contract include strep throat, Hemophilus influenza, viral gastric infection, and tuberculosis. Although curable, these chronic illnesses still take their toll on the sex addict and his or her family.

Finally, the increased stress created by their addictive behavior exacts a heavy physical toll on sex addicts. It often leads to such persistent physical problems as recurring headaches or backaches, stomach ailments, nightmares, sleepless nights, and constant fatigue.

Sex addiction truly is a disease that affects the addict's mind, body, and spirit. Continued exposure to STDs wears down sex addicts physically, and continued exposure to the other risks brought on by their addiction wears them down mentally and spiritually as well.

Although the awareness and practice of protective sexual measures may reduce the risk of developing and spreading sexually transmitted diseases, the only truly effective way for a sex addict to protect himself or herself and his or her family from these infections is to finally stop denying reality and seek help for the illness that leads to all other illnesses: sex addiction.

When Disease Leads to Discovery: Will Loved Ones Acknowledge the Disease or Deny It, Too?

Unless a sex addict contracts AIDS, picking up a sexually transmitted disease could possibly result in a positive outcome. It almost always forces the addict to face the fact that he or she just might be accountable for his or her actions. In fact, we have seen at least one case in which picking up a disease actually led a sex addict to seek help for his problem. Unfortunately, this is not always the case. When Don caught gonorrhea, for example, he did briefly consider the possibility that his own sexual behavior might be stupid, but nonetheless focused most of the blame on the woman who gave him the disease.

Even addicts forced to confess their infidelities because they have picked up a disease do not necessarily change as a result of the disease or the discovery of their secret life. "I never actually admitted to my wife that I had had sex with anyone else," Todd says, then corrects himself. "No, that's wrong. I did admit it once, but only because I had picked up something. I was really sorry I'd given her something. But, to be honest, I was more sorry that I had to confess it. It was awful, a nightmare. I couldn't believe it, but I had to tell her, and she just couldn't handle it."

All too often, a sex addict's disclosure to his or her spouse or partner follows this pattern. The addict feigns remorse for the infidelity but feels real remorse only because the problem has finally had to be brought out into the open. As we shall discuss in the next two chapters, more often than not, the addict's spouse or lover is almost as eager as the addict to ignore or cover up the problem.

Sex Addiction Is a Family Disease

II

6

IS THERE A STRANGER IN THE HOUSE?
Living with a Sex Addict

The first time we saw Molly, she reminded us of a fragile porcelain doll. Just 5 feet 2 inches tall, the plump, pretty, thirty-six-year-old mother of two sons has a lovely, clear-skinned, rosy-cheeked face framed by a mop of soft red-brown curls. As she sat before us for the first time three years ago, that face and her green eyes were completely expressionless. When Molly came to us, she had already been married for fourteen years to Hank, the insurance salesman and sex addict we described in earlier chapters of this book.

Perhaps you noticed that most of the sex addicts you read about earlier were or had been married—not just for a year or two while the addiction was temporarily under control, but for ten, fifteen, or even twenty years. They managed to maintain their marriages, have homes in the suburbs, raise children, and convince all outside observers that they had an ideal home life while actively pursuing sexual highs, sometimes on a daily basis.

To do this, they had at least one accomplice, and usually several. Family members, especially spouses like Molly, unwittingly enable sex addiction to continue and progress by denying the existence of the problem or downplaying its seriousness, assuming responsibility for anything the addiction has prevented the addict from doing, and upholding a code of silence and secrecy both within the family and outside it.

How could anyone even unwittingly make it easier for a sex addict to continue acting out for years on end? If you are a co-dependent, you may already know the answer. But it took Molly three years of treatment—including participation in our weekly therapy group for spouses and loved ones of sex addicts—to figure out why she had put up with and covered up Hank's sex addiction.

"I honestly did not know what I was getting into when I married Hank," Molly insists, and for the most part, her statement is accurate. In the beginning, she knew very little about Hank at all. "We met when he was transferred to this area by the insurance company we both worked for," she explains. "He was so handsome and charming. Half the women in the office were dying to go out with him. Right off the bat, I felt really special, really privileged because he chose *me.*"

A compulsive overeater since early adolescence, Molly had waged a lifelong battle against obesity. When she met Hank, she had just lost thirty pounds and was thinner than she ever remembered being, but her image of herself had changed very little. "I had never been confident about attracting men," she says. "Because of the weight thing, I pretty much settled for whoever I could get. Mostly moody, distant guys who needed a lot of mothering, but ended up leaving me because they said I smothered them." So Molly played a little hard to get with Hank—at least at first.

"He definitely swept me off my feet," she reports. "He went all out to win me over. He was so sweet and attentive, a complete gentleman. There were days I honestly could not believe that this handsome, bright, funny ex-football star was wining and dining me and telling me he had been looking for me his whole life. I felt that way too, like I'd finally found the man who made me feel complete and good about myself. He could get any girl he wanted, but he picked me. It was such a wonderful feeling. I never wanted it to end."

As you can see, Molly's self-esteem quickly became attached to her relationship with Hank. Her conviction that—because of Hank—she felt special, complete, worthwhile, and truly loved for the first time in her life set the stage for all that would follow. The more time she spent with him, the more Molly adored Hank, and the more terrified of losing him she became.

After they had been dating for a year, a salesman from Hank's old district office paid a visit, and Molly overheard him chiding Hank about his many sexual adventures. The other salesman alluded to a trail of broken hearts that Hank had left across his old sales territory and asked Hank if he'd slept his way across the new state yet. Molly went into a panic, obsessively worrying that Hank was dating other women and would ultimately choose one of them over her.

"It was making me so nuts that I just had to ask him about it," she says. "But before I could, he volunteered the information that he had done a lot of running around before he met me, but that I had changed him. He thought he must have just been looking for the right woman. He swore he actually got down on his knees each morning and thanked God that he had finally found me. Then he got down on his knees and proposed."

This episode confirmed Molly's belief that their relationship was "special, almost sacred," and that her love for Hank was powerful enough to overcome any obstacle. Hank believed this also. He was truly convinced that he was a new person. He thought his obsession with sex was cured, and she thought that she and her love had reformed him, ending his days of running around, forever. With the stage set for the *folie à deux* that would follow, Molly and Hank got married.

"I started noticing changes in Hank right after our first son was born," Molly recalls. "But I didn't really know what they meant. It was a tough time for us. The economy was bad and I had stopped working, so Hank was always worried about money. And Billy was sick a lot, so I was just exhausted most of the time. I'd also gained a lot of weight during the pregnancy. Between being tired and being self-conscious about my body, I really wasn't that interested in sex. But mostly I thought Hank's moods were just his way of adjusting to the changes in our life. I thought he'd get used to the way things were, and the mood would pass."

It didn't, and after their second son was born, Molly found a credit card receipt from a sleazy hotel and a matchbook from a pickup bar with a woman's name and number written on it. Once again, panic set in, and she stewed in her own juices for several days before Hank returned from a business trip. Just like the last time Molly had tried to confront Hank, he beat her to the punch.

"He walked in the door looking like he hadn't slept in days," she remembers. "He immediately told me he had been with another woman and begged me to forgive him. I swear he was more upset than I was. He actually cried. I felt bad for him, and I just thought 'These things happen. He's been under a lot of stress lately and he's really sorry. It will never happen again.' "

So Molly forgave him and tried to forget the incident had happened at all—until the next time. Then she not only forgave him but started thinking that she had "done something to push Hank into another woman's arms." She went on a crash diet, dyed her hair blond and read a half-dozen sex manuals in hopes of enticing her husband to get what he wanted at home rather than looking elsewhere for it. "But he just kept on having affairs and one-night stands," Molly told us.

By the time their boys were in school, life in their home was ruled by Hank's compulsive behavior and Molly's obsession with finding some way to stop it. She seduced him, gave him the silent treatment, played on his guilt, checked up on him throughout the day, and assumed responsibility for taking care of anything she thought put pressure on him and led him to act out. She made sure no one outside the home suspected anything was wrong and thought she was sheltering her sons from the painful realities as well.

At first, Hank confessed each infidelity, and she confronted him each time she found tokens from an adult bookstore, women's phone numbers, ticket stubs from XXX-rated movies, lipstick on his shirt collar, or pornographic magazines hidden in a drawer. "I went through a suspicious period. I'd go looking for these things and confront him. He'd apologize and say, 'I don't know what got into me. It won't happen again.' But it always did.

"After a while, I stopped looking. I didn't have to. Hank had always been a really private, moody person, but before, during, and after one of his little sex binges, he was especially moody, just really depressed and guilt-ridden. Then he'd snap out of it and be okay for a while. I would pacify him as much as I could, trying to make the good periods last longer, trying to make sure the kids or money problems or other things didn't upset him."

Eventually, Molly resigned herself to her plight, persuading herself that Hank's behavior was normal for a guy and that life was not so bad in spite of Hank's infidelities and peculiarities.

"I just focused on the good things," she says. "Our kids, our home, the things we did at church, and the way people would always tell us how much they envied us. They thought we were really lucky, really happy and stable. It was very important for me to hear that. I devoted myself to making sure everyone kept right on thinking we were the Ozzie and Harriet of the '80s."

Molly might have maintained this pretense indefinitely if a magazine article about sex addiction hadn't started her thinking that Hank might be an addict. "I really didn't think so at first. But for some reason, I clipped the article and kept it."

It came in handy several months later when she walked into her husband's den and found her sons poring over Hank's collection of porno magazines. "I just lost it. All I could see was my sons growing up to be sex addicts. I mean, Hank's father had molested Hank's sisters, and Hank couldn't get enough sex no matter what he did. And now, the boys were starting, or that's what I thought, anyway."

Molly called Hank, who was out of town on business (interrupting his latest one-night stand), and told him she "couldn't live like this anymore." Then she dialed the hotline number listed in the magazine article she had saved. The hotline referred her to us, and Molly entered treatment. Hank refused to get help and continued his pursuit of sexual highs until the couple separated eighteen months later.

Now, two years later, they are discussing a reconciliation, although Molly is ambivalent about the reunion. Hank has abstained from his compulsive sexual behavior for six months now, but she still is not sure she can trust him.

"I'm not sure I can trust myself, either," she sighs. "I was really as sick as he was and even though I'm better, I'm not sure I'm really well yet."

CO-DEPENDENCY

Molly's story dramatizes the fact that, like all addictions, sex addiction is a family disease. The addiction itself, whether or not the addict or anyone else in the family openly acknowledges it, is the central and most powerful force governing that family, the unspoken and often unrecognized focus of all family interaction. Denial and secrecy become the unwritten rules everyone follows. Almost always motivated by the best of intentions—to protect the family and help the addict overcome the problem—family members, especially spouses and lovers, are as obsessed, and sometimes more obsessed, with the sex addict's behavior than he or she is.

Spouses like Molly minimize their own needs, shut off their emotions, and censor their conversations, all in deference to the unacknowledged lord of the manor: sex addiction. Paralyzed by their own fears, family members unwittingly enter into a secret pact with the addict, one that perpetuates the illness and prevents change. Soon enough, they are, as Molly put it, "as sick as he is."

The disease suffered by those closely involved with sex addicts is called co-dependency—a term first used to describe the painful condition suffered by family members of alcoholics, but one that applies equally in all addictions. As any addiction progresses, co-dependents—not just spouses and partners, but children, parents, and siblings as well—tend to focus almost exclusively on the addict in the family, tailoring their own lives to revolve around the addict and the addiction. Their disease is progressive, too. The more the addict becomes obsessed with sex or alcohol or food, the more co-dependents become obsessed with the addict and his or her behavior.

Co-dependents are essentially "addicted to the addict," and develop many of the same personality traits: denial of the disease, secretiveness, an inability to express feelings, strong fears of abandonment and rejection, and a marked resistance to change, to name just a few. Some co-dependents, because they were raised in homes where one or both parents were addicted, already have some of these characteristics by the time they begin their relationships with sex addicts. Others develop these tendencies in direct response to their addict's behavior.

We have found without exception that whenever the sex addicts we treat are married or involved in long-term relationships, their spouses or lovers are indeed co-dependent. Molly most certainly was. What's more, her potential to become addicted to the addict was clear from the outset of her relationship with Hank. Because of her own out-of-control eating disorder as well as influences from a childhood that revolved around her father's alcoholism, Molly suffered from low self-esteem. All her sense of her own worth and uniqueness hinged on Hank and their relationship. To lose him would mean once again to lose herself and "feel empty and miserable." She was not about to let that happen.

Molly's determination to hang on to Hank and her own identity as the woman he loved and married, no matter what the cost, is shared by most co-dependents. So are several other aspects of Molly's marital history, including:

- ignoring, downplaying, or making excuses for various warning signs of sex addiction,
- taking action only after a traumatic event has occurred or a tearful confession has been made,
- obsessively trying to reform the addict or cover up the problem because acknowledging it creates a painful conflict between ideals and reality.

WARNING SIGNS OF SEX ADDICTION

Sex addiction, like all other addictions, does have its warning signs: clues that *could* prompt family members to insist that the addict get help before the disease progresses any further or get the co-dependents to seek help for themselves. Although in many ways more subtle than the obvious progression of an alcoholic's drunkenness or a compulsive gambler's dwindling financial resources, the signals of sex addiction are not invisible.

When they look back over the history of their relationships, however, many of our co-dependent patients can now identify longstanding patterns and many specific incidents that pointed to the problem of sex addiction. At the time, however, those few who even saw the clues took no action to find out what they meant. Only in retrospect, and through their own recovery, did the following warning signs become apparent to our co-dependent patients.

If you are not a sex addict, and your therapist, a relative, or a friend has given you our book, you may not yet want to admit the possibility that someone close to you might be a sex addict. And certainly, you may be right. However, try to keep an open mind while reading this chapter. If you recognize someone you love in the description of sexually addicted behavior, or if you see yourself in the accounts of these co-dependents, you should open yourself to the possibility that sex addiction might be part of your life.

If, on the other hand, you have bought this book for yourself, you most likely already suspect that you or someone you love may be a sex addict. This crack in the wall of denial indicates that you are ready to look at your situation from a fresh perspective. You may recognize yourself, your girlfriend, your husband, your child, or your parent in the following checklist of warning signs.

Of course, we don't want our readers to become unnecessarily alarmed or start to see sex addiction where no addiction exists. Let us make clear from the outset that *none of these warning signs definitively indicates sex addiction,* especially when only one sign is observed rather than a pattern of interconnected signs. A single sign may point to a problem of *some kind,* particularly if either partner is unwilling to

SEX ADDICTION IS A FAMILY DISEASE

acknowledge or discuss it. However, we urge readers to be careful not to jump to conclusions, based on what they read here.

Regular, Unexplained Time Lapses: Sex addicts frequently disappear for extended periods of time, offering little or no excuse for their absences. Hank, for instance, would often tell Molly he had been meeting with a troubled friend or had stopped off at a shopping mall and lost track of the time. Other sex addicts don't even bother to justify their unpredictable latenesses or periodic disappearing acts.

Sara, thirty-two, recently divorced her husband of ten years and went back to work after devoting herself completely to raising three children and protecting her husband's and family's reputation. Her life revolved around her husband's alcoholism and his compulsive affairs. Both addictions lead to unpredictable behavior and frequent unexplained absences. Sara remembers, "Joe spent a lot of time traveling. But even when he was in town, plenty of nights he wouldn't come home until two or three o'clock in the morning. He didn't call, and he never said where he'd been. He got nasty if I asked, so I didn't."

Most compulsive behaviors take addicts away from their homes and families for hours on end, not just once in a while, but regularly, day after day. As the disease progresses, these absences become more frequent and more pronounced. Cheryl, whose husband is in our Thursday-night recovery group, separated from him for six months as a first step toward undoing more than a decade of co-dependency. During the separation, she got her first job since college and independently supported herself and her two children. With new-found confidence, she recently reconciled with her husband, who no longer "goes off for two or three days at a time, never calling or coming home at all." Previously, however, because her co-dependency and denial were as pronounced as his addiction and denial, when her husband did come home, Cheryl had accepted any excuse he gave her, no matter how lame.

As we mentioned in earlier chapters, sex addicts habitually come up with alibis for the time they use to indulge their sexual obsessions. By accepting any and all excuses, co-dependents reinforce this addictive behavior as well as create their own patterns of denial.

Lapses in Efficiency: The pursuit of sexual highs and fantasizing about those highs often take time away from work or impair the addict's ability to concentrate on work. As a result, addicts don't get promotions or pay raises, watch their work performance plummet, and sometimes even get fired. Indeed, Cheryl's husband lost half a dozen jobs during the three-year period when his addiction was at its peak. She explains, "His mind would be a million miles away. He couldn't think about anything but sex and the problems it was causing. It got so bad that he just couldn't function. He couldn't do the work."

As the addiction saps the addict's energy and preoccupies his or her thoughts, difficulty holding down a job often leads to persistent financial problems. Co-dependents may mistakenly believe that this symptom is the real problem. Sara, for instance, thought that her husband drank and cheated because "he was constantly switching jobs. He'd always start out enthusiastically and work hard, but then he'd lose interest really fast. Things wouldn't happen the way he wanted, or the job just wasn't what he expected it to be. He'd get very impatient and discouraged. Then he'd just up and quit, start over someplace else.''

Actually, Sara's husband quit each job just as he was about to be fired. His three-hour disappearances (while he cruised through the city masturbating in his car) were never tolerated for long by any employer. However, like many co-dependents, Sara persisted in blaming problems at work for the addiction, when, in fact, the reverse was true.

Because nothing sustains the addict's interest for very long and the only constant is the obsession with and pursuit of sexual highs—his or her efficiency and involvement in other areas of daily living dwindles, including the marriage, home life, and the relationship with children. Most co-dependent partners automatically take up the slack, burdening themselves with extra responsibilities to make up for the sex addict's inefficiency.

Rapid and Unpredictable Mood Changes: Closely linked to their deteriorating efficiency, sex addicts frequently experience drastic and apparently unexplainable mood changes, both before and after feeding the addiction. Although most spouses and lovers find this emotional instability hard *not* to notice, they only guess at its source. Molly, for example, thought Hank's moodiness after the birth of their older son "was just how he adjusts to changes at home or at work. He just has that kind of personality. He takes things very personally and worries a lot. Even day-to-day things can be depressing for him.''

It is quite common for sex addicts—after procuring a prostitute, masturbating several times in a row, or coming home after a one-night stand—to feel down or discouraged. Consumed by guilt, shame, and self-disgust, they withdraw emotionally from their families. Then, just as inexplicably, they snap out of it. These mood swings are so rapid and so frequent that those closest to the addict are likely to agree with Cheryl, who says, "He was like Jekyll and Hyde—very hot and cold. And I know now that he was the coldest when he was in the middle of a binge.''

As the illness progresses, the moodiness increases and the addict puts more and more distance between himself and his family. Obsessed with sexual fantasies before acting out, and filled with remorse afterward, sex addicts spend enormous amounts of time literally "staring at the walls," as Sara and many other spouses would say. "His mind was a million miles away,'' she elaborates. "And he didn't want to be interrupted.''

In some instances, addicts lash out at family members who inadvertently intrude on sexual fantasizing. In addition, unconsciously looking to justify their behavior, addicts become irritable and extremely critical. "All of a sudden, he wouldn't be satisfied with anything at home,'' Sara recalls. "He'd get really picky, try to stir up arguments. He had absolutely no tolerance for anyone or anything.''

Many co-dependent spouses and lovers accept the addict's moodi-

SEX ADDICTION IS A FAMILY DISEASE

ness as "just the way (s)he is." Those who actually question addicts about their moods are coldly rebuffed and eventually stop asking.

Other Compulsive Behaviors: The vast majority of sex addicts we have treated are compulsive in other areas in addition to sex. Many are alcoholics or drug addicts, workaholics, binge eaters or bulimics, compulsive gamblers, neat freaks, or perfectionists. These other compulsive behaviors are easier to identify than sex addiction, and they can sometimes serve as clues to what twenty-seven-year-old Jenny calls "the big picture."

Jenny, a very successful architect, recently ended a six-year, live-in relationship with a young artist who was an alcoholic as well as a sex addict. "I never could understand why he wasn't able to control his drinking when we were at a party or in any type of social situation," she says. "When I started wondering about the drinking, a whole lot of other things came to me, like how he couldn't meet a woman without trying to pick her up. It was all part of the same thing. It was all out of control."

Few co-dependents make such connections on their own, although a number of our patients became aware of sex addiction after another of the loved one's addictions was discovered and treated. "About four years ago, my husband got picked up on a DWI charge and had to go to some AA meetings," reports Cheryl, who, as a way of encouraging her husband, started attending Al-Anon meetings. "When he stopped drinking, the sex binges got a lot worse, and I mentioned that to one of the women I'd gotten really close to at Al-Anon. She said that maybe he was a sex addict. I'd never heard of that, but it made me want to find out more."

Since sex addiction is still an unfamiliar notion to most people, other addiction recovery programs are often the first source of information about the disease for addicts and co-dependents alike.

Unfortunately, most couples fail to get even this far, and if they do break through their denial and stop covering up the other addiction, they may focus all attention on the other disease they have acknowledged, allowing sex addiction to remain hidden indefinitely.

Family History: As we explained in Chapter 3, sex addicts were frequently raised in families where at least one parent was an addict or abuser. Even though growing up in an addictive or abusive home does not necessarily mean that children will become sex addicts, when combined with other warning signs, information about a partner's family history provides valuable clues about his or her compulsive behavior. For instance, when Sara tried to trace her husband's drinking problem back to his childhood, she discovered a connection of a different kind. "My father-in-law drinks very seldom, because his own father was an alcoholic and that really affected him," Sara explains. "But he's been married six times, and he shows some of the same traits as my husband, especially when he's around women."

Linking past history to present behavior can be extremely difficult, however, because many sex addicts absolutely refuse to talk about their childhoods, have lapses of memory due to the repression of traumatic incidents, or paint the same rosy (and false) picture their family presented to outsiders. Nonetheless, spouses or lovers who do know of addiction or abuse in their partners' backgrounds should take these clues into consideration, especially if they have already observed other sex-addiction warning signs.

Significant Changes in Sexual Behavior: "Our sex life has had so many ups and downs," Molly says, describing a phenomenon noticed by nearly every man or woman who has ever been in a long-term relationship. Over the years, any couple's sex life changes and is influenced by everything from job stress to childbirth. However, when sex addiction is involved, changes in sexual behavior tend to be quite drastic. In some cases, moved by his own insatiable lust, a sex addict's desire for sex with his long-term partner will increase dramatically and he will push for more sex more often. In other instances, addicts—driven by their own guilt and powerful fears of abandonment—will run from intimacy and lose all interest in sex with spouses or live-in lovers. Other addicts, who are frantically indulging their sexual needs outside of the relationship, claim to be too tired to make love. Some develop performance problems like impotence, because they can become aroused only by their specific sexual rituals.

Sex addiction also alters the nature of the addict's sexual expression. Again, the way most people express themselves sexually evolves and changes over time, and certainly, a varied sex life often enhances relationships. However, the changes we are referring to, including various attempts to get partners to participate in their sexual rituals, are not aimed at improving the relationship or pleasing anyone but the addict. Some addicts we have treated have succeeded, for instance, in convincing their partners to have sex with someone else while they watch and indulge their voyeuristic urges. Others introduce heavy bondage into their marital sex lives or develop a sex-on-demand mentality that leaves their partners feeling like prostitutes. Of course, spouses or lovers can and do refuse to participate. However, few partners ever actually question the sex addict's sudden interest in new types of sex.

Sara's husband, Joe, for instance, indulged his sexual compulsions outside the relationship for the most part. His activities included voyeurism, exhibitionism, and masturbating in his car while parked in public parking lots or on busy downtown streets. His sexual euphoria was heightened by the added risk of possibly getting caught in the act.

Had Sara known this, she might have been less confused when "Joe would hit me up for it ten minutes before my parents were coming over, and I'd be thinking, 'What's *wrong* with you? My parents could walk in on us and what would they think?' " Sara never got around to asking why Joe picked such inopportune times to get sexually aroused. Just saying no "would make him really angry at me," she explains. "Then he would say that I *never* wanted to have sex or that I wasn't fulfilling his needs."

Many sex addicts make their demands work to their advantage both when their partners give in to them and when they do not. Addicts determine the rules of the game, and place their partners in no-win situations. Lovers or spouses who acquiesce to their demands give

138

addicts yet another sex object to use in their rituals, while those who refuse give them yet another excuse to seek sex outside their relationships.

Even when addicts don't demand different kinds of sex or more frequent lovemaking, their partners often notice certain attitude changes. "It wasn't anything obvious, just this feeling I had," Molly says about her husband, Hank. "It just felt weird. Something weird was going on between us." Molly later learned that Hank was rarely "with" her during sex. Instead, he was wrapped up in his own sexual fantasies.

Physical Evidence: Physical evidence of infidelities or other secret sexual pastimes includes anything from a little black book listing names and phone numbers of unfamiliar men or women to coins or tokens from adult bookstores; a cache of pornography to an enormous phone bill revealing dozens of calls to 900 sex-line numbers; credit card receipts for rooms at nearby motels to ticket stubs from XXX-rated movie theaters. Most co-dependents of sex addicts have found such items at least once. And more often than not, they have dismissed such evidence almost as easily as they overlooked or explained away erratic moods and any of the other signs we have already described.

Indeed, most sex addicts are quite adept at explaining physical evidence of this sort, and most co-dependents are more than willing to accept the stories they are told. Besides, the discovery of physical evidence places spouses and lovers in a truly gray area. It actually may *not* indicate a serious problem, or even a problem of any kind. Sometimes, phone numbers are just phone numbers of friends or colleagues; sometimes, pornography is just a relatively harmless indulgence; sometimes, as Sigmund Freud reputedly said in reference to dreams, a cigar is just a cigar.

Of course, co-dependents grab onto this possibility as a drowning man grasps a life preserver. They hang on for dear life to even the slightest chance that nothing is *really* wrong. Many co-dependents try to ignore physical evidence completely, putting whatever they discovered back where they found it and banishing it from their minds. Others confront the sex addict, and immediately accept their partners' apologies, embarrassment, indignation, and sometimes histrionic displays at face value, convincing themselves that it will never happen again. But, of course, it does.

Like the alcoholic forced to pour bottles of alcohol down the drain under the watchful eye of a frustrated spouse, the sex addict plays along with the drama while it unfolds, then goes out to pursue yet another sexual high. Getting caught and having to perform acts of contrition only leads the sex addict to be more careful the next time.

If You Do See These Signs . . .

Don't read too much into them.

As we have tried to make clear, none of these signs definitely identifies anyone as a sex addict. On the other hand, if any of these signs are part of an ongoing pattern in any relationship, a problem of some kind probably exists. That problem may not be sex addiction, however.

Do try talking about the signs themselves.

Because of the addict's well-honed denial defense mechanism, attempts to discuss unexplained absences, family histories, sex-life changes, or any other signs will rarely uncover sex addiction. Discussing the disturbing signs is still highly recommended, however, because spouses or lovers may discover that another problem does exist that lies elsewhere. Their partners may be worried about their jobs or their physical health. They may be struggling with their attraction to another man or woman, or feeling left out since a baby was born. Perhaps they simply did not know how to approach the subject until they were asked directly about it. What they have to say may bring relief or it may be painful, but most importantly, it may not relate to sex addiction.

Do try to have an honest and caring discussion, but *don't* stage an interrogation.

No one likes to be put on the hot seat. Sex addicts or not, people get angry, defensive, and uncommunicative when they feel they are being accused, tried, and found guilty right there on the spot.

Do focus on specific behaviors and observations.

You may want to try saying something like, "I've noticed this, this, and this recently. You know I care a lot about our relationship and I'm really concerned about you. Is anything wrong?" Then, make sure to give the other person a chance to respond in his or her own way, without making him or her feel overly defensive.

Don't present vague suspicions or prematurely drawn conclusions. Blurting out, "You're a sex addict, aren't you?" is no way to open a discussion. For one thing, the other person may not be a sex addict. For another, such accusations almost always drive real problems further underground. You may recall from the last chapter that Todd pretended to resent his wife's suggestion that he might be having an affair and convincingly played the part of an innocent victim who had been falsely accused. He knew, just as the other sex addicts know, that the best way to take the heat off and quickly return to their old ways is to react to accusations with vociferous denial and anger. The heated argument that follows resolves absolutely nothing.

Don't make other accusatory "you" statements.

Saying, "You're sick!" "You never do anything but mope around the house!" or "You are irresponsible and unreliable!" will shut down the lines of communication, not open them.

Do try to use "I" statements or "we" statements.

People tend to be far less defensive when a conversation begins with "I've been confused by the changes in our sex life and I think it might help to talk about it," or "I'm concerned about how quiet and tired you've seemed lately. Is something wrong?" or "I worry that something bad has happened to you when you don't come home until late." (By the way, "I think you're a sex addict" is *not* an "I" statement.)

If attempts to talk about problems do not reveal sex addiction or if they get nowhere at all, but your concerns continue, *do* get help for yourself. Anyone who feels hurt, angry, confused, or frustrated by his or her partner's behavior—whether or not the partner is a sex addict—can benefit from professional help, even if the other person refuses to get help. Checking out your impressions with an expert, seeking guidance from a therapist who specializes in sex addiction, or participating in a self-help group for co-dependents of sex addicts (S-Anon or COSA, both listed in Appendix B) has enormous value whenever any problem—sex addiction or not—has taken its toll on the individual and the relationship.

Unfortunately, most people who are involved with sex addicts seek help only after they reach a point of utter despair and hopelessness. They postpone hitting this bottom for as long as they can by shutting their eyes to even the most obvious signs of sex addiction and devoting themselves to maintaining an illusion of normalcy, in much the same way that addicts themselves maintain their illusion of control. Most co-dependents keep their blinders on until a traumatic event forces their eyes open.

TRAUMATIC EYE-OPENERS AND THEIR AFTERMATH

Because co-dependents generally want to believe the best about their spouses or lovers and above all else want to preserve their relationships, they are able to overlook a great deal of suspicious behavior. However, catching the sex addict in the act—seeing a lover come out of a cheap hotel with another man or woman, walking in on a spouse who is in bed with a child's best friend or little-league coach, discovering one's partner peering through binoculars at a neighbor while masturbating—will shatter even the most powerful illusion of normalcy and break through even the most fortified wall of denial. Refusing to accept that a problem exists simply will not work after you have picked up a sexually transmitted disease from your partner, learned of a partner's arrest for, or heard a partner's confession of, "perverted" sexual behavior. It would take not only denial, but amnesia to blot out such realities.

Yet, believe it or not, even these traumatic events may not lead to any lasting change in the addict, the co-dependent, or the relationship. Although a spouse or lover who finds a "smoking gun" will invariably demand an explanation from his or her partner, such confrontations—whether they occur once or many times—rarely guarantee that the couple will deal with the actual problem of sex addiction.

Reeling from the Blow

A traumatic event serves as a slap of awareness in the co-dependent's face. Co-dependent or not, no human being we have ever encountered has been able to walk away from such events and pretend they never happened—or at least not before taking some sort of action.

And co-dependents *do* take action. If nothing more, they tearfully or furiously confront their partners. Yet—because they have a remarkable ability to believe the best about the sex addict while blinding themselves to the worst—after the initial uproar, co-dependents tend to automatically accept the sex addict's excuses or rationalizations and quickly return to the status quo. Because they didn't *really* want to know about the addiction in the first place, co-dependents find it easy to believe addicts when they say "It only happened this once" and then promise that "It will never happen again." More often than not, co-dependents believe such boldfaced lies even when they have ample physical evidence or other clues that it has happened before.

Ellen, who, up until three years ago, had been married to Todd, the investment analyst and compulsive womanizer we have previously described, suspected almost from the outset that Todd was unfaithful to her. She did not confront him with her suspicions, however, until she found a bundle of classified ads he had written for singles newspapers. "To say I didn't react well would be an understatement. I just went to pieces. I screamed. I yelled. I cried. I went through his drawers, the glove compartment of his car. I made him empty his pockets right there in front of me. It was an unbelievable scene."

It was the kind of scene many of our co-dependent patients have participated in. Hurt, angry, sad, and scared to death that their whole world is crumbling around them, spouses and lovers unleash their pent-up emotions on their partners. Although many of our patients claim they didn't know exactly what they were feeling, all agree that the one emotion they definitely experienced was shock. This was true even for co-dependents who had been harboring suspicions about their partners. "It was a nightmare," Ellen recalls, shuddering. "I wanted to pretend it wasn't true, but I couldn't."

When in this state of shock, some co-dependents explode in an uncontrollable, sometimes violent rage. Several years ago, Rebecca, a forty-three-year-old commercial artist, walked into the bedroom of her family's summer home and found her husband in bed with another woman. "I went completely crazy," she later told us. "I had a metal tennis racket in my hand and I started beating both of them with it." When the tennis racket broke, Rebecca went into her son's bedroom and retrieved a baseball bat. Swinging it wildly, she drove her husband and his lover out of the house. Then she took the sheets and blankets off the bed, carried them outside, and set fire to them in the middle of the front lawn. For days, she considered sending the woman a bill for the use of the summer house. "I would have done it, too," she claims, "but I didn't know her address."

Although few co-dependents go to the extremes Rebecca did, they almost always go to pieces the way Ellen did, and for a time they are completely disgusted with the addict, feel revolted, and want as little as possible to do with him or her.

Shock is experienced by all co-dependents, but once it wears off, the emotions they feel cover a wide range. Some remain enraged and outraged, while others respond with tears and sadness. Some turn their anger inward and blame themselves for the sex addict's compulsive behavior.

Others do not express their feelings at all, becoming numb and confused about how they *should* react to the trauma.

Sara first learned about her husband's sexual activities outside the home when he confessed to her after developing a physical problem he feared might be a sign of a venereal disease. "I didn't feel anything, really," she claims. "Although I spent a lot of time thinking about how I should be feeling. I'd always said, 'If I ever caught my husband cheating, that would be it. He'd be out the door.' But when it actually happened, I didn't really want to do that. I didn't know what to do."

Sara did what so many co-dependents do after the smoke has cleared. She tried to comfort and take care of her husband, because "I knew he was suffering. I knew it was really hard for him to tell me about his problem." She selflessly focused her attention and energy on her husband, putting her own feelings on the back burner while she tried to help him overcome his guilt. "I felt sorry for him," she explains. "I believed that he felt really bad about what he had done and that he was genuinely sorry about it."

Sara even managed to find a positive side to the crisis. "I thought it might even make our situation better. I remember telling myself, Now I don't have to worry anymore. I figured the whole scene had made enough of an impact to keep him from ever cheating again, so I didn't have to worry anymore about what he was doing when he was out on the road. I just put it out of my mind. I told myself it was over and done with, that I could get on with my life—just like it used to be."

For anyone, the most natural reaction to *any* crisis is to try to return to normal as quickly as possible and go on as if nothing had happened. Psychologists call this stage after initial shock, outward adjustment. The outward adjustment stage, which is necessary and temporary for most of us, is usually detrimental to addicts and co-dependents. It may take six days, or it may take six months, but addicts ultimately go back to their compulsive behavior, and co-dependents shut their eyes once more.

After reacting with an immediate explosion, co-dependent spouses, lovers, children, siblings, and parents settle back into their old routines. Rarely does anyone delve deeper into the problem or take any action to resolve it. Again and again, the pattern of shock and confrontation is followed by rapid return to the status quo. The addict knows exactly what will happen each time he or she is caught, figures there will be no lasting consequences, and thus has no reason to alter or abandon addictive behavior.

Don, the chronic masturbator who was molested by his brother when he was young and, in turn, as a teenager molested his niece, wonders if this pattern contributed to his later addiction. "My mother found out what I was doing to my niece and confronted me," he says. "She told me, 'If you've got a conscience, it must be killing you.' Then she said, 'I'm not going to tell your sister this time, but if you ever do that again . . .' and never did say what she would do. That was it, and it was never mentioned again, although I did molest my niece again a couple of times. Sometimes, I think I might not be the way I am today if my mom had done more. I don't know."

We will never know whether Don might have grown up differently if his mother had reacted differently. However, we do know that returning to the status quo, and once again denying the problem, merely perpetuates it. Each time a traumatic event occurs, addicts and co-dependents have an opportunity—and a reason—to get help and begin their recovery. Each time they waste that opportunity and choose to go on as if nothing had happened, the addiction progresses.

The sad truth of the matter is that addicts and co-dependents pass up one opportunity for change after another. For example, Cheryl first learned of her husband's compulsive behavior when, convinced that he was going to turn his life around, he voluntarily confessed that he had been having an affair. Describing a scene quite similar to one Hank and Molly had, Cheryl explains, "He came home one night and right out of the blue started telling me that he had been sleeping with somebody else. Someone he had met at work, I think. It's hard to remember now, because there wound up being so many other women. But anyway, he cried and I cried, and he said he was sorry and I believed he really was sorry. In fact, I still think he *was* sorry, then and all the other times, too. It's just that being sorry didn't mean he wouldn't go out and do it again. I didn't know that at the time, though."

Dozens of times over the next three years, Cheryl's husband had affairs, confessed his sins, and begged Cheryl's forgiveness. Each time, Cheryl "figured that would be the end of it. He'd never do it again." But he always did, and Cheryl went right on forgiving him for as long as he went on confessing to her. After a while, he stopped confessing and Cheryl stopped forgiving. She simply looked the other way.

THE WAR BETWEEN IDEALS AND REALITY

Although co-dependents seem to shut their eyes effortlessly to the warning signs of sex addiction and easily revert to their old routines after briefly reacting to traumatic events, they are often, in fact, experiencing a great deal of inner turmoil. Deep inside the psyche, a war is being waged between their romantic or religious ideals about how their lives and their relationships *should* be and the reality of what they are. Their intense need to hang on to the illusion of perfect love and perfect families almost always wins out over the intense pain caused by the reality of their situations. To maintain the former, they deny the latter, and in doing so become unwitting accomplices to the addiction's destructiveness.

In particular, the co-dependents we've treated tend to have an extremely high emotional investment in their families and their relationships. Molly, for instance, found the idea of divorcing Hank completely unacceptable. "Some people walk down the aisle thinking if things don't work out they can just get a divorce, but that wasn't what I was raised to believe," she says. Actually, Molly's own parents had divorced when she was in her early teens, creating a great deal of turmoil within the family, as well as garnering the shock and disapproval of outsiders.

"I was raised such a strong Catholic," she remembers. "Divorce was presented as such a sin, such a complete failure. My parents' divorce was the first and only one on either side of the family, and it was just devastating. I think some of my relatives are still talking about it. I didn't think it was right then, and I don't believe that it's right now." As a result, Molly entered marriage with the absolute certainty that she would never consider divorce as an option "no matter how bad things got."

Many co-dependents echo this sentiment, although their reasons may not be the same as Molly's. "No matter how bad it gets," most co-dependents tenaciously hang on to the relationship they've got. This unflappable determination to *make* the relationship work stems, in part, from the fact that co-dependents, like sex addicts themselves, generally have a very poor self-image. Because they have little or no sense of their own intrinsic worth, they may consider themselves lucky to have a relationship at all.

Even though she was bright, attractive, and highly regarded for her work as an architect, Jenny, like most co-dependents, doubted her ability to sustain herself on her own and only felt good about herself when she was involved in a relationship. "I desperately needed my lover's time and his attention," she admits. As nearly every other co-dependent has done, rather than risk the possibility of losing the relationship, Jenny shut her eyes to her boyfriend's compulsive affairs and alcoholism.

Most co-dependents extend this judgment of their own worth by their ability to maintain their relationships with their entire family. Indeed, many seem to have no identity at all apart from their roles as lover or spouse and parent. Obviously, if co-dependents have so much of themselves and their lives invested in their immediate relationships, they are going to find it extremely difficult and frightening to face problems in those relationships.

Lynn was astute enough to recognize the serious problems in her relationship the instant her boyfriend suggested that she have sex with another woman while he watched. As she put it, "All these warning buzzers went off in my head." She ended her relationship immediately and came to see us not just to cope with what had happened but because she was afraid she would attract sickos, as she called them, for the rest of her life.

Lynn, whose father had privately humiliated her with his molestations and publicly humiliated her mother by having affairs "that everyone in town knew all about" throughout their marriage, recalls that her mother was single-mindedly devoted to the family, so much so that she was virtually blind to the damage actually being done within the family.

"My mom always said her greatest fear was being alone. To her, life with my father, no matter what he did, was still better than being alone. She just wouldn't take the problem seriously, even though it was literally killing her. The whole time we were growing up, she insisted we were this happy little family. I knew darn well we weren't because my dad was molesting me, and as it turned out he was molesting my sister and brother, too. But we all played along. Mom dressed us just so, and when company came over, we all acted like nothing was wrong. She gave everything she had to keeping up this pretense, this big monster of a lie, and I swear that's what killed her, all that stress and anxiety.''

As family therapists, we naturally place a high value on families. Yet, when devotion to the family reaches the extremes to which Lynn's mother took it, where this all-consuming belief in the sanctity of the family makes it impossible to acknowledge real problems within that family, everyone involved is damaged.

In addition, the enormous stakes that co-dependents have in their relationships make the possibility of change terribly frightening to them. Almost everyone resists change to a certain extent, but co-dependents tend to view change as inherently dangerous. As a result, they have a strong need to maintain the family and the relationship *as is* rather than take the chance that change might rob them of what little they do have—and they have very little, indeed.

"In a lot of ways, I guess I knew exactly what I was doing," admits Sara. "It was kind of a trade-off. I tolerated his behavior so I wouldn't have to try and survive on my own. I didn't think I could do that. I couldn't work to support myself and still be able to spend time with the kids when they were young. And I really wanted to do that. I didn't want to give that up, so I gave up other things instead."

Sara chose to devote herself to her children at all costs. But her children were not really the issue at all. Like many co-dependents, Sara made this choice out of insecurity and the fear that she was incapable of surviving on her own, a terror that forced her to shut her eyes to the real problems in her relationship.

Co-dependents also tenaciously resist change because they *do* reap some benefits from their relationship with sex addicts, if only the security of having some sort of relationship, however destructive. They are also reluctant to recognize sex addiction because if the addict has to change, everyone in the family must change, too. And co-dependents have no way of telling where those changes may lead. If Sara had demanded that her husband deal with his addiction, for example, he might have agreed and entered a recovery program—a positive change; but he might have refused and left her. The possible destruction of the relationship was one Sara felt unable to risk. What's more, if her husband recovered, Sara would lose her role as caretaker, which, as you will see in the next chapter, was the only role Sara had ever known. Either way, Sara thought she would lose—her relationship, or her identity and function in the relationship. Many, many co-dependents fear such a possibility.

Co-dependent spouses and partners often have another strong motivation for denying sex addiction. Many a co-dependent-to-be has an idealistic image of the sex addict and of what the relationship between them will be like. Certainly, co-dependents are not the only people who think this way. Our culture—through its educational and religious institutions as well as the media, especially television—unabashedly encourages such romantic ideals. Whether we grew up watching *Father Knows Best* or *The Brady Bunch,* or continue to watch the idealized version of the family on *The Cosby Show,* most of us have been bombarded with unrealistic images of what family life *should* be.

Most of our co-dependent patients eagerly bought into this romantic ideal. Admitting a problem as serious as sex addiction obviously means they have failed to measure up to their idyllic vision of relationships and families. They find it nearly impossible to admit such failure. Long after she had learned of her husband's sexual compulsions—some of them criminal—Cheryl was still unable to reconcile her husband's uncontrollable sexual appetite with her idealistic image of the man she chose to marry. "My husband thinks that his sexual behavior was wrong, too," she says. "He really is a person with morals. He really has very high standards and strong values."

Cheryl's husband, like most sex addicts, did indeed have a strong sense of morality and impeccable values. But because, as Cheryl would go on to say, "He wasn't acting out what he believes," those impeccable values and romantic ideals were no more than a flimsy façade, a mask for the addict to hide behind. The same can be said of co-dependents. Their inflated opinions of their spouses or lovers and their romantic ideals about relationships and families—which they uphold no matter what—are false fronts disguising a real and dangerous disease as well as the many serious problems going on inside the family.

"I just didn't want to believe it," Cheryl sighs. "I knew what a good marriage should be like, and I'd always *said* that I wouldn't take a husband who was unfaithful to me. But that was the least of what I took. Every time something else happened, I would think, 'Oh no, this is the one thing I could never put up with.' But I put up with it for eighteen years."

Perhaps you have noticed the similarity between Cheryl's statement and those made by sex addicts themselves, who often say *"This* is the one thing I'll never do," then go ahead and do it. In numerous ways, co-dependents are mirror images of addicts. As you will read in the next two chapters, co-dependents' personalities and behaviors are almost exact reflections of addicts'.

7

ADDICTED TO THE ADDICT: The Co-Dependent Personality

"I guess you could say I'm a natural-born nurturer," Sara chuckles. Although no one is actually born with the ability and desire to nurture others, it has been a vital part of Sara's identity since early childhood. The oldest of four children, Sara assumed responsibility for rearing her siblings and running her family's household because her parents, who owned their own business and worked long hours, spent very little time at home.

Now, at thirty-two, Sara is still most comfortable when she is taking care of others. She arrives early for Monday-night sessions of our group for co-dependents of sex addicts, makes the coffee, and always brings in a batch of homemade cookies or cupcakes. She stays late to collect the empty styrofoam coffee cups and crumpled napkins, and to straighten the chairs. Perhaps because anyone who encounters Sara senses that she is compassionate and trustworthy, other group members call her between meetings and pour their hearts out. Strangers stop her on the street to ask directions. Everyone, from her children's teachers to the cashier at the grocery store, tells their problems to her.

Sara even looks like the proverbial earth mother, with her straight brown hair parted in the middle and her big brown eyes brimming over with sympathy and understanding. Fairly tall and full-busted, her body is all soft curves and cushiony comfort. It is easy to imagine her with a child nestled in her lap or with an apron tied around her waist in the kitchen of a cozy, immaculate house in suburbia.

Sara can kiss a child's bruised elbow and make it all better. She can listen to the most tragic tale of woe and convince the taleteller that everything will be all right. If something is broken, Sara believes it is her responsibility to fix it. She ignores gray clouds, preferring to see the silver lining—even when there isn't one. Absolutely nothing is so dreadful or so out of control that hard work, self-sacrifice, and a positive outlook can't improve it. However, this belief, ingrained in Sara since early childhood, was sorely tested and ultimately shattered during ten years of marriage to Joe, a sex addict and alcoholic.

"I grew up knowing what hard work was," Sara says, smiling proudly. "Everyone was expected to work hard, my parents who worked twelve and fourteen hours a day in their own business and us kids, too. We all had to contribute if the family was going to run smoothly and if we wanted to have the better things in life. We were given a tremendous amount of responsibility for taking care of ourselves and taking care of the house because our parents really couldn't be around a lot of the time. When other kids were outside playing or sitting around watching TV, we were inside doing our chores—or at least I was. I didn't think it was healthy for my younger brother and sisters to be inside all the time, so I sent them out to play and did the chores myself. I really didn't mind.

"The message I remember getting from my parents was that you had to make sacrifices to get anything you wanted in this life. And now, I think maybe I learned that lesson a little *too* well."

By the tender age of ten, Sara had already learned that others' needs—her younger siblings', for instance—were more important than her own, as well as to sacrifice her own happiness for the greater good of the family. She also came to believe that it was her responsibility to "take up the slack whenever other family members couldn't get the job done."

"Because my mother worked every bit as hard as my father and was usually exhausted when she came home, I pretty much filled in for her. Childhood for me was child care and housecleaning and having dinner on the table when Mom and Dad came home."

Although Sara denies feeling any resentment toward her mother for abdicating the parenting responsibilities, she does say that she felt closer to her father, whose approval she sought constantly.

"I was always trying to make my dad happy," Sara admits. And her father seemed happiest when Sara was playing "little adult." Indeed, he often treated her as if she were not a child at all but an adult peer and trusted confidante. "My father shared a lot of his intimate thoughts and feelings with me, a lot of personal things about his life and his relationship with my mother. There were things he told me that I really didn't want to hear about, like their sex life, which definitely was not the greatest. He would tell me how frustrated he was sexually. Hearing that made me feel really nervous inside, but at the same time, knowing he trusted me enough to tell me those things felt really good."

Already a parent surrogate for her siblings, Sara, in many ways, also played the role of her father's wife. Although, as far as we know, Sara's father was never actually sexual with her, through his self-disclosure—which crossed the usual boundaries of the parent-child relationship—he did convey certain messages about male sexuality that influenced Sara's later relationship with her sex-addicted husband. "One thing my father always got across, that he always stressed, was that a man *has* to have sex. That all these pressures build up inside him, and he has to be able to relieve himself."

Having played little wife and mother for most of her childhood, Sara was extremely well prepared to play them as an adult. Indeed, Sara herself sees her marriage as simply a continuation of the roles she already had down pat. It should come as no surprise, then, that one of the things that attracted Sara to Joe was that he seemed to need someone to take care of him. "He reminded me of a vulnerable puppy dog," Sara comments, sharing her first impression of Joe. "He was really sensitive and unsure of himself. Things never seemed to go right for him. Something always happened just when he was about to get something he was looking forward to—like the time he was down to the final cut for his high school basketball team and he tore a ligament in his knee, or the time he had to interview for a job he really wanted but his car broke down and the interviewer didn't believe his story. I always told him his luck would change, tried to build up his confidence. He's really bright and creative. I saw all this potential, you know."

Sara believed very strongly in Joe's potential and never stopped believing in it—not even after years of watching him jump from job to job, dive into silent, sullen funks for weeks at a time, and sometimes become totally incapable of functioning at home or at work. She remained loyal and optimistic long after he first confessed his infidelities, and even after he was acting out sexually in many ways on almost a daily basis. Sara believed just as strongly that her love and nurturing could bring out Joe's potential. If she just worked hard enough, remained determined and optimistic enough, sacrificed enough for her husband and children, everything would turn out all right. She refused to admit defeat. Instead, for ten years she single-mindedly devoted herself to her family, shut her eyes to the problems of Joe's alcoholism and sex addiction, and not only convinced herself that her idealistic vision of the perfect family and the perfect marriage was a reality, but worked overtime to convince others that this was true.

THE ROOTS OF CO-DEPENDENCY

As therapists, we are often asked why *anyone* would put up with compulsive sexual behavior for years on end—especially after discovering physical evidence or catching a partner red-handed. People who are not involved with sex addicts or addicts of any other kind often say, "Boy, if I found out my husband was masturbating ten times a day or caught my wife having affairs or heard that my lover was arrested for exposing himself or suspected he was committing incest, he'd be out the door so fast it would make your head spin! I wouldn't wait around to find out if he was going to do it again. No way. One strike and you're history! Anyone who stays in that kind of relationship has got to be crazy!''

Actually, most of our co-dependent patients have expressed the same sentiments at one time or another. The words are easy enough to say, but no one honestly knows what he or she will do during a crisis until it happens. Actual discovery—and a wide variety of other factors—changes everything, and the judgmental attitudes expressed by people who are *not* in the same boat often motivate the co-dependent to remain silent.

Like anyone else, co-dependents react to relationship and family problems with the coping skills and attitudes they learned from childhood role models (most often their parents), religious teachings, and messages conveyed by the culture in which they live. Indeed, the values co-dependents have taken to heart—reverence for family and the importance of maintaining family ties, virtues such as responsibility, loyalty, humility, patience, and helping others, to name just a few—are universally held in high esteem.

The difference between co-dependents and the rest of the population is that co-dependents almost always take their values to extremes. Respect for the family becomes selfless, single-minded devotion to the family. Taking responsibility for one's own actions is extended to feeling personally responsible for everything and everyone, including other people's behaviors and emotions. Simple loyalty becomes blind or misplaced loyalty, prompting co-dependents to stand by their loved ones at all costs. Helping others becomes fanatical self-sacrifice, even to the point of real martyrdom.

Why do co-dependents cross the boundary between universally accepted values and fanatical ones, until they have completely lost their ability to see themselves as separate from their families and their addictive relationships? A number of different forces come into play to cause this. First of all, like sex addiction, the predisposition to become co-dependent, as well as the actual traits of co-dependency, have their roots in the past, particularly in childhood. Sara, for instance, learned at a very early age to regard other people as *more* important than she was and needing *more* nurturing than she did. By the time she met Joe, she *habitually* put other people's needs and desires first.

Although some co-dependents encounter traumas during early adulthood and adapt to these crises by adopting co-dependent traits, most learned these thought and behavior patterns in their own homes during childhood.

Family Histories

As we do with sex addicts, when we begin treating a co-dependent we take an extensive family history. Very often, we find remarkable similarities between their childhoods and those of sex addicts. In fact, in a couple made up of one partner who is sexually addicted and one who is co-dependent, we may discover that both grew up feeling personally inadequate, unable to honestly express emotions, and possessed by a strong need to be in control—even though they did not necessarily experience the same problems during childhood.

For example, early in her recovery, Cheryl, the co-dependent described previously, told us, "I guess I knew my family loved me, but I never felt like I was worth much. My parents said they loved me, but if I was worried about something or feeling insecure, they didn't really do anything to reassure me. I never heard them brag about me. I can't remember a single time they complimented me, although it seemed like they were always criticizing me." When Cheryl's husband entered treatment several months later, after the couple had separated temporarily, he used almost the same words to describe his own recollections of childhood.

Cheryl's husband had a mother who was addicted to prescription tranquilizers and a father who had affairs, eventually left the family, and ended up marrying several times. Cheryl, on the other hand, reports no addictions among her family members, but recounts that her "rebellious older sister always kept the family in trouble." More importantly, she remembers that "My sister made me feel worthless. She was always putting me down. She knew exactly how to get to me, and I was a really sensitive kid to begin with. She had me completely convinced that I was ugly, stupid, and a total loser."

Co-dependents, like sex addicts, frequently grow up feeling inept and unlovable as a result of the events that occur in their childhood homes. In Cheryl's case, her sister was the one who verbally and emotionally abused her, although her parents' lack of support and encouragement did reinforce her sense of worthlessness. The pain Cheryl felt was as real and as long lasting as her husband's, even though he endured severe beatings from his stepfather and listened to his bitter, resentful mother tell him time and again how much better her life would have been if he had never been born.

The problems in a co-dependent's childhood home take their toll regardless of their source or severity. And co-dependents, just like sex addicts, sometimes find those problems quite difficult to identify because, unlike abuse or addiction, they did not seem like problems at the time. Sara, for example, never gave a second thought to playing mother to her siblings and being the "woman of the house." It didn't seem at all strange to her that her father shared his most intimate thoughts and problems with her. Not only did constant caretaking seem perfectly normal to her, she rather enjoyed it. As it does for most co-dependents, assuming all those extra burdens and adult responsibilities made Sara feel special and important—just as she would years later when she was mothering her alcoholic, sex-addicted husband.

Some co-dependents can trace their own behavior and attitudes to verbal, sexual, or physical abuse suffered during their childhoods. Others felt persistently neglected by their parents. Still others, when they finally look back on the past objectively, recognize other family members' addictions, compulsive behaviors, or inappropriate treatment.

"Oh, my family is compulsive, all right," Molly acknowledges with a laugh and then a sigh. "My father's an alcoholic, and his wife is a heavy drinker. My sister is compulsive about cleaning and polishing things. She washes her hands until they are just about raw. I compulsively overeat, and I'm obsessed with keeping my life in order. I get confused and edgy when things are disorganized. It's either total control or total chaos as far as I'm concerned."

When you realize that Molly's home life was shattered by her father's drinking and extramarital affairs, and that her parents' ultimate divorce turned what little order there was into chaos, it is easy to understand her obsessive need for order and control—a need shared by many co-dependents and sex addicts as well. Children raised in chaotic environments frequently develop a strong desire for order in their lives, as do children raised in *overly* controlled families, who learn it through the example set by their parents. Sex addicts fulfill this need with the illusion of control they get during their sexual rituals, while co-dependents fulfill it by attempting to cure or control the addict and maintain an illusion of normalcy both within and outside their homes.

More often than not, co-dependents learned how to cope with family problems by observing their parents. In homes where both parents were addicts or abusers, chances are that they took turns covering up for each other in co-dependent ways. And if just one parent were an addict or abuser, you can be sure the other was a co-dependent. From co-dependent parents, children learn to keep their feelings to themselves and to sacrifice their needs for the greater good of their families, as well as develop an inflated sense of responsibility and the confidence that they can overcome any obstacle through sheer will and perseverance.

Although Molly's mother divorced her husband when Molly was twelve, she retained many of the co-dependent traits she had developed during the marriage. "My mom had this attitude that no matter what happened, she could handle it," Molly recalls. "Because she was a single parent for so many years, she really did handle a lot of things on her own. It was how she lived and how she taught us to be. You just did what you had to do. The problem might seem enormous, but you never gave up."

If there is one impression from childhood that the majority of our co-dependent patients share, it is the sense that they had no real childhood at all. Many, like Sara, assumed adult roles at an early age because of their parents' absence or addictions. Others, like Molly, felt their childhoods were stolen from them because of some traumatic event. For one reason or another, most co-dependents had to grow up quickly and learn to fend for themselves. Most feel proud that they were able to take on these adult burdens while they were still children. Unlike sex addicts, who grow up doubting their ability to handle the demands of adult life and take little responsibility for anything, including their own actions, co-dependents reach adulthood believing, "The more responsibility I take on, the better I am."

However, when it comes to taking on adult responsibilities, children, especially those with co-dependent personalities, seldom know where to stop. These "little adults" respond to any call for support and assistance, and do their best to solve any problem. Indeed, they come to believe their greatest value as a person, perhaps their only true value, comes from caretaking and problem solving. What's more, when parents, like Sara's father, inappropriately use their children as sounding boards for their own emotional or even sexual frustrations, the boundaries that define the parent-child relationship get blurred or disappear altogether.

As most co-dependents do, Sara came to regard herself as her father's one true and loyal friend—which was just how she would one day regard herself in relation to her husband and children. Driven by this extreme loyalty, Sara and many other co-dependents are reluctant to act when they discover a problem since they view even questioning the object of their devotion as a betrayal.

If you are interested in examining your own past for possible clues to co-dependency, you can do so by completing the Family History Questionnaire at the end of Chapter 3. Pay particular attention to how you responded to family problems and crises, the times you might have accepted more responsibility than you could handle as a child, and whether you gave yourself permission or enough time to be playful or childlike. These seem to be a few of the more significant facets of the co-dependent personality that develop as a direct result of family interactions during childhood. Yet, there are many other personality traits and outside influences that contribute to becoming co-dependent—and staying that way.

Crossing the Line: When Self-Sacrifice Becomes Martyrdom

In countless ways, ours is a culture that encourages co-dependent behavior. For one thing, as we pointed out earlier, many of the values and virtues that serve as a foundation for co-dependency are also the foundation for Judeo-Christian religions and the Puritan work ethic that predominate in Western society. Indeed, some co-dependents point to Biblical teachings about enduring suffering with patience and humility to justify their own behavior. Cheryl, a Christian fundamentalist, believed that putting up with her husband's affairs was the morally correct thing to do. "At the time," she recalls, "I truly believed it was my Christian duty to stay in that marriage, no matter what happened."

Some Christian denominations actually preach that spouses should surrender their own will and martyr themselves in order to save their spouse or the marriage. Although we frequently advise co-dependent patients who have strong religious beliefs to seek comfort and guidance from members of the clergy, this same clergy has also pointed out to several co-dependents, women in particular, that they promised to "endure" their spouse's compulsive sexual behavior when they recited their marriage vows. Men and women alike have been told that they have the ability to "save" their partners and the obligation to keep trying no matter what happens. This concept is one of the central beliefs of co-dependency in the first place.

Co-dependents find it difficult enough to curtail their self-destructive patterns of self-sacrifice. To change, co-dependents must essentially turn against themselves. If they also think that their old behavior is God's will, they may believe that seeking their recovery means turning against God. What will co-dependents have left if they renounce themselves *and* the religious teachings they have clung to all their lives? Very little, they think, so little that change becomes all the more frightening and unacceptable. Those encouraged by their clergy to go on martyring themselves often suffer in silence for decades.

And the truth is that suffering in silence will not save the sex addict because sex addicts almost always interpret silence as permission to continue the addiction. We have yet to treat a sex addict who witnessed the pain suffered by a self-sacrificing spouse and therefore developed greater respect and sympathy for the co-dependent, or changed his or her own compulsive behavior in any positive way. Indeed, each time a co-dependent stoically puts up with the addiction, the addict merely sees another opportunity to get away with what he or she has been doing all along.

Learning to "Stand by Your Man" (or Woman)

In addition to religious teachings, cultural expectations also play a role in encouraging co-dependency. Cheryl, for example, had recently begun to make significant changes in her co-dependent behavior when her husband, also in recovery, landed a new job with a large corporation. "The new company is very family-oriented," she explains. "The whole family is expected to be part of the company team, especially the wives. We're supposed to support our husbands in everything they do for the company. Help them get ahead, help the company get ahead, make sacrifices for the greater good—now where have I heard *that* before?"

The traditional view of sex roles has men sacrificing themselves in the outside world to provide for and protect their spouses and families, while women sacrifice themselves to nurture and care for their loved ones in the home. Again, co-dependents, especially those raised before the 1960s, tend to exaggerate these traditional values, losing their own identities while carrying the notion of self-sacrifice to an extreme. Co-dependents who adopted the less traditional values advanced by the feminist movement also sacrifice themselves, maybe even more so than their more traditional counterparts. They try to be superwomen or supermen: assuming *all* responsibility both at home and at work.

Addict and Co-Dependent: Interlocking Puzzle Pieces

Diane, a forty-three-year-old pediatric nurse whose mother was an alcoholic, married a man who compulsively sought out sex with prostitutes. "I really think my husband's addictive tendencies were what attracted me to him in the first place," she reveals. "I didn't know exactly what he was doing, but so many things about him touched off this reaction in me that I assumed was love. Now, I think it was just recognition. In dozens of ways, he was just like my mother. Obviously, I was a co-dependent long before I met him.''

Most co-dependents—influenced by families, religion, and society in general—have absorbed co-dependent traits into their overall personalities. The caretaker, the problem solver, the martyr, and every other co-dependent role is incorporated into their identities. They do not know—and have never known—any other way to be.

The same holds true for sex addicts. Indeed, in many of the couples we've treated, the sex addict and the co-dependent are such perfect mirror images of each other that we can't help thinking they were destined to find each other. Each fulfills the other's neurotic needs in important ways. Sex addicts need to be constantly reassured that someone cares for them, while co-dependents need to be constantly reassured that someone needs them. Their marriage contracts are agreements to change and be changed, since sex addicts sincerely believe that the relationship will remove their need to indulge in addictive behavior, and co-dependents, although seldom aware of the specific problem at this point, sincerely believe that their nurturing, devotion, and determination can fix anything.

"I never really believed in self-fulfilling prophecies," Molly sighs. "But my dad ran around on my mom and wound up marrying his ex-mistress. My mom bent over backward to take care of him and keep the family together, but wound up divorced and alone. Maybe I always had it in the back of my mind that the same thing would happen to me, too. I know I was always afraid it would.''

Of course, the values and behaviors Molly had learned in the past, rather than her frightening thoughts that the past would repeat itself, led her to marry an addict. Because of their family histories and interpretation of religious and cultural messages, by the time potential co-dependents and potential or active sex addicts meet, they have become flip sides of the same coin, interlocking pieces of the same puzzle, each equipped to supply what the other is missing.

MIRRORING ADDICTIVE BEHAVIOR

Not all of our sexually addicted clients are married or involved in long-term relationships. And we treat many co-dependents without treating or even meeting their sexually addicted partners. Yet when couples do come to us—even when the co-dependent sought help months before the addict, or the addict was court-ordered into treatment and his or her partner came to us much later—we are always struck by the similarities in their backgrounds, behavior, and attitudes. And we can't help but notice that over the years they were together, they became even more alike. As addiction and co-dependency progress, partners become virtual mirror images of one another. When one acts, the other reacts. By the time most co-dependents enter a therapist's office or join a self-help group, their self-talk, their coping behaviors, their denial and secretiveness, and their overall emotional state either precisely replicate or perfectly complement the addicts'. They even have their own obsessions and rituals.

Co-Dependent Self-Talk

Vicki, a thirty-year-old social worker, wound up in our office after her live-in boyfriend, a compulsive voyeur, was arrested and referred to us for treatment. She is a painfully thin woman prone to hand wringing and chain-smoking. Employed by a public child welfare agency, it is quite common for her to work late into the night and on weekends—not because this is expected of her, but because she gets deeply involved with every child on her caseload and worries about them almost all the time. "She acts like she's personally responsible for protecting every kid in the county," her boyfriend complained during one group session.

Indeed, Vicki does feel personally responsible for many things that are beyond her control, including everything bad that has even happened to her or someone she loved. "I never really thought I was worth much," she told us soon after we met her. "In fact, I thought there was really something wrong with me, something that made people want to stay away from me. My father left our family when I was just a little girl. And before I was married, I had a boyfriend and we were very serious, but he left me, too. And, of course, my husband took off after we'd been married less than two years. It was just one thing after another, and all the bad feelings from one situation carried over into the next. They just got stronger, until I was completely convinced that all people, men especially, would always leave me." As a result, rarely does a day go by without Vicki thinking, "I'm completely unlovable."

Co-dependents, like sex addicts, suffer from low self-esteem. Telling themselves they are unlovable is just one of many ways they keep their feelings of worthlessness alive. Many co-dependents are persistently nagged by a sense of inadequacy. Because they held themselves personally accountable for everything that happened in their families, whenever anything went wrong—and something always did—they thought, "I can't do anything right" or "I let everyone down. I'm a horrible person." As adults, co-dependents continue to assume enormous burdens, encounter problems, and repeat to themselves the negative self-talk that originated during childhood. What's more, their inability to control the sex addict's behavior and the fact that sex addicts frequently go outside the relationship for sexual gratification reinforce the belief that they are inadequate and unlovable.

In addition, various personal insecurities lead many co-dependents to believe that "other people are better than I." For instance, Diane, the pediatric nurse who grew up with an alcoholic mother and married a sex addict, always felt unattractive, even though she was actually a very pretty woman. Her husband's compulsion to have sex with prostitutes reinforced this feeling. From Diane's perspective, even prostitutes were more attractive to her husband (and therefore better) than she was.

Indeed, virtually everything sex addicts do and say feeds co-dependent self-talk, making it even more negative. Any fears that co-dependents harbor increase as sex addiction progresses. For instance, the sex addict's tendency to be cold and distant confirms the co-dependent's belief that "nobody really cares." And because co-dependents tell themselves "I have to make myself useful. I need to be needed," their self-esteem plummets each time sex addicts fail to respond to their attempts to take care of them.

What's more, when sex addicts lash out at those closest to them, usually because they feel burdened by the weight of their guilt, their words echo whatever negative self-talk co-dependents already hear in their own minds. "My boyfriend was very intimidating, very critical," says Jenny, the architect whose alcoholic boyfriend tried to sleep with anyone who caught his eye. "I was already trying to make it in a very competitive field and wondering if I could cut it. I was absolutely petrified of screwing up. I'd be home ten minutes and do *something* he didn't approve of and, of course, he'd let me know it. My nickname used to be Asshole."

To make matters worse, the slightest hint that all may not be well in their relationship, if it gets through the wall of denial at all, creates enormous inner turmoil. Because their identities depend so much on their relationships with others, co-dependents tend to automatically blame themselves for their partners' compulsive sexual behavior. "Whatever self-confidence I had went out the window after I found out my boyfriend was sleeping with other women," Jenny reveals. "I was feeling so damn inferior anyway, I figured I must have done something to drive him to it. Even after I found out he had a problem—and having to sleep with three and four women a day was really *his* problem, not mine—I still kept thinking back over everything that had happened between us, wondering what I had done wrong."

In addition, co-dependents feel like failures for not living up to a myth that they, as well as many people who aren't co-dependent, sincerely believe: "I should be able to satisfy all of my partner's needs." Upon discovering that their spouses or lovers are having sex with other people or repeatedly indulging in masturbation, voyeurism, or other essentially solitary sexual acts, co-dependents assume—as almost anyone would—that they have failed to satisfy their partners' sexual needs. Nothing pushes more panic buttons or bruises more egos than feelings of sexual inadequacy or failure. As a result, acknowledging the compulsive sexual behavior deals a severe and excruciatingly painful blow to the co-dependent's already beleaguered self-image. In fact, it is so painful that co-dependents sometimes turn reality inside out, seriously considering the possibility that they are the ones with a problem. Jenny voices this feeling when she says, "There were plenty of times, after I first found out, that I actually convinced myself that *I* was the one who had abnormal feelings about sex, not my boyfriend."

Adding to the pain that comes with the feeling of failure to meet the partner's needs is the co-dependent's sense that he or she has been

betrayed by the addict. Because most co-dependents come across their
partners' compulsive sexual behavior long before they know anything
about the disease of sex addiction, they take that behavior very personally, reacting with hurt and horror to what they believe the sex addicts
are doing to them personally. Of course, this heightens the fears of
abandonment and rejection co-dependents have harbored since childhood. "The pain was absolutely unbearable," Sara winces. "I kept
thinking that if he cared about me at all, he would want to come home to
me and wouldn't go out looking for other women. Every time he slept
with another woman I felt like he had stabbed me with a knife. Every
little sick sexual thing he did was like hearing him say that he didn't love
me. Sometimes, I thought he actually hated me, since he always seemed
to be hurting me."

When the reality of their partners' sexual compulsions cause such
tremendous pain, is it any wonder co-dependents prefer to maintain their
romantic illusions? When considering change means admitting they have
failed in countless ways, is it any wonder co-dependents reject change as
an option? When their fear of being abandoned and alone is the most
powerful fear they have, is it any wonder that co-dependents build an
impenetrable wall of denial around themselves and their families?

DENIAL

Denial offers co-dependents a handy escape route. They bury their
fears and silence their destructive self-talk by minimizing or making
excuses for the sex addicts' behavior, convincing themselves that no
serious problem exists in their relationships and, in some cases, denying
that anything out of the ordinary ever happened at all.

Unlike many of the other men and women we treat, Lynn recognized
and did something about her boyfriend's sex addiction when she saw the
very first sign of it. However, she clearly remembers her mother's
remarkable ability to ignore her father's compulsive extramarital affairs.
Her father was a minister and "apparently everybody in the church knew
about his affairs," she explains, "but we didn't. I was twenty or twenty-
one when I found out, and based on my mother's behavior when we were
kids, I assumed she never knew. She sure never acted like she knew. I
was shocked when she told me she had always suspected it. I guess she
just couldn't face it."

Lynn's mother was able to shut her eyes to the incestuous behavior
going on inside the home as well. For many years, Lynn's father went
through the ritual of first spanking her brother or Lynn—ostensibly for
some infraction of the strict house rules—and then "comforting" them
by sexually molesting them. Although her mother never said a word about
it, Lynn feels certain she knew. "Of course, my mother would be at the
other end of the house whenever it happened. And we *did* live in a huge
house, but *I* always knew what everyone was doing. I just know that she
knew and didn't do anything about it."

Apparently, not even the maternal instinct to protect her children was enough to make Lynn's mother give up her romantic illusions about her husband and her family. Her unconscious denial mechanism protected her from facing that which was too psychologically painful to face.

Constantly telling themselves, "What I don't know won't hurt me," co-dependents often completely cut themselves off from the reality of their situations and later say that they were living in a fog. And those co-dependents who witnessed during childhood the devastating effects of addiction or divorce have even more invested in maintaining the illusion of the close-knit, problem-free family. Like Molly, who grew up in the shadow of her father's affairs as well as her parents' unthinkable divorce and swore, "I'm not going to let that happen to me," many co-dependents simply cannot face the fact that their most dreaded fears are coming to pass because of their partners' addiction. As a result, co-dependents, again mirroring the sex addicts themselves, create and take up residence in a fantasy world, where everything is the way it's supposed to be.

"I just couldn't let myself dwell on it," Sara explains, justifying her need to deny reality. "My husband traveled so much. He had so many opportunities to pick up women. What was I supposed to do, hire a private detective to keep an eye on him? I couldn't do anything, and I would have been a nervous wreck if I had let myself worry about it all the time."

Cheryl explains her reasons for denying the problem. "I *had* to believe it would never happen again. If I thought he was lying when he said it would stop, if I admitted he was going to continue cheating on me, I would have to think about leaving him, and I knew I couldn't do that."

Denial eventually leads co-dependents to move from merely shutting their eyes to the addiction to becoming unwitting accomplices to it by actively hiding the problem from others and repeatedly covering up for the addict, sometimes even justifying his or her behavior in their own minds. "I had a million excuses," Sara now admits. "I never really denied he was a heavy drinker, so I figured whenever he picked up a woman, he'd been drinking. I told myself the alcohol took away his inhibitions, made him feel aroused, and also that because of the alcohol he didn't really know what he was doing. Or I'd remind myself of the kinds of situations he was in, being on the road, going down to the hotel bar for a couple of drinks. I always told myself the woman came on to him, and when you've got some girl hanging all over you, *and* you've been drinking, it's pretty hard to say no. I had a lot of other stories, too, but they all added up to the same thing. It was just a one-night stand or a one-time fling. It happens. It doesn't mean anything, and it certainly wasn't anything to end a marriage over or carry on about."

Co-dependents who justify addicts' behavior to themselves almost always end up staunchly defending their partners in front of others. Once again, they become interlocking pieces in the addiction puzzle. If the addict leaves a chink in the wall of denial, the co-dependent fills it—by covering up for the addict's behavior or concocting elaborate excuses for it. Indeed, co-dependents often want to deal with the addiction even *less* than addicts do and will sometimes continue to deny the magnitude of the problem or pretend it does not exist long after addicts themselves have admitted that they are out of control—thus undermining the addicts' recovery as well as their own.

And in protecting themselves, their families, and their partners, co-dependents end up denying more than the addiction itself. Just as sex addicts often refuse to acknowledge any needs except sexual ones, co-dependents deny all of their own needs except for the need to serve and take care of others. Almost universally, co-dependents place their need to please other people, and especially to please their spouses or lovers, above all other needs. They sacrifice all else in order to be of value to others—which is the only way they know to feel valuable themselves.

Sara, for instance, says she "always felt like I had to make amends, to give up something, if I wanted to have anything. I literally cut back on things that I needed to make up for what my husband did. When he started getting into porno movies, and hanging out at adult bookstores, and God knows what else, he was going through money like you wouldn't believe, and his sales commissions were way down, too. Since we were so short on money, I cut back the household budget. I denied a lot of things to myself and the kids. And because I did that, Joe got to go on doing what he wanted."

Like most co-dependents, Sara felt that it was her responsibility to be available for her husband "just in case he needed me," and she thought it was her duty "to always do a little extra for the kids" and spend more time with them to make up for their father's inconsistency and absences. Eventually, she had absolutely no life of her own.

Emotional Withdrawal or Volatility

"My mother always had a smile on her face," Lynn recalls. "She never let anyone know that what my father was doing was hurting her in any way." Like many sex addicts, most co-dependents are stoic, unwilling—and eventually unable—to express their feelings—or even feel them. In response to her boyfriend's constant affairs, Jenny says she "started putting up walls, shutting off my feelings. Whenever I thought about the other women, I'd get so frustrated and angry and really hurt that after a while I just pushed it all down deep inside. I wouldn't allow myself to feel anything."

When a person seeks sex outside of a relationship, *any* spouse or partner feels hurt and angry. These feelings are intensified for co-dependents, who feel they will lose their own identities and the little self-worth they have if they lose their relationships or cannot please their partners.

Like the addicts with whom they live, co-dependents sometimes experience wild mood fluctuations, getting angry, irritable, impatient, or bursting into tears without warning or for no apparent reason. "We always thought my mother was a little crazy," a young woman named Kate once told us. Kate came to us for help with an eating disorder and, during the course of her treatment, revealed that for as long as her parents were married, her father had had affairs that her mother always knew about but did not openly acknowledge until several months before she filed for divorce. "Obviously, she was angry at my dad because of the affairs. But she couldn't say that, especially not at the dinner table in front of her children, where most of these scenes happened. So, she would start picking on my father about something really trivial. We could never understand what she was so upset about, but the next thing we knew, she was yelling, and then she would just fall apart, race upstairs to her bathroom, and run the water in the sink so we couldn't hear her crying."

When such outbursts occur, they usually come as a shock to everyone involved—even to the co-dependents who, for the most part, consider themselves very levelheaded, not prone to emotionalism. Actually, such explosions are inevitable.

Self-sacrifice, especially when it does not have the desired effect of changing the addict or solidifying the relationship, almost always leads to resentment, which in turn leads to anger—an emotion co-dependents find particularly uncomfortable. Whether they unconsciously fear that expressing anger and other negative emotions will lead to abandonment or they learned during childhood that unpleasant feelings should be kept to oneself, co-dependents bury these emotions and keep them buried for as long as possible.

For instance, when Cheryl first came to us for treatment, we asked her if she ever felt angry and what she did when she was angry. "You know, I'm not sure I've got any anger," she replied. "Maybe God has kind of taken it away."

Months later, she admitted, "I told you that because I really didn't think it was right to feel angry. Expressing anger wasn't a Christian thing to do. You were supposed to turn the other cheek. So, that's what I tried to do. I guess I just stuffed it all the way inside me for all those years."

Although a small percentage of co-dependents get stuck in an angry mode—screaming, criticizing, and browbeating their partners incessantly—most bury negative emotions and stuff them down inside themselves the way Cheryl did. But feelings do not disappear just because someone chooses not to express them. If anger and other negative emotions do not bubble over during periodic explosive outbursts, they eat away at co-dependents from the inside—often leading to severe depressions or, we believe, physical illnesses.

Yet, burying their feelings is the only way most co-dependents know to survive. Life with any addict is an emotional roller-coaster ride. Every loop and turn brings more loneliness, pain, fear, sadness, frustration, or anger. It seems that the only way to get off the ride is to tune out, anesthetize oneself, or literally refuse to feel anything at all—which is why, when we ask co-dependents how they feel, virtually every one of them replies, "Numb."

Secrets and Cover-Ups

For most co-dependents, burying their true feelings is more than a self-service protecting them from constant pain. It is yet another form of self-sacrifice. They put on a happy face and present a cool, calm, collected, and cheerful façade to protect their partners, their children, and the family image.

"From all outward appearances, we had the perfect marriage," Molly explains. "My husband even had his family convinced that I'd turned out to be this 'good little wife and mother,' even though they'd had their doubts before we got married. Hank was an elder in the church, for Pete's sake. You couldn't get more upstanding than that. But what people saw from the outside and what was actually happening were obviously two different things."

After Molly sought help for her co-dependency, she realized that she had also contributed to that image. "The truth is, I played the part of the good wife and mother extremely well," Molly says now. "I did my best to make Hank look like the good husband and father. Heck, I wish I had a dime for every time I told people how much he suffered when he had to travel and be away from the boys and me. When his sales were dropping off, I even started asking everyone I met about their insurance coverage, trying to get him leads, so he wouldn't lose his job. And I tried to mold my kids into perfect children. I was one of those mothers who never let anyone see her kids with a hole in their jeans or a scuff mark on their shoes. There was a lot of pride involved. I wanted people to think my family was okay."

Many co-dependents step effortlessly into the role of co-conspirator because they regard themselves as very private people by nature and grew up with the utmost respect for the idea that "You don't air your family's dirty linen in public." What's more, as lifelong people-pleasers whose identities hinge on other people's responses to them, co-dependents constantly ask themselves, "What will people think of me if they find out?"

Co-dependents consume an enormous amount of their time and energy trying to prove to themselves and others that everything is just fine. Even though they almost never feel normal, they *always* try to act normal. As chief co-conspirators in an elaborate cover-up, they hide the secret from children, parents, and friends. Like grizzly bears guarding their cubs, co-dependents will go to any lengths to protect the family image.

Some, like Cheryl, routinely lied for their partners. "He would stay home from work, with such a 'hangover' that he couldn't get out of bed, and I'd call his boss and say he had the flu or that some relative had died," she remembers. "Or he might stay out of town two or three days more than he was supposed to. And I'd go to social functions without him or to church without him and tell the same lies to anyone who asked where he was. He missed so many planes, you just wouldn't believe it. I don't even remember all the stories I told to airlines people so he wouldn't lose his discount fare and have to explain it to the auditor at work. I lied for him every day of the week. I'm so good at cover-ups I could get a job with the CIA."

But again, co-dependents are not just helping addicts save face. They are protecting their own image as well. They are sincerely concerned that friends, relatives, and business associates will think negatively about their partners, but they are even more afraid that people will judge *them* harshly. "There were plenty of times when Hank and I were out in public and he was being loud or obnoxious, and I would think 'I should just let him be a jerk. People can just think whatever they want to think,' " Molly says. "But I was always too embarrassed to do it. I'd always wonder what they were going to think of *me* if I didn't do something. So I'd try to get him away from whoever he was pestering, tried to smooth things over, just keep him out of trouble as much as I could."

By protecting the addict's image and reputation, and "keeping him out of trouble," as Molly put it, co-dependents hope they can avoid guilt by association. Already feeling ashamed and guilt-ridden because they believe they have failed to meet their partners' needs and their own expectations, co-dependents naturally prefer not to have other people know they have failed as well.

Even more significant is the sense of satisfaction many co-dependents feel when they successfully protect their loved ones from shame or ridicule. Remember, co-dependents desperately need to be needed—a need they can fulfill by shielding addicts from harm.

ENABLING

Whenever co-dependents attempt to rescue the addicts they love, both by downplaying the problem in their own minds and hiding it from others, they actually enable the addiction to continue. With the best of intentions, they eliminate or cushion the impact of any consequence addicts might otherwise suffer as a result of their compulsive sexual behavior. And in doing this, co-dependents remove any reason for the addict to seek help or even want to change. They want to protect the addict, but instead protect the addiction.

And as that addiction progresses, rescue attempts become more frantic and frequent. Looking back after the fact, most co-dependents can barely believe the extremes they went to in their well-meaning but misguided attempts to protect their partners. Cheryl still shudders when she recalls, "I did all sorts of things to get him off the hook, really crazy things. Once, he left his wallet at a hotel in a really sleazy, dangerous part of town, and he thought maybe someone had turned it in to the police, and if he went to pick it up, they would arrest him—which was crazy to begin with. But I was the one who was really crazy, because I drove down there and got it back for him. I should have said, 'Look, that's your problem. You handle it.' But I didn't. I never did."

In situations like the one Cheryl described, co-dependents' overdeveloped sense of responsibility gets the better of them. As they have done so many times before, they step right in and handle everything. It *is* what they do best after all, but it absolves the addict from *his* responsibility and clears a path for the addiction to continue.

Isolation

"I could never make plans to get together with my family or with other couples," Vicki complains. Her live-in boyfriend was arrested for voyeurism, but indulged in various other sexual activities as well, leading to sudden disappearances and prolonged unexplained absences characteristic of all sex addicts. It wreaked havoc with what little social life Vicki, a workaholic, did have. "I never knew where he would be or when to expect him back. If I did make plans, it would be just like him not to show up."

Because sex addicts might disappear without warning or be too withdrawn and depressed after a sex binge to socialize with other people, if co-dependents want a social life, they must be willing to go places and do things without their partners, and most prefer not to. Most co-dependents rarely even think of doing anything to please themselves and would agree with Vicki, who says, "I couldn't enjoy myself if he wasn't there. I'd spend the whole time wishing he was there, not to mention wondering where the heck he was." Other people would wonder about that too, once again putting the co-dependent in the stressful position of having to lie or make excuses for the addict.

In addition, socializing with other people puts co-dependents in settings where they may be tempted to share more than superficial information about themselves. Although well guarded by their denial, there is always a chance something will prompt them to let something slip out, and co-dependents will not risk that. They often think that "If I start opening up about myself, it will be impossible to prevent others from knowing that I have this problem. And if they know that, they're sure to reject me. They'll think something's wrong with me." As you may recall, this is precisely what sex addicts think in social situations.

Although both addicts and co-dependents tend to keep conversations as superficial as possible, some co-dependents have plenty of meaningful interactions in which they play the sympathetic listener while the other person does all the talking. Sara, who was one of those co-dependents who listened to everyone else's problems but never revealed her own, says, "Plenty of people told me their troubles. And sometimes afterward, they would apologize for dumping on me, and I'd say, 'Oh, I don't mind.' I really didn't, because as long as they were talking about *their* feelings and *their* problems, the heat was off me."

Like addicts, co-dependents find that the problem and the need to keep it a secret creates an impenetrable wall between them and other people. "I never had any real friends," Molly sighs. "Because I could never be truthful with anybody. After a while, it was just easier to keep other people at a safe distance. Even when I did go to church or social functions, I made a little bit of small talk and then walked away. I was really lonely most of the time."

Like sex addicts themselves, co-dependents believe, "I'm the only one with this problem." And so they also believe there is no one they can turn to for help or comfort.

CO-DEPENDENT OBSESSIONS AND RITUALS

In the previous chapter, we mentioned that co-dependents are literally addicted to the addict. Their addiction can be most clearly seen through the obsessions and compulsions they develop as time passes.

With a trace of bitterness in her voice, Cheryl says, "My whole life revolved around him and his problems. Nothing else took precedence in my mind. I was absolutely obsessed with what he was doing and what I could do to stop it." The addict does indeed become the co-dependent's obsession. Just as sex addicts are preoccupied with and distracted by their sexual fantasies, co-dependents are preoccupied with thoughts about the addicts and what they might be doing at any given moment. At times, they are unable to concentrate on anything else, and no matter how they try to banish them, their obsessive thoughts keep returning. "Night after night, I would stare out the window," Diane remembers, "just waiting for him to come home."

Co-dependents' persistent uncontrollable thoughts focus on more than where the addict is and what he or she might be doing. They are equally, and perhaps more, obsessed with doing whatever it takes to preserve the relationship and satisfying the addict's every need—often to the point of sacrificing *all* of their own needs. "My only goal in life was to make him happy," Diane continues. "We went where he wanted to go, did what he wanted to do. My life was scheduled around his schedule, and I never gave it a second thought. I never once thought, 'What is he doing for me?' Why should he do anything for me? I was nothing."

Co-dependents also develop obsessive fears about some kind of harm coming to their partners. "It really scared me when he didn't come home on time," Sara recalls. "I was always convinced he'd been in an accident or gotten beaten up in a bar or murdered. Sometimes, when I had fixed dinner and was waiting for him to come home, I'd be sure the phone was going to ring, and the police or someone from a hospital was going to tell me something had happened to him. I even imagined myself going to the hospital, seeing him all covered with blood while they wheeled him down to surgery, or going to the morgue to identify his body."

As you can see, a co-dependent's obsessive thoughts can be as elaborate as a sex addict's fantasies—and they are every bit as persistent. Ultimately, co-dependents are compelled to do *something* to relieve their pain and anxiety. Molly's story, related in the previous chapter, demonstrates this connection. Soon after Hank's first confession, Molly became obsessed with what Hank was up to and went through what she called her suspicious period—compulsively looking for clues, going through drawers, searching Hank's car, and insisting that he empty his pockets in front of her. Diane also felt compelled to "find out what was really going on."

"I've never really gone *in* anywhere and tried to catch him," Diane says, "but I'd look for his car, driving by hotels or bars where I thought he might be or past the office to see if he was where he was supposed to be. The whole time I was out trying to check up on him I was very wound up, my heart was beating real fast, my head was buzzing so loud I couldn't hear myself think. I was like a zombie. I had to do it. I had to know, even though I really knew more than enough already.''

Diane's words should sound familiar. They are almost exactly the words sex addicts use to describe the trancelike state they enter during their sexual rituals and precisely the way anyone with an addiction explains the overpowering urge to engage in compulsive activity.

Every day, Howard, a forty-six-year-old plumber, comes home from work and immediately starts looking for packs of cigarettes or cigarette butts. His wife, who normally did not smoke, would always have a cigarette at the end of her compulsive masturbation ritual or after having sex with anyone but him. Of course, if he found what he was looking for, Howard, like most other co-dependents, rarely did anything about his discovery. Sometimes, he confronted his wife with the evidence, but even then, he accepted any excuse she gave him, or listened to her promise she would never do it again, and immediately exonerated her. Although co-dependents may claim otherwise, their compulsive rituals are rarely aimed at actually bringing about change in the addict or their relationship. For co-dependents—and everyone else—compulsions are a largely unconscious attempt to relieve their own anxiety, albeit only temporarily.

Though finding out everything they can about the sex addict's actions may ease a co-dependent's fear of the unknown, or allow a co-dependent to feel as though he or she is doing something about the problem, it invariably creates new tensions. Each new discovery creates even greater doubts and anxiety. And co-dependents know only one way to relieve that stress: by turning back to their own compulsive rituals. Co-dependents' compulsions can be far more extreme than Howard's and Diane's. We have treated several co-dependents, for example, who actually tapped their spouses' phones or hired private investigators to follow them.

Lynn recalls that her mother made at least one particularly drastic attempt to find out what her husband was doing: "I was dating a cop at the time," Lynn relates. "And my mother had him put on a disguise, rent a car, and spy on my dad. He followed my dad and this lady and got the license number of her car. One Sunday, we spotted that car outside the church, and all three of us waited for the woman to come out and walk over to the car. My mom said it was just who she thought it was, but she didn't actually do anything. Just knowing her suspicions were correct seemed to be enough to satisfy her.''

Although co-dependents will repeatedly say, "I hate myself when I'm doing it,'' they keep right on doing it, often persuading themselves that they are taking steps to resolve the problem. But, like Lynn's mother, they aren't doing anything constructive at all.

Like sex addicts themselves, co-dependents get trapped in an endlessly repeating pattern. Or as Cheryl, whose obsessive thoughts and compulsive rituals influenced her every move for eighteen years, expressed it, "It was like my husband and I were on a roller coaster.

Sometimes, it was the pits, and then everything would seem to be okay. But we always shot down into the pits again. Always.''

Sitting on the Sidelines

We'd like to turn for a moment to a metaphor we hope will help you understand how sex addiction affects the co-dependent in general. Think for a moment about people who are devoted fans of a sports team that perpetually ends its season in last place. Those fans are intensely dedicated to their team, get completely caught up in each game, and identify so strongly with the players that each loss ruins their day. And since their team seems to lose day after day, entire seasons of their lives are ruined.

As the game unfolds before them, the rabid fans sit in the stands, observing every play, but taking little action other than letting out an occasional jeer or an even rarer cheer. They try to transfuse their team with their own desire for victory by yelling or booing or having pep rallies. But when it comes right down to it, they have absolutely no control over what happens on the playing field. However, if anyone else dares to criticize *their* team, these blindly loyal fans rush to its defense, rationalizing the players' errors and making countless excuses for the losses. They live vicariously through their team, actually feeling the agony of defeat and endlessly pursuing the elusive ecstasy of victory.

But no matter how much it *feels* like real involvement, theirs is really a superficial attachment. They are involved in the game, but because they are not part of the team, they have no control over the game's outcome. And, in spite of suffering throughout a losing season, they invariably renew their season tickets and sign on for yet another year of humiliation and frustration.

Every aspect of this metaphor precisely parallels the experience of men and women who are involved in relationships with sex addicts. They sit on the sidelines while the addicts execute the plays and rack up the losses. Days and years of their lives are ruined, as they frantically try to get into the game and influence the addicted players' actions. Perhaps saddest of all, while co-dependents focus all their attention on the game and the players (on the addiction and the addicts) their own lives pass them by. They lose track of their own needs and lose sight of their own identities. They never think to look at what they can do to change themselves and make their own lives more satisfying. And ultimately, they sink into hopelessness and despair.

Powerlessness and Despair

"I really didn't know what to do," Sara confesses. "I didn't want to nag. I didn't want to challenge him about it, because I told myself he had to learn how to handle the problem himself. Besides, I thought if I got angry or confronted him with what he was doing to me and the kids, it would piss him off and he would leave us."

Paralyzed by their fear of abandonment, desperately afraid of being alone and seeing any expression of anger as foreign and dangerous as well, co-dependents take no substantial or positive actions to change anything in their lives. They are frozen as well by fear of the unknown— a fear that plagues all of us when we are faced with making major changes in our lives. This fear is intensified for co-dependents, who believe they are nothing without their relationships. As a result, they often convince themselves that the painful relationship they have is better than no relationship at all—leaving them no choice but to endure their suffering.

A feeling of powerlessness comes over co-dependents and they ultimately come to believe that "There's nothing I can do to change this." And so they wait for something else to change the situation for them.

"When Joe started to rant and rave, I just sat there and let him get it out of his system," Sara sighs, but then a flash of awareness hits her, and she lets out a hearty laugh. "I was waiting, all right. I was waiting for him to get *everything* out of his system: the drinking, the women, the yelling, everything."

As the addiction progresses, co-dependents actually lose the capacity to act independently. They don't act; they react. Yet, they sincerely believe they are doing everything in their power to make the situation better. Ultimately, they realize that no matter what they do, they cannot change the sex addict. This is one of the few truths in the co-dependent's tape loop of negative self-talk. Unfortunately, rather than persuading them to try to change themselves, the realization of their powerlessness to change the sex addict sends them deeper into the abyss of despair.

Cheryl now realizes, "I would confront him. He would admit it, or he would make up something. It didn't matter. Confrontation never helped at all. It just made him feel guilty. But then, he'd felt guilty all along, and it had never stopped him."

Whether they confront their partners with the evidence they've gathered, cry and beg, threaten to leave, extend themselves beyond the breaking point to make life as stress-free as possible, or make sure their partners suffer no negative consequences for their behavior, co-dependents repeatedly fail to change addicts and eventually stop trying. Cheryl did. She says, "It got to the point where I thought, Why confront him? It's not going to accomplish anything. He's not going to admit it, and even if he does, he's not going to stop. So why bother?"

Hopelessness and despair become their constant companions as co-dependents repeatedly fail to achieve an impossible goal: changing another person. They really are powerless to *make* sex addicts stop being sex addicts. But because they devote so many years to attempting to reform the addict and many more to concentrating on their failure to do so, co-dependents overlook the one thing they *can* change: their own attitudes and behavior.

8

STUCK ON THE MERRY-GO-ROUND: Co-Dependent Roles and Reactions

The children were bathed and ready for bed. The day's last load of laundry had been sorted into neatly folded piles. There were still dinner dishes to do, but once they'd been washed and the kitchen cleaned, maybe, just maybe, Cheryl could relax.

Cheryl sighed as she trudged down the hall toward the kitchen. It had been a long day, and there was nothing she wanted more than to curl up on the sofa with her husband, watch some television, and share the little details normal married couples talk about at the end of a long day. Cheryl hated to admit how long it had been since she and Sam had spent a quiet evening at home simply enjoying one another's company. But maybe, just maybe, tonight would be different.

Cheryl tried not to think about the look Sam had had on his face when he'd walked through the door earlier that evening. That look had told her that the last thing he wanted to do was stay at home with her. He had sulked silently all through dinner, staring glassy-eyed into space, not even noticing the meal she had cooked or how desperately the children tried to get his attention. He would have been out the door by now if she hadn't hidden his car keys, hoping that maybe, just maybe, his mood would pass.

It had not, she realized as soon as she entered the kitchen and saw him frantically yanking open drawers and rooting through them to find his car keys. He wheeled around to face her. "Give me my keys," he growled.

Cheryl ignored him and stepped toward the kitchen table, intending to clear away the dinner dishes. He blocked her path. She tried to step around him. He grabbed both of her arms, squeezing the flesh so tightly that Cheryl knew there would be bruises to hide in the morning. Again, he demanded that she return the keys. Again, she said nothing. He shook her and yelled horrible things. She showed no emotion.

"You can call me every name in the book," she told him, "but you are not leaving this house to go looking for some little tramp to have sex with. Not tonight. I won't let you."

Sam glared at her—then pushed her away. She lost her balance and fell to the floor. He turned and slammed his fists on the table in frustration. Angrily, he swept the dinner dishes onto the floor. Some shattered. Others landed upside down in pools of tomato sauce and grape soda. Then he stormed out of the room.

Crying, Cheryl got to her feet and followed him. "Why are you doing this to me?" she asked, over and over again. Sam stared straight at her, but it was clear he really did not see her or hear her at all. After a moment or two, he turned away, picked up the telephone, and called a cab.

"Then he walked out the door and did what he'd wanted to do all along," Cheryl said, concluding her tale with a long, deep sigh. A decade after the actual incident occurred, Cheryl sits rigidly in a straight-backed chair and haltingly recounts the details of her "worst nightmare come true."

Through the entire story, Cheryl has stared intently at her hands, nervously sliding her wedding band up and down her finger. Now that the tale has ended, she looks up at us sadly, tears filling her pale blue eyes. "Maybe I shouldn't have taken his car keys," she says. "But I had to do something, didn't I?"

Hiding the car keys is only one of many things Cheryl felt she had to do and actually did during eighteen years of marriage to a sex addict.

At forty, Cheryl is a slim, attractive blonde whose perfectly put together appearance belies the fact that her entire married life has been one "nightmare" after another. The very first time we met her three years ago and at every subsequent meeting, Cheryl has been stylishly dressed, with every hair in place and her makeup expertly applied. Even her jogging suits look as if she'd just ironed them and are worn with tasteful but expensive gold or diamond jewelry, much of it given to her by her husband, Sam—who, like many sex addicts, assuaged his guilt by plying her with gifts, even when he could not really afford them. Cheryl takes pride in presenting an absolutely impeccable image to the people around her and once told us that "every one of my married friends envies me." Maintaining a perfect façade was yet another way that Cheryl compensated for her husband's compulsive sexual activity.

A member of our Thursday-night group for sex addicts, Sam claims to have had hundreds of one-night stands while married to Cheryl, including at least one during their honeymoon in the Bahamas, when he snuck a young woman into their hotel room while Cheryl was sunbathing on the beach. Although Sam pursued sexual highs in many forms, Cheryl was obsessed only with his affairs and admits, "I was willing to try *anything* to get him to stop sleeping with other women."

"At first, I tried to please him," Cheryl recalls. "I tried to do everything right—to fix better meals, be a better housekeeper. I tried to always be pleasant, to smile at him and be cheerful. I never burdened him with any kind of problem. If something went wrong, I handled it myself. I went through a really long period of taking care of everything—the kids, the house, the bills. A couple of times, I had to borrow money from my parents to make ends meet, and I didn't mention it to him. I got this idea in my head that if everything went smoothly, and nothing put pressure on Sam, he wouldn't feel the need to have sex with other women."

Cheryl's caretaking extended to covering up for Sam's indiscretions and shielding him from the consequences of his actions. But when pleasing and protecting Sam did not have the desired effect, Cheryl resorted to more and more drastic measures. "I tried to retaliate. I thought I could make him feel bad about what he was doing, and if he felt bad enough, he would stop. I used guilt, telling him he was destroying me and the kids. I screamed and yelled and cried and pleaded with him. I remember one time when I actually got down on my knees and begged him not to leave the house. Sometimes, I would refuse to have sex with him and sometimes, I would beg him to have sex with me. If he would just have sex with me instead of with other women, I would do anything he wanted. I actually told him that. I stooped that low. I just groveled and begged and bargained for years and years. Until I was completely humiliated."

In previous chapters, we emphasized that co-dependents rarely take positive steps or act in a constructive way to resolve the problems created by sex addiction. However, this does not mean they do nothing at all. Indeed, as Cheryl did, co-dependents try everything they can think of to control the uncontrollable. They will yell and badger, induce guilt, monitor everything the addict does, try to create the perfect home environment, withhold sex, or cater to the addict's every sexual desire.

These and the many other strategies co-dependents try, at best, delay the addict's pursuit of sexual highs for a short while. Invariably, as Sam did, sex addicts find a way to "do what they wanted to do all along." Yet co-dependents keep plugging away. Desperately seeking to curtail their partners' compulsive sexual activity and squelch their own feelings about it, they employ every trick in the book *except* what might actually bring about positive change: accepting that they are powerless to stop the addict and getting help for themselves.

FOUR CO-DEPENDENT ROLES

Of course, not all co-dependents react to their partners' addictive behavior in exactly the way Cheryl did. Some never get beyond denial, continuing to ignore the existence of a problem or its impact on them, cutting off their feelings until they are *alienated* from everyone around them and strangers even to themselves. Others get angry and stay angry, becoming relentless critics and *bullies*. Still others endlessly bargain with their partners, changing themselves, handling problems, shielding the addicts and *managing* every aspect of daily living the way Cheryl did. Finally, some co-dependents blame themselves for everything their partners do, *martyring* themselves day in and day out until they are mired in severe depression.

Co-dependents tend to settle into certain response patterns. Indeed, through our work with the families of sex addicts, we have noticed that co-dependents seem to play one of four clearly defined roles throughout their relationships with the addicts—instinctively adopting the role that most comfortably fits the individual personality and immediate circumstances or mirrors the roles they observed their own parents playing during childhood.

The Alienated

Alienated co-dependents perpetually hide their heads in the sand. They deny that a problem exists at all, or they deny that the problem has an adverse effect on them. They ignore their own feelings of pain, anxiety, frustration, or anger as well as the addict's behavior.

Vicki, the social worker we introduced in the previous chapter, played the alienated role for years. She did not want to believe she had fallen in love with a sex addict who quite often preferred to be out peeping through windows or masturbating in his car, rather than to be at home with her. "I always had this sense that I should have known better," she sighs, "that I should have seen it coming because of my professional training."

But there was more than that involved. Having already been abandoned by her father at a very young age and suffered one broken engagement and a divorce, Vicki's self-talk constantly reminded her that "anyone I love will abandon me." When she actually got involved with someone who confirmed this self-talk, she simply refused to face the fact that her greatest fear had come true. Even though her boyfriend was essentially abandoning her each time he left the house in pursuit of another sexual high, Vicki "didn't want to deal with it. I didn't want to think about it at all."

The alienated role can only be played with the addict's cooperation. If Vicki's boyfriend had confessed his compulsive sexual activities the way Molly's or Cheryl's husband did, Vicki would have been unable to keep up the pretense for long. But since Vicki's boyfriend was an extremely introverted, emotionally distant person in general who did not want to talk about the problem any more than Vicki did, she was able to remain completely out of touch with reality for years.

Vicki, like many alienated co-dependents, also used her own compulsions to escape the lion's share of pain she felt. Already a workaholic, extremely emotionally involved with her clients and working sixty hours a week or more, Vicki simply buried herself deeper in her work whenever stress on the home front threatened her illusion of the perfect relationship. Other alienated co-dependents may resort to compulsive overeating, spending, gambling, drinking, or drug use to bolster their denial—thus harming themselves as well as allowing their partners' addiction to progress.

The Bully

Bullying co-dependents attempt to control their own frustration and anguish by lashing out at any available target. Tough, aggressive, and often sarcastic, bullies have the hard-nosed attitudes of street fighters and try to control addicts' behavior by belittling and punishing them in countless ways.

Kim, a thirty-nine-year-old marketing executive, constantly berated her husband, a compulsive voyeur who also frequented prostitutes. Even before she knew the details of her husband's sexual behavior, Kim attempted to shame him into behaving the way she wanted. Dissatisfied with their sex life and failing to see any noticeable improvement over a period of months, she would taunt, "Why don't you want to make love? What are you, a homosexual?" Once she learned specific facts about her husband's sexual rituals, she flew into a rage. "You're sick!" she told him. "You're crazy!"

Bullies do not limit their words of anger and disgust to the addiction alone. They criticize constantly and become furious over minor matters. Shooting darts randomly, bullying co-dependents pick on sex addicts for both real and imagined offenses. What's more, they let loose their limitless wrath upon anyone who crosses their path—children, aging parents, bank tellers, anyone. Miserable themselves, they spread misery wherever they go and make no attempt to control their tempers. When they aren't actively expressing their rage, they can be sullen, cold, and silent.

And, of course, bullying has as little—or even less—impact on the addict as denial does. While the alienated co-dependent's blindness to the problem allows addiction to continue unchecked, the bully's brutality gives the addict yet another reason to seek solace through sexual rituals.

The Manager

Consciously or unconsciously, managers devote their energies to attempting to bargain with addicts, trying to benevolently take over or manage their partners' lives. By smoothing out all the rough spots in the addict's path, managers believe that addicts will automatically stop pursuing sexual highs and no longer feel the need for them.

Although Cheryl's attempts to control her husband's compulsive behavior often bordered on bullying, she was essentially a manager who "took over a lot of responsibilities that should have been his." She assumed that "He worked and it was my responsibility to take care of everything else. And I did. He came home and sat down to a great meal, and everything was taken care of. He didn't have to worry about anything at home." After a while, he didn't have to worry about anything at all—including the consequences of his addiction—because Cheryl, in her ever-expanding management role, "handled anything that came down the pike."

Kind, cheerful, effective, and efficient are words any outside observer would use to describe managing co-dependents, who seem to be at their best during a crisis. Even though plenty is wrong, and their worlds are literally crumbling around them, managing co-dependents somehow continue to smile and carry on as if everything were just fine.

Each time they fail to control their partners' behavior, they simply try harder, employ a new tactic, assume more responsibility, and manage more effectively. Molly, drawing upon various childhood experiences that taught her she could "handle anything" and should "never give up," was hellbent on "taking care of this poor soul."

"I kept track of things for him, what he was wearing, where he was supposed to be at certain times, what he needed to do during the day, what he was saying to people—those sorts of things," she explains. "Then I'd check up on him to make sure that he did what he told me he was going to do—just like I do with the kids."

Although we regularly treat co-dependents who play other roles, the manager role is the one adopted by the majority of our co-dependent patients. In fact, frequently, both bullies and martyrs have first attempted to manage their partners' lives for months or years before switching to these other roles. Like Molly, managing co-dependents often call what they do "mothering," but their behavior is actually that of caring wardens who monitor every move the addict makes and step in to take over at the first signs of trouble. They not only fail to manage their own lives but also provide sex addicts with an unobstructed path and a perfect cover for addiction to continue.

The Martyr

"My mother was always very submissive," says Lynn, who was both a witness to and a victim of her minister father's sex addiction. "My dad made all the decisions. He never asked my mother's opinion about anything. She never expressed an opinion, as far as I remember, rarely even said how she felt. She'd just go along with my dad. He abused her constantly. He said horrible things to her, really put her down. And although I don't know it for a fact, I think he beat her. She always said the bruises on her arms were from her diabetes, but they might not have been. He was definitely capable of beating her, and my mother was definitely capable of taking it and covering it up. She did that her whole life. He treated her like dirt, and she took it. And in the end it killed her. Her death certificate reads: death due to stress and anxiety."

Lynn's mother was a martyr. Often believing they deserve the abuse heaped on them by their partners, martyring co-dependents passively endure an enormous amount of pain and suffering. Years of submission and the damage done by sex addicts who "treat them like dirt," as Lynn put it, destroy any trace of positive self-esteem. Lacking the confidence to risk change, martyrs turn all emotions inward and become severely depressed. They hope their suffering will make their partners feel guilty or sympathetic, and thus prompt them to abandon their addiction. This does not happen. Martyrdom does no more than trap co-dependents in their own depressions and turns them into doormats that addicts are more than willing to walk all over, time and again.

Of course, none of these roles is etched in stone. Some co-dependents combine aspects of different roles to create a hybrid role. For instance, Cheryl, who tormented Sam by hiding his keys, punished him by withholding sex, and often retaliated by heaping on guilt and mercilessly berating him, might be considered a bullying manager. In addition, many co-dependents shift their roles as time passes. Managers, frustrated with their failure to control addictive behavior, become bullies or sacrifice themselves so completely that they become martyrs. Once Vicki, who spent years as an alienated co-dependent, faced the truth about her boyfriend's voyeurism and public masturbation, all of her pent-up anger and resentment exploded, and she became a relentless bully. Co-dependents will even bounce back and forth between roles—moving from the extreme self-control of the manager to the out-of-control anger of the bully and back again, for example—until they wonder if they are going crazy.

SIMILARITIES AMONG ALL FOUR ROLES

Although each co-dependent role relies on different coping strategies, all four roles share a number of common characteristics.

- *All role players suffer from low self-esteem.* Alienated co-dependents run from their own sense of being inadequate and unlovable. Bullies cope with their own misery by making others miserable. Managers believe they are worthwhile only when they are taking care of others. And martyrs truly believe they are destined to be abused and victimized.
- *All co-dependent roles mirror the addict's behavior patterns.* Co-dependents and sex addicts fall into patterns of behavior that invariably complement each other. Alienated co-dependents have cold, closemouthed partners whose secretiveness and emotional distance makes denial easier. Bullies have partners who feel guilty and disgusted with themselves, believing the cruelty and criticism heaped upon them is their just desert. Managers have partners to take care of and rule over, finding them in sex addicts who are moody, remorseful, and likely to repeatedly confess their sins. And martyrs have addicted partners who abuse and dominate them.
- *Role playing extends beyond the interaction between co-depen-*

dents and addicts. Behavior patterns become ingrained habits that permeate all aspects of the co-dependents' lives. Alienated co-dependents become estranged from everyone around them and cope with any problem through denial. Bullies intimidate everyone they meet. Managers try to take care of everyone's problems, and martyrs feel helpless all of the time, often trying to elicit pity from everyone they know.

- *None of the roles works*. All simply enable co-dependents to avoid dealing directly with the addict and the problems caused by the addiction. All prevent co-dependents from looking honestly at themselves and the destructiveness of their co-dependency. All are simply another way for co-dependents to persuade themselves they are doing something to solve the problem, when in reality they are merely helping to perpetuate it.
- *All roles are part of the co-dependency merry-go-round* that keeps co-dependents from completing the grieving process they began when they saw the first sign that their real relationship did not match their romantic ideal of the perfect relationship.

TRAPPED IN THE GRIEVING PROCESS

The death of an ideal has the same impact as any other significant loss, and co-dependents' feelings and reactions are almost identical to those of people who face their own deaths from terminal illnesses or grieve over the death of a loved one. However, co-dependents, although suffering real losses—the death of their idyllic picture of family life, the loss of trust in their partners, the deterioration of their own sense of adequacy and control—are unable to make it all the way through the grieving process as it is described by Elisabeth Kübler-Ross in the book *On Death and Dying*.

Kübler-Ross organizes common human responses to death or other losses into five stages of mourning: denial, anger, bargaining, depression, and acceptance. Co-dependents go through the first four stages time and time again. Typically, co-dependents deny sex addiction for as long as they can. Then, confronted with irrefutable evidence, they explode in anger. Attempting to reform addicts, co-dependents bargain with them. And when bargaining—in whatever form it takes—fails to control the addict's sexual compulsions, co-dependents plunge into depression.

They may come this far into the cycle countless times, but it can take years for them to reach the final stage of acceptance—if they reach it at all. Unable to accept that their partners' behavior is part of the disease of sex addiction—which they cannot control—and unwilling to let go of the romantic vision of their partners and their relationships, co-dependents try the same solutions over and over again, cycling back through the earlier stages of grieving until they burn out, bottom out, or end up as sick as or sicker than the addict.

178

Denial

We have already discussed denial in great detail in previous chapters of this book. Although we cannot overemphasize the role denial plays in addiction and co-dependency, we do not wish to belabor the point. So we will mention here only one additional—and crucial—aspect of denial: the co-dependent's denial that his or her relationship with the addict will have to change.

Those co-dependents who break through the wall of denial and admit the existence of a problem at all tend to concentrate only on that problem, blocking from their conscious awareness all other aspects of the relationship and their own behavior. This narrow focus enabled Cheryl to tell us, "Sam and I always got along so well. Everything about our marriage was okay except this one thing."

Later in treatment, Cheryl was able to admit that many other aspects of her eighteen-year marriage were not okay at all. Sam's inability to hold down a job for any length of time created financial insecurity for the entire family. The way Cheryl handled everything increased Sam's sense of inadequacy and left Cheryl feeling resentful. The couple rarely talked about anything but their problem, and they participated in few pleasurable activities together. Sam did not share in child rearing. Their sex life was unsatisfying and stressful—to mention just a few of the other marital problems this couple encountered.

No, Cheryl and Sam's relationship was not okay, but like most co-dependents and their addicted partners, they were extremely reluctant to admit that they had to make changes in that relationship. Co-dependents in particular cling to the myth that "If we got rid of this one little problem, if my partner would just stop what he or she is doing, we would have a good relationship and a happy family."

Indeed, a couple *does* have to address the addiction before they can effectively work on the other challenges in their relationship. However, recovery from the addiction will not cure all of the problems in the relationship or in the family. Moreover, by concentrating all their energy on the problem, co-dependents are still denying the loss of their romanticized ideals, refusing to accept their powerlessness over the addiction or to acknowledge their own need for help.

Anger

As we mentioned in earlier chapters, a traumatic eye-opener, such as catching the addict in the act, can temporarily obliterate this denial. Co-dependents, reeling from their discoveries, immediately get angry— as anyone in such a situation would. However, co-dependents' anger rarely brings them any closer to accepting reality. For one thing, many co-dependents are afraid to express anger and keep it bottled up inside. And even those who do articulate their anger usually limit it to a single explosion. "Get out! To hell with you! Don't touch me!" they scream, reacting only to their immediate circumstances, then quickly returning to the status quo.

Also, because they are compulsively driven to protect their partners, co-dependents are reluctant to express anger toward them on a day-to-day basis. "I hardly ever blamed my husband for what he was doing," Cheryl says. "I really believed that he didn't want to do it. He couldn't help himself."

On one level, Cheryl is correct. Sex addicts are not in control of their behavior. Yet, their partners have every right to feel angry about the pain and problems the compulsive behavior causes. And the anger does not just go away. In many cases, co-dependents misdirect any ongoing anger or outrage they feel, attacking others while continuing to protect their partners. Like Sara, who blamed her husband's countless infidelities on the women "who were always hanging all over him," co-dependents frequently reserve the lion's share of their rage for their addicts' sexual partners. Others get angry at their partners' bosses for piling on the pressure at work, at themselves, at their children, or at any other person or circumstance they believe forces addicts to act out their obsessions.

Or co-dependents focus their anger on behaviors other than the sex addiction itself. Cheryl, for instance, had no trouble blaming her husband for their financial state. "We almost went bankrupt," she says. "And that wasn't anyone's fault but his."

Similarly, Sara would "stay off the topic of sex. It was just too touchy for both of us. I'd get angry about his drinking, instead." Indeed, she harped on her husband about his drinking whenever she was angry about anything he did.

Except for bullies, however, who express nothing but rage, most co-dependents, Sara and Cheryl included, rarely allow themselves to vent their anger at all. "It happened, it's over and done with," they think. "There's nothing I can do about it, so why get angry now?"

Because they are afraid of looking too closely at the addiction and what it is doing to the relationship, co-dependents gloss over their anger, limiting it to brief explosions over immediate circumstances or periodic sniping at their partners about anything but the real problem. Occasionally, they take their anger one step further and punish the addict by withholding sex.

SEX AS A WEAPON

After each new discovery of a partner's sexual activities outside the relationship, co-dependents, whether they express their anger or bury it, back away from their partners. They temporarily withdraw their emotional support, limit communication to brief conversations on superficial topics, and almost always refuse to have sex—at least for a short while.

Withholding sex from their partners could certainly be considered a reasonable response to the legitimate anger co-dependents feel upon discovering compulsive sexual activity. Indeed, Cheryl and many of our other co-dependent patients regard withholding sex as an appropriate punishment for acting out sexually. But it is also a form of self-protection. Being used sexually, being treated like a prostitute or sex object by the addict, realizing that during sex the addict is off in some fantasy that does not include them—all this leaves co-dependents feeling hurt, rejected, and sometimes disgusted. Anyone would find it difficult to get in the mood for sex while feeling such unpleasant emotions. And sometimes co-dependents simply get tired of the sex addict's unrelenting pressure for sex and assert themselves by saying no. Regardless of their motivation, because co-dependents fear that their own sexual inadequacies drove the addict outside the relationship in the first place, they seldom withhold sex for very long.

Indeed, our experience with co-dependents has shown us that most resume having sex with their partners long before they really want to. Anger and revulsion are overridden by the co-dependent's sense of duty and the fear that their partners will use their refusal as an excuse to go back out and engage in their compulsions again. Sara explains her willingness to continue having sex with her husband in spite of her anger by saying, "I could never understand how he could go out and do what he did and then come home and feel like he wanted to have sex with me right away. Sometimes it made me angry, especially because I felt like I wasn't supposed to question it. I was brought up to believe when a man wanted sex, a good wife obliged him. Obviously, I could only fake so much. But even when I was feeling no desire at all, I went along with it."

Some co-dependents don't just withhold sex but also contemplate having affairs of their own. Bullying co-dependents are most likely to have affairs out of anger and a desire for revenge. For instance, Kim's philosophy was, "What's good for the goose is good for the gander," and she had several affairs prior to divorcing her husband. Other co-dependents may give themselves permission to have their own affairs because they long for affection, want to reaffirm their own attractiveness, and are vulnerable to any interest shown to them by other men and women. Still others wonder, "What does (s)he see in it?" and may give in to their curiosity and have sex outside their monogamous relationship.

While one co-dependent may bury all angry feelings, another may explode briefly or snipe at his or her partner about anything but the real problem, and a third may use sex as a weapon, no co-dependent, prior to beginning recovery, ever sorts out the reasons for angry feelings or resolves them. Anger is bottled up for the next go-round in the grieving cycle, preventing the co-dependent from reaching the all-important acceptance stage.

Bargaining

As Cheryl's story at the beginning of this chapter demonstrated, co-dependents will try anything and everything to control the addict's behavior. They desperately want to hear their partners promise to reform. No matter how many times they have heard such promises before, no matter how often they have proved to be empty and meaningless, they will bully, shame, and manipulate addicts into making them. Co-dependents can go on bargaining indefinitely because they persistently convince themselves that "This time will be different."

Depending on the role they are playing, individual co-dependents bring different strategies to the bargaining table. The bullying co-dependents we have treated take an aggressive stance, bombarding their partners with insults. This approach simply amplifies addicts' negative self-talk, which they almost always silence by engaging in their sexual rituals.

Other co-dependents may try to force their partners to confess or constantly remind them of their indiscretions, often enlisting children or other family members in their efforts to shame sex addicts into abandoning their compulsive behavior. Still others, like Cheryl, humiliate themselves, hoping their partners will be moved to reform after witnessing the suffering they have caused. "I can remember one Sunday afternoon," Cheryl says. "I knew he was going to go off somewhere, and I literally cried and begged him not to leave. He was so cold and heartless. He was just going to do what his mind was set on." Guilt and shame rarely stop sex addicts from doing what their minds are set on, as Cheryl puts it. Indeed, compulsive sexual rituals are what addicts use to anesthetize such feelings in the first place.

Of course, if sex addicts feel guilty enough, they may do some bargaining of their own, attempting to compensate for their sexual behavior by buying lavish presents for their partners or for their children, for instance. Diane's husband, a high school principal who compulsively had sex with prostitutes, always followed a sex binge by going on a spending spree, buying expensive gifts for his wife and children. "He always spent more than he earned, bought things we didn't need," Diane recalls. "He liked to be extravagant with me. And whenever he hadn't been spending much time with the kids, he compensated by giving them some special treat. Once, he just walked in the door waving airline tickets and said, 'Everybody get packed. We're going to Disney World.' I guess it eased his conscience to give like that."

Diane never refused her husband's special treats and by accepting them without making it clear that such gifts do not fix anything, she was unwittingly promoting his addiction. Because, in the addict's diseased mind, giving the family presents gives him or her permission to act out again.

Another popular bargaining tool is the threat. Virtually every one of our co-dependent patients has threatened to end the relationship at least once and usually many times. "If this happens one more time," they say, "I'll leave. I'll take the children with me and you'll never see them again." But co-dependents are not really willing to act on those threats— and their partners know it—so they have no impact whatever. Indeed, each time co-dependents cry wolf, they prove to their partners that they can indulge in their obsessions without having to face the consequences of their actions.

Managing co-dependents, like Jenny, whose boyfriend could not resist the urge to sleep with every woman he met and sometimes had

SEX ADDICTION IS A FAMILY DISEASE

three or four quickies a day, convince themselves that "It will all work out in the end. If I put enough effort into this relationship, he will come around. He will see that I'm right, that he doesn't need to keep having affairs. Then everything will be just fine."

Managing co-dependents' bargaining chip is themselves. To reform their partners, managers try harder and harder to please them. Believing that "If I do something differently, it won't happen again," they strive to be all things to the sex addict: spouse, parent, confidant, therapist, boss, servant, and lover. "I guess I thought that if I kept loving him and forgiving him, one day he would just stop," Diane confides.

By bending over backward to meet the addict's every need, co-dependents think the partner will no longer need his or her sexual rituals. With this wishful thought in mind, some co-dependents attempt to meet the addict's every sexual need, too.

SEXUAL BARGAINING

The belief that "If I were sexier, he or she wouldn't need anyone else" is behind all forms of sexual bargaining. Operating under this false belief, many co-dependents try anything they can to make their addicts happy sexually.

"I blamed myself," Diane confesses. "I couldn't stop thinking, 'Well, maybe if I do this or that or the other thing, he will be happy with me.' " As you may recall, Diane had always doubted her attractiveness, even though she was quite pretty by anyone's standards. As her husband turned more and more often to prostitutes for sex, she naturally assumed that he found them more attractive and "went through a period when I was constantly trying to improve myself, to make myself look the way I thought my husband wanted me to look."

Our co-dependent patients have gone on dangerous crash diets, dyed their hair, gotten face lifts, tummy tucks, and breast implants all in a vain attempt to please their partners sexually. Once again mirroring sex addicts' behavior themselves, for many co-dependents looks become everything.

As we mentioned earlier, having sex on demand is also part of the bargain for co-dependents who believe handling everything themselves will cure sex addiction. As Sara would put it, "When he wanted to have sex, we had sex, whether I wanted to or not. That's what constitutes being a good wife." And Sara, like most co-dependents, believed that being a good wife would prevent her husband from going outside their relationship for sex.

Thinking "If I really care for my partner, I have to do this," co-dependents often martyr themselves sexually, doing what their partners want, no matter how humiliated it makes them feel. Alice, a forty-five-year-old editor, whose husband has not yet sought help for his compulsive masturbation and dependence on prostitutes, recently told us that whenever she has sex with her husband she feels completely revolted. Yet, she has never turned down any of his sexual overtures.

Many co-dependents strive to be supersexual in order to hold their

183

addicts' interest. Upon discovering Hank's infidelities, Molly bought a half-dozen sex manuals and read them cover to cover. Indeed, the co-dependents we treat have been willing to try almost anything to satisfy their partners sexually, including watching porn videos, having oral or anal sex, or experimenting with sadomasochism, even when they felt uncomfortable or indeed disgusted while engaging in these activities.

We have also treated co-dependents who, at their partners' urgings, have tried partner-swapping, threesomes, or having sex with another person while the sex addict watches—all behaviors far outside their own standards for acceptability. Without realizing it, when co-dependents participate in sexual acts that they find extremely distasteful, they become yet another sex object to the addict and reinforce the addict's diseased self-talk, which already tells him or her that "I can make it happen. I am in control. I can get the sex object to do whatever I want."

Like all other tactics, sexual bargaining fails to cure the addict. In fact, catering to the addict's sexual needs usually works to the addict's advantage. Sex addicts gain ground, knowing that they can continue to have sex with the co-dependents *and* act out in other ways as well. Moreover, in attempting to play out sex addicts' fantasies and thus satisfy the addicts' sexual urges, co-dependents fail to anticipate that a sex addict's lust is insatiable, that addiction is never satisfied. Their partners' sexual appetites are bound to increase as the addiction progresses, escalating to involve activities that co-dependents find even more distasteful—requiring them to further humiliate themselves, all to no avail.

As you can see, all this bargaining, sexual and otherwise, brings about absolutely no positive change in the addict. If anything, it gives addicts further justification for their behavior while exempting them from responsibility for their actions. In addition, it does devastating damage to co-dependents themselves. Between humiliating themselves and repeatedly failing to reform their partners, they chip away at their self-esteem day in and day out. And as long as they believe that "This time it will be different," and are willing to stoop lower and lower to prove their point (no matter how many times they fail), co-dependents will not be able to accept sex addiction for what it really is—a disease that is beyond their control. However, they *will* easily move into the next stage of the grieving process: depression.

Depression

"No matter what I did, no matter how hard I tried, nothing changed," Cheryl whispers. "There were days when I lost all hope. It was so painful. I just didn't think I could live with the pain for another minute. Sometimes, I honestly didn't want to live at all. If it hadn't been for the kids, I think I might have tried suicide. I thought about suicide plenty of times. I prayed for God to let me die. But then I thought I had to live, because of the kids, because in spite of it all, I still loved Sam."

Although all co-dependents may not reach the point Cheryl did and contemplate suicide, most do experience profound depression. Every emotion they feel, every doubt, every failure, gets turned inward and unleashed on their increasingly defenseless psyche, leaving them feeling hopeless, helpless, and utterly confused.

"It was all so confusing to me," Jenny admits. Initially, she denied that her live-in boyfriend's endless string of sexual liaisons with other women bothered her. Then she did everything she could to reform him. Nothing worked, "but I kept trying and trying and trying. When one thing failed, I tried something else, and it failed, too, until I was in a constant state of turmoil. I didn't understand what was going wrong."

Like Jenny, few co-dependents can understand why they keep failing to reform their partners or improve their relationships. They cannot escape the thought that they have "done all the right things, but none of them worked." As if caught in quicksand, the harder they struggle to extract themselves from the painful situations they are in, the more hopelessly mired they become. As they continue to lose ground, co-dependents, rather than express their frustration, succumb to feelings of inadequacy. "If you're doing everything that you can possibly do," Sara explains, "and that still doesn't cut it, you can't help but feel inferior. You think making your marriage work is just beyond your capabilities, that there must be something really wrong with you because you can't live up to what's expected of you as a wife and mother."

Unaware that they have been attempting to do the impossible—single-handedly cure sex addiction—co-dependents' sense of failure and inadequacy creates overwhelming guilt. Diane, the pediatric nurse whose husband is a high school principal, sincerely believed that "It was my fault that he was running around like that."

"I thought, 'I'm not pleasing him,'" she recalls. "He kept telling me, 'It's not you. It's my problem.' But I couldn't accept that. I felt so guilty that I just tried even harder to please him."

While Diane's husband tried to relieve her guilt feelings, other sex addicts actually reinforce co-dependent guilt. For instance, Sara's husband encouraged her feelings of sexual inadequacy, which already consumed her. "I remember times when we were having sex and I wasn't really into it for one reason or another, he would say something like, 'You can't do anything right,' or 'If our marriage ends, it's going to be because of our sex life.' I felt horrible."

With or without their partners' assistance, co-dependents continue to lose faith in themselves and their own abilities. Like Vicki, the social worker, who believed that because of her professional training she should have recognized her boyfriend's addiction even before she got involved with him, co-dependents endlessly replay scenes from the past, looking for the signs they missed and telling themselves "I must be really stupid" or "I was a fool not to see that this was bound to happen." Constant thoughts of past and present failures reinforce their feelings of worthlessness, and co-dependents repeatedly remind themselves that "I must really be a horrible person to let this happen."

Such feelings grow to enormous, unbearable proportions when mixed with the remorse or disgust co-dependents feel about prostituting themselves or engaging in sexual acts they personally find reprehensible. "I'm just as sick as my partner. I had sex that way, too," they think, wishing they had not given in to the addict's demands. Being unable to turn back the clock and change the past only increases depression.

Profound discouragement and brutal self-criticism of past mistakes give way to self-pity. "Why me? Why is something so terrible happening to me?" they wonder. "I'm trying, I'm caring, I'm doing so much. This shouldn't be happening." But it is happening, and co-dependents are plagued by their assumption that their partners have not gotten better because they themselves are not trying, caring, or doing enough.

Co-dependents swing back and forth between complete inertia and frantic activity. Sometimes, they feel like helpless victims and can barely take care of themselves and their children. At other times, they feel compelled to try and try again and resume the denial, anger, or bargaining they used in the past—all the while isolating themselves and gearing up for their next bout of depression by directing all negative feelings inward.

Moreover, because they have no sense of a boundary between themselves and their partners, co-dependents sink and slide with the sex addicts. "When I think of what I've been through with him—it really has been hell," Molly laments. "It's been a lot of hurt and pain and questions. Who am I? Why did I marry him? Why did I let this go on for so long?"

Feeling ashamed, powerless, and bereft of all hope, co-dependents are often led by depression to tolerate more abuse, strike more futile bargains, and endure more humiliation. Overwhelmed and thinking, "My life is devastated," they hit bottom many times before finally accepting the loss of their ideal relationships and admitting that their partners' compulsive sexual activity is beyond their control.

At first, most co-dependents view such acceptance as a defeat, the ultimate proof of their own failure. Yet, acceptance is a gift, an open door co-dependents can step through to begin their own recovery. Indeed, recovery from co-dependency begins the moment co-dependents finally accept that sex addiction is a family disease and are able to say, *"My partner is a sex addict. I am powerless to control his or her behavior and my own life has become unmanageable because of the disease."*

9

NEW VICTIMS, NEW PLAYERS: The Children of Sex Addicts

"My dad is a tyrant, a dictator, a sick, sick man and he infected all of us: my mother, my brother and sister, me. My mom's dead, and the rest of us are all sick in our own ways because of him," Lynn says. From behind large, black-rimmed glasses, her eyes flash fire.

More bitterness bubbles to the surface as twenty-nine-year-old Lynn explains, "He's a minister. His business is saving souls. And that's what he said he was doing when he physically and sexually abused us—saving our souls, driving the devil out of us. Let me tell you, if there was a devil living in our house, it wasn't us. It was him."

Lynn is the highly organized and efficient producer of a local TV talk show and the oldest daughter of a sexually addicted father and a co-dependent mother who played the martyr role right up until her death five years ago. A childhood rife with brutal beatings and degrading sexual molestation by her father was not all Lynn had to endure. Her father had countless extramarital affairs with his female parishioners, and her mother denied and covered up for them all, frequently suffering stress-related illnesses as a result.

In treatment with us for nearly a year, Lynn—for the first time in her life—is examining the impact of growing up in a home ruled by sex addiction. Although she has been expressing a great deal of anger and resentment in recent therapy sessions, these and all other emotions still seem foreign and frightening to her. Like all children of sex addicts, Lynn was conditioned not to talk about the family problem or anything else of substance, not to trust herself or anyone else, and not to feel anything at all. The first time we met her, we could clearly see that she had learned these lessons very well.

Carrying a briefcase and glancing at her wristwatch, when Lynn marched into our office for the first time, she wore a conservative suit with a crisp white blouse buttoned all the way to the top of its high collar. Her dark hair was cropped short, and she wore little makeup and no jewelry. As she calmly took a seat, crossed her long legs, and folded her hands in her lap, Lynn looked more like someone who had come to sell us a copy machine or discuss our insurance coverage than a woman seeking help for problems dating back to a seriously troubled childhood. Indeed, Lynn was downright businesslike. She sized us up coolly and got straight to the point.

"I attract sick men," she said bluntly. "I want to stop. If you can't help me, tell me now, and I'll try someplace else."

When we pressed for a bit more information, she impatiently recounted what she considered to be the pertinent facts of her life history. She had recently ended a relationship with a man who wanted her to have sex with another man while he watched. Only after she had kicked him out of her apartment did she learn that he had a criminal record for voyeurism and that he had been banned from the television station where she worked for exposing himself to a news anchorwoman. Before that relationship, Lynn had been married to an alcoholic who beat her. "And I only married him to get out of my father's house," she explained, matter-of-factly adding that her father also beat her and began sexually molesting her when she was seven years old.

As Lynn saw it, her problem was simple and clear-cut. Her past was obviously repeating itself, and she wanted it to stop. She wanted to have a normal relationship with a normal man, and she wanted us to help her do that—"without dredging up all the garbage from my past." But because her past—as the child of a sex addict—was inextricably linked to her present and future, she had to look back. With our urging, she did.

"The first time my father got sexual with me, it seemed innocent enough," Lynn recalls. "We were wrestling on the floor, just playing around, and he started rubbing my crotch. I told him not to do that, and he stopped. He said he was just fooling around, and I believed him. I didn't tell my mother or anything like that. It didn't seem like that big a deal."

But, soon after this incident, Lynn's father initiated a ritual that would occur up to several times a week for the next ten years.

"Sometime between the time he got home and dinnertime, something would happen to set my dad off," Lynn continues. "It could be anything—or nothing. There were times when I could have sworn I didn't do what he said I did, but I couldn't argue with him, or I'd pay for it later."

Lynn could not predict what would set off her father and was powerless to prevent the madness that followed. Whether her transgression was real or a figment of her father's warped imagination, nothing altered the ritual itself. Her father calmly informed Lynn that she would get spanked later, "and then we all went back to playing a good Christian family," she says. "We ate dinner together; did our homework; had family devotions around our parents' bed."

An evangelical minister, Lynn's father ran a strictly religious home. Each night, the family—which included one brother and one sister, both younger than Lynn—knelt in the parents' bedroom while Lynn's mother told a Bible story, her father read scripture, and everyone prayed.

"It was really nice," Lynn sighs. "Really peaceful and I always thought, 'Maybe it won't happen tonight. Maybe we'll just say our prayers and go to bed.' "

But Lynn's hopes were never realized—and the dramatic difference between these moments of idyllic family devotions and what occurred afterward was simply mind-boggling. While her mother went off to the other end of the house to put her sister to bed, her father took Lynn, and sometimes her brother, down to the garage.

"He kept a big board there," Lynn says, and although her voice betrays no emotion, tears glisten in her eyes and her lip quivers. "As soon as he would walk into the garage, it was like a switch in his brain flipped on, and he went into a rage. He'd hit us with the board, not caring where it landed. If we cried, he hit harder and longer. He would go on and on about the devil and the wages of sin until he wore himself out and threw down the board. That was our signal to get out of there and go to our rooms."

Knowing her father wasn't through with her yet, Lynn lay on her bed wide awake and waiting. After her mother was asleep, her father would slink into the bedroom.

"He'd turn on the light and make me lift my nightgown so he could see the places he hit me. Then he would whisper about how much he loved me and how everything would be okay and how he was going to make me feel much better. That's when he would start fondling me and rubbing and kissing me all over. I just squeezed my eyes shut and tried to pretend I was someplace else, that none of this was happening."

This ritual and others occurred at unpredictable intervals the entire time Lynn lived in her father's home. There were countless incidents of spontaneous physical abuse witnessed by the other family members as well as other forms of sexual molestation and degrading invasions of Lynn's privacy.

"By the time I got to be a teenager, I was scared to death of my dad," Lynn reports. "My heart would race the minute I heard his car pull in the driveway because I never knew what kind of mood he would be in or what he might do. And by then, I really thought I was going crazy, because part of me knew things were really bad, really out of whack, but the other part of me played along with everyone else. We all played a good Christian family and acted like nothing was wrong at all."

They put on a very convincing act. "No one suspected a thing," says Lynn, who was perhaps the most persuasive actress of all. She excelled in school, was active in the church youth group, and dated regularly. She went away to college, convinced that her ordeal was finally over, but when she came home for her three-month summer break, "things were worse than ever."

"I don't think I consciously went looking for a way out," Lynn says. But when she began dating an assistant professor seven years her senior, and he asked her to marry him, Lynn "jumped at the chance." She quickly regretted her decision as her husband's drinking problem worsened, and the beatings he inflicted upon her occurred more frequently. Yet, with a lifetime's worth of training in co-dependency behind her, Lynn stayed in the marriage for five humiliating years, finally filing for divorce on the first anniversary of her mother's death. "I didn't want to end up like her," Lynn sighs. "But the truth is, I didn't know any other way to be."

Lynn truly did *not* know any other way to be. Every single thing she knew about living and relating to other people she had learned in the topsy-turvy, terrifying, and unmanageable world that revolved around her father's sex addiction.

Of course, not all children of sex addicts are pulled into their parents' sex addiction as directly and injuriously as Lynn was. However, *any* child who grows up in the presence of sex addiction—whether aware of the specific nature of the problem or not—suffers the effects of the disease. After all, they spend nearly every day observing and interacting with the two most influential figures in their young lives, and one is obsessed with sex, while the other is obsessed with the addict. Neither parent has much attention left for the child.

Often neglected, abused, and fearful, the children of sex addicts feel deprived, fear abandonment, and are unable to trust others—just like their parents. They grow up feeling insecure and unworthy of love—just like their parents. And sadly, by the time they reach adulthood, the children of sex addicts have fallen into many of the same patterns as their parents. Co-dependent and sexually addicted parents teach their children the rules, behaviors, and attitudes by which they live their own lives, and in the process unwittingly breed a new generation of victims and players, co-dependents and addicts.

DON'T TALK

Children of sex addicts learn at a very early age that unless a subject is safe and essentially trivial, they simply don't talk about it. For one thing, neither sex addicts nor co-dependents talk to *each other* about the sex addiction even though it is the central focus of their lives. They are not about to discuss it with or in front of the children. But more importantly, little communication of any kind goes on in homes where sex addiction exists.

"Everyone always kept everything inside," says Jane, the adult child of a sexually addicted mother who had compulsive affairs for more than twenty years. Now twenty-five, and a recovering alcoholic, Jane recalls, "Anything that wasn't small talk, anything that went below the surface, was kept private. And I was better at keeping the lid on than anybody. I was the little entertainer of the family. I'd try to set the tone, try to get people to laugh and make light conversation that wouldn't cause arguments. I thought it was my job to make every day a happy day for everyone in my family."

As hard as she tried, Jane could not achieve this goal. There are few truly happy or conflict-free days in a family with a secret. The first and foremost family rule is that the family secret *must remain secret*. No one is allowed to lift the lid and look inside, not even inside themselves. As we have explained previously, neither the co-dependent nor the sex addict wants to acknowledge the well-kept secret of addiction and thus be forced to take action to truly resolve the problem.

Hiding It from the Kids: Deceit as Protection

In most cases, both sex addicts and co-dependents take great pains to keep their children from knowing about the family secret. As a rule, due to their obsessive need to protect the image of the entire family, co-dependents work much harder than their partners to shield their children from the truth. They cover up their own anguish as well as cover for the addict, making excuses for their partners' moodiness, absences, and unreliability.

Jeffrey, a construction worker, simply goes off and has his affairs, without saying a word or even bothering to lie to his wife, Peg, who knows by now exactly what he's doing but continues to get him off the hook with their children. Rescheduling a meal to compensate for Jeffrey's lateness is a routine occurrence in their household, as are the lies Peg tells her kids whenever they ask about their father's absence. "Daddy would like to be here with you," she tells them, "but he has to work late to make money, so you can have all the nice things you enjoy so much."

Ironically, Jeffrey's addiction has taken so much time away from his work that the family is in deep financial trouble. All those nice things they enjoy, the high lifestyle they continue to live—in spite of the fact that they are on the brink of bankruptcy—are part of a bigger lie. Desperately trying to keep up the family façade, Peg now lies about money and many other things besides the addiction itself. Indeed, dishonesty often is a way of life for sex addicts' families—and sometimes a cooperative effort.

"On our report cards, if we got anything less than a B, we were sure to get beaten," Lynn recalls. "In the last quarter of sixth grade, I had gotten a D in math. Mom knew Dad would kill me, so she changed the D to a B to save me. My mother would do things like that to protect us. But, at the same time, she would pretend that nothing was going on, that there was nothing to protect us from. It was really kind of strange."

Indeed, many things seem "kind of strange" to children whose parents are sex addicts and co-dependents. If kids themselves comment on one or both parents' behavior—mentioning an increase in tensions or arguments, for instance—both parents band together to silence them. Frequently, both partners claim that they have *not* been arguing or fighting at all, presenting a united front to contradict what children have witnessed with their own eyes and ears. Other parents do not address their children's concerns at all, but simply order them to drop the subject.

For instance, Hank, who years later found out that his sex-addicted father had molested his sisters, recalls that any time a problem arose, his parents simply refused to discuss it. "When my sister was eleven, she must have tried to tell my mother what my father was doing, because my mother dragged my father to talk to our priest. I don't know what the priest actually said, but they told my sister that he said to forget about it. I heard them tell her not to bring it up again. And that was the end of it."

Whether they are told flimsy lies, repeatedly have their observations refuted, or are ordered outright not to discuss certain topics, children of sex addicts usually end up wondering if they are losing *their* minds. "Gee, I thought I knew what happened. But they're telling me it never happened. What's going on here?" they ask themselves. Not knowing who or what to believe and often deciding that their parents—being grown-ups—know better than they do, children of sex addicts ultimately learn not to trust their own perceptions, thoughts, and feelings.

What Kids Know—and How They Find Out

Sex addicts, and especially co-dependents, sincerely believe that their lies and deceptions protect their children. Yet, shielding children from the truth about the addiction doesn't shield them from its consequences. Not talking about a problem never makes it go away, and children almost always know that *something* is amiss. Although they may not know precisely what is wrong with their families, they can feel the tension in the air around them.

Witnessing the roller-coaster ups and downs in their family relationships makes life seem like an unsolved—and unsolvable—mystery for children of sex addicts. They know something is wrong, but they don't know what. They feel anxious, insecure, and unhappy, but they don't know why. Since they have no reliable standard of comparison, they simply cannot figure out what is happening in their homes.

Yet, many children do find out about their parent's sex addiction sooner or later. When the addict actually victimizes a child the way Lynn's father did, children know precisely what the problem is—although they may never let on that they know. However, the vast majority of children who discover the exact nature of the family's problem do so when they accidentally stumble upon the truth. For example, Laura, today a nursing student, was ten years old when she learned of her father's sex addiction by picking up the phone and hearing her father's sexually explicit conversation with one of his many lovers. Traumatized by the discovery, Laura immediately decided she could not hurt her mother by revealing what she had heard. Not knowing whom she *could* tell, Laura kept her knowledge to herself. In this way, her father's secret became her secret as well—a tremendous burden for a ten-year-old to bear.

Occasionally, sex addicts reveal their secrets directly to their children. Jack, a twenty-eight-year-old plumber, remembers that throughout his childhood his father would disappear for days at a time, offering little or no explanation for his absences. Jack naturally wondered where his father went and what he did during these disappearances. He found out at age seventeen, when his father invited Jack to join him on one of his mystery weekends. Jack was stunned to discover that for all those years his father had been photographing and participating in sexual orgies, which involved women, other men, and even animals. Why Jack's father decided to initiate his son into his sexual rituals we'll never know, but Jack raced out of what he calls "that house of horrors" feeling embarrassed, humiliated, and angry. Yet, like Laura, Jack never told his mother or anyone else about his father's secret sexual activities until he began recovery and talked to us.

We have seen a few cases where co-dependents have been the ones to provide the children with the details of the addiction. In what is usually a desperate ploy to humiliate and control their partners, co-dependents may angrily fling open a trunk full of porno magazines and inform children that *"This* is why your daddy and I fight all the time." Or they may have their children dial the addict's out-of-town hotel room and ask "Are you alone or are you doing nasty things with someone again?" This type of behavior obviously creates a host of new problems for kids, especially for young children, who do not have enough basic knowledge of sexuality to process the information. Indeed, revelations made in anger may prove even more confusing for youngsters than the long silence they had previously endured.

If they do not stumble upon the truth, or learn it directly from their parents, most children of sex addicts recognize how different their families are from others only after they leave their childhood homes. The first thing they notice is that other families are not governed by the special rules that are by now second nature to them. "In college, I started watching my friends and how they interacted with their parents," recalls Jane, whose mother had had one affair after another during Jane's childhood. "They were free to tell their parents if they were mad or didn't like something that they were doing. That never happened in my family."

In some cases, however, even after getting away from the diseased environment of an addictive household, children may remain oblivious to the problem. In fact, having come to rely on denial in the same way their sexually addicted and co-dependent parents do, these children may not acknowledge the existence of any family problems at all. Such was the case for Fran, who had not lived at home for seven years when she, her fiancé, and some friends spent a weekend with her family at their seaside house. Throughout the weekend, Fran's father blatantly came on to his daughter's friends. When Fran's fiancé mentioned this, she excused her father's behavior by saying, "That's just how my dad is." Even when one of her friends arrived on the beach in tears because Fran's father had cornered her in the kitchen and groped at her breasts, Fran insisted that her father must have rubbed up against the girl accidentally and that she was making a big deal out of nothing. Fran was so determined *not* to acknowledge what any outsider could easily see that she never spoke to that girlfriend again and eventually broke off her engagement, because "A man who couldn't accept my father could never accept me."

Keeping Up the Façade

Regardless of what or how much they know about the exact nature of the family problem, children of sex addicts are expected to participate in maintaining the family's image. Most often, they act as unwitting accomplices, doing what is asked of them in order to win their parents' approval or avoid their wrath. However, if children do know specifics about the problem, they knowingly and actively participate in the cover-up. That is because a child's first reaction to a parent's sex addiction is likely to include profound embarrassment. Thinking that "If the other kids at school knew, they'd make fun of me," children immediately decide that keeping the family secret completely hidden is the only way to avoid ridicule or rejection from their peers—which all children, even those without serious family problems, fear.

"We all played along, following Mom's lead, I guess," recalls Lynn, who had cooperated in maintaining the family façade even before her father first molested her at age seven. "At holiday time, when we went to visit our relatives, we all acted really happy. One big, happy, well-adjusted family, that was us. Of course, by the time we got home, we all had headaches or were sick to our stomachs from the stress involved. It was a lie and we knew it, but we had to make sure no one else knew it."

For children like Lynn, lying was an integral part of daily living. In fact, sometimes those lies are so convincing and so constant that children actually forget they are not the truth. "My father once caught me daydreaming while I was supposed to be doing my homework," Lynn continues. "He grabbed my hair and slammed me into the desk so hard that I chipped my tooth. When anyone asked about my tooth, he told them I chipped it diving into the shallow end of a swimming pool. I had to tell people that, too, and you know, even though I know it didn't really happen that way, to this day, I can actually see myself diving into that pool, hitting bottom, and chipping my tooth."

In this and other ways, many children of sex addicts transform the family's façade into reality in their own minds—which is why so many of the adult children of addicts we treat sit in our offices and insist they had normal, happy childhoods. They sincerely believe it themselves until the layers of protective armor they donned as children are finally peeled away.

DON'T FEEL

Donna, at twenty-nine a wife and mother herself, is the daughter of a sexually addicted mother who used her as a confidante, endlessly and explicitly sharing the details of her numerous sexual obsessions. "My mother thought every man in America couldn't wait to have sex with her," Donna says flatly. "Lord knows she was ready and willing to oblige them. She had a thing for men's bodies. We'd be out someplace, and she'd stare at every guy that walked by. She'd poke me and say, 'Get a load of that ass. I bet that guy is really hung.' She said it loud enough for anyone to hear, too. And then later on, after my dad left her, and even after she married my stepfather, she would go out to this country-and-western bar and pick up guys and sleep with them. When I got home from school, she sat me down and told me exactly what happened. Every detail."

Donna's mother erased the boundaries that define the parent-child relationship in much the same way that Sara's father did when he told her his wife wasn't meeting his sexual needs. But unlike Sara's father, Donna's mother spoke openly *only* about sex, keeping all else hidden. She revealed nothing else about herself, expressed no other emotion, and expected her daughter to do the same. Any sign of sadness, anger, or even happiness on Donna's part was greeted with fury from her mother. "Oh, grow up!" she would say. "Stop being a baby!" Clinging to the last threads of a relationship with her mother, especially after her father had left the home, Donna dared not risk her mother's wrath or rejection. Being emotional caused trouble, young Donna decided, and she didn't want to make trouble. To this day, Donna simply does not know how to express emotions appropriately.

Keeping Emotions Inside

"To be part of our family, you had to be strong," Lynn said, explaining her family's philosophy. "And strong people don't cry—no matter what. If I cried while my dad was spanking me, I got spanked more. I also got spanked again if I cried when my brother cried. We did whatever we could, pinched ourselves, to keep from crying. And crying wasn't all we couldn't do. If I ever said that I was unhappy or hurt or gave any indication that I thought I wasn't being treated fairly, I got hit, punched, pinched. In my house, you paid for feeling anything, so I kept it all inside."

Although not all children of sex addicts received such severe punishment for expressing their emotions, most tell us they suppressed their emotions because they too feared verbal or physical reprisals. Whether they are beaten, angrily chastised as Donna was, or ridiculed for having feelings at all, children of sex addicts learn what Lynn learned: to keep it all inside. Sexually addicted and co-dependent parents reinforce this lesson through example. In most cases, the only emotion parental role models regularly express is the sort of rage Lynn so chillingly described earlier in this chapter.

Moreover, children of sex addicts seldom actually *want* to feel anything—especially not the confusion, insecurity, and self-doubt that result from their parents' secretiveness. Plagued with a swarm of unanswered questions about what is wrong with the family, children tend to assume they are the ones at fault. They tell themselves "I must be a truly rotten son or daughter" or "I must be crazy" or "I'm the problem; everything would be okay if it wasn't for me"—all thoughts that dredge up the most painful of emotions. Indeed, children who feel responsible for all family problems often become extremely despondent, especially when parents inadvertently or knowingly exacerbate the child's negative self-talk.

"The closest I ever came to wanting to kill myself was in seventh grade," Lynn reports. "My mom was very sick, and my dad took us aside and told us that because of us she was going to die, that she was sick because we had been such bad kids. I had thought that anyway, but when he said it was true, I just hated myself even more."

For Lynn and countless other children of sex addicts, this childhood depression, left untreated, all too often persists throughout their entire lives. Frustrated by their parents' unreliability, feeling the sting of their abuse, and having their trust shattered by parental lies and deception, these children develop some decidedly negative feelings about their parents as well as themselves. They instinctively know that "good children aren't supposed to feel this way about their parents." Already fearing parental abandonment and disapproval, they become truly terrified by the thought that "If my parents knew what I really think of them, they'd surely leave me." To ward off this terror, most children of sex addicts take the safest route available: they completely block out all negative feelings about their parents.

To make matters worse, as the addiction progresses, these children are often drawn into the power struggle between their parents and feel enormous pressure to take sides in family disputes.

"Growing up, I always saw my mother as the good cop and my father as the bad cop," Hank recalls. "And I had to side with the good cop, because the bad cop was rotten and abusive to both of us." Yet, Hank's mother did nothing to protect him from his father's abuse or even to soothe him afterward. "That made me angry," he says. "But I couldn't get mad at the good cop, or at least I never thought I could."

Forced to choose a hero and a villain, Hank, like other children of sex addicts, could not and still cannot comprehend his own ambivalence toward the chosen hero—his mother. Yet, such ambivalence is found in every human relationship. No matter how much you love someone, he or she will sometimes hurt or infuriate you. And, no matter how much you hate or fear someone, he or she will occasionally do something that pleases you. Most of us accept this as a matter of course. After all, no one is perfect. But children of sex addicts cannot cope with ambivalence at all. Forced to take sides at such a young age, everything is black or white to them. They simply cannot deal with shades of gray.

One parent—usually, although not always, the nonaddict—becomes the absolute hero, while the other parent becomes the absolute villain. In this child's-eye view of the world, Supermen and Wonder Women can have no flaws; therefore, the child can have no negative feelings toward them. Unable to *admit* bad feelings toward the heroic parent and afraid to *express* bad feelings toward the villainous parent, these children try even harder to keep their dangerous emotions buried deep inside.

Lost Emotions Lead to Lost Identities

An intrinsic part of childhood is the freedom to be unabashedly emotional. Children experience life at full throttle, traveling the emotional spectrum many times in a single day—often to the amusement of the more reserved adults around them. Sadly, the demand to rigidly control all emotions from a very early age robs the children of sex addicts of their freedom to ever be kids at all.

Physically punished or verbally abused if they dare to cry, much less throw a tantrum, with no adult available to model appropriate emotional expression, and often afraid of their own feelings about themselves and others, children of sex addicts kill their natural feelings, and as a result, freeze their emotional development. Feelings that were merely suppressed during childhood are entirely lost by the time the offspring reach adulthood.

At twenty-nine, Donna still bottles up all emotions and keeps them hidden deep inside herself until she can force them down no further and they explode. In fact, these explosions of apparently unprovoked anger and frustration were what first brought her to us for treatment. She sought our help because she was venting her rage on her newborn baby—slapping, hitting, and shaking him repeatedly. She had been in treatment for only a few weeks when it became apparent that Donna still had the raw, unrestricted emotions of a little girl. She had stopped herself from feeling at the age of six, and once she found a safe place in which to examine her feelings, she discovered they were exactly as she had left them, completely untouched by maturity or life experience.

Children of sex addicts lock up their emotions and throw away the key, hiding from their conscious awareness anything with the potential to hurt or frighten them. In fact, many children of addicts suffer from a sort of selective amnesia. They not only block out their feelings about certain events, but also their recollection of the events themselves. As twenty-five-year-old Jane puts it, "I see my life in two segments. The first segment is my childhood, and it seems like a dream that never really happened or a movie that happened to someone else. I'm not really in it. I don't have any feelings about it. In fact, there are lots of things I don't even remember, although my dad and my brothers tell me they really did happen."

Emotions play a critical role in forming children's identities and have the potential either to build or to destroy self-esteem. Feelings cue us in to the appropriate way to respond to a given situation, give us a better idea of what is important and what is not, and influence all of the decisions we make. Because they rarely know what they are feeling at any given moment, and may not even recognize that they are feeling anything at all, children of sex addicts respond erratically, blow things out of proportion or give them less credence than they warrant, and tend to be extremely indecisive—all factors that influence how they relate to other people and how they will perform in the real world. Stripped of their emotional barometers, children of sex addicts have a difficult time figuring out what to do and, more important, who they are.

As a result, like adult co-dependents, the children of sex addicts use well-rehearsed roles to take the place of fully developed identities. In *Another Chance: Hope and Health for the Alcoholic Family,* Sharon Wegscheider-Cruse identifies the roles adopted by children in alcoholic families as: the family hero, the scapegoat, the lost child, and the mascot. In their attempts to improve the situations in their homes, children of sex addicts often take on these same roles.

- *The Family Hero,* usually the oldest child, shoulders much of the burden for making sure the family functions perfectly—taking care of other children (and parents), cleaning house, cooking meals— responsibilities generally neglected by both parents. The hero also tries to be perfect in other areas, doing everything in his or her power (and attempting many things that are not) to hold the family together.
- *The Scapegoat,* who abandons all hope of achieving the perfection that the hero strives for, acts out at home, in school, and in the community, often taking the heat off the sex addict by getting into serious trouble and becoming the readily available target for family anger and frustration.
- *The Lost Child* tries to avoid conflict completely by withdrawing physically and emotionally from the rest of the family, disappearing into the woodwork and out of harm's way.
- *The Mascot,* usually the youngest child, actively attempts to lighten the atmosphere of the gloomy home, easing tensions and taking attention away from the family problem with comic relief and a relentlessly sunny disposition that masks his or her own sadness.

Like adult co-dependent roles, these roles are neither constant nor rigid; children alter their coping strategies to fit changing circumstances. For example, if the family hero leaves home for college or to get married, another child will often step into the vacated role, no matter what his or her previous role had been.

Adopted unconsciously, in most instances, these roles furnish children with their only concepts of personal identity, and often bolster their ailing self-esteem as well. Roles allow children to feel they are doing their part to keep the family running as smoothly as possible. Lost children will literally go out of their way to avoid adding to family tensions, while mascots try desperately to lift everyone else's spirits. Even scapegoats, in drawing attention away from parents' problems and focusing it on their own actions, help maintain the status quo. And of course, family heroes draw their only sense of self-worth from their attempts to keep the household together.

Lynn, for example, played the part of family hero while growing up, taking care of both her siblings and her increasingly depressed mother. She readily admits that the role helped her feel useful and important. "Every day I would check with my mom to see what needed to be taken care of. I went to the grocery store, I helped with the housework. I thought of myself as Superchild. I could do twenty things at once. Of course, I neglected myself, my diet, exercising. I overcommitted myself at church and school. I tried to do everything for everybody, especially my mom. It was a lot of responsibility, but I really thought my mom and my family would fall apart if I didn't do those things."

Later in treatment, Lynn would confess that she felt relieved when her mother died and lifted the worrying and caretaking burden from her shoulders. Children of sex addicts generally do feel relieved when they no longer have to play the roles they adopted as children. Yet most continue to play them well into their adult lives, long after the roles have outlived their usefulness. Like characters in search of an author, the children of sex addicts often leave home typecast in their circumscribed roles, unconsciously looking for someone else with whom they can play their familiar parts. All too often, they find them, as Lynn did when she married an abusive alcoholic and later lived with a sex addict.

DON'T TRUST

In addition to becoming increasingly alienated from themselves, children of sex addicts become alienated from others. Experiences that have already taught them not to trust themselves or their parents convince them not to trust anyone outside the well-guarded family circle, either.

Consistency is a prerequisite for building trust. Children learn to trust themselves through experimentation with the laws of cause and effect. They learn that certain actions on their part will consistently be met with certain reactions by others. They learn to trust others by observing their behavior patterns, noticing that in specific situations or in general, other people react to them and to each other in ways that are reasonably predictable. But no such consistency or predictability exists in homes ruled by sex addiction.

"I grew up in a mine field," says Hank, whose sex addiction created a similarly explosive environment for his own sons, a situation he hopes he still has time to correct. "I always had this sense that things could blow up at any moment. And I never really knew what would trigger it."

Unable to predict, and thus without hope to prevent, the next explosion, Hank grew up in a constant state of anxiety. Other inconsistencies left him totally baffled about human behavior and relationships. "It always threw me for a loop when I saw my parents kissing," Hank continues. "My dad was hard on my mother and would hit her and yell at her. I didn't know what to make of it, how he could be all lovey-dovey one minute and hit her the next."

Cheryl thinks her husband's sex addiction and her own co-dependency must have had a similar effect on their children. "Sam wasn't a bad father really, but he was gone a lot and that kept him from having a close relationship with them. Even when he was home, sometimes he acted like he didn't want to be around them. For one thing, when his mind was on sex, he couldn't even carry on a conversation. And after a binge, he would sulk around the house like a sick puppy dog. Then we'd make up, or he'd snap out of it and act like nothing had happened. Bingo, just like that, we were a normal family—going out for pizza, to ball games, having barbecues—until the next crash. It was like a roller coaster."

Co-dependents often prove to be as untrustworthy as their addicted partners. As Cheryl admits, her husband was not alone in neglecting and sending mixed messages to their children. "Over the years," she says, "it got harder for me to concentrate on the kids. I was too preoccupied with Sam's problem. I realize now that when I was upset with Sam, I also acted upset with the kids, snapping at them, and being very critical. Then I'd catch myself and go to the opposite extreme."

Both the addict and the adult co-dependent fluctuate unpredictably between loving and hateful behavior toward each other and the children. Both undergo rapid mood swings, bewildering their children with their inconsistencies. Their unpredictability and unreliability, as well as their inability to provide the basic nurturing that their children need, makes both parents unworthy of trust. Moreover, sex addicts and co-dependents, who don't trust each other at all, set an example of basic distrust for their children to observe and emulate.

Sex addicts and co-dependents also lose their children's trust each time their words and deeds contradict each other. Just as Hank was baffled by his father's ability to kiss his mother one moment and abuse her the next, children of sex addicts do not know what to make of parents who preach family togetherness, but then disappear without explanation, or who forbid their children's tantrums, but freely indulge in their own.

Children also have their trust shattered by the no-win situations in which they find themselves when one parent's message contradicts the other's. Lynn recalls that her father insisted that the children show her mother respect by always saying yes, ma'am and no, ma'am. "But after my dad would leave, my mom would say, 'Don't say that to me. It's too formal.' So when he wasn't there, we wouldn't say it, and when he was, we would. Only sometimes we'd forget—and get whipped for being disrespectful."

Lynn found herself caught in the middle: if she trusted her mother's words, she risked her father's wrath; but if she obeyed her father's commands, she risked offending—and in her mind, losing—her mother. Trying to reconcile such conflicting messages and inconsistent rules for acceptable behavior, children desperately try to figure out which parent to trust and often decide it's safer not to trust either one.

Isolation: Carrying Distrust Outside the Home

Fed a steady diet of distrust at home, children of sex addicts inevitably distrust people outside the family as well.

Whether or not they have direct knowledge of a parent's sexual activities, children of sex addicts rarely invite their playmates or school friends into their homes. It is just too risky. Something might happen to let their playmates know what children of sex addicts already suspect—something is terribly wrong with their family.

Children of sex addicts also become isolated because, like their parents, they lack the social skills needed to get along well with others. Rarely, if ever, have they seen their parents take steps to make friends with other people. In fact, they have often observed their parents change dramatically in the presence of outsiders, putting on a happy face and telling little white lies or fantastically false stories to make sure no one suspects the truth about them. Also like their parents, children of sex addicts constantly fear that something terrible will happen if they ever let down their guard.

Because of this fear and because they have only the vaguest notion of how to relate to others their own age, children of sex addicts often play roles with their peers in much the same way that they play roles within their own families. They become the class clown, the troublemaker, the bookworm, the dumb jock, or just one of those invisible kids who never says much or does much to let others know he or she is even in the room.

Their behavior with other children often mimics their parents' behavior toward them or toward each other. They may repeatedly deny they are sad or upset although their body language and tone of voice scream that they are—thus pushing away friends who want to get close to them. They may explode with little or no provocation, flying into a rage and getting into countless fistfights. And they may try to assume responsibility for or take control of every situation, becoming little managers and little bullies. Children of sex addicts, already schooled in distrust, lose the ability to allow relationships to develop spontaneously and naturally. They seldom give themselves a chance to get to know other people—to discover their individual needs and desires, their likes and dislikes—because they have learned in their own families to disregard others' feelings the way the addict does or to try to control others the way the co-dependent does. As a result, like their parents, these children often find themselves with lonely and isolated feelings that persist throughout their lives—just as the habits they learned at home continue to keep them from having satisfying adult relationships later on.

DON'T BE SEXUAL

When family life revolves around sex addiction, both parents, equally troubled by their sexual relationship, provide their children with an extremely negative impression of sex. Although, in most cases, neither parent ever speaks to their children frankly about sex, their own behavior speaks louder than any words ever could.

Even when they do not actually know about the sex addict's compulsive sexual behavior, children cannot help but observe their parents' coldness and indifference toward each other. Or, like Hank, they observe as much or more abuse than affection between their parents and form the impression that neither parent truly values the other. Most never get to see sexual expression, even in its most innocent form of touching and caressing, as a special part of a loving, adult relationship. Children of sex addicts seldom associate sex with warmth, respect, or intimacy.

In fact, children often either absorb their parents' unhealthy attitudes about sexuality or react to those attitudes by adopting ones at the opposite end of the spectrum. For instance, Donna, who was forced to listen to "every disgusting detail" of her mother's sexual obsessions and activities, finds sex repulsive. "She ruined it for me," Donna sighs. "She made it dirty and disgusting. I have sex with my husband, but I grit my teeth and turn off my mind the whole time."

And when their parents send mixed messages about sex, children often wind up as confused about sexuality as they are about everything else. "My father told me I had to get my mind off boys and get my mind on work," Lynn recalls. "That I was his little girl. He was the only one I needed to worry about. But then he would contradict himself and tell me that he wanted me to be popular with boys. He'd go from one extreme to another, and so would I. Even now, I go through periods where I just don't want to deal with men. And then I'll go through periods where the most important thing to me is dating and having a boyfriend. I'll be absolutely desperate to attract a man, any man."

Given contradictory messages when they are given messages at all, and lacking healthy adult role models, children of sex addicts often have extreme difficulty distinguishing between appropriate and inappropriate sexual behavior. As you may recall, Hank's father punished him severely and utterly humiliated him for playing doctor with a neighbor's child, a form of youthful sexual exploration many children try. This experience, combined with the relationship between his parents he observed throughout his childhood, left Hank with the impression that all sexual behavior was inappropriate—a belief that contributed to the development of his own sex addiction.

Although she is not a sex addict, Jane also came to believe sexual expression of any kind was unacceptable. "For one thing, my parents were real strict abut the way I dressed," Jane reports. "Anything I wore, dresses or slacks, had to be really conservative. I wasn't allowed to wear what other girls my age wore. They said I would look like I was easy. They wanted to make sure no one mistook me for a tramp." By forbidding her to wear clothes that were in style, because they might give the impression that she wanted to have sex, Jane's parents managed to convince her that having sexual feelings was inappropriate. Many of the children of sex addicts we treat grew up with the same impression.

Of course, some of our patients came away from their childhood homes with a different mind-set altogether. Given no guidance about what was and was not appropriate, they adopted an attitude of "You never know unless you try it," having purely sexual relationships during their early teenage years, long before they were emotionally ready for them.

The children of sex addicts, having never witnessed much communication, affection, or commitment in an adult relationship, often carry into adulthood a fear that they won't be able to have a healthy sex life, either. Indeed, they may view sex as a destructive force rather than a constructive one and believe that "Sex is a problem in any relationship." And their fear may become an unconscious self-fulfilling prophecy, creating or contributing to various sexual problems in their adult relationships.

Incest: The Worst Possible Sex Education

While all children of sex addicts learn not to talk, not to feel, not to trust, and not to be the least bit comfortable with their own sexuality, no one has those lessons driven home more painfully than victims of incest.

- Incest violates all barriers between appropriate and inappropriate sexual behavior and creates enormous confusion and often an overwhelming fear of sexuality in its victims.
- Incest makes children's negative self-talk much louder and more damaging to their sense of self-worth. Victims of incest feel dirty, different from other people, abnormal, and as if they had done something terribly wrong.
- The act of incest generates unbearable guilt in its victims. They know that what is happening between them and their parent is wrong, yet they may, at times, feel physically pleasurable sensations; they may like and even crave the tenderness and affection they receive during these sexual encounters; or they may feel valued and important for having been singled out as special, as the abuser's favorite. Incest victims almost always assume their own emotional needs and/or personal faults caused their parents to become sexual with them. They believe the incest is their fault.
- In spite of such thoughts on the child's part, incest is always initiated by the adult, who has sex with the child against his or her will. Manipulating the child, playing on the child's vulnerability, and often terrorizing the child, the adult shatters the child's sense of security and personal control, totally destroying the victim's ability to trust. Unable to trust those they should be able to trust completely, many incest victims vow never to make themselves vulnerable again.
- Incest victims' fear and distrust extend to everyone in the family. Because the nonaddicted parent usually denies and covers the sex addict's actions, the victimized child has no one to turn to for

comfort, no one with whom to share the dreaded secret, and feels totally isolated.

Incest victims, like other children of sex addicts, often keep the secrets of the past hidden throughout their lives. But old wounds will not heal unless they are examined and treated. Children of sex addicts and especially incest victims repeat their pasts and suffer enormous pain as a direct result of their childhood experiences.

THE NEXT GENERATION

The survival techniques, coping strategies, and defense mechanisms adopted by children of sex addicts almost always outlive their immediate usefulness. The lessons learned in a sex addict's household do little to prepare children to survive or succeed as adults in the world outside their childhood homes. Indeed, the only thing families ruled by sex addiction do well is prepare children to become addicts and co-dependents themselves.

Although not all children of sex addicts develop their own addictions or marry addicts, many do. In fact, when you consider that the two most influential role models in these children's lives—the sex addict and the co-dependent—train them so thoroughly in compulsive and co-dependent behaviors, it is remarkable that any of these children manage *not* to follow in their parents' footsteps.

Hank, the son of a sex addict now recovering from his own sex addiction, sums it up this way: "The more I learn about my father's sex addiction, the more afraid I am that I'm going to do what he did. I get scared that I might be locked into repeating his mistakes. I'm sure the whole time I was growing up, it influenced me and I didn't know it. And I worry about how my addiction, and my attitude toward work, and my moods have already influenced my kids. Every time I look at my sons, I ask myself if they are going to be sitting in a group like this when they get to be my age."

Hank and countless other sex addicts have learned that the only way to stop perpetuating the cycle of addiction and co-dependency is to work on their own recovery and to encourage family members to pursue recovery themselves. For sex addicts, people living with or married to sex addicts, and children of sex addicts, there is a way out. There is help available for every member of the addictive family.

Recovering from Sex Addiction

10

THE FIRST STEP:
Reaching Out for Help

"It's a miracle I'm alive today," Don says, then shakes his head. "An honest-to-God miracle. Three years ago, I was a sorry excuse for a man, a man who had just about lost everything he could lose. I wanted to die, but I didn't have the guts to pull the trigger—and I consider that a miracle, too."

Like many other men and women who have sought and found help for their compulsive behaviors through self-help programs and professional counseling, Don—a big, broad-shouldered black man with close-cropped hair graying at the temples—calls himself a "gratefully recovering addict." When the fifty-year-old federal parole officer compares how he once was to how he is now, he does indeed feel enormous gratitude—and relief. He no longer looks in the mirror and sees "a sorry excuse for a man," but he never lets himself forget who that man was, what he did, and how low he got before he reached out for help.

"My whole world was crashing down around me," Don recalls. "My marriage was falling apart. I don't think my wife and I had spoken more than three civil words to each other in months, and I was sleeping in one of the kids' old rooms because she wouldn't let me near her. I'd watch her leave the house for work every morning, cleaning other people's houses like she had to do when we first got married. She was back doing that because I was drinking and whoring away my paycheck. We couldn't pay our bills. We were so behind on mortgage payments that we were about to lose the house. The kids were grown and gone. Those were supposed to be the good years, the easy years, but because of me, because of my disease, they were hard years, a living hell."

By this time, Don was in the final stages of alcoholism and had been compulsively masturbating for almost thirty years. "I don't know why my wife stuck with me as long as she did. I wouldn't have done the same for her. But she'd been through so much by then, I guess maybe she asked herself whether it was worth bothering to kick me out and live alone."

Don's wife had stayed with him through thick and thin, through week-long drinking binges, in spite of all of Don's affairs and strange unpredictable moods. The daughter of an alcoholic who also had a way with the ladies, she was literally born into co-dependency and was not particularly surprised when her own married life turned out to be just like her mother's. Until Don's addictions began threatening the couple's financial security, she often told herself that she was comparatively lucky. Don worked steadily, and he didn't beat her or abandon her and the kids.

But with each passing year, Don, firmly in the grasp of alcoholism and sex addiction, slid further downhill. "I started having problems at work. I just couldn't do my job anymore. I was responsible for all these guys on parole, and I didn't know where the hell half of them were or what they were doing. And when I think about it, it was amazing that I knew that much. I polished off a six-pack of beer before I got to my desk in the morning. Lunchtime, I went home and put porno tapes in the VCR and masturbated, then stopped off at a bar for a couple of stiff drinks. Dinnertime, I drank some more, and I spent the night going from bar to bar until I found a woman to take me home. I'd roll in at two or three in the morning, get a couple hours' sleep, and start the whole routine over again. I figure in a twenty-four-hour day, I slept, ate, and worked maybe eight hours and the other sixteen were turned over to my addictions."

Don was suspended from his job after one of the parolees whose whereabouts and activities were a mystery to him went on a crime spree. He masturbated until his penis bled and became infected. Too embarrassed to go to a doctor, he attempted to treat it himself, ending up with a urinary tract infection. His long-suffering wife went to stay with her sister, leaving him alone in the house to drink and masturbate and watch porno movies. By the time he was called back to work, he had "gone over the edge."

Don explains, "I was sick from the drinking. I was sick about my marriage. My kids refused to have anything to do with me, and at work my supervisors—kids half my age—were watching me like hawks. I was so anxious, I couldn't concentrate at all. Everything was happening at once, and I was really depressed. Something had to give. The pressure was so strong that I thought the only way to stop it was to kill myself."

Don owned a gun, and one night three years ago he took it out of his nightstand drawer, fully intending to use it on himself.

"I was sitting on the bed with the gun in my lap," he says. "A fifth of bourbon was already half gone, and I poured myself another one—for courage. Then I picked up the gun and held it to my head, but my hands were shaking so bad that I couldn't hold the damn thing, much less pull the trigger."

Don, with the gun still nearby, drank himself into a stupor and fell asleep. "I woke up a couple of hours later, rolled over, and saw the gun. And it scared the hell out of me. I guess I forgot what I'd been planning to do, or maybe I remembered and figured out I didn't want to die. But something got through to me. This voice in my head kept saying, 'Think, Don. There's got to be something else you can do.' And that was the miracle of it, because as drunk and depressed as I was, I *did* think of something. I remembered a guy from work who'd been a drunk and stopped drinking. I called him right then and there at four in the morning, and he came over."

The next morning, Don's co-worker took him to a hospital, and he checked into a detox unit, beginning his recovery from alcoholism and later from his sex addiction.

"And, you know," Don recalls, rubbing his chin and shaking his head in wonder, "that guy who saved my life wasn't the least bit surprised to hear from me. He said, 'I knew you'd hit bottom sooner or later.' Now, I thank God I hit bottom when I did. Because if I hadn't, I wouldn't have gotten help, and I wouldn't be alive today. I know that sounds melodramatic, but it was that clear-cut. Get help or die."

HITTING BOTTOM

Although the moment of truth—when a sex addict or co-dependent finally acknowledges that the addiction has become unmanageable and reaches out for help—is not always as clear-cut as the one Don experienced, that moment arrives sooner or later. The decision to seek recovery from the disease of sex addiction is not always so obviously a matter of life or death as it was for Don, but it is almost always a decision that gets made only after addicts and co-dependents recognize that they have hit bottom, that they literally cannot take the pain and agony anymore.

It almost always takes a broken marriage or relationship, a lost job or ruined career, an arrest or some other tragic loss, to open an addict's or co-dependent's eyes and create a true awareness of the damage done by the addiction. Some will even experience these traumas several times over before taking positive steps toward recovery. Although neither co-dependents nor addicts think of it in such rational terms, the losses must outweigh the gains before either will acknowledge and do something about the insanity of addiction. They must hit bottom before they can climb out of the hole in which the addiction has buried them.

Every person—addict or co-dependent—has his or her own individual "bottom." The luckier ones hit a relatively high low, as George did. "I always knew that I wasn't happy," he says. "But the turning point came when I couldn't pay my bills."

George, a well-paid hotel-chain staff supervisor, spent mind-boggling amounts of money on phone sex services and prostitutes. He had just turned twenty-five when he realized "I was in a complete financial mess. All my credit cards were charged right up to the limit. My phone bills were astronomical. I earned a substantial paycheck, but every penny was spent before I got it. I was a regular at the credit union, and one day the loan officer asked, real innocently, what I was doing with all my money. He probably thought I was on drugs or something, but it did get me thinking. I just said to myself, 'Wait a minute, there's something dramatically wrong here. I'm a fairly responsible individual. I shouldn't be up to my ears in debt.' It finally sunk in that all my money was going to my little hobbies, and the amounts kept increasing. I tried to cut back on my own, but I couldn't. So even though it was a real blow to my ego, I went to my company's employee assistance program, and they sent me here to get help."

Financial troubles or problems at work are what a number of our patients tell us caused them to finally hit bottom. For others, it takes a run-in with the law to instigate any lasting change. Mitch, for example, was arrested, not just once or twice, but several times before he recognized that his addiction was creating completely unmanageable problems in his life. His lawyer referred him to us for treatment.

Many of the sex addicts and co-dependents we treat hit bottom after the addiction has disrupted or destroyed their marriage or primary relationship. Molly, for instance, had threatened to leave Hank many times during their marriage, but because she never made good on her threats, Hank never took them seriously. Finally, two years ago, Molly, who had already entered a recovery program, insisted on a separation and literally moved Hank out of the house. Hank was shocked, but also relieved.

"I think I almost wanted someone to force me to change," he admits now. "In the back of my mind, I knew I had to change. After a while, it got so hard to work and keep track of all the lies. It was completely overwhelming, and I wanted some peace again."

Unfortunately, the stress of his lifestyle was not enough to convince Hank to seek help. "I don't know if I ever would have changed if Molly hadn't left me. When she left, I finally realized how important my marriage and my kids were. I was willing to go to any lengths to get her back and to get my life back."

Co-dependents also find the seemingly irreparable damage to their relationships a powerful motivation to change. "I had just lost all respect and trust," Cheryl says sadly. With the support of friends she made at Al-Anon and another self-help group for co-dependents of sex addicts, Cheryl separated from her husband for six months, reconciling after he entered a recovery program himself. "There was nothing there by the time I left. I had to leave. It was the only way to save myself."

Yet, other sex addicts and co-dependents separate, divorce, and even remarry several times without hitting bottom. The marriage or monogamous relationship simply does not mean enough to either partner for them to view its dissolution as a significant loss or persuasive reason to change their behavior. Indeed, for a significant number of our patients, Don included, it took several serious problems occurring simultaneously to create enough of a crisis to drop them to rock bottom and convince them to pursue recovery.

No matter what pushes them over the edge, when sex addicts or co-dependents hit bottom, they suffer severe depression, sometimes contemplating suicide as Don did, or even attempting it. This depression is accompanied by a tremendous sense of powerlessness. Broadsided by the loss of something they value a great deal, addicts or co-dependents finally realize that their way of doing things isn't working, that it has utterly failed. Or as George puts it, "There comes a point where you can either keep on running away from reality or you can finally face it—and do something about it." Fortunately, George and the other sex addicts and co-dependents who have shared their stories in this book chose to stop running and start recovering.

If before or after reading this book you have come to believe that you are a sex addict, a co-dependent, or a child of a sex addict, you may very well be the first member of your family to recognize the damage done by the addiction, and to hit your individual rock bottom. Even if no one else in your family has yet acknowledged an intolerable loss, you may know that *you* need help for the problems addiction has created in your life. You do not need to wait until other family members hit bottom, too. We encourage you to seek help *for yourself*.

Because addiction touches every member of the family, whether you are a sex addict yourself or live with a sex addict, the addiction has had an effect on you, inflicting wounds that you have a right to heal, whether or not anyone else in your family chooses to heal their wounds, too. If you are a co-dependent who has hit bottom, pursue recovery for your own sake, not because you want the rest of your family to follow your example. If you are an addict, enter a recovery program for your own sake, not just because your family has pressured you into it. *You* can recover. *You* can change your life—if you are willing to reach out for the strength, encouragement, and guidance of others who have been where you are now, or seek help from professionals who are trained and experienced in the treatment of sex addiction.

HELP IS AVAILABLE

Help Comes in Many Forms

You take the first step toward changing the compulsive habits and patterns in your life when you realize that you cannot take care of *everything* on your own. You must reach out for help. Fortunately, a variety of self-help organizations and forms of professional therapy are available to help everyone in the family improve their lives—together or separately. In Appendix B of this book, you will find a list of the national headquarters or hotlines for a variety of resource organizations that can assist in your recovery. You can also ask your family doctor or member of the clergy or contact other local resources—community mental health centers, for example—for referrals to groups or agencies in your area that specialize in the treatment of addictions.

Because sex addiction encompasses such complex psychological issues—sexuality, childhood fears, undeveloped social skills, and deep-seated negative self-talk—we believe that a combination of *self-help* and *professional help* is the most beneficial route to recovery. The ideal treatment program would involve individual, marital, family, and/or group therapy with professionals experienced in sex addiction therapy along with participation in a self-help group. In addition, we often encourage our patients to obtain additional support through churches, synagogues, or other community organizations, particularly if they already have affiliations with these groups.

Finally, whenever compulsive sexual behavior has involved contact with another person, *we strongly advise both sex addicts and their partners to have complete gynecological or urological examinations* to find out whether either or both have contracted any sexually transmitted diseases (see Chapter 5 for more information).

Change Takes Time and Effort

One of our patients came up to us after a group meeting recently and complained, "I must not be getting much out of these groups. I'm always in turmoil when I leave."

Like many others before him, this patient wanted recovery to be a comfortable experience. But we told him, and now tell you, "That's the point of recovery programs: Something that happens during a group or individual session stirs you up and sticks with you when you leave, forcing you to deal with what you feel and how you act outside these rooms."

Without constant reminders about where they have been and where they could be again, it is all too easy for sex addicts and co-dependents to reactivate the denial they relied on in the past. Most need a thorn in the side, the voices of self-help group members or therapists, to keep them moving toward recovery and to prevent them from returning to their old ways of thinking and behaving.

We hope you recognize and are willing to accept the fact that recovery does not happen overnight. Indeed, recovery is a lifelong growth process. After all, it took a lifetime for addiction and co-dependency to develop and essentially become a way of life. Now, recovery must be given time to become your new way of life.

Yes, the road is long, but recovery is not as unbearable a chore as you might think. It might help to consider what one of our sex-addicted patients once told us: "Every time I think I don't have the energy to get well, I remind myself of all the energy I put into being sick for all these years. I have the energy all right, I just have to decide how to use it."

Although difficult at times, recovery requires only a willingness to grow, a commitment to try, and the determination to keep moving in a self-improving rather than a self-destroying direction. By taking recovery in small steps, one day at a time, you can avoid returning to the path of addiction or co-dependency, a path you already know leads nowhere. Once you embrace recovery, you will find many others willing to help you stay on course every step of the way.

Self-Help Groups for Sex Addicts and Their Families

For both sex addicts and co-dependents, anonymous support groups—modeled on the Twelve Steps recovery program of Alcoholics Anonymous (AA)—provide an invaluable service. Members of anonymous fellowships help one another recover by openly sharing their own experiences and feelings, and nonjudgmentally listening to yours. Their generosity immediately erases the idea that "I am the only one with this problem."

"Going to meetings helped me to realize that lots of people are going through the same things I am," says Diane. "It helps me just to talk about it and to hear other people talk about it. Even when I think, Well, my experience was not exactly like theirs, something seeps in. I may not even know it, but later it comes back to me and helps me get through the rough moments."

Diane, whose husband compulsively had sex with prostitutes, is in a self-help group for co-dependents, but her sentiments are echoed by Hank, who is in a group for addicts. "Understanding that I wasn't alone was very important," he told us. "I always felt so bizarre, that what I did was some wild thing in me and couldn't be dealt with. When other people said, 'Yeah, me too. I did that too. I thought that way too,' that was helpful and hearing how they changed helped even more."

Equally important to recovery, self-help groups offer you a safe place—a supportive group of your peers—in which to finally share your own story. "Just to be able to talk about it, just to get it out, was a terrific release," Mitch explains. "Everything had been locked up inside for so long. I was afraid to let it out, but it was killing me to keep it in. This tremendous weight was lifted when I could talk frankly about myself and my addiction."

The opportunity and the encouragement to express yourself genuinely and truthfully will no doubt be a unique and new experience for you—so new, in fact, that you may actually need the group to help you do it. Although other members will not censure you for anything you do say honestly, they may remind you to be *really* honest if you fall back into patterns of self-justification and denial, lies they recognize because they used to tell them, too. You can't con a con, and members of self-help groups often cut through the deception and dishonesty behind which sex addicts and co-dependents habitually hide.

If you are a sex addict, three different organizations—Sexaholics Anonymous (SA), Sex Addicts Anonymous (SAA), and Sex and Love Addicts Anonymous (SLAA)—can support you in your recovery. And if you are a co-dependent, S-Anon or Co-dependents of Sexual Addicts (COSA) meetings can help you change your life. Check the telephone book to find out about the groups meeting in your area or call the national hotline numbers listed in Appendix B of this book.

Cheryl, who attends both Al-Anon and S-Anon meetings, says, "The groups helped me not to fall back into my old patterns *and* showed me new ways to cope." Using AA's Twelve Steps as they apply to co-dependency, Cheryl "realized that all I was doing was enabling Sam to continue in his addiction. I thought I was in control but I wasn't. I had to change my way of thinking and acting. The Twelve Steps and the people in the groups helped me do that."

In addition to introducing you to the Twelve Steps and new strategies that can take the place of addictive or co-dependent behavior, support groups—with members available at meetings or by telephone on a twenty-four-hour basis—allow you to talk about your concerns and work through crises immediately, anytime day or night—a service most professional therapists cannot offer. In many areas of the country, self-help groups meet every day, or even several times a day, and particularly during the early stages of recovery, many sex addicts and co-dependents need this kind of daily contact. Group members generally exchange telephone numbers and call each other between meetings. Also, most anonymous fellowships encourage new members to choose sponsors: more experienced members whom they can contact anytime, day or night. A sponsor is neither a critical surrogate parent nor another easily manipulated co-dependent. He or she has something you want—recovery that is further along than your own. They will share it with you and provide emotional support, but *only if you ask for it.*

Self-help groups—as the name implies—reinforce an important concept of recovery: You have to do your part to help yourself get better. No one else can *make* you recover. It is your responsibility to keep coming back to meetings and to reach out to your sponsor or other recovering addicts or co-dependents when you need help. This may not be easy to do at first.

Hank, for instance, went to SA early in his recovery effort but only recently began to use the self-help group to its full advantage. "I made some progress," he says. "I wasn't acting out as much, but I wasn't really recovering, because, at first, I wasn't willing to do the work involved, particularly working with my sponsor."

While Hank was stumbling along, taking half measures instead of fully committing himself to recovery, no one tried to force him to follow the Twelve Steps program. If you don't want to work at recovery, no one in a self-help group is going to make you work at it. However, when you do give the recovery program a chance and work the Twelve Steps to the best of your ability, you will reap the extraordinary benefits it can offer, as Don has.

"I've been going to SA meetings for two to three years," Don explains. "When I listen to other people, I always hear myself. For instance, at one meeting this guy said, 'I play it safe. I do just enough to get by and don't break new ground if I can possibly help it.' And I thought, 'Hey, that's me. That's what I think. That's what keeps me from doing anything new.' And after that, I really made an effort to try new things.

"Something like that always happens at SA meetings," Don continues. "SA reminds me that recovery is an ongoing process. It keeps me green, as they say—lets me know that the problem never goes away completely. But I can deal with it as long as I'm willing to go to meetings."

Other Self-Help Groups

Most of the self-help groups that deal exclusively with sex addiction have only been founded within the last twenty years. And although the number of SA, SAA, SLAA, S-Anon, and COSA groups continues to increase rapidly, some communities have not yet established groups meeting every day. As a result, many sex addicts and co-dependents cannot attend as many meetings as they may need or want. Our patients find it helpful to supplement their participation in these groups by attending AA or Al-Anon (a self-help organization for co-dependents of alcoholics), which hold meetings seven days a week in most areas of the country.

Many sex addicts or co-dependents also suffer from other addictions that cause problems as serious as those caused by sex addiction. Naturally, we encourage these patients to attend the self-help group(s) that address those addiction(s): Overeaters Anonymous and O-Anon for compulsive overeaters and their families; Gamblers Anonymous and Gam-Anon; Narcotics Anonymous and Nar-Anon; Debtors Anonymous and Spender Menders for compulsive spenders; and many others. Information about these groups can be found in Appendix B of this book.

Particularly for sex addicts and co-dependents who have a drinking problem or live with an alcoholic, membership in AA or Al-Anon, as Don attests to, is indeed essential. "AA is really important to me," Don acknowledges. "It's my lifeline. I'd never be able to control any of this if I were still drinking."

To obtain the additional support they need, many of our sex-addicted patients attend AA meetings even if they are *not* alcoholics. By substituting the word "sex" when hearing others talk about alcohol, they are able to benefit from the experiences, strengths, and hope of recovering alcoholics.

"At AA meetings, I get a real feel for how the Twelve Steps work," explains Bill, who is not an alcoholic. "There are usually people there who are really working the steps, really dealing with things. And even though they don't have my problems, I can learn how to deal with my problems by paying attention to how they cope with theirs."

Although more helpful than not, the benefit of AA groups for nonalcoholic sex addicts is somewhat limited. The AA program, like the other self-help programs that copied its model, depends on honesty, but sex addicts rarely acknowledge their *real* reason for being there. For one thing, in a room full of people who are not sex addicts and may know little or nothing about sex addiction, it is taking quite a risk to say, "I am a sex addict." Those who have taken this risk have met with varying success: some received an open, welcoming response, while others encountered hostility and self-righteousness—attitudes that only reinforced their sense of shame and isolation. But most of the sex addicts we've treated who attend AA meetings either remain silent, listening but not sharing their own experiences, or discuss their problems with alcohol when they really are referring to masturbation or affairs or compulsive sex. Unfortunately, these equally unsatisfactory approaches prevent them from using AA meetings as a safe place where they can openly talk about their compulsions without feeling ostracized or alone, a place where they can develop their social skills and improve their ability to trust others.

Fortunately, we believe that as awareness of the problem increases, the number of self-help meetings geared specifically toward sex addiction will grow. In the meantime, listening to AA or Al-Anon members does provide a day-to-day resource to help strengthen sex addicts' and co-dependents' own resolve to recover.

Resources for children tend to be even more limited in number. Although several organizations exist that provide support to adult or teenage victims of incest—Incest Survivors Anonymous and Survivors of Incest Gaining Health, for example—we know of no self-help groups specifically geared to helping children cope with a parent's sex addiction. Most often, Alateen—an organization of peer support groups for children of alcoholics—is the only self-help resource available to them.

However, as Sean, a patient of ours who regularly attended Alateen meetings during the 1970s, sees it, children of sex addicts are likely to be accepted into and helped by Alateen. "I don't think they'd face the same sort of tension as, say, a sex addict in an AA group," he says. "I know in our group, we had a number of regular and semiregular members whose parents had other problems. Our group never turned anyone away."

Professional Group Therapy

Although self-help groups contribute enormously to recovery from sex addiction and co-dependency, we have found that most addicts and co-dependents—children as well as adults—also need the psychological expertise that professionally led therapy groups can provide. Like self-help groups, group therapy offers a safe place where addicts or co-dependents can practice honest communication without fear of reproach. In fact, with a therapist present to facilitate interaction, group members can take greater risks than they might in a self-help group.

"I always thought that if I told my friends I was homosexual, they'd find a way to get rid of me," Mitch confides. "That's one area where our group sessions helped me a lot. I got to test out my thinking and see how people actually reacted. I could say, 'I'm a homosexual. What do you think of that?' It was still uncomfortable, but I wanted to know the truth one way or the other. Even when some people reacted negatively, it didn't kill me the way I thought it would. Actually, I learned a lot from discussing it with straight people and found out that most people who know don't really care. I had always thought it would affect my life badly to let someone know. The group helped me realize that I was who I was and also how to express myself and my feelings to someone else.''

Although group therapy does not serve as a twenty-four-hour support network as self-help groups do, it can help you recover in ways support groups cannot. Group leaders with psychological expertise furnish you with specific tools and useful insight, especially in the areas of emotions and self-talk. As therapists, we encourage our patients in group therapy to explore a deeper level of their feelings. In a manner that would be totally inappropriate coming from a peer in a self-help group, we push and prod them to reveal themselves more completely—to the group as well as to themselves.

While self-help groups rely on sharing honestly and listening openly without pushing or advising, therapists provide *direction* for both the group and each individual. For instance, we not only encourage members to fully examine their negative self-talk, but also act as expert guides, suggesting ways to alter and improve that self-talk and patients' overall self-image.

Finally, although self-help groups indirectly improve sex addicts' and co-dependents' social skills, group therapists can offer actual instruction in assertiveness skills, mutually beneficial rules of communication, and how to give appropriate feedback. Through guided interaction with each other, group members put these skills into practice, as well as learn how to respond appropriately when someone else shares pain or makes them angry.

If anyone in an anonymous fellowship meeting tried any of these therapeutic techniques, resentments would fly. But in group therapy, it is precisely the role of the professional therapist to use them. An objective leader, clearly identified as the expert guide for the group, provides focus and structure for group meetings and allows flexibility and the cross-pollination of ideas while still keeping the group from wandering too far afield.

Having the helpers clearly distinguished from the helpees was particularly beneficial to Hank, who, like many sex addicts and co-dependents, tended to keep up his façade as big-man-on-campus in self-help groups where many members were constantly looking for someone who seemed to know what he or she was doing.

"In my SA group, I sort of set myself up as a leader," Hank admits. "I wasn't able to share very openly, because every time I wanted to share something negative, I would think, 'I can't. There's a new person here who is going to wonder what good the program does if someone like me was still having such a rough time.' "

In a professionally led therapy group, Hank not only got to share and learn from his rough times, but was no longer able to hide behind the familiar know-it-all façade that was hampering his recovery.

Individual Therapy

In many cases, sex addicts and co-dependents need more attention than either professionally led group therapy or participation in self-help groups can offer. The group process, though extraordinarily helpful to recovery, cannot provide the intensive focus on one individual's specific problems that both sex addicts and co-dependents so often need. The time limitation imposed by even a two-hour group meeting, whether professionally led or peer supported, simply does not permit in-depth examination. In fact, if any one person's problem takes up the entire session, it is almost always destructive for the group as a whole.

Individual therapy is especially helpful if you are already abstaining from your sexual rituals or acting much less co-dependent, but still feel depressed or plagued by unresolved problems from your past or current relationships. You may need the personal attention individual therapy can give you, as well as the chance to concentrate on the specific issues that influence your recovery. By digging deeper and learning more about yourself, you become even less likely to slip backward into past compulsive patterns.

"Individual therapy lets me go as far as I'm willing to go to get things out," says Don. "I can talk specifically about what ails me. The more I find out about myself, the more sure I am that I just can't act on things the way I used to."

A good therapist, experienced in the area of sex addiction and the family, can gently and skillfully help you uncover feelings you may have buried a long time ago and come to terms with past events that still cause you intolerable pain and guilt. Both Donna, whose destructive relationship with her sex-addicted mother kept her from experiencing her own emotions, and Lynn, who was sexually abused by her father, needed individual therapy to sort out conflicts from the past. Visualization, role playing, and writing exercises designed specifically for the individual patient helped both women get in touch with their emotions and build self-esteem. For Lynn, a devout Christian, one such exercise involved imagining herself having a conversation with Jesus in which he told her what he loved about her. Other patients benefit from writing a letter to one of their parents. Expressing their emotions about that person can be therapeutic, whether the patient actually sends the letter or not.

If sex addicts or co-dependents are having difficulty in one particular area, individual therapy lets them focus on that area again and again, slowly peeling away the layers, session after session. This worked well for Sara, who needed individual support to rid herself of the guilt she had carried with her since childhood.

"Nobody can cut right through to what's really going on the way my therapist can," Sara says. "He listens and when guilty things start coming out of my mouth, he says, 'Well, why would you feel guilty about that?'

or 'Do you think that's not a normal way to feel?' And he never lays on the guilt the way other people do. He doesn't come at me with all of these 'You shoulds' and 'You shouldn'ts.' He lets me work it out within myself.''

In addition, many patients feel more comfortable sharing hidden parts of themselves in one-on-one therapy. Sex addicts and co-dependents, who have difficulty trusting anyone, often find it somewhat easier to build trust in one person, the individual therapist, than to trust an entire group of people. Without the safety and one-on-one relationship found through individual therapy, certain facts and feelings would never come to light or be dealt with effectively—because it seems too scary to bring them out in front of a group.

Couples and Family Therapy

Because sex addiction, like all addictions, is a family disease, whenever possible the family as a whole needs to work together on recovery. Both sex addiction and co-dependency involve distorted relationships and problems of communication with other people. If each individual in the family or relationship deals with recovery separately, some parts of the problem do not get treated. In couples therapy or family therapy, professional therapists treat the couple or family as a unit. In a sense, the couple or family *is* the patient—and therapy addresses the problems and difficulties unique to that relationship, just as individual therapy deals with the unique problems of the individual.

In addition, because all members of a sex addict's family habitually deny and minimize their own and each other's actions, new facts and feelings that might not be revealed by individuals can be observed during couples or family therapy, especially those attitudes and behaviors that block intimacy in the relationship.

We believe it is important to mention that couples therapy is not intended to keep that couple together at all costs. Some people discover through couples therapy that their relationship is beyond repair. After achieving a certain amount of growth through therapy, the couple may decide that the best choice for everyone involved is to dissolve the relationship. Moreover, we often conduct couples therapy with husbands and wives who have already separated, to help them resolve the problems that disrupted their relationship and learn not to fall into the same traps in the future.

Family therapy as we practice it takes several forms. We usually start family therapy only with the immediate family—the sex addict, his or her spouse or partner, and their children, if any. When possible, we expand the family group to include the adult patients' parents and the siblings willing to participate in the process, which we call family-of-origin therapy. Although initially frightening, including their parents in their recovery can be enormously beneficial for sex addicts and co-dependents. Family-of-origin therapy gives sex addicts and/or co-dependents their first and perhaps only opportunity to communicate safely with their parents in a new way, from the standpoint of their own progressing recovery.

Family-of-origin therapy almost always provides eye-opening information to the therapist. By observing how parents and adult children treat and respond to one another, the therapist gains insights that can be used to further a sex addict's or co-dependent's recovery. But even more importantly, when compassionately and skillfully conducted by the therapist, family-of-origin therapy rids patients of the ghosts and goblins from the past, clearing up many misperceptions and relieving countless fears that have haunted addicts and co-dependents since childhood, as well as paving the way for better relationships with their parents and siblings in the future.

Workshops, Conferences, and Bibliotherapy

Although they cannot take the place of self-help groups or professional therapy, workshops, seminars, and conferences addressing a wide variety of issues relevant to sex addiction and/or co-dependency can enhance your recovery. Courses and workshops teaching assertiveness, communication skills, meditation, Bible study, and stress reduction, to name just a few, can help improve specific areas of your life that addiction and co-dependency have damaged. Unfortunately, as many bad seminars exist as good ones. However, recommendations from friends, peers in your recovery program, therapists, and members of the clergy will improve your chances of finding a truly helpful seminar.

Many of our patients have also drawn enormous benefits from attending national or regional conferences, getting together with other sex addicts or other co-dependents from all over the country. Because the people who take part in these conferences usually have a great deal of experience in Twelve Steps programs, they can offer new insights and positive role models showing how recovery works. Bill, for instance, attended the International Sexaholics Anonymous conference and came away with the sense that "We're in this thing together," renewing his commitment to and hope for long-term recovery.

Another supplementary resource that our patients have found helpful is bibliotherapy—a program of reading books that address specific areas of their lives that need improving. In conjunction with ongoing therapy, reading some of the better literature available about sex addiction and co-dependency can provide unique insight and understanding, as well as make the time between therapy sessions as productive as therapy itself.

We recommend Patrick Carnes's *Out of the Shadows* (originally published under the title *The Sexual Addiction*), for example, to every sex addict and co-dependent we treat. Those who take the time to read Carnes's book—and now, we hope, our book as well—inevitably experience what we call the "Aha!" response: They recognize themselves or their partners on the pages they read, and think, "So that is what's going on," or "So there is a way to change things." This can be a tremendously powerful experience, helping both sex addicts and co-dependents realize that they are not alone and not destined to eternally be at the mercy of the disease.

In addition, workbooks like *The 12 Steps: A Way Out,* which we use as a guide for our compulsive patients' Twelve Steps work in group therapy, provide a structure for working on recovery issues. Workbooks, with their step-by-step approach and clear overview of recovery as a whole, are particularly helpful for those sex addicts and co-dependents who get nervous about what they are doing and where it is leading.

Most importantly, reading reinforces the idea that recovery is an integral part of everyday life. It cannot be confined to several hours a week spent in self-help meetings or therapy sessions. Reading is one of the many activities we recommend to keep recovery on course between group and therapy sessions.

In Appendix A of this book you will find the resources we consider to be some of the better recovery literature available, including books that our patients have consistently found helpful. You may also want to seek additional suggestions from personal contacts you meet through your recovery program: your sponsor, family therapist, psychologist, physician, or member of the clergy.

As with workshops, some books can do more harm than good. Please keep in mind that although reading will add a great deal to your recovery program, it does not take the place of other helpers. To think that you could just read yourself out of addictive or co-dependent patterns of thought and behavior is foolhardy—and dangerous. Reading does not enable you to practice honesty, develop social skills, really work on personal relationships, or give you the nurturing and support you need from others, whether peers or professional helpers—all of which are essential to recovery from addiction and co-dependency.

Community or Church Involvement

Whether recovering from sex addiction or co-dependency, it is extremely important to build ties outside the immediate circle of your peers in recovery groups. Community and church activities offer you opportunities to improve your social skills, express your thoughts and emotions, feel a sense of belonging and productivity, and, most importantly, strengthen the long-neglected spiritual side of your life.

Many recovering sex addicts and co-dependents find acceptance and a sense of belonging by participating in charitable or civic organizations, their child's school programs, or various community causes. They discover that they further their own growth by getting involved in something that matters strongly to them, something that adds meaning to their life and helps others. These activities also bring previously isolated addicts and co-dependents together with people who share similar community values.

Many of our sexually addicted and co-dependent patients also draw support—and find a sense of belonging and people who share their interests—by strengthening the informal support network they already have with their friends. Jenny, the young architect, did this when she needed support to leave her sexually addicted boyfriend. "I sought out my own support group, you might say: friends whom I was close to who would go and do things with me," she explains. "I knew that they accepted me, that they loved me for who I was. I think that's really the only thing that saved me, knowing that other people who came in contact with me really liked me. They were the ones who got me to try to stick up for myself and to be a little more aware of situations that they could see that I couldn't. They helped me see that I might be justified in feeling angry or hurt, that it wasn't just my overactive imagination. Something really was wrong."

Establishing a network of close friends, both inside and outside the immediate circle of recovery, not only provides support and reassurance, but also relieves the intense loneliness and isolation both sex addicts and co-dependents commonly feel.

For some of our patients, the strongest sense of connectedness arises from involvement in their churches or synagogues. We have treated sex addicts and co-dependents of many religions, and we have found that calling upon their religious beliefs and reconnecting with a spiritual community helps sustain recovery. Some patients have chosen to find a new worshipping community to better help them in their recovery.

"Getting involved with the church helped me a lot," Bill acknowledges. "It wasn't so much that I could talk about my problems, but I knew I was accepted. I have a lot of friends there. I get reinforcement that I'm liked, that I'm okay. I'm not one to preach religion to anybody. But it's very important to me, and if I lose it, I can slip into some very serious problems. It sets a foundation for living for me, a solid base. No matter how bad things get, there are going to be other people here that I can make friends with."

As it did for Bill, spiritual growth can play a vital part in establishing a foundation for your recovery, but spiritual growth alone will not bring about a complete recovery. Some addicts take refuge in churches that preach recovery from emotional illness through religious beliefs alone. Yet, a church that ignores the mental, emotional, and behavioral aspects of the disease of sex addiction can be as destructive to recovery as a therapist who dismisses the importance of spirituality. No matter how deeply felt their religious convictions, both sex addicts and co-dependents consistently behave in ways antithetical to their moral beliefs. And without help and support, this pattern of betrayal will continue.

Taking Care of the Body

Recovery from addiction and co-dependency involves not only the mind and spirit, but also the body. Exercise and physical activity relieve stress in a more productive, less damaging manner than engaging in compulsive behavior—and also help those in recovery feel energetic and alive. Physical exercise becomes a release—a new, healthy high, if you will—free of the destructive repercussions of compulsive behavior.

In addition to advocating regular exercise, we encourage all sex addicts and co-dependents to be completely screened for any sexually transmitted diseases. Women should consult a gynecologist, and men, a urologist or specialist in infectious diseases. Perhaps you, like many of our patients, feel uncomfortable with the idea of revealing your fears about having picked up a disease because of your own or your partner's compulsive sexual behavior. Keep in mind that a doctor's records are completely confidential, so anything you say in your doctor's office will stay there. Besides, the embarrassment or even humiliation involved is nothing compared to leaving a harmful or deadly disease undetected and untreated.

If you are a co-dependent whose sexually addicted spouse or lover has not begun to pursue his or her own recovery, we even more strongly urge you to have yourself checked for sexually transmitted diseases and, for your own safety, to refrain from sex with your partner as long as he or she continues to indulge in compulsive sexual behavior that involves other people. If you must have sex with an active sex addict—whether out of a sense of duty or your own desire—make sure to use a condom and one of the spermicides containing the chemical nonoxynol-9. Even these protective measures are not foolproof, however, so to continue having sex with an active sex addict could be extremely detrimental to your health—or deadly.

CHOOSING THE RECOVERY PROGRAM THAT'S RIGHT FOR YOU

With so many recovery options available to you, how do you choose the one that is right for you? Although we advise a *combination* of self-help support groups and professional therapy, your first reaction to the idea of getting professional therapy may be to worry about the cost—especially if sex addiction has already put a dent in the family bank account. If the cost of treatment concerns you, call your community mental health center. It should be able to refer you to a therapist you can afford.

But the state of your finances should not be the only criterion for selecting a therapist. It is best to find one who has experience in treating sex addicts and their families. In fact, if your only choice for treatment is between a professional with *no* expertise in sex addiction and a self-help group modeled after the Twelve Steps of Alcoholics Anonymous, we recommend the self-help group. Fortunately, with the enormous number of options available, few people are forced to make this choice.

Choosing the Right Therapist

Ideally, you should choose a professional with expertise in and understanding of sex addiction. Before we were educated about sex addiction and accumulated experience treating the disease, we might have taken a more traditional, and for sex addicts, less beneficial approach ourselves. Chances are that we would have decided, "Well, the *real* problem isn't the behavior. That's just the symptom. The real problem is chronic depression or an unresolved problem with the patient's father or mother," and delved into those issues while all but ignoring the compulsive behavior itself. This traditional therapeutic approach simply does not work when it comes to sex addiction. Neither does traditional family therapy, which we might also have tried in the past, thinking, "If we improve personal relationships, these other things will take care of themselves."

Therapists who minimize compulsive behavior—whether sex addiction or co-dependency—seeing it only as a symptom of a larger problem, rather than as a disease itself, become professional enablers. They unwittingly allow the addiction to continue by not focusing on the true disease, and by giving addicts and co-dependents new justifications for their behavior. Since they are chronically depressed, have unresolved conflicts from childhood, or are having an adjustment reaction to adult life, the addicts or co-dependents can't help doing what they do—at least, that's how certain therapists see it.

Therapists untrained in sex addiction are not the only professional enablers. Sara encountered one when she went to a gynecologist because she feared she had contracted a venereal disease from her husband. Her doctor minimized the problem. " 'Well,' he said, 'it happens to the best of them,' " she recalls. "It never occurred to me that it wasn't the most helpful thing to say. In fact, I used it to excuse my husband's behavior for a long, long time." Although he no doubt intended to ease her fears, the doctor's well-meant comment allowed Sara to retreat back into denial.

Like co-dependents themselves, professional enablers always mean well, but they end up simply perpetuating the addiction. "I first sought help just a few years into my marriage," Hank admits. "I went to a young pastor who had some training in psychology. He told me, 'Well, you're just in this particular stage of life, and it's nothing to worry about. It, too, will pass quickly. Everybody's struggling. Here are some tools that will open your eyes.' Then he gave me a couple of psychology books, and that was that."

By assuring Hank that he was just going through a stage, rather than treating the compulsive behavior as a serious problem in its own right, his pastor essentially allowed him to go right on doing it, confident that it would go away on its own. Other clergy members who sincerely urge prayer and Bible study alone as the answer to sex addiction or encourage co-dependents—or even victims of incest—simply to forgive the addict's behavior also unintentionally help perpetuate the addiction.

Fortunately, the growing number of books, conferences, and seminars on the disease is helping more and more therapists, doctors, and clergy members become knowledgeable about sex addiction and the family, reducing the chances that you will encounter professional enablers when you seek help. If you do not know of a therapist who has experience and expertise in treating sex addicts and members of their families, ask someone in one of the helping professions if they might be able to refer you to one. A good therapist always refers a patient to another therapist if he or she does not have the expertise necessary to treat a particular problem, and we receive referrals from other therapists for precisely that reason: to deal specifically with sex addiction and the relationship between a sex addict and his or her family.

Even within this specialized field, there are a number of different approaches to treating sex addiction, and one approach may work better for you than another. As a result, you may find a therapist who has expertise in sex addiction, but still feel that this particular therapist is not helping you.

If you feel so uncomfortable with your therapist that it detracts from your recovery, find another therapist. But don't give in to the temptation to decide this on the basis of one session. Most people—whether or not they are sexually addicted or co-dependent—feel uncomfortable just reaching out to a therapist for help. Your discomfort may very well be the result of being in therapy for the first time rather than a problem with a specific therapist. Take the time to develop trust and a working relationship with the therapist, giving yourself at least several sessions before deciding to look for another one.

If, after several sessions, you still feel the therapy isn't working, ask your therapist to recommend a colleague who uses a different treatment approach, one you might find more helpful. Your therapist will not be surprised or upset if you do this; such a request is a common occurrence.

Beware, however, that it is all too easy to justify continuing your addiction or co-dependency with the excuse that "I can't find the right therapist." If you truly want to get better, you will keep looking until you find the right therapist among the many who are knowledgeable about sex addiction.

Choosing the Right Group

Just as individual therapists have their own personalities, groups—whether peer supported or professionally led—have their own particular style, too. Even within the same organization, individual groups may have very different characteristics, and different people may benefit more or less from a specific recovery group. We have heard both praise and criticism of every type of self-help or therapy group.

Often, the effectiveness of a particular group depends on the personality of the individual. Although they attended the same groups, for instance, Bill and Don came away from the experience with very different impressions. "For some reason, I've never gotten much out of the local SA groups," Bill complains. "In fact, the down stories just brought me down to the point where I wanted to act out again. Sometimes, people would talk nonstop about their slips, drawing out all the gory details. I didn't feel like anybody was getting well. I didn't see the Twelve Steps program and how it worked." For Bill, who had a lot of ambivalent feelings about giving up his compulsive behavior in the first place, going to SA meetings only linked him with other partners in crime. He felt drawn to those group members who minimized slips and excused away the continuation of compulsive behavior. For Don, however, contact with those same people strengthened his own resolve to get better. "The most frightening thing I ever saw was a nineteen-year-old boy who was further gone than anybody I'd ever seen. He looked like he was in his thirties. He had these bizarre mannerisms, almost looked like he was twisted. He had this telephone sex thing going, all day every day with his girlfriend. He actually said, 'I think it's too late for me.' After listening to him, I knew I had to do whatever I could to stop myself from ending up like that."

Female sex addicts often have a particularly hard time finding the right support group for them. Just as fifty years ago, in the early days of Alcoholics Anonymous, most AA members were men, most self-help meetings for sex addicts today have a largely male membership. "Women sometimes come to SA meetings, but all they see is men," explains Don. "They start talking and say, 'I'm not sure I belong here,' and they really do, but they never come back."

While many women feel uncomfortable in these groups today, we suspect that the number of women actively participating in sex addiction self-help groups will increase dramatically over the next decade, and we agree with Don, who says, "If half those women had stayed, we would have a dozen women in our group alone." Male or female, to build trust in a group, you must attend more than just one meeting.

Co-dependent groups also have their own particular personalities, determined in large part by the individuals who regularly attend meetings. Cheryl recalls that "One particular S-Anon group really turned me off. Everybody there was divorced and talking about their exes. I couldn't really relate. I was trying to hold a marriage together, not break it apart. That meeting just didn't give me any tools to move ahead. Fortunately, I tried other meetings and found some with women who had stayed with their husbands. I got a lot out of hearing them tell where they had been and where they are now."

Like Cheryl, you may need to try more than one group before finding the one that's right for you. But again, don't make hasty judgments about how useful a group will be to your own recovery. We recommend going to six to eight meetings of a particular group before making a firm decision about whether or not it helps. To select the best group for you, look for one in which you feel comfortable to openly express your feelings and discuss your experiences. Sharing with others can be the cornerstone of your recovery, so, if you honestly believe you can't share in one group, look for another.

Likewise, every therapy group has its own distinctive flavor. For example, one of our groups is not limited exclusively to sex addicts, but includes a mix of people who engage in a variety of different compulsive behaviors: sex addicts, child abusers, alcoholics, wife batterers, and others. Although the members of this group do not share the same compulsion, they do not look down their noses at one another.

In our groups for addicts and co-dependents, at each session, a different member discusses how one of AA's Twelve Steps applies to his or her own life. Afterward, the other members of the group give detailed feedback about what they have heard. The remainder of the session is devoted to working on the immediate issues that one or more of the members bring up for discussion. By dividing the session between examining one of the Twelve Steps and dealing with the current anxieties of group members, we address both short-term and long-term recovery issues. We run groups for other patients in different ways, but we have found that a disciplined approach to the Twelve Steps combined with psychological guidance is the most helpful form of group therapy for compulsive people.

However proud we may be of our method's effectiveness, we do not claim that it is the right approach for everybody. There simply is not one universal answer for recovering from addiction or co-dependency, and our groups have their critics. Janet, for example, who wants and needs far more individual attention than she gets in the group, sometimes finds meetings frustrating. "I wish we could work more on an individual basis," she complains. "The Twelve Steps work takes too long. Sometimes, when I get there, I have lots of things built up inside me, and I want to get them out and get some input."

Because we believe the Twelve Steps to be critical to recovery, we do place a great deal of emphasis on that program. But, although Janet recognizes that working on the Twelve Steps is important to her recovery, she benefits more from a smaller group and one-on-one therapy, where she gets more of the individualized attention she needs.

When you find a group in which you feel comfortable, continue to attend as long and as often as it assists you in your recovery. As you progress in your recovery, your own needs will change and, as new members come and go, the characteristics of the meetings you attend may shift, too. A particular meeting that helped you for a long time will sometimes stop serving your individual needs. If you are thinking of leaving a group, however, we would strongly urge you to get as much feedback as possible from people you trust. You should avoid making this critical decision entirely on your own. Bounce it off your therapist, or even the group itself, to make sure you are not trying to rationalize a return to compulsive behavior. If you are certain you aren't, your friends and advisers may very well agree that you could use a change. If this is the case, you need not feel ashamed or guilty about wanting to change groups or deciding to switch to individual therapy, instead. Even if you cease going to individual or group therapy, however, we do recommend that you continue attending a self-help group, such as SA or S-Anon, indefinitely.

If there is one rule of thumb for choosing a recovery program, this is it: *If it doesn't help you, don't go back. But if it does help you, embrace it, and make it part of your new life.*

11

THE TWELVE STEPS:
A New Way of Living for Both
Sex Addicts and
Co-Dependents

The Twelve Steps of Alcoholics Anonymous, originally developed to help men and women recover
from alcoholism, serve as the foundation of vir-
tually every effective self-help group that addresses addictive, compulsive, or co-dependent behavior—from Gamblers Anonymous to Overeaters Anonymous, from Al-Anon to Nar-Anon. The most successful
recovery programs for any addiction—including sex addiction and co-
dependency—use them. Valuable tools for everyday living, the Twelve
Steps are useful for nonaddicts as well. In fact, we use them to guide our
own lives.

THE TWELVE STEPS OF ALCOHOLICS ANONYMOUS

1. We admitted we were powerless over alcohol—that our lives had
become unmanageable.

2. Came to believe that a Power greater than ourselves could restore us
to sanity.

3. Made a decision to turn our will and our lives over to the care of God,
as we understood Him.

4. Made a searching and fearless moral inventory of ourselves.

5. Admitted to God, to ourselves, and to another human being the exact nature of our wrongs.

6. Were entirely ready to have God remove all these defects of character.

7. Humbly asked Him to remove our shortcomings.

8. Made a list of all persons we had harmed, and became willing to make amends to them all.

9. Made direct amends to such people whenever possible, except when to do so would injure them or others.

10. Continued to take personal inventory and when we were wrong promptly admitted it.

11. Sought through prayer and meditation to improve our conscious contact with God *as we understood Him,* praying only for knowledge of His will for us and the power to carry that out.

12. Having had a spiritual awakening as the result of these steps, we tried to carry this message to alcoholics and to practice these principles in all our affairs.

If you are a sex addict or a co-dependent, the Twelve Steps offer you a set of principles to guide you to a new way of thinking and relating to others, free you from compulsive behavior, and move you toward a more peaceful, serene, and sober life.

Although the Twelve Steps are common-sensical, they are not easy. Each step builds on the one that precedes it. As an addict or a co-dependent, you develop an understanding of the First Step and begin applying it to your life before moving to the Second, the Second before continuing on to the Third, and so on. However, you need not *completely* grasp one step—or *completely* incorporate it into your life—before beginning work on the next. In fact, recovering addicts and co-dependents work on the Twelve Steps continually, returning to particular steps again and again throughout their recovery as their own progress and life experiences bring new and deeper meaning to steps they have previously taken. Recovery is a lifetime's journey traveled one day at a time.

On the pages that follow, we present an overview of the twelve steps as they apply to sex addiction and co-dependency. Our words in print will give you a working understanding and the basic flavor of the Twelve Steps. Yet, the Twelve Steps are best learned by experiencing them and sharing the insights gained by those who have worked through them before you. This is achieved by attending Twelve Steps recovery program meetings and interacting with your sponsor and other recovering addicts or co-dependents. Consider the following as merely a framework upon which to build your understanding of the Twelve Steps.

ADAPTATION OF THE TWELVE STEPS TO SEX ADDICTION AND CO-DEPENDENCY

1. We admitted we were powerless over lust—that our lives had become unmanageable.

2. Came to believe that a Power greater than ourselves could restore us to sanity.

3. Made a decision to turn our will and our lives over to the care of this Higher Power, *as we understood Him, Her, or It.*

4. Made a searching and fearless moral inventory of ourselves.

5. Admitted to our Higher Power, to ourselves, and to another human being the exact nature of our wrongs.

6. Were entirely ready to have our Higher Power remove all these defects of character.

7. Humbly asked our Higher Power to remove our shortcomings.

8. Made a list of all persons we had harmed, and became willing to make amends to them all.

9. Made direct amends to such people wherever possible, except when to do so would injure them or others.

10. Continued to take personal inventory and when we were wrong promptly admitted it.

11. Sought through prayer and meditation to improve our conscious contact with our Higher Power *as we understood Him, Her, or It,* praying only for knowledge of our Higher Power's will for us and the power to carry that out.

12. Having had a spiritual awakening as the result of these steps, we tried to carry this message to others and to practice these principles in all our affairs.

APPLYING THE TWELVE STEPS TO YOUR LIFE

The First Step: We admitted we were powerless over lust—that our lives had become unmanageable.

The first step provides the foundation for the entire Twelve Steps program—and opens the door to recovery. To take it, you admit that a problem exists, recognize that the problem has had a negative effect upon you, and reach out for help. Sex addicts must hit bottom and admit they are powerless to control their own lust. Only then will they reach out to a self-help group or therapist for help. Co-dependents must admit that they are powerless over the addict's lust. Only then will they stop vainly trying to control their partners and seek help for themselves. Before *you* can take the first step, you must acknowledge that all your old ways haven't worked—and will not work in the future, that you are stuck in the thoroughly unmanageable cycle of addiction or co-dependency.

Like everything else in your life, once you hit bottom, denial has stopped working, and you recognize the high price paid for your compulsive behavior. Among other losses, you have lost control, if you ever had control. Your obsession with your own lust or the addict's lust has seeped into and wreaked havoc on your work, your marriage, child rearing, finances, your physical and mental health—virtually every area of your life. Admitting this is the essence of the first step.

Of course, we all prefer to think that we *do* have control over our own lives—and especially over our actions in areas as sensitive as sexuality and personal relationships. Therefore, we find it not only difficult but also discouraging to admit powerlessness over compulsive behavior.

It helps to remember that sex addiction is a disease. Any recovering alcoholic will tell you that while other people can control their own drinking without help, people who have the disease of alcoholism cannot. Similarly, people suffering from the disease of sex addiction cannot control their lust—and the people who are close to them cannot control it for them, either. Just as you cannot arrest a disease like diabetes through mere strength of will, you simply cannot control addictive lust through willpower alone. You know this from your own experience. Your life is littered with the broken promises you made while you repeatedly and ever more desperately tried to control your own and/or the addict's behavior.

"I always believed that I was in control. Always," Todd admits, "but I'm not. If I *really* was in control, how could I let myself live my life the way I lived it? Still, I *tried* to control everything in my life, and when I couldn't, I put the blame on other people and circumstances."

Actually, the disease of sex addiction created the circumstances that Todd once blamed for his compulsive behavior. And ultimately, those circumstances—including a broken marriage and instability at work—forced Todd to admit his powerlessness over his own lust. As Todd did, you may find it extremely difficult to believe that the control you tried so hard to maintain was no more than an illusion. It is a truly terrifying thought. After all, if you cannot trust or rely on yourself or your own willpower in order to recover from sex addiction or co-dependency, whom or what *can* you trust? Once you truly recognize your own powerlessness and honestly realize that all you tried to do in the past has come to naught, you are ready to seek the answer to that question.

The Second Step: [We] Came to believe that a Power greater than
ourselves could restore us to sanity.

You have admitted that you cannot cure yourself. You are powerless to control your own or your partner's compulsive behavior. You have cried out for help. Is there someone or something that can actually help you? There is, and your work during the second step involves defining the source of that help and preparing yourself to accept help.

By now, experience has repeatedly taught you that you cannot stop your addictive or co-dependent behavior by deciding at a particular moment, "Okay, I'm just not going to do it anymore." And since you can't stop by yourself, you have no choice but to reach out to someone or something else for help. It is time to acknowledge that a power stronger than your own willpower is essential to your recovery. Indeed, if you cannot control your own addictive and co-dependent behavior, your only hope for recovery is to recognize and turn to a power higher than yourself for help.

The second step requires more humility than most sex addicts or co-dependents have exercised in the past. Acknowledging that controlling compulsive and co-dependent behavior takes more than their own resources, honestly admitting that they *cannot* do it without help, is the hardest part of step two for most of our patients. Sex addicts and co-dependents often harbor grandiose illusions about the strength of their own will, believing that they can control both events and other people, almost to the point of Godly omnipotence. This belief has to go, because sex addicts or co-dependents who see themselves as their own Higher Power are constantly tempted to keep trying to control their addiction or co-dependency on their own, often setting up tests for themselves the way Bill did when he repeatedly tried to prove he could drive through the local red-light district wihout picking up a prostitute. These tests always fail—as you well know—and instead of verifying your power, they leave you all the more vulnerable to the self-destructiveness of your own uncontrollable impulses.

You will find it impossible to take the second step if you have not *really* taken the first, if you have not *really* admitted your own powerlessness or put aside your stubborn willfulness to battle your addiction or co-dependency to the bitter end—without support or assistance from anyone else. To recover, you must abandon the image of yourself as a self-contained unit, an island unto yourself. You must ask for and receive help from a Higher Power. Whether you decide the source of that power is God, your recovery group, or something else entirely, you will need it in order to feel a greater connection to others and realize that life has not irrevocably pitted you against the world.

In our work with addicts of all kinds, and specifically with sex addicts and co-dependents, we have witnessed again and again that the *only* way to recover is to rely on a Higher Power. This spiritual pilgrimage, which we believe is a necessary part of recovery, includes coming to terms with the meaning and purpose of life in general and your own life in particular, as well as examining both what is important in your life today and what you have sacrificed in the past because of your obsession with sex or the sex addict.

The spiritual dimension of your life may be one you have never fully experienced before, one you have not previously taken the time to examine fully. Doing so now is most certainly worth the effort involved. Belief in a Higher Power, along with helping you center your life, offers you a new feeling of serenity and peace, a sense that you fit in with the rest of the universe.

The genius of the Twelve Steps program is that it doesn't spell out the meaning of a Higher Power for you. It does not tie the spiritual dimension of recovery to a particular theology or religion, or single out one conception of a Higher Power as *the* answer. Instead, it urges you to examine the question yourself, to define the concept in a way that makes sense to you personally.

Most of our sex-addicted and co-dependent patients do choose to envision their Higher Power as God. Powerless to control their behavior on their own, they often decide that change will require a power that is not only greater than their own, but greater than any human power.

But the Twelve Steps program does not demand that you believe in God *per se*. If you are an agnostic or an atheist, nurturing the spirit and developing a personal relationship with a Higher Power may simply mean exploring how you fit in and act as part of the rest of the universe and with other people. For instance, Sean, an agnostic and an adult child of an alcoholic, visualizes his Higher Power as "a group of people holding hands around a table," a picture he drew at age twelve during an Alateen meeting. "And for me, that still serves as my Higher Power," he says, "the love and support that exists among a group of people, although not necessarily from one specific person. It's nothing tangible, and I certainly don't see a single figurehead, but I draw strength from feeling that connection with other people."

We have also worked with many sex addicts and co-dependents who, when taking their second step, announce, "For now at least, my Higher Power is *this* [SA or S-Anon or SAA or COSA] group."

No doubt, your personal spiritual beliefs are as important to you as ours are to us, and we in no way intend to foist our particular views on you or anyone else. However, we both refer to our Higher Power using the word God, and our perception of God's wisdom and benevolence tends to be built upon Judeo-Christian religious values and teachings. We personally believe that Biblical teachings fit in well with the Twelve Steps program. As just one example, to help our like-minded patients better understand the battle between their desire to recover and the force of their obsessions and compulsions, we might cite the Bible passage in which Paul says, "The good that I would do, I do not," which we believe aptly describes the painful dilemma faced by most sex addicts and co-dependents. We believe that there is no dichotomy between sound theology and sound psychology.

If you believe in God, the second step encourages you to *reexamine your relationship,* and in doing this you may find it helpful to consult a member of the clergy with knowledge of the Twelve Steps program. For a high percentage of our patients, the religious training they received in their childhood homes was confusing and constrictive, leaving them with many unresolved conflicts in this area. And because few of these patients gave much thought to theology or the spiritual side of themselves during adulthood, they find themselves stuck with the negative conception of God they formed as children.

And in our opinion, certain visions of God can indeed be destructive to an individual's self-esteem, hampering instead of sustaining recovery. For example, addicts and co-dependents who perceive God as a punishing, overbearing figure find it practically impossible to develop the kind of healthy, nurturing relationship with a Higher Power that recovery programs depend upon. This conception of God as an angry and abusive parent, waiting for you to sin so he can condemn you to burn in Hell, only amplifies the neurotic, destructive guilt that fuels compulsive behavior and blocks recovery.

On the other hand, as we see it, the conception of God as a passive, all-forgiving sugar daddy can be equally detrimental to recovery. The automatic redemption preached by some religions and spiritual movements leads many addicts to believe that their actions in this world carry no consequences, that they need not be accountable or feel responsible for their behavior, and thus leaves them with no real motivation to change.

We believe that a balanced conception of God as a Higher Power includes the vision of a caring and helpful God, yet one who reinforces the notion that self-destructive or hurtful actions do carry consequences. If you find yourself stuck with a vision of a God that actually stands in the way of your recovery, making it hard for you to allow a Higher Power into your life, a member of the clergy may be able to help you deal with the concept of a Higher Power in a more constructive way.

We have included this personal statement about our views on God to give you a sense of where we're coming from, not to convert you to Christianity as we practice it or to talk you out of your own faith, whatever it may be. We don't have the one right and perfect answer any more than anyone else does and merely hope to spark you to think about your own relationship with a Higher Power.

Although defining their concept of the Higher Power that can restore them to sanity often takes a great deal of time and effort, most of our sexually addicted and co-dependent patients quickly grasp a concept of what sanity is. Having hit bottom, they can finally see the *insanity* of their past behavior in a glaringly bright light. They are finally aware that their obsessions made them unable to manage their own affairs and filled them with impatience, worry, and depression. For example, Andy, who picked up a prostitute on the day before his wedding, knew his behavior was crazy. And Cheryl, who searched her husband's pockets every morning, knew her behavior was crazy. Indeed, both voluntarily labeled their actions dumb and insane.

Yet, sex addicts must deal with the question of sanity and sobriety differently than addicts in most other Twelve Steps programs. "There's always an ongoing debate as to just what constitutes sobriety," concedes Don, who is also an active member of AA, where the issue of sane behavior—never taking another drink—is more clear-cut. "Everyone tries to identify sobriety on their own terms because, for one guy, it may mean not going to a prostitute; and for another, not going to a bookstore; and for another, not masturbating. It's always strange for me to hear someone say they masturbated, but don't see that as acting out. Maybe some of them can masturbate, but I know I can't. For me, sobriety means not masturbating."

The truth of the matter is that sex addicts, who must define their own sobriety based on their past compulsive behaviors, walk a dangerously fine line. While no one advocates negating your sexuality entirely, you must constantly take care not to allow denial and self-deluding rationalizations to dictate your definition of sanity in such a way that you continue compulsive behavior.

The Third Step: [We] Made a decision to turn our will and our lives over to the care of this Higher Power, as we understood Him, Her, or It.

At first reading, the third step may seem to promote passive resignation, a new version of letting problems take care of themselves. It does not. Indeed, the third step involves two tasks: letting go and turning over to your Higher Power those things beyond your control *and* actively working on every aspect of your own recovery that you do have the power—and the responsibility—to improve.

Once you take the first step and admit your powerlessness over your own or your partner's sex addiction, you have nothing to lose and everything to gain by turning the problem over to the care of a Higher Power—asking that power to remove your obsessions and help you resist your compulsions. But turning your will and your life over to a Higher Power never, ever releases you from *responsibility* for doing what you can to repair your relationships, communicate honestly, straighten out your financial situation, or anything else that will further your recovery.

"When I find myself worrying about something that's out of my control, I pray that an answer will be provided," Todd explains one way this step works. "It takes a lot of pressure off me, which is good, since pressure makes me want to act out. Besides, all the worrying about things I couldn't do anything about was a real waste of time. I can use the time to work on the things I can change, like taking care of my health, and being a better father to my kids, and not screwing up at work."

As Todd has learned, turning over the areas of your life that you can't control means you no longer need to consume time pointlessly worrying. Yet, you still have a will of your own. You will need to yield to your Higher Power control over your own or the addict's lust. You will *not* stop making rational adult decisions. The third step asks you to find a balance. In doing this, many sex addicts and co-dependents take their lead from the Serenity Prayer: "God grant me the serenity to accept the things I cannot change, the courage to change the things I can, and the wisdom to know the difference."

Every day, indeed every moment of every day, presents new opportunities to make individual decisions about circumstances still within your control. In fact, many of the choices you face do not require a

Higher Power's assistance at all. However, as you have learned time and time again, in the area of your greatest vulnerability—sex addiction or co-dependency—you *cannot* control these decisions by yourself, through your own will.

The third step gives your Higher Power an active role in your life and the potential to make an enormous contribution to your recovery. In the past, when your own will conflicted with the will of a Higher Power, when you wanted to act out sexual rituals that went against your moral values, for instance, or when you covered up for your partner in spite of your beliefs about the value of honesty, your will won the battle. By giving your Higher Power a prominent place in your life and letting it influence your decisions, you will be less likely to behave in ways that are antithetical to your own values.

"One of the hardest things to change was always trying to do things *my* way," Bill admits, "always wanting what I wanted when I wanted it exactly the way I wanted it." As Bill discovered, the decision *not* to act on your own will, but to accept God's will or what you perceive to be your Higher Power's will, is indeed difficult—but necessary. The stubborn and self-destructive willfulness that Bill described is what allowed your addiction or co-dependency to turn your life upside down, and that attitude must change. Recovery depends upon acting according to the *highest* part of yourself, rather than willfully abandoning yourself to the lowest.

The third step also asks you to find a balance between dependence and independence, which sex addicts and co-dependents, as flip sides of the same coin, seldom experience prior to beginning their recovery. Sex addicts deny their dependence on other people, channeling all of their needs for affection, nurturing, and acceptance into their compulsive sexual behavior. Co-dependents, on the other hand, deny their independence, sacrificing their needs for productivity, recognition, and individuality so they can hold on to their relationship with the sex addict. Both paths are linked to their overpowering fear of abandonment and create a void that a relationship with a Higher Power can help fill.

Or as Bill puts it, "Now that I've learned that I used my sexual rituals to avoid bad feelings and to keep from worrying about my problems and a whole lot of other things, I want to meet some of those same needs through my relationship with God, praying for guidance instead of worrying obsessively about my problems, meditating instead of getting myself all riled up, going to church instead of going out to peep through people's windows."

We feel it is important to warn you, however, that the third step, and the program in general, carries with it the risk of becoming dependent on a Higher Power in an unhealthy way. Obviously, you would be going too far if you were to turn over your mind to a religion or a God or a group and say, "Take care of me. Do everything for me. Whatever you say, that's what I'll believe." Do not forget that *you still need to function independently as a responsible adult*.

The third step also raises an issue you may be reluctant to confront:

your ability to trust. You cannot turn to a Higher Power—be it God or a group—for help unless you trust that Higher Power, unless you are willing to let down your habitual defenses and make yourself vulnerable. For sex addicts and co-dependents, such vulnerability is taken to mean exposing yourself to the rejection you so strongly fear. A leap of faith is required. If you give it a chance, *faith* in a benevolent and sovereign God, a compassionate group of your peers, or some other Higher Power can remove and replace your *fear* of abandonment and, gradually, your fear of life itself. In fact, our patients and we ourselves have found that the more we trust our Higher Power, the easier it becomes to trust and be open and honest in every area of our lives.

The Fourth Step: [We] Made a searching and fearless moral inventory of ourselves.

After years of denial and rationalization, your recovery depends upon your ability to be open and honest with yourself as well as others. Helping you do this, the fourth step involves thoroughly and fearlessly examining your own thoughts, feelings, behaviors, relationships, and so on—actually taking a written inventory of your personality and your lifestyle, your strengths, and your weaknesses.

Throughout this step, you must work tenaciously to flush habitual denial and rationalizations out of your system and deal with your real personality and your real behavior. The roots of sex addiction or co-dependency must be exposed, not just the obvious, surface issues of compulsive or co-dependent behavior. Searching your soul relentlessly, you ask yourself:

- What are the aspects of my personality that encourage me to indulge my sex addiction or co-dependency?
- What attitudes and emotions trigger my compulsive sexual behavior or co-dependent behavior?
- What fears am I escaping through my sex addiction or co-dependency?
- What resentments do I use to justify my behavior?
- What strengths have I overlooked as I buried myself deeper and deeper in my addiction or co-dependency?

From years of experience, we can tell you that the areas most often left out of this self-examination are the ones that our sexually addicted and co-dependent patients most need to come to terms with—ideas, attitudes, and emotions that they have kept hidden longest and thus find most frightening to look at in the light of day. Yet, the fourth step will not have a healing effect unless you unearth the fears and feelings that you shut off or hid from yourself and others long ago—as far back as your childhood.

The fourth step is not easy, but it is absolutely nonnegotiable. Because half measures will not significantly advance your recovery, to move forward you must form a clear and complete picture of your individual strengths and weaknesses. And, if you do, in fact, scrutinize your life honestly and thoroughly, a great weight will be lifted off your shoulders, as it was for Mitch. "One of the biggest things I've learned in recovery is to deal with myself and the other people around me; to be comfortable with myself, to know who I am really," he explains. "Before I took my fourth step, I lived in a fantasy world. I don't do that anymore. I can't . . . I was running away from the lies and running right into a deathtrap."

Before taking an honest and searching inventory, Mitch felt like a fraud—and nearly every sex addict and co-dependent feels the same way. As Mitch pointed out, an enormous sense of relief comes from knowing who you really are and being able to live your life as a whole person who has the problem of sex addiction or co-dependency, rather than rejecting huge portions of your own identity and filling the gaps with compulsive or co-dependent behavior.

The fear that accompanies fourth-step inventory taking seems overwhelming at times. You can relieve some of that fear by reminding yourself of the reason you are facing up to your faults and weaknesses: to pinpoint the characteristics you want to and *can* change. You are *not* stuck with your old patterns of co-dependency or sex addiction forever. Each time you identify a negative characteristic, remember that "This is only one part of me. I don't have to go on this way. With the help of a Higher Power, I can change."

To take a complete and useful inventory, look closely at your past, as far back as early childhood—not to blame others for your problems, but to discover how some of your deep-seated beliefs arose. You will, no doubt, see that most of your self-destructive attitudes developed as a result of specific situations or circumstances encountered at an early age, when you were not equipped to deal with them constructively. You cannot change these events, but you can change your self-talk, beginning by adding to your repertoire this new message: "I am honest with myself."

Try to maintain a well-rounded perspective, remembering that you are a *whole* person, not just an addicted or co-dependent person. In fact, because sex addiction and co-dependency tend to color every aspect of the way you see yourself, you are quite likely to overlook the positive attributes you do possess. Don did. Even though he had already worked the first three steps as part of his recovery from alcoholism, when Don came to his first therapy group meeting, he could describe himself only in negative terms: "I screwed up my life, I've ruined my marriage, I'm unlovable," and so on. When pressed to come up with something positive, he offered only his wife's observation that he was good with the kids.

But what Don's wife had told him was not necessarily what he believed. To fully recover from his addiction, Don could not continue to judge his own worth by what other people said about him. It took a good twenty minutes for Don to come up with just three positive things to say about himself: "I *am* intelligent, I *am* a good worker, and I care about my kids."

Like Don, you may find affirming your positive qualities as difficult as pulling teeth. But to get better, it is absolutely essential that you open your eyes to your positive traits as well as the negative ones. Remember that negative self-talk is what fueled your compulsive behavior in the past. Beginning with your fourth-step inventory, you identify the positive attitudes you can use to overcome the negative. What's more, awareness of your strengths sustains you in recovery, making sure the flaws you must face and deal with do not overwhelm you or discourage you from continuing to make progress.

"It's really tough," George admits. "I'm trying to learn to like myself at the same time that I'm looking at my character defects under a microscope. It helped to say, 'Sure, some big mistakes were made here, but it's okay. I don't have to make those mistakes anymore. Life goes on.' "

Life does go on, and it goes on differently than it did before you began your recovery and realized that your sex addiction or co-dependency defines only *part* of what you are, not your entire identity. Yes, you do have a problem over which you are powerless, but you also have good qualities and intrinsic self-worth, which serve as the foundation for your future. Indeed, your recovery will be built upon these strengths, which you will draw upon to overcome your weaknesses. Of course, you must first fearlessly look at both.

The Fifth Step: [We] Admitted to our Higher Power, to ourselves, and to another human being the exact nature of our wrongs.

The fifth step, which asks you to actually speak about what you wrote in inventory form during the fourth step, begins the process of repairing the damage done by your addiction or co-dependency. Previously alienated from yourself, others, and your Higher Power, when you share your own pain and the wrongs you committed as a result of your disease, you get closer to others and to your Higher Power. The fifth step opens a door, allowing your Higher Power and at least one other person to understand what is really going on in your life, an understanding they must have if they are going to help you recover.

The fifth step is the first one that requires you to speak out loud, to put into words how your addiction or co-dependency has affected you and those close to you. As a result, you effectively declare an end to the secretiveness that kept you isolated, locked away with your addiction or co-dependency. If you are like most sex addicts and co-dependents, you have almost always believed that the world would come to an end and you would self-destruct if you ever told anyone about your addictive or co-dependent behavior and the damage it has caused. The fifth step powerfully demonstrates that another person can actually know about and understand your personal or family secret, without harshly judging you or rejecting you.

Of course, it is of the utmost importance to choose an appropriate person with whom to share your wrongs. First and foremost, you have to trust that person to keep whatever you say in his or her confidence. Next, because you won't find it easy to express the ways you injured yourself and others, you should choose someone with whom you already feel comfortable. And, since feedback plays an important part in your fifth-step work, try to choose someone who will be tough enough to truthfully tell you what he or she thinks and feels about your admissions.

Most of our patients prefer to take the fifth step with another member of their recovery group or with the group as a whole. By this time, they have grown to trust their fellow group members, know that they can offer honest feedback, often based on similar experiences of their own. For the same reasons, you too may choose to take the fifth step with someone in your recovery group.

However, we caution you *not* to select another sex addict or co-dependent who is not in recovery or who is just beginning his or her own recovery. Such a person is the worst possible choice, as Bill discovered. As we mentioned earlier, Bill initially felt drawn to the SA group members who were least committed to recovery. Merely going through the motions himself, he at first chose to share his wrongs with these buddies, who of course assured him that the injuries he had inflicted were no big deal, that his behavior was not that much of a problem. For Bill, these "partners in crime" actually gave him more encouragement to act out, instead of providing the feedback and support he needed to pursue his recovery.

To avoid making the same mistake, select someone you respect, preferably someone further along in recovery than you, whose feedback will carry more weight. His or her acceptance of you—flaws and all— effectively teaches you that you can safely interact with others honestly, instead of always trying to manipulate them or convince them that your carefully constructed façade is who you really are.

In addition, you will give up any illusions about being able to manipulate your Higher Power. You simply cannot fool God, if God is your Higher Power. And if you regard a group of your peers as your Higher Power, you will quickly find out that you can't fool them either, since they have already been where you are now.

What's more, as you describe your actions and attitudes to others, they become real to all of you and harder to deny or justify. The fifth step gets you to see the damage done by your addiction or co-dependency more clearly and concretely. This tangible proof of past insanity, as well as the unconditional acceptance of at least one respected confidant, strengthens your determination *not* to repeat your past mistakes and motivates you to try harder than ever *not* to blow your recovery.

The Sixth Step: [We] Were entirely ready to have our Higher Power remove all these defects of character.

The first five steps toward recovery change you, making you, among other things, more honest with yourself and others. They also instill in you a desire to be even better, making you aware of the need for *more* change. By the time you reach the sixth step, you are able to identify what you are feeling at any particular moment, to recognize the emotions, attitudes, and events that used to trigger your compulsive or co-dependent behavior, and to experience new feelings and new relationships that were impossible for you to maintain in the past—all of which contribute to your desire *not* to let your compulsiveness victimize you in the future.

The awareness developed during the first five steps gets you ready for a new way of life. The sixth step poses the question of how ready you really are. It asks:

- Are you really ready to do something about the problem?
- Are you willing to abandon the self-destructive defense mechanisms that sabotaged your previous efforts to change and the obsessions that made your life unmanageable?
- Are you prepared to actually accept the help necessary to repair the damage done by addiction or co-dependency?

The first five steps encouraged you to become a more detached and objective observer of your own defects and thus paved the way for lasting change. But actually changing compulsive or co-dependent behavior requires even more hard work.

When "entirely ready" to change, you no longer need to resist the force of your Higher Power. If you have not yet done so, during the sixth step, you will abandon the thought that "I should be able to do this on my own." Look back on all those times when you struggled to change on your own. You cannot help but see that, despite your best efforts, you returned again and again to your self-destructive behavior patterns.

You first surrendered your life and will to a Higher Power when you took the third step. The sixth step represents a new level of surrender: taking a hard look at how you resist change and abandoning those old familiar defense mechanisms in favor of more open, courageous attitudes toward change. Old habits and unproductive ways of thinking die hard, however. You may be tempted to continue blaming others for all of your problems, for example. But as long as you do that, you cannot truly recover. The sixth step asks you to *stop* thinking that "I can't help being who I am and doing what I do. The things other people did to me and the way life treated me made me what I am today, and I'm stuck with that." It encourages you to *start* thinking that "Perhaps I was treated badly and maybe given a raw deal, but that does not mean I have to stay the way I am. I can look at myself honestly today and with the help of my Higher Power be different and better than I used to be."

The sixth step reminds you that, even though you may have allowed it to do so in the past, compulsive behavior does *not* define your entire identity. The disease of sex addiction or co-dependency and the flaws you recognize in your character are *parts* of you, not *all* of you. They are defects, not the end-all and be-all of who you really are.

With the fourth and fifth steps, you identified and revealed to others the games you play and the defense mechanisms that keep you tangled up in your addiction or co-dependency. These are the defective or unhealthy parts of your personality and your lifestyle. You may no longer want them, but you are probably reluctant to give them up, nonetheless. As destructive as they have proved to be, they are your only known survival tools, and the thought of going on without them naturally makes you feel anxious and afraid. The sixth step gets you to face your fears head-on, as you ask yourself:

- When I no longer have compulsive or co-dependent behavior to fall back on, how will I cope with stress?
- If I give up my flawed but familiar patterns, what will sustain me as I struggle to live my life and deal with everyday problems?
- Do I really trust the strength of a power greater than myself to get me over the rough spots while I learn new ways to think and act?

Answering yes to the last question lets you take on new challenges with a more relaxed attitude and more willingly give up the character flaws that locked you into your addiction or co-dependency.

The Seventh Step: [We] Humbly asked our Higher Power to remove our shortcomings.

Like the third step, the seventh step, though it may seem to encourage passive resignation, requires action on your part. The seventh step is not a quick fix. Your problems and shortcomings will not disappear with the snap of a finger, just because you ask your Higher Power to remove them. Praying to God, if that's the way you conceive of your Higher Power, offers an alternative to obsessively worrying about your problems and compulsively acting in ways that make problems worse instead of better. However, it does not remove your responsibility to do everything within *your* power to change.

Indeed, in order to get better, you must do what *you* can while letting others do what they can. To recover, you will need the assistance you ask for and receive from a Higher Power, combined with what you do for yourself and the help you accept from other people. The humility that is one of the cornerstones of the Twelve Steps program must be balanced with self-assertion—the determination to do your part in your own recovery. Tipping the scales either way—exaggerating the importance of yourself or of others—can undermine your recovery instead of furthering it. In increasing your humility, you do not get rid of your self-determination entirely. You do give up the self-centered control that has characterized your past behavior.

In fact, one of the major goals of recovery is to move away from the self-centeredness of addiction or the selflessness of co-dependency and move toward *healthy selfishness*. But how do you define, no less adopt, such an attitude? To begin with, realize that there is very little that we do that is not essentially selfish. When you get right down to it, human beings are generally motivated by their own self-interest—a normal, acceptable motivation as far as we, as psychologists, see it. In fact, as we mentioned earlier, recovery itself must be motivated by self-interest if it is to succeed. Sex addicts who pursue recovery to placate others, or because they are pressured into it, and co-dependents who do not want to change themselves, but instead hope their actions will make their partners change, rarely, if ever, get better.

On the other hand, like anything else, self-interest can be taken to extremes, becoming the sort of self-centeredness that leads you to believe you have omnipotent powers or are in control of everything all the time—and therefore have the right to do whatever you want regardless of the consequences. That attitude must change if you intend to recover from sex addiction or co-dependency.

Such an attitude change was crucial for Hank, who, through his seventh-step work, has begun to develop a sense of accountability and responsibility he never before possessed. He is beginning to realize that the world does not owe him a great life and that he cannot mope around or indulge his compulsions every time he does not get exactly what he wants. "I am trying to have some discipline," he explains, "and find the courage to tackle all these things. I would love to be able to view myself as a courageous person who does what it takes, does the right things to get whatever I'm after. I'm trying not to expect things to just happen, and at the same time, trying not to give up too soon and resign myself to living without them."

In addition, the seventh step helps you to strike a balance between what you can do to advance your recovery and what you must leave to your Higher Power. Drawing upon the wisdom of the Serenity Prayer, this step asks you to muster "the courage to change the things you can," while humbly trusting your Higher Power and others to do the rest. It gives you your first opportunity not to behave in the old manner, not to react the way you used to react. You now have the option to act in accordance with the will of a Higher Power.

Finally, relying on a Higher Power gives you a sense of security, reducing the fears and negative self-talk that kept you stuck in your addiction or co-dependency. Relieved of these, and able to pray or talk honestly with others instead of focusing on your obsessions or acting out your compulsions, you move forward on the road to recovery.

The Eighth Step: [We] Made a list of all persons we had harmed, and became willing to make amends to them all.

Asking you to identify the actual damage you inflicted upon yourself and others while in the throes of addiction or co-dependency, the eighth step both reinforces the idea that you are accountable for your past actions and motivates you to change your harmful attitudes and behaviors. In taking this step, you finally face your mistakes and accept responsibility for them, paving the way to overcome the guilt and shame that alienated you from others and kept addiction or co-dependency alive.

Through eighth-step work, you learn to stop running from responsibility, to stop hiding your shame behind compulsive or co-dependent behavior. When your disease controlled your behavior, you bottled up the guilt you felt for having hurt someone else, frequently turning it inside out and developing resentment toward that person. You then used your resentment as an excuse to continue your original behavior, getting caught up in a vicious, virtually inescapable cycle.

The eighth step shows you how to release yourself from this trap, *replacing the urge to resent the people you have harmed with a productive outlet for alleviating the guilt that feeds your resentment.*

Also, in the past, when the time came to face someone you had harmed or to accept the consequences of your actions, you ran away from responsibility and even entirely withdrew from relationships. However, as you now surely recognize, this type of withdrawal did not improve matters at all. Indeed, it only created ever more powerful fears of abandonment and rejection. With the eighth step as a guide, you can now work through your resentments and attempt to resolve your problems *within* your relationships instead of trying to deny or escape both through compulsive or co-dependent behavior.

In listing those injured by your compulsive behavior, remember to include *yourself* as well as others. You must be willing to make amends to yourself, too: by not being as hard on yourself as you have been in the past, and by resolving to stay in recovery and avoid relapses.

It is also important to guard against letting the list of people you have harmed destroy your newly restored sense of self-esteem. Keep in mind that, yes, through your past behavior, you *have* hurt other people, *but* in most instances, you will be able to make amends and, even more important, be able to avoid repeating those mistakes again and again. You cannot reverse your past actions, but you can talk directly with some of those people you hurt in the past, heal old wounds, complete unfinished business, and resolve to discontinue past practices. In doing this, you keep history from repeating itself and begin to overcome the guilt and self-loathing left over from your old way of life.

The Ninth Step: [We] Made direct amends to such people wherever possible, except when to do so would injure them or others.

Having identified both the people you harmed and the ways you harmed them, you reach the ninth step, which asks you to go to those people directly, admit your mistakes, and attempt to repair whatever damage you have done. Of course, all of us wish we could simply go back and change the past, rewriting history so that painful events never happened at all. But you live in the real world now. In recovery, you no longer pretend that your ideal fantasies are reality. You face facts, gratefully acknowledging that, even though you cannot change the past, you *can* do something about the present and future. One of those facts is that the ninth step will not be easy.

"I finally told my wife some significant truths about what had gone on over the years," Hank says with a sigh of relief. "She knew I had been unfaithful to her, but she didn't know how often. I even told her about the episodes with men in the porno movie places. There was a time I couldn't imagine ever telling her those things, but I did. I felt I had to. It was tough, but we got through it."

It is truly difficult and takes an enormous amount of courage to approach someone you've hurt and admit the error of your ways. Although the ninth step should involve face-to-face communication whenever possible, you may be tempted to find an easier, softer way to do it, by writing a letter, for example. You can write that letter as a way of collecting your thoughts, but if you want to truly reap the benefits of the ninth step, you will sit down face to face with those you've harmed. If you try, but still cannot get out the words, hand the person what you have previously written, explaining, "I'd like you to read this, because I can write it more clearly than I know how to say it."

Whether you speak them out loud or write them, simply confessing your sins directly to those you've harmed will *not* in itself repair the damage done. Your words of contrition are only a starting point for further discussion. Find out how the person feels about what he or she has just read or heard. Answer questions, and elaborate on what you were able to say or put down on paper. Remember that making amends involves more than uttering apologies. A commitment to change your behavior is required as well.

Obviously, you may never be able to fix *everything* you did, but you *can* repair some of the damage that resulted from your addiction or co-dependency. Merely acknowledging that you hurt someone won't take away the pain, for example. However, if you admit you inflicted that pain *and* share what you know about your disease, while still accepting responsibility for your actions and allowing the person to express his or her feelings, you can open a line of communication and begin to improve the relationship between the two of you.

But please, take care not to expect too much in return. You only have the power to openly acknowledge the harm you have caused in the past and to do your best to behave differently in the future. You *cannot* control the way other people respond or react to your past actions or your present attempts to make amends. Realistically speaking, you will not be able to rebuild all of your relationships. Some of the people you've hurt in the past will no longer want to have a relationship with you. And the people who do want to continue their relationships with you may very well need time and support—and lots of both—before they are able to forgive you or trust you again.

But then, the amends you make when you take the ninth step should *not* be made in order to get something in return. The purpose of making amends is to validate and, if possible, ease the *other people's* pain.

Keep the above priority in mind when trying to decide whether or not it is appropriate to made amends directly. If confessing to the harm you've done will make *you* feel better, but make another person feel worse, do not inflict further damage on that person. If trying to rectify past wrongs will prove destructive to another person in any way, don't do it. For example, it would be detrimental (and dumb) to go up to a friend—or even a stranger—and say, "I'm really sorry, but I slept with your husband" or "I slept with your wife, but it's all over now. I hope you aren't hurt."

On the other hand, do not employ rationalizations to convince yourself to avoid making direct amends when they truly need to be made. To make sure you are not copping out, we recommend asking your therapist or another self-help group member for advice.

If you can't directly address the person you've harmed, you can still release your own disabling guilt. If making amends to someone directly would cause more harm than good, use a surrogate—someone else—to hear your admissions. In the confidential, trusting atmosphere of a therapy session or a self-help group, confessing to the damage you have done will allow you to demonstrate that you aren't simply justifying your fear of facing the person, and it will also help you get beyond your guilt. This is especially important when the person you've harmed has died. Obviously, you cannot talk to that person directly or actually do anything to repair your relationship with him or her. Yet, you can still talk through these issues with someone who understands and cares about you, and thus avoid repeating your past mistakes in your future relationships with others.

The Tenth Step: [We] Continued to take personal inventory and when we were wrong promptly admitted it.

Recovery is a lifelong process. The tenth step is the first of three steps that solidify your commitment to a new way of life, bolstering your determination to deal in new ways with yourself, your Higher Power, and other people.

Realistic and pragmatic, Twelve Steps programs take into account the fact that people in recovery sometimes slip and backslide. The tenth step, which encourages you to take daily inventories of your actions and emotions, helps halt slips and backslides before they become full-blown relapses. Bill explains that "I take daily spot-check inventories of myself to look out for any signs that I'm trying to manage too many things myself, or slipping into any of my old patterns. I try to find out if I'm feeling angry or resentful or fearful or pressured or frustrated or lonely, because any of that could set me off, get me to act out again. If I know what's happening, I can do something more constructive about it."

When you do encounter the inevitable slip-up—in emotion, attitude, or behavior—it's important *not* to say, "Well, that's it. I'm back where I started. I might as well just give up." Instead, if you stumble during the course of your recovery, stand up, brush yourself off, and look back at the distance you have already covered. Think of emotional or behavioral slips—falling back on old patterns—as signs telling you to return to one of the earlier steps and work through it again. Perhaps you need to redo the third step, to work harder at giving up your willfulness. Still clinging to a character defect, maybe you need additional work on the sixth and seventh steps. Or you may need to review your fourth-step inventory— something the tenth step encourages you to do regularly.

Although you can expect to slip up occasionally and slide back into old habits at least once during your recovery, you will not lose all you've gained and wind up scraping bottom again if you promptly admit your

247

wrongs and seek additional help *immediately after any and all slips*. By taking the tenth step, you no longer keep the self-destructive secrets that imprisoned you in your past behavior patterns. In addition, taking regular personal inventories helps you stay honest—with yourself and others.

"Honesty and humility are what make my program work," Bill acknowledges. "Honesty is the biggest thing. Before, I would hide everything, keep it all to myself. Whatever I did, peeping or whatever, I wouldn't own up to it. I'd look straight at people and lie . . . Now, I just face people and square things with them before it all gets out of hand."

As Bill discovered, honest self-examination keeps you in touch with the feelings that can trigger undesirable behavior. And redressing wrongs immediately improves your relationships with others, demonstrating the credibility and integrity that allow them to trust you.

Having already learned how to deal with your past mistakes in a constructive way, you can do the same with your current slip-ups—as soon as they occur. Recovery proceeds slowly and imperfectly: one day at a time, one step at a time, one choice at a time. If you deal with your mistakes as soon as you make them, you won't refill your warehouse of guilt and negativity.

"If you stop working on your program when you start slipping, it's easy to get back into all your old behaviors," Bill warns, sharing a lesson he learned through experience. "I slipped all over the place at first. It took me a long time to figure some things out. Now, if I harm someone in some way, I make amends to that person right away. Then I can go on with my daily living, instead of spending a whole lot of time being worked up about my mistakes and wanting to do something I shouldn't, just to get away from the pressure and the guilt."

For Bill and countless other recovering addicts and co-dependents, taking the tenth step gave them a way to pull themselves out of backslides instead of pushing themselves further into them.

The Eleventh Step: [We] Sought through prayer and meditation to improve our conscious contact with our Higher Power, as we understood Him, Her, or It, praying only for knowledge of our Higher Power's will for us and the power to carry that out.

Taking the eleventh step makes your relationship with your Higher Power part of your day-to-day life, in much the same way that the tenth step got you to incorporate inventory taking and admitting your wrongs into everyday life. Many of our patients had to go back and redo their second and third steps before they were able to take the eleventh, reminding themselves that their Higher Power had been there for them even before they asked for help, and reinforcing their conscious awareness that they are not alone.

The eleventh step asks you once again to examine your perception of your Higher Power. Do not be surprised if regularly thinking about the existence of and your relationship with a Higher Power prompts you to think about a lower power as well. Life in recovery is a constant struggle between the part of you that wants to do healthy, constructive things and the part that wants immediate gratification of every need. To sustain your recovery, you must constantly be on the lookout for the impatience to get what you want instantly and the frustration you feel whenever your schemes are thwarted. Taking the eleventh step means that, instead of allowing the lower power to determine your actions—as you did when your sex addiction or co-dependency held sway—you appeal to that Higher Power within you and surrender to its will when making decisions today.

"I'm not trying to push anything on anybody. But every morning I say the Serenity Prayer, Hail Mary, and the Lord's Prayer," Bill says. "I just try to have a peaceful minute to myself. And for some reason, when I don't take that time, I seem to have a lot more problems all during that day. But when I do, it seems to get me off on the right track." For Bill, this daily ritual of prayer and meditation replaced his negative ritual of compulsive behavior. Although Bill, reared in the Catholic faith and still a Catholic today, naturally based his new ritual on his own religious beliefs, many recovering addicts and co-dependents have found similar motivational rituals to be helpful. Some read brief inspirational—although not necessarily religious—passages and contemplate their meaning, while others focus on some personal affirmations—positive self-talk that reinforces their sense of self-worth. In whatever form it takes, meditation and other efforts to strengthen your conscious connection with a Higher Power establish a positive, life-affirming ritual that can keep you from slipping back into your old, self-destructive habits.

The Twelfth Step: Having had a spiritual awakening as the result of these steps, we tried to carry this message to others and to practice these principles in all our affairs.

The twelfth step embodies the principle that made AA and all the Twelve Steps programs enormously successful in attracting and helping people with addictive and co-dependent behavior: the realization that the best way to help yourself recover is to reach out and offer help to someone else. The underlying message of the entire Twelve Steps program is that *"We are in this together."* And helping somebody else move toward or stay in recovery increases your ability to recover yourself. While helping others, you reaffirm the importance of your own recovery, and constantly remind yourself of all the things you need to do to continue moving in the right direction. As Bill sees it, "In the Twelve Steps program, I can help others, and know that they will help me when I need help. If I can make their struggle easier, I will, because that makes my struggle easier, too."

Because we have noticed time and time again that the help we give the patients who come to us for therapy ends up helping us live our own lives as well, we know firsthand that the twelfth step works. For one thing, while helping others work on their recovery, there is no way to avoid examining the issues that also apply to our own lives. And guiding our patients through the twelve steps—which we have learned work on life problems other than addiction and co-dependency—prepares us to

249

courageously take on new challenges, honestly acknowledge our own flaws, and more effectively and compassionately deal with other people. As therapists, we may be more tuned in to certain things than other people are, but the twelfth step has virtually the same healing effect on everyone who takes it.

Recovery through the Twelve Steps makes a tremendously positive impact on your life, and as a result, you naturally feel excited and eager to carry its message and share its miracles with others. However, your zeal, if not tempered by sensitivity to others' feelings, can sound like preaching. You may unwittingly lead others to think you are saying, "I am better than you." It is always best to tread lightly when introducing the Twelve Steps program to other people.

Discovering that you can have a positive impact on others and play a useful role in a community is healing in itself. Being an active part of something larger than yourself keeps the excitement of your recovery alive and makes the struggles you went through all the more meaningful. This effect was experienced by all of the recovering sex addicts and co-dependents who shared their personal stories with you through this book. When Bill, George, Hank, Molly, Cheryl, or Lynn sat in our office and spoke with the tape recorder running, they were doing twelfth-step work—sharing their experiences, strength, and hope with you, and possibly attracting you to the idea of pursuing recovery yourself.

Of course, the best way to work the twelfth step is to commit yourself to making *your* recovery a way of life. The most comprehensive of all the steps, the twelfth encompasses all of the others and outlines them as not merely a prescription for recovery from the specific problems of addiction or co-dependency, but as a guide to use in all of your affairs. This involves a commitment not to keep secrets anymore, to continue examining yourself and turning to your Higher Power and others for help, to promptly admit your wrongs, and to deal with yourself, others, and your Higher Power openly and honestly.

Taking the twelfth step naturally reminds you of all the work that is involved in recovery from addiction and co-dependency. It points out that recovery is a never-ending process, that no one who has been a sexual addict can ever honestly say, "I used to be a sex addict, but I'm not one anymore." The same holds true for co-dependents.

From the perspective of someone who has not yet begun working a recovery program, the tasks that lie ahead seem monumental, perhaps even impossible to achieve. Every recovering addict or co-dependent thought so before taking the first step. Yet, looking back on their recovery, those who stuck with it would not go back to their old ways. They have found sanity.

"I used to think that my life could only turn out one way," says George. "I mean, since puberty, I had been masturbating excessively. So by the age of twenty-four, I thought, 'Well, that's what I'm going to do for the rest of my life. I'll never be happy. I'll always be the way I am now.' What a tremendous relief it was to find out about recovery, to see that through the Twelve Steps and with help from other people, my life could be different."

12

FOR THE SEX ADDICT:
Tips for Staying on the Road to Recovery

The Twelve Steps described in the previous chapter will guide you on a lifelong journey down the road from sex addiction to recovery. Continued participation in a Twelve Steps recovery program, as well as individual or group therapy, will help you adjust to your new way of life. However, as we've mentioned before, the journey itself will not be easy, effortless, or without occasional setbacks. The roots of sex addiction—including negative self-talk, difficulty coping with stress, and dependence on sexual highs to feel good and escape the problems of daily living—date back to childhood and can undermine your best, most sincere efforts to change. Consequently, to achieve a full and lasting recovery, you must:

- Zero in on and revise your own negative self-talk, developing a more positive self-image and a more trusting vision of other people.
- Learn to recognize when you are feeling anxious, to identify the sources of stress in your life, and to use new coping skills, instead of relying on compulsive sexual rituals to relieve or release the tension you feel.
- Rethink your old ideas about sexual behavior and human sexuality, replacing your destructive attitudes and beliefs with constructive

ones and your unhealthy dependence on sexual highs with a healthy dependence on other people and a Higher Power.

In this chapter, we offer specific suggestions for achieving these goals as well as tips for making sure the inevitable slips and backslides do not steer you too far off your road to recovery.

IMPROVING SELF-TALK

When they take their initial steps toward recovery, most sex addicts are virtually drowning in a sea of negative self-talk. With the pain of hitting bottom still fresh in their minds, they can barely see beyond their problem. Day in and day out, they tell themselves, "I'm really sick," "I've been so stupid," or "I've hurt everyone close to me." Unlike the negative self-talk they tried to silence through compulsive sexual behavior, this self-talk is neither an overreaction to life in an imperfect world nor a distorted version of the messages they received from their parents during childhood. It is based on reality and, although quite painful, it is a sign of progress.

Identify and Affirm Your Positive Qualities

After years of denial, now, for the first time, you are viewing sex addiction realistically. Unfortunately, acknowledging the impact addiction has had on every area of your life will dredge up some distressing thoughts and feelings that will overwhelm you *if you let them*. To endure this period of extremely negative self-talk, you must remind yourself of your positive qualities and try to come to the same conclusion Don arrived at: "Maybe I'm not such a bad person after all," he declared several months after joining our Thursday-night therapy group. "I have done a lot of good things in addition to the bad things."

Here is an exercise to help you recall your own positive qualities and begin to improve your self-image. On a blank piece of paper, write five or ten times "I am _____" and as many times "I am a good _____." Then, fill in the blanks with *your* individual strengths, writing positive statements such as:

"I am getting better."
"I am a good listener, understanding, and sympathetic."
"I am more than just sex and lust."
"I am a good friend."
"I am an okay person."
"I am worthwhile."
"I am lovable."

Deafened by the roar of your own negative self-talk, at first, you may strain and struggle to come up with even one admirable trait to list. But keep trying until you come up with at least half a dozen—preferably

RECOVERING FROM SEX ADDICTION

more—positive things to say about yourself. Putting your positive qualities into words helps you recognize that you are many things besides a sex addict—you are also a parent, a spouse, a friend, a son or daughter, a brother or sister, an employee or an employer, a citizen, and so on. Although sex addiction may have had an impact on some or all of these areas, in nearly every instance, you have done good things in these areas as well. And, through your recovery efforts, you have the ability to be even better, as Bill's list of positive attributes reflects.

"I am feeling better about myself through the work I've been doing," Bill wrote. "I am building my self-esteem. I am more self-confident than I used to be. I am able to recognize that I have some talents and abilities. I am not constantly putting myself down anymore, and I am not negative about other people. I am someone whom other people like, and I am able to make new friends."

To make the words you have written more real to you and more powerful, after completing your list, read it aloud. Share it with your therapist or members of your recovery group, people who will verify and support your good points—and perhaps suggest a few more. And the most healing use of this list is to keep it or memorize it, reaffirming your strengths by going over and adding to the list each day or anytime you are feeling especially negative about yourself.

An All-Purpose Affirmation: *"I deserve to recover."*

Because hitting bottom leaves you feeling hopeless and helpless, you may have to tell yourself over and over again that your life is *worth* restoring. Yes, you do have a serious problem, and yes, over the years it injured you and others. *But you are not beyond help.* You have the right to try to feel better. You *deserve* a chance to recover. Seek help and stick with it, even if your partner is unwilling to get help, too, or discontinues his or her treatment soon after beginning it. The advice we give codependents applies to sex addicts as well: get help *for yourself,* through self-help groups and/or professional therapy. *You* deserve to escape the cycle of sex addiction.

WHEN YOU DO SOMETHING TO HELP YOURSELF, YOU FEEL BETTER ABOUT YOURSELF

Entering a recovery program and starting to change your behavior in turn changes your self-image. You prove to yourself that, although you are powerless over your lust, you *do* have the power to seek help and use it to recover. "I can do something about this addiction. I can break old habits and live without old rituals," you realize—and that feeling does wonders to improve your self-talk. In addition, in recovery you learn things about yourself that contradict your previous point of view.

"I used to think that I was really awkward and inept when it came to talking to people," Mitch admits. "It was what I honestly believed at one time, but I found out it wasn't true. I saw how people in this group actually liked me and thought I was basically an okay guy. They even told me I was pretty articulate and interesting. Therapy helped me realize that, in general, most people who meet me like me, and now I sort of like me. I didn't think I ever would.''

The Twelve Steps recovery program itself helps change your self-talk. Taking a complete fourth-step inventory, one that lists your strengths as well as your weaknesses, does this directly, but each of the other steps also improves your self-image in one way or another. The ninth step, for example, which allows you to make amends to people you have harmed in the past, reinforces the idea that you have the ability and strength of character to make a situation better. Building a relationship with your Higher Power and the people in your recovery group increases self-worth by eliminating loneliness, isolation, and doubts about your ability to get along with other people, while the twelfth step shows you that you can actually be a positive role model for others. Indeed, each of the twelve steps helps you restructure your self-talk, which in turn helps you put compulsive sexual rituals behind you.

Of course, your self-talk, like your recovery itself, will have its ups and downs. Self-criticism, put-downs, and pessimism are habits that won't change overnight. Be patient and, whenever you feel yourself slipping into old patterns of negative thinking, reach for your list of positive attributes and work with it.

Don't Make Promises You Can't Keep

While in the grip of sex addiction, you repeatedly promised to change and broke every promise you made to yourself and to others. This made it impossible for others to trust you or for you to trust yourself. Moreover, each broken promise turned up the volume on your negative self-talk, reinforcing your feelings of inadequacy. You will begin to trust yourself again and stop reneging on your commitment to change, once you learn *not* to promise more than you can deliver.

In fact, all you can really promise is to follow your recovery program, one day at a time. If you keep that promise, your increased honesty with yourself and others, your changed attitudes and behavior, and your abandonment of compulsive sexual rituals will make you truly trustworthy for the first time in years.

Don't Expect Too Much Too Soon

As a rule, most sex addicts set unreasonably high expectations for themselves, and judge themselves quite harshly each time they fail to meet those standards. If you, too, expect perfection or set unrealistic goals for yourself, you are setting yourself up for a fall. You are not perfect. You will always fail to achieve perfection and be frustrated by your own failure. This frustration may very well drive you back to old behaviors, flaunting in your face yet another broken promise and another reason not to trust yourself. So, instead of trying to be perfect, work on feeling more comfortable with yourself as you really are and really can be—imperfect but constantly improving.

Listen to Your Gut Feelings

"In my recovery, the biggest thing I've learned about myself is that I can trust my own instincts," George explains. "Everything I think or feel is not weird or sick. In fact, if I pay attention to my feelings, how I'm responding emotionally to certain situations, I can almost always figure out how to handle that situation. My feelings usually tell me what is the best thing to do."

As George shared his emotions with others in his recovery group, he began to see that they weren't as weird, or as dangerous, as he had once believed. Others had the same fears and feelings. You will, no doubt, make the same discovery. And, as you become more tuned in to your own feelings, you will learn, as George did, that they can help you make decisions about how to behave in various situations.

If you feel anxious, for instance, that will alert you to look for and deal with whatever might be causing your anxiety. Feeling sad or angry—so-called negative emotions, which you once believed were "bad" to feel at all—almost always point to a problem within yourself or in one of your relationships. Knowing this, you can address that problem, before it reaches crisis proportions.

Accept That Other People Are Imperfect, Too

True recovery from sex addiction requires a new outlook about the world around you and the people in it. A partial shift in your attitude happens automatically. As you come to recognize your own self-worth, you also begin to appreciate the fact that others have intrinsic worth, as well—even though they, like you, are not perfect.

Before beginning your recovery, you, like many sex addicts, tended to judge others harshly, expecting them to live up to the same unrealistic standards that you had set for yourself. But, other people are imperfect, too. They also have their faults. Life is not just a struggle for *you;* it's a struggle for everyone, and no one meets all of life's challenges flawlessly. Everybody makes mistakes. To improve your relationships with other people—and your own self-talk about your ability to get along with others—you must learn to let them make those mistakes, and stop condemning them for not being what neither you nor they can be: perfect.

A Little Compassion Goes a Long, Long Way

"Through SA, I found out that many, many people have addictions, unhealthy relationships, and compulsive tendencies," Hank acknowledges. "Before, when I had my holier-than-thou attitude, I would have looked at them and acted disgusted or judgmental. Now, I feel for them. I know what they're going through."

As it did for Hank, being part of a self-help or therapy group teaches you that other people also have problems, both similar to and different from your own. You begin to realize that, like you, other people are *more* than their flaws. And most importantly, through your experiences with others in recovery, you learn how to respond compassionately to other people when they are in pain or having problems, lessons you can then apply to your life and your relationships outside the group.

Define Your Own Place in the World

Sex addicts often believe that everybody knows their secret and judges them harshly because of this knowledge. In recovery, they find out that they are *not* the focus of everybody's attention, that the world does *not* revolve around them and their problems. As part of your recovery, you must realize this, too.

Other people have their own worries and interests. Your problem is not a priority in their lives, as Don learned. "Talking to everybody about my problems isn't right," he says. "It makes some people uncomfortable, because they have to cover up themselves, pretend they don't understand or don't have problems themselves. But that's okay. It's better than what I used to think, which was that people wanted to know, that they speculated about it behind my back and were always keeping an eye on me. Of course, that was all in my own mind."

In fact, most people have little interest in keeping an eye on you so that they can criticize or judge you. What's more, very few people, if you give them the chance to understand you, will label you a pervert or a weirdo. You simply must give up the old idea that "Everybody is out to get me." Involvement with a self-help recovery group will help you see that this bit of negative self-talk simply is not true. In fact, you will hear new self-talk saying, "Other people are valuable to me," and even, "There are some compassionate, nurturing people in my world, available to help and encourage me."

Life Isn't a Prizefight

"I know now that I don't have the right to put people through bad stuff, and they don't have the right to put me through bad stuff," Hank concedes. "I used to think people had the right to push me around and hurt me. I was always waiting for them to do that, always on the defensive, waiting for them to throw the next punch."

Hank went through life with his "dukes up," and saw himself as fending off one opponent after another. Yet, when you set yourself up against the world, the way Hank used to do, you at best win a battle or two, only to inevitably lose the war. If you truly want to rid yourself of destructive self-talk, you must take a less adversarial, less hostile view of others, recognizing their good qualities and affirming them in much the same way you identified your own strengths through the exercise we included earlier in this chapter.

In fact, you may want to try the following exercise with the people in your life with whom you are the closest, starting perhaps with your spouse or partner. Sit facing each other, and take turns saying what you like about yourselves and what you like about each other. Someone who cares about you may see some good qualities that you have overlooked. In turn, you are able to see more of the good in someone you once feared would hurt or abandon you, as well as to strengthen the relationship between you. Although, for the sake of your recovery, neither of you should depend too heavily on the other person's assessment to determine your own self-image, you will decrease hostility by looking at each other's positive attributes. Again, old habits die hard, and if doing this exercise seems unappealing, or you fear it will lead to an argument instead of greater closeness, you need not do it or can choose to do it in the presence of a therapist.

You will also dispel the myth that you stand alone in opposition to the rest of the world if you extend the same openness and honesty you practice within your recovery group to people outside. Indeed, you just might find that other people also treat you kindly and can also be supportive. If you give others a chance, you may even be able to honestly admit that "I am loved and accepted by others."

Adopt a More Forgiving Attitude

"I keep hearing that I had a miserable childhood, but now I'm an adult, and it's my choice to be miserable or not to be. Well, I don't get it. When did it become all my fault?" Robin's words, spoken bitterly soon after she began treatment for both her sex addiction and an eating disorder, reflect a struggle common to all recovering addicts.

Robin, who had an alcoholic father and a chronically ill mother, has many legitimate reasons for feeling angry—and *your* anger or resentment at your parents, your spouse or lover, your children, or anyone else may be justifiable also. You certainly have a right to express such feelings and an obligation to work through them. Yet, there comes a time when you simply have to stop blaming other people for all of your problems and stop using what others did or still do to you as an excuse for indulging in compulsive sexual rituals. If you want to get better, you must devote your energy to correcting *your own* defects, instead of concentrating endlessly on the faults of others. Events that occurred in the past and the actions of others today are beyond your control. Turn them over to your Higher Power and get on with your recovery. Replace finger pointing with forgiveness: the same forgiveness that you hope to receive from those you've harmed.

Mitch, whose father physically abused him throughout his childhood, also has plenty of reasons to feel angry. However, because his sex addiction forced him to seek help, Mitch was able to acknowledge and then release his anger, allowing him to accept his father as "a human being who was doing the best he could under the circumstances." While his siblings still can't stand to be near their dad, Mitch, through hard work and dedication to recovery, is able to say and believe, "I am worthwhile. Others are worthwhile. The world is worthwhile."

A Few Words about Trusting Others

More often than not, the people you care about also care about you. Trusting them enough to let them show it, however, will not be easy. Chances are that you spent your childhood and lived your adult life believing that you could "Trust nobody." Indeed, just the thought of trusting other people frightens you—perhaps convincing you not to try. But try you must.

Building trust, like recovery itself, is best taken one small step at a time—first daring to trust your therapist or the other people in your recovery group, then rehearsing interactions that involve trust. For instance, in the safe environment of our therapy groups, we sometimes stage role-playing exercises, rehearsing a real-life situation with other members of the group standing in for specific people in a given patient's life. After running through the scene, group members join us in providing honest feedback about what we have seen, offering encouragement and advice, and sharing our own experiences of similar situations. This kind of exercise gives sex addicts an opportunity to practice and develop the communication skills they will use when they actually risk trusting another person.

Really putting yourself on the line and trusting someone else is indeed a risk and takes an enormous amount of courage. Because you cannot control that other person's actions or reactions, you are obviously leaving yourself wide open to the ridicule, rejection, or abandonment that terrifies you. In fact, if you are like most sex addicts, you have spent most of your life trying to avoid this sort of vulnerability. Now, you want and need honest human relationships. The problem is that they all carry with them the possibility of being hurt. Recognizing the dangers involved, you muster your courage and move forward in spite of your fears.

But please, take intelligent risks. Choose carefully—especially at first—those with whom you will risk vulnerability. During the early, often shaky stages of recovery, the safest people to trust with important facts about yourself are your therapist, members of your support or therapy group, or your partner if he or she is actively seeking recovery from co-dependency.

Once you have learned that you can trust the people who know about or share your problems, try trusting people outside this small circle, again proceeding slowly and recognizing that building trust involves a step-by-step process. Be patient. Share yourself prudently, while you discover through experience whom you can and cannot trust. The "Don't trust" rule that governed your childhood kept you trapped in the cycle of sex addiction for many years, but blindly trusting everyone is not the answer either, as Bill discovered. "It feels so good to finally get things out in the open that sometimes I feel like telling everybody I know," he explains. "I've got to tell myself, 'Wait a second, pull yourself together.

You can't say this stuff to just anybody. You're going to blow somebody away.' ''

When you come across someone who proves to be untrustworthy, it is going to hurt. But don't let one or even several bad experiences convince you that you will never be able to trust anyone or even that the specific person who failed you can *never* be trusted at all. Remind yourself that you had the courage to risk trusting somebody else in the first place—no matter how a particular situation turns out.

Each risk you take makes it easier to take another. Eventually your old "Don't trust" self-talk will give way to a fresh new idea, one repeatedly verified by real-life experience. You will come to believe, "I can share myself with others."

COPING WITH STRESS

You will be making a grave error if you think that *all of your problems will disappear just because you are recovering from sex addiction*. In fact, most addicts find that immediately after abandoning their compulsive rituals, coping with the stresses of daily living is even tougher and more painful than ever before.

Grief

When you discontinue your compulsive sexual rituals, you lose the defense mechanism that once protected you from the realities of your life, the false shield you once used to ward off pain and anxiety. For perhaps the first time in your life, you must face the reality of both old and new problems, without your first line of defense to protect you. Until you learn new coping skills, you will feel a strange, nagging emptiness— a real loss. You will also experience both profound sadness and deep anger over having to give up your sexual highs. Although self-destructive, they did bring at least momentary pleasure and were a big part of your life.

Turn to your self-help or therapy group for the support you most definitely need while you mourn the loss of your compulsive rituals. People who have already gone through this stage of recovery will let you know that they too felt and survived the anger or depression, irritability or moodiness, that you will experience as you learn to live without sexual highs. Knowing that they got through this stage will help you get through it, too. And once you get beyond your grief, they can suggest ways to deal with stress without resurrecting your compulsive sexual rituals.

Recognize the Stress in Your Own Life

Before you can employ new coping strategies, you must learn to recognize anxious feelings and identify sources of stress in your life. Sometimes stress can be easily traced to specific situations—job pressures or a family crisis, for instance—but many sex addicts also experience a more nebulous, free-floating anxiety. As George puts it, "I can usually tell that I'm stressed out, but I don't always know why." Yet, by carefully observing your emotional responses, you will often find that even this generalized anxiety springs from a specific source.

Pay attention to "bad" feelings and the reappearance of any old impulses or cravings. Review the events that occurred over the past few hours or the past few days. Did they put pressure on you? Did they remind you of similar situations, ones that turned out disastrously in the past? Did they resemble events or interactions that used to occur in your family during childhood? By asking yourself such questions, you gain a better understanding of how events, even the ones that seem insignificant at first glance, can produce stress and tension.

Reduce Day-to-Day Pressures

Once you are able to identify the sources of stress in your life, you may decide to reduce day-to-day pressures by avoiding certain stressful situations or even making major changes in the way you live your life.

"Professionally, I've always gotten better jobs than I was qualified for," Todd now realizes. "That was really stressful because I constantly felt like I was in over my head and that people were going to find out I didn't really know what I was doing. I've been looking for a new job where I can start out just learning the job and later move into a management role. I want to have a solid base to work from, instead of going straight to the top and blowing it."

Like Todd, many recovering sex addicts, in order to reduce work-related stress, choose to change jobs, especially if their present job involves spending time alone in a car or in out-of-town hotel rooms. Such settings, which triggered sexual fantasies and rituals in the past, are just too tempting and stressful for most sex addicts to handle. Holding down such a job might very well jeopardize their recovery—which is why Bill, who used time spent in his car to fantasize and cruise around looking for prostitutes, realized it would be foolhardly to keep his position as a Health Department inspector and asked to be transferred to a desk job within the department. Just as recovering alcoholics stop going into bars and compulsive gamblers stay away from casinos, recovering sex addicts must identify and, whenever possible, avoid the places that triggered their sexual rituals, as well as circumstances that create undue stress—so that they are not tempted to cope through sexual behavior.

Reduce the Pressure You Put on Yourself

Of course, you probably put more pressure on yourself than other people or external events ever could. The day-to-day stress everyone experiences quickly gets out of hand when magnified by your own internal reaction to it. Particularly stressful is the expectation of doing more than humanly possible and doing it perfectly—a lesson Bill learned with the help of his therapist and his support group.

"I have this tendency to make these long lists of things to get done during the day," he acknowledges. "They get too long, and I can't finish everything the way I want to. Until recently, it never occurred to me to set some things aside to do another day. Now, I try to do that, because I really get myself into trouble when I forget that I can only get so much done in one day."

Once again, a group of understanding people can save you from the stress you create for yourself without knowing it. They will notice that you are falling back into your old patterns before you do, point out the ways in which you set yourself up to fail in your relationships or other situations, and constantly remind you that you don't have to do *everything* perfectly or all by yourself.

Learn New Relationship Skills

If you are a sex addict, relationships have always been a source of stress in your life. Giving up the sexual highs you once used to cope with that stress initially leaves you feeling even more anxious than you felt before. You can no longer rely on a co-dependent to bend over backward to meet all of your needs. You cannot continue the self-absorption that kept you isolated from other people and allowed you to live in your own little fantasy world. And you must be careful not to indulge your own co-dependent tendencies.

As children, most sex addicts observed both compulsive and co-dependent strategies for dealing with the tension in their homes. When they reject compulsive behavior as a coping mechanism, they are tempted to fall back on their second line of defense: co-dependent behaviors, such as assuming responsibility that is not theirs, excessively worrying about pleasing others, attempting to manage other people's lives, or trying to rescue others. As any recovering co-dependent can tell you, these strategies work no better than addictive ones.

Instead, to reduce tension in your personal relationships, learn to treat other people as equals deserving of respect and compassion, neither accepting responsibility for all of their problems or blaming them for all of yours. This will require new skills—communication and effectiveness skills that you can learn from therapy, self-help groups, reading, and training workshops or courses.

Learn Stress Management Skills

No matter what you do to reduce day-to-day pressures at home, at work, and in your personal relationships, you will still experience stress. For as long as you live, life remains a challenge—demanding that you live up to adult responsibilities and adjust to unforeseen circumstances. This means you will always have to cope with stress, and as a recovering sex addict, you must cope without resorting to your old compulsive sexual rituals. Fortunately, alternatives for managing stress are plentiful.

You can take stress reduction courses, learn relaxation techniques, or use biofeedback machines or hypnosis to lower your stress level. You can release tension through exercise—jogging, tennis, golf, swimming, or joining a health club, for example. Exercise produces an important physical release, but also allows you to redirect emotional energy and clear your mind of worries about work, relationships, money, recovery, or anything else that bothers you.

You may have to shop around for the technique that best suits you, but we strongly recommend that you find some way to release physical, mental, and emotional tension without causing harm to yourself or others. For instance, you can yell (as long as you don't yell directly at someone) or you can take out your aggressions on a punching bag. A hobby of some kind can take your mind off your worries. And, as the Twelve Steps suggest, you can reduce anxiety caused by the things you cannot control by turning them over to your Higher Power and perhaps developing a positive ritual of prayer or meditation each morning. Anything that enables you to relax and doesn't hurt anyone is going to help you resist the urge to pursue sexual highs.

Talk About the Things That Cause Stress and Tension

One of the best ways to release tension is to talk about it. Bill, for one, has learned that "I constantly put pressure on myself. I worry about being needed, about friends, about people liking me, finances, you name it. One worry leads to another until they are all rolling around in my head. When I start getting that way, I find someone to have a healthy talk with. I keep a list of names and numbers in my wallet, and if things start getting out of control, I call some people. That's the thing that saves me from myself."

Talking to supportive friends or other recovering addicts can save you, too. You can also call on these people to join you in activities that distract you from obsessive worrying, or you can get involved in group activities sponsored by churches, synagogues, or community organizations. And if you want to deal directly with the tension you are feeling, go to a recovery group meeting or call your sponsor or therapist.

Mitch sums up the value of this emotional support and how important it is not to isolate yourself any longer when he says, "I can slip back into my isolation mode very easily, but I don't want to. If I'm hurting and my friends ask me to go out somewhere, I could say 'No, thanks, I want to be alone.' But when I'm alone, I hurt more. When I start getting into self-pity—feeling sorry for myself—I have to make myself be around other people, keep busy, do things at home, go out with friends. It doesn't really stop the feelings, but it keeps me from doing something stupid because of them."

OVERCOMING YOUR DEPENDENCE ON SEXUAL HIGHS

"Actually stopping the behavior is the hardest thing," Keith asserts. Although many areas of his life have improved since he came to us for help for compulsive sexual behaviors that ran the gamut from obscene phone calling to anonymous encounters with men in adult bookstores, Keith is "still struggling with the desire to do what I once did. I don't do those things anymore," he says. "But I still feel like I could. Lots of times I want to."

Like a recovering alcoholic who still craves a drink, a recovering compulsive overeater who is always one bite away from an eating binge, or a recovering drug addict who still savors every detail of the highs, recovering sex addicts miss the euphoria and escape of their compulsive behavior. As Keith noted, not indulging in old sexual rituals is indeed the hardest part of recovery.

But don't forget that those rituals came close to destroying you and everyone close to you. That is why you sought help in the first place and why you want to change. Through your recovery program, you learn to understand yourself, improve your self-image and your view of others, and find new ways to deal with stress—all worthy achievements themselves. Yet, the primary goal of recovery is to change your compulsive sexual behavior. These other changes serve that purpose, making your former rituals unnecessary and unappealing.

Be Careful Not to Replace One Compulsion with Another

Many of the sex addicts we treat indulge in at least one other compulsion besides sex addiction. Wayne, for instance, is a recovering cocaine addict, and Robin has an eating disorder. Cheryl's and Sara's husbands were both alcoholics and sex addicts. So was Don. In fact, Don's compulsive masturbation and womanizing got worse *after* he stopped drinking. Although sex addiction had always been part of his life, its seriousness became apparent only when he sought help for his alcoholism. The reverse occurs for many sex addicts. If they do have another addiction, it frequently intensifies when they start to deal with the sex addiction.

Stripped of one defense mechanism against pain and anxiety, you too may find yourself relying on other equally destructive compulsive behaviors. In fact, the insight you gain from your Twelve Steps program for sex addiction may be what convinces you that you are indeed addicted in more than one area. And, obviously, you can't let that addiction rule your life the way sex addiction did. If you hope to recover, you must get help through self-help groups or professional therapy for that addiction, too. The national headquarters for a variety of self-help organizations that address other addictions and compulsive behaviors, as well as groups for addicts' family members, can be found in Appendix B of this book.

Develop Healthy Dependencies

By now, you know that your dependence on sexual highs was extremely harmful, but not all dependencies lead to self-destruction. In fact, your recovery is built upon a healthy dependency on your recovery program, on other people, and on your Higher Power.

For as long as you find it helpful, depending on a Twelve Steps program is a very positive "addiction." It brings you together with others, rather than isolating you the way sex addiction did, and encourages you to face problems instead of running away from them. Getting hooked on recovery enhances your self-esteem, your relationships, and your life. It is a healthy dependency.

Combining professional therapy, self-help groups, and involvement with religious or community groups reduces the risk of becoming overly dependent on one source of strength, support, and relief—although you need not worry too much about that. As you internalize the lessons of your recovery program, you will eventually grow out of your dependency on that program, even though you may always maintain your connection to others in recovery and continue going to meetings to make sure you stay on the right track.

Learn About Human Sexuality and Sexual Behavior

Recovery from certain addictions—most notably, compulsive overeating, compulsive spending, and sex addiction—requires addicts to abstain from compulsiveness without giving up the behavior entirely, challenging them to replace destructive patterns with constructive ones. This task is particularly demanding for sex addicts who missed out on appropriate sex education during childhood. With only limited information about how men and women react sexually and because most, if not all, of your own sexual experiences have centered on your compulsive sexual ritual, you may not know what constructive sexual behavior is. What's more, having never allowed emotional involvement or honest communication to be part of your own sexual experience, you may believe that others regard sex the same way you do: as a source of purely physical pleasure. Clearly, you have a lot to learn.

The need for basic sex education is one reason that we recommend professional treatment for sex addicts—in addition to self-help support groups. A professional whose experience includes sex therapy as well as treating sex addiction can help patients:

- learn to be nurturing and sensual, discovering the value of touching and being touched, both physically and emotionally.
- practice communicating and respecting their own and their partners' sexual needs.
- discover new, deeper ways of sexual expression, leading to mutual satisfaction.

All of the sex addicts we have treated needed this sort of sexual retraining in order to incorporate constructive sexual attitudes and behavior into their recovery.

Develop More Patience

Like most sex addicts, you may view verbal communication between sexual partners and physical foreplay as pointless activities. After all, you reason, they only delay gratification. Todd, for instance, often compares sex to a business deal. Closing the deal excites him. Everything that leads up to the closing is dull and routine, and he has little patience for it. He and other addicts feel the same way about sex. They want immediate gratification and become impatient with anything that might postpone it. Likewise, your obsession with instant gratification was one of the forces behind your addiction. To resist being pulled back into compulsive sexual rituals, you will have to slow down, delaying gratification to reap the benefits of a healthy sexual relationship.

The patience to communicate with your sexual partner, to find out what he or she enjoys, to enjoy the physical and emotional sensations that lead up to orgasm, in addition to the orgasm itself, actually improves sexual satisfaction, rather than detracting from it. More importantly, you will feel good about yourself and your partner, instead of ashamed and guilty.

Enhance Communication and Social Skills

Healthy sexual relationships grow out of healthy personal relationships, which require certain social and communication skills. Your therapist and/or a self-help group can help you learn how to relate to people on a more personal level than you have in the past.

At first, practice socializing in nonsexual ways, getting to know others as whole people rather than viewing them as objects to be included in your sexual rituals. "Go to the movies," Bill suggests. "Try to get to know the person, talk about personal lives, just develop friendships. It's not as hard as I thought it would be to just say goodnight and not think, 'I didn't make it with them, so I'm a failure.' "

If you are single or divorced, practice just dating, like Bill, getting to know someone you think is interesting or attractive for reasons other than lust alone. And if you are married or involved in a long-term relationship, practice treating your partner as if he or she were a date, talking, listening, and getting to know each other again.

For the sake of your own recovery and self-esteem, you want to have relationships with whole people, distinguishing between sheer lust and genuine interest in another person, between the lust that almost destroyed you and the love that can help you—and your partner—grow.

Both a healthier understanding of sexuality and improved social skills teach you that a relationship is an important part of sex. And this new world of complete relationships will ultimately bring more meaning and satisfaction to your life than your fantasy world and sexual rituals ever did.

What to Do and What Not to Do: A Difficult Question

Because they don't know how to define constructive sexual behavior, when sex addicts begin their recovery, they need someone to tell them what is or is not permissible, to help them learn a new set of rules for sexual conduct. Yet, it is impossible to issue a blanket statement that would cover all possible situations. The question of what sexual behavior is appropriate, and what is not, needs to be addressed on an individual basis.

Because you, like all sex addicts, must abstain completely from certain behaviors, but *not* from all sex, you must come up with your own personal definition of being "on the wagon." If you examine yourself honestly, you will recognize your own addictive patterns—whether they involve masturbation or pornography or voyeurism or something else— and you will know which activities to avoid. Sobriety means abstaining from compulsive sexual behavior. You must decide which of your sexual behaviors is compulsive and which is not. This decision seems to be most difficult to make when the sexual behavior in question is masturbation.

Although some recovering sex addicts insist that all masturbation is inappropriate, not only for themselves but for other sex addicts as well, we take a more moderate approach. We view *occasional* masturbation to be permissible for *some* sex addicts if, and only if, two nonnegotiable conditions are met. Fantasies during masturbation must *not* be destructive to one's relationships or recovery; and fantasies during masturbation must be restricted to the addict's spouse or partner.

By now, you know enough about yourself and your past behavior patterns to recognize destructiveness when you see it. If masturbation detracts from or takes precedence over a good physical, emotional, and spiritual relationship with your spouse or lover, or if it leads you to fantasize about pornography, or prostitutes, or the kind of other addictive sexual activities you used to practice, do not indulge in it. And the truth of the matter is that, at least during the early stages of recovery, you will not be able to meet these criteria and therefore should not masturbate.

Remember that, in the past, your addiction to certain sexual behaviors has wreaked havoc on every area of your life and that indulging in certain behaviors, even though those behaviors may be perfectly acceptable for other people, will have the same effect today. You are a sex addict and have to live by sexual rules that are different from the ones other people live by. Any sexual behavior that leads to secrecy or guilt, hurts anyone—including yourself—or is accompanied by obsessive fantasies is against the rules. Don't do it. And don't allow denial or rationalizations to influence your judgment, convincing you to do something you know is not okay for you—even if it might be okay for someone else. Let the Twelve Steps, your therapist, and the people in your recovery or therapy group guide you, helping you stay in reality instead of slipping back into denial.

The Issue of Monogamy

Appropriate sexual behavior for a sex addict includes a commitment to monogamy. Most of our sexually addicted patients tell us that, to sustain their recovery, they must limit themselves to having sex within a monogamous relationship. They cannot sleep around, carry on even one affair, or even fantasize about being with someone else while having sex with their spouse or lover. We wholeheartedly agree with this idea. However, we are not making a *moral* judgment when we say this. We are not saying that all people should be monogamous. That is an individual value choice. We are being pragmatic—and realistic.

As a sex addict, you have a problem relating to people. You have turned people into sex objects, depersonalized your relationships, manipulated, managed, and misled others. Indeed, by definition, sex addiction involves an avoidance of the honesty, intimacy, and trust unique to monogamous relationships. Certainly one pervasive goal of recovery is to live your life differently than you did when you were ruled by your addiction, and one way you will do this is to commit yourself to a monogamous relationship, a commitment that extends to your fantasies as well as your behavior.

Maintaining more than one sexual relationship at the same time impersonalizes those relationships, usually involves dishonesty, and often re-ignites your interest in sex for its own sake—all danger zones for a sex addict. Yet, monogamy may be brand-new for you. For example, even during his marriage, Bill (who is now divorced) was never monogamous. And George, whose sexual pursuits were limited to masturbation, phone sex services, and prostitutes, has never had—at the age of twenty-six—a serious, committed relationship of any kind. If you find yourself in a similar situation, you may be tempted to latch on to the first person you date, jumping into a relationship you don't really want in order to get the sex you do want. You must exercise patience. Get to know and trust the other person, employing your new communication and social skills to build the sort of honest, intimate relationship you truly *want* to commit yourself to.

You may be surprised to hear that in most of our cases a sexually addicted patient has actually felt relieved when told to have sex only with a partner, if he or she had one—and if not, not to have sex at all. After years of believing that sex was the most important thing in their lives—and at the same time witnessing what the compulsive pursuit of sexual highs was doing to their lives—it was a revelation to learn that they could live without sex, that they didn't *have* to act out sexually in order to survive. In fact, rather than feeling restricted, these patients felt liberated. Recovery gave them permission *not* to have sex, not to give in to their nagging obsessions and compulsions. Recovery gave them permission to feel good about other areas of their lives.

SLIPS, BACKSLIDES, AND BINGES: TIPS FOR HANDLING RELAPSES

Like any journey, recovery seldom proceeds in a straight, uninterrupted line. Most sex addicts slip back into their compulsive sexual rituals at least once—and often more than once—during the course of their recovery. Chances are that you will, too. Slips *can* turn into backslides, binges, and full-blown relapses, *but they do not have to.* Anytime you step off the road to recovery, you are faced with a choice. You can get right back on track, or you can wander further off course. Here are some tips to help you choose the former and prevent the latter.

Do Not Regard One Mistake as a Complete and Utter Failure

"I had been sober for a while when I had a slip and it really blew me away," Hank admits. "I felt like I was right back where I had started. When people at SA asked how much sobriety I had and I had to say twenty-four hours, it just drove home this feeling that I was starting over from scratch. I really questioned whether I could get it together again, whether I had what it takes to recover."

Viewing a single reoccurrence of compulsive sexual behavior as a complete and utter failure—and believing he was right back where he had started—set off a barrage of negative self-talk and left Hank feeling hopeless, as if he were incapable of recovering from his addiction. It prevented him from reclaiming his sobriety and resuming work on his recovery, leading to months of sexual acting out before getting back on track.

You can learn from Hank's mistake. If you slip back into old rituals, do not assume that one slip means you are all the way back at ground zero. Instead, tell yourself, "I am having some period of recovery, despite periods of regression." You *have* made improvements since beginning your recovery program, and you can continue to make progress as long as you don't allow the negative self-talk and feelings of failure that accompany a slip to steer you too far off the course you have chosen: recovery from sex addiction.

Just Because You Can Expect Slips, Do Not Give Yourself Permission to Slip

Yes, breaking past patterns of compulsive behavior is difficult. And yes, you can reasonably expect to slip once or several times during your recovery. But please, do not use that information to justify continuing your compulsive sexual behavior.

People who slip repeatedly—going on sexual binges and then shrugging off their behavior with the claim that "Nobody's perfect" or acting out at regular intervals and pointing to the fact that "I'm not doing it as much as I used to"—are not truly committed to recovery. Perhaps they have not actually hit bottom yet and need to lose even more before they can take recovery seriously. Members of Twelve Steps programs have seen this syndrome before and may even tell someone to go out and do what he or she thinks they want to do. "Get it out of your system," they say. "Then come back when you *really* want help."

In many cases, this reverse psychology works. You are free to do what you want. When you realize that, you may also realize that you do not *really* want to do what you've done in the past—or to suffer the consequences you now know come with it. You can freely choose to commit yourself fully to recovery.

Do Not Make Recovery Your New Obsession

While some sex addicts do not take recovery as seriously as they should, others go to the opposite end of the spectrum, obsessively worrying about the possibility of falling back into old compulsive patterns. They reduce their interaction with the outside world, fearing that almost any activity will trigger a compulsive episode. They work their program compulsively, spending so much time going to meetings, making phone calls, attending workshops, and reading about their problems that their work life and personal relationships suffer—in precisely the same way they did when the pursuit of sexual highs was the obsession. If you constantly worry about relapses and feel compelled to build your entire life around avoiding them, obviously, your life will be no more manageable than it was before.

Turn those worries over to your Higher Power and work your program faithfully, but not compulsively. Trust that with the help of other people and your Higher Power, you will be able to survive your mistakes and resume your recovery.

Reach Out for Help Immediately

"I am a sex addict. I may be recovering, but I'm still a sex addict and always will be a sex addict," Hank says. "I can slide all the way back into the gutter at any time. If I slip, I have to come in here or go somewhere and tell somebody. That way, I can get back on the track. If I don't get help right away, I'll keep slipping and sliding all the way back to square one."

Don agrees with Hank's point of view and adds, "The problem is that once you act out, you don't feel like going to a meeting. Your first thought is to keep other people from knowing what you did. You want to isolate yourself or pretend it didn't happen. If you go to a meeting and don't say anything, you feel like a hypocrite, and if you don't go to a meeting, you feel like a failure. Either way, you usually want to act out again. That's why they say 'keep coming back,' because if you don't, you're going to reach for more and lose your whole recovery."

When you slip, don't reach for more—reach for help. Don't wait. Talk to your sponsor or your group, contact your therapist, and get back into recovery as quickly as possible. Trying to hide slips instead of accepting responsibility for them eats away at your recovery. Sooner or later, you will have to deal with your behavior. You can do it now, immediately moving back toward sobriety, or you can go through another extended episode of sex addiction, which will leave you worse off than ever before. In this light, we hope you can see that it makes sense to reach out for help immediately after you slip.

Do Not Turn a Slip into a Binge

A common pitfall experienced by many of our sexually addicted patients is thinking, "Well, I've already screwed up. I might as well go all the way." This sort of diseased thinking sends you off on a binge that immediately begins to affect every area of your life. "It's like a chain reaction," George explains. "When I'm slipping, I get depressed, my room starts to get sloppy, dishes start to pile up in the sink, I start to eat a lot of junk food, I don't cook for myself, I lie around in front of the TV. I think, 'Damn, here I go again,' and just keep right on going."

Again, rather than prolonging the agony, it makes sense to get right back on the wagon, making immediate amends to anyone you've hurt through your compulsive behavior, and not being too hard on yourself, either. As George has learned, remind yourself that *recovery does not entail perfection. You're recovering from something. It's a coping mechanism, and it's going to take time and patience to learn to live without it.*

RECOGNIZE THAT RECOVERY GETS EASIER TO KEEP THE LONGER YOU HAVE IT

As your recovery progresses, you will find yourself slipping less and less often. You learn to trust yourself and others, and you have less need to turn to sexual highs to feel good. You learn new coping strategies and can handle stressful situations without relying on compulsive sexual rituals. In time, sticking with your new way of life will be easier and more appealing than going back to your old one. If you work the Twelve Steps to the best of your ability, heed the suggestions we've included in this chapter, and employ the tips for handling relapse that we have given you, recovery will become a habit—a healthy one that completely replaces the unhealthy habits of the past.

13

FOR THE
CO-DEPENDENT:
Finding a Balance

When you seek recovery from co-dependency, you—like the sex addict—embark upon a life-long journey. Guided by the Twelve Steps and strengthened by experiences in therapy and self-help programs, you move one day at a time and one step at a time toward a new way of living. We do not need to tell you that the path you have chosen will not always be easy to follow. It demands hard work and challenges you to replace old attitudes and behaviors with new ones, as well as make some difficult choices about the way you live your life. Like sex addicts, who must abandon the compulsive sexual rituals they employed to escape from powerful fears and painful emotions, you will be asked to give up something: your lifelong habit of focusing all of your attention and energy on the addict and other people so that you do not have to face yourself.

Obsessively worrying about other people, putting their needs before your own, and trying to control their every move has not worked. You know that now. Your co-dependent rituals, like the addict's compulsive ones, have not only failed to change your partner, but have destroyed *your* self-esteem and rendered *your* life unmanageable. Yet, as ineffective and self-destructive as your old ways are, they have given you a certain sense of security and control, and if you are like most of our co-dependent patients, you will resist letting go of them. Moreover, in order to embrace recovery and move on to a fuller life and healthier relationships, you must accomplish two tasks that are unique to recovery from co-dependency. You must:

- finally work all the way through your grief over the losses you've suffered as a result of your partner's sex addiction and your own co-dependency.
- develop an attitude of detachment, clearly defining the boundaries between yourself and other people as well as determining what is your responsibility and what is not.

These tasks, along with suggestions for using recovery to its fullest advantage, are the subject of this chapter.

DO IT FOR *YOU*

Because you have taken a back seat to others for much if not all of your life, you are liable to find the first step toward recovery the most difficult to take. You must make a commitment to *your own recovery,* to recover *for yourself,* whether or not your sexually addicted partner wants to change or decides to seek help. Indeed, you can only embrace recovery when you take your eyes off the addict and take a long, honest look at yourself; when you stop trying to control the uncontrollable—the addict's behavior—and work on changing your own behavior.

Seeking help as a ploy to get your partner to follow suit, or joining a self-help group in the hope of learning new techniques for controlling or changing your partner, is *not* a step toward recovery. It is yet another act of co-dependency. The addict's recovery is *not* your responsibility. You are responsible for your own recovery. And contrary to the perverse advice of your negative self-talk, *you* deserve to get better—just for yourself.

"BUT I CAN'T JUST SIT BACK AND WATCH HIM DESTROY HIMSELF"

Whether your partner is a man or a woman, trying to change a sex addict is a hard habit to break. But as you progress with your own recovery, your partner's self-destructiveness actually becomes more obvious to you and more painful to witness. However, if you find you are repeatedly determined to try at least one more time to get through to the sex addict, you may want to look into a therapeutic technique called family intervention.

Family intervention consists of a sophisticated, carefully planned, and well-rehearsed confrontation designed to get an addict into treatment. The actual intervention involves a group of people who are close to and/or respected by the sex addict—you, other family members, friends, and perhaps an employer, doctor, or clergy member. *Under the supervision of a trained family intervention specialist,* these people explain to the addict in no uncertain terms exactly the sort of behavior they have observed, how they feel about it, the harm it has done to them, and why they can no longer support or ignore it. The intervention specialist then explains the treatment alternative that has been arranged for the addict, leaving him or her to accept or reject the help being offered.

Intervention will not work and can, in fact, do more harm—unless conducted by somebody with expertise. Ask your therapist or family doctor for the name of a trained intervention specialist who is knowledgeable about sex addiction. In addition, we recommend that you make headway with your own recovery before attempting an intervention because *you* will need strength, support, and self-assertiveness to do your part in it.

STAYING TOGETHER OR SPLITTING UP: AN EMOTIONALLY CHARGED QUESTION

Regardless of what your partner does or does not do to recover from sex addiction, you may reach a point in your own recovery where you consider the question of continuing or ending your relationship with the sex addict. If your fear of being alone which has fueled your co-dependency for years rears its ugly head now, it may be powerful enough to sabotage your recovery.

Many a co-dependent has abandoned all recovery efforts after thinking: "Look what's happening here. I'm getting better, but my relationship is getting worse. I'm going to end up alone, without any relationship at all—and that's just what I didn't want to happen." Convincing themselves that the cost of recovery is too high, such co-dependents drop out of therapy or stop attending self-help group meetings and soon slide back into their old behavior patterns.

We urge you not to make the same mistake. Yes, chances are that as your own recovery progresses unhappiness with your relationship will increase, especially if your partner is *not* in recovery. Recovery does change your perspective. For the first time, you can realistically appraise the relationship's strengths and weaknesses. Although painful, the return of objectivity is a positive sign. Before, you felt *compelled* to hang on to your relationship at any cost. Now you can *freely and consciously decide* to continue that relationship or end it.

However, the question of whether or not to continue your relationship—which is discussed in detail in the next chapter—is not one you have to answer when you first enter your recovery program. Later, having regained some strength and sanity, you will be better equipped to choose the course of action that is best for you. For now, just keep in mind that your *fears* about making that decision have the potential to divert you from your own recovery. Don't let them.

FINALLY DEALING WITH YOUR GRIEF

A sense of loss is nothing new for you. You felt it the first time you were confronted with evidence of the sex addict's behavior. Recovery drives home the point, forcing you to recognize that you have lost not only the ability to trust or influence the sex addict, but the ability to control your own life, as well. Your romantic vision of the world, your relationship, and your partner dies a slow, painful death—and you grieve that loss.

In the past, because you did not allow yourself to feel the emotions that accompany loss and did not constructively express and release those emotions, you got stuck in one of the stages of grief. Now, with recovery as your goal, you must work your way through all the stages. You cannot do this alone. Professional treatment, in particular—but also involvement in a recovery group that encourages you to discuss your feelings openly—will help you work through the stages of grief, disarming the denial defense mechanism so you can move through the remaining stages of anger, bargaining, depression, and finally, acceptance.

You do not necessarily go through these stages in order and need not wait to complete one before beginning to work on another. For instance, if you enter recovery in a state of depression, you will have to take steps to relieve your depression before you can work through anger or replace destructive bargaining with a healthier approach. Or you might have to learn to accept yourself as a whole person—with both positive and negative qualities—before you can believe you deserve to work through the other stages. Or, as Cheryl did, you might strike and adhere to a healthy bargain about what you will and will not accept in your relationship before you feel any anger at all. However, regardless of the order in which you proceed through the stages, you *will* have to push your way through all of them.

YOU HAVE A RIGHT TO FEEL ANGRY

Getting angry and expressing anger is a terrifying prospect for most co-dependents, but an absolutely essential part of recovery. Although you have spent most of your life denying and burying anger, it has always been there under the surface waiting to get out. When you finally do let it out, the extent of your anger may surprise you.

Indeed, it will sometimes seem as if there is no end to your anger, and, like many of our co-dependent patients, you may find yourself thinking, "I'm so mad! I'm furious all the time. I swear I must be losing my mind." Rest assured that you are not going crazy. Your rage is a normal reaction to real circumstances. You have endured years of pain, uncertainty, and frustration. You have earned the right to feel angry.

You can expect to rail against the unfairness of it all—especially the disease of co-dependency that is forcing you to go through this grueling process called recovery. Chances are that you will furiously berate yourself—for failing to control your partner's behavior, for not realizing your powerlessness sooner and seeking help for yourself years ago. But most of your anger, at least at first, is likely to be directed at your partner. Indeed, there will seem to be no limit to your rage when you are diligently working on your own recovery while your partner refuses to get help.

And don't be surprised if you are equally incensed at a partner who makes a sincere effort to recover and actually begins to get better. Filled with righteous indignation, more than ready to make the addict pay for all the pain he or she has caused, the wind gets knocked out of your sails by a partner who admits mistakes and is willing to make amends for them. This turn of events was particularly frustrating for Kate, a thirty-four-year-old social worker, who was absolutely furious that her husband started getting better just when she was ready to make him "face the music."

"I don't think he's hurt as much as I've been hurt, and I want to even the score," she explains. "I'm always thinking of ways to get back at him. I just keep thinking that he should have to pay for what he did, that he should suffer the way I had to suffer."

If you have not yet begun your own recovery, or are just beginning it, you may not understand this kind of rage and desire for revenge, or believe *you* could ever feel it. However, the truth of the matter is that after you have bottled up anger for so long, it does tend to explode in this way—which is all the more reason to seek help to work through it. Professional guidance and support from a self-help group teach you to express and release anger without causing further damage to your relationship or hampering your recovery.

LEARN TO EXPRESS ANGER CONSTRUCTIVELY

You have the right to *feel* angry. You don't have the right to hurt yourself or other people by endlessly and impulsively venting anger or outrage and acting out revenge fantasies. Contrary to the messages you received during childhood and lived by as an adult, anger is not inherently destructive. Expressing it will not irreparably damage you and your relationships. In fact, releasing anger can be healing and healthy—if you express it appropriately.

In counseling sessions, we use a Gestalt technique to teach our patients to express anger constructively. We set up two chairs, leaving one empty and having the patient sit in the other. Pretending that the empty chair is someone the patient is angry at, the patient talks to that "person," expressing just how angry he or she is. In this way, patients get to vent long-repressed anger, learning that doing so will not destroy them. It also opens a discussion about what might happen if patients expressed anger to real people the way they expressed it to the empty chair, paving the way for them to learn new, more constructive ways to communicate emotions in real-life situations.

Of course, this exercise works best in a therapist's office or with a group of people whom you trust. Since you will not always be in such a setting when you are ready to explode, consider calling your Twelve Steps program sponsor, or another group member, or writing out your angry thoughts, rather than lashing out impulsively at the nearest target.

By putting anger and other emotions into words, and receiving feedback and support from other people, you will eventually be able to express anger directly to the sex addict or others—honestly sharing a deeply felt emotion in order to open doors for further communication, rather than just blowing off steam or intentionally inflicting pain. In addition, you will begin to recognize those things you can take action to remedy and those you will have to release and turn over to your Higher Power.

FIRST YOU LET IT OUT, THEN YOU MOVE BEYOND IT

Working through the anger stage of grieving takes more than feeling anger and expressing it. In fact, if all you do is vent your rage, you are liable to get stuck—stewing in your resentments and becoming the *bully* type of co-dependent we described in Chapter 8. To avoid such an obvious pitfall, ask yourself: What steps can I take to leave anger behind and get on with my life?

- If you're angry with yourself, what changes can you make that will relieve your anger?
- If you're angry with someone else, how can you communicate your anger clearly, so he or she will know how you feel?
- If there is something that person can do to avoid angering you in the future, how can you negotiate reasonably—giving him or her an opportunity to meet your needs without sacrificing self?
- If there are resentments you cannot resolve through negotiation, can you ask your Higher Power to remove them? Are there techniques—exercise, punching pillows, shutting yourself in the bathroom and yelling—that can relieve the tension anger brings with it?

To move beyond anger, search inside yourself for the answers to these questions. Seek advice from your therapist and fellow recovering co-dependents. Then, act accordingly.

Recognize That You *Will* Feel Angry Again—and Again

Finally dealing with the rage you once denied—and working through the anger that is part of grieving for your many losses—does not mean you will never feel angry again. Even though you never before realized it, feeling angry is a normal part of everyday life. In addition, anger at your partner and about the diseases of sex addiction and co-dependency will most certainly return from time to time.

As you move through recovery, you remember painful events and recognize injustices that you did not notice at first. And, if your partner slips back into compulsive rituals after a period of recovery, your fury is likely to return with full force. Fortunately, you now have the tools to work through the anger that once frightened you—acknowledging it, releasing it, and getting beyond it *when you feel it*, instead of bottling it up as you did in the past.

276

BARGAINING

As you may recall from Chapter 8, getting stuck in the bargaining stage of the grieving process turns you into a *managing* co-dependent who vainly attempts to curtail the addict's compulsive sexual behavior by assuming responsibility for every detail of daily living. Before embracing recovery, nearly every bargain you struck diminished you. No matter what extreme you went to, your partner did not change. And you were left feeling drained and utterly powerless.

In recovery, any and all bargaining you do should have the opposite effect. Healthy bargaining helps you attend to your needs rather than neglect them. It gives you the power to live your own life and the freedom to identify the behaviors you will not tolerate any longer, including the addict's endless pursuit of sexual highs.

Establish Some Nonnegotiable Ground Rules for Your Relationship

When you committed yourself to recovery, you committed yourself to doing what is best for *you*. This commitment does not end when you leave your therapist's office or your recovery group meeting. It carries through to your behavior in your relationship. Since it is clearly not in your best interest to continue covering up for the addict, catering to your partner's every whim, or using any other humiliating bargaining strategy, you must stop doing these things—and let your partner know that you *will not tolerate or in any way support his or her compulsive sexual behavior.*

The first and most critical ground rule for your relationship is: "I will not work to maintain or improve our relationship if you will not work on yourself and your recovery from the disease of sex addiction." Like all healthy bargains, this one presents your partner with a choice and clearly defines the consequences of certain behaviors. If your partner stops acting out, you will work with him or her to rebuild the relationship. If your partner continues to act out, he or she can expect no support from you; there will be no more action on your part to protect your partner from the consequences of his or her behavior.

Sometimes, although not always, this ground rule leads to a physical separation. Molly, for instance, chose not to live under the same roof with Hank as long as he continued to act out. Her bargain was clearly defined and nonnegotiable: She would not be there for him at all—emotionally or otherwise—unless his compulsive affairs stopped.

Moreover, when Molly separated from her husband, she communicated her position clearly, so that Hank knew exactly where she stood. She told him, "Since I'm really concerned about our financial picture, I want a legal separation. If you go for help and stop doing what you've been doing sexually, and if you show me you really want us to be together, then we'll talk about whether or not we want to get together again. It's up to you. You do whatever you want. But, for my own sake and the kids', I refuse to ride this emotional roller coaster anymore or deal with the financial insecurity of living with you the way you are now.''

Of course, you do not *have* to separate from your partner to make a healthy bargain work. However, to keep from sliding back into co-dependent patterns, you *must* take a stand—and stick to your end of the bargain. And certain ground rules about sex should definitely be part of the bargain, especially if your partner's sexual acting out involves indiscriminate contact with any number of sexual partners. The health considerations alone give you the right to say, "You have to get sober and stay sober before I will have sex with you again." Even when a sex addict who previously engaged in high-risk sexual behavior enters recovery and is abstaining from compulsive rituals, we advise you to avoid sexual contact with him or her at least until you are positive your partner is free of sexually transmitted diseases and has not contracted the HIV (AIDS) virus—which will require at least two tests, one immediately and one two to four months later.

Any ground rules you establish must last for the duration of your relationship, not just for one day or one week—and they should cover any behaviors associated with addiction, not just compulsive sexual acts. For instance, several months after Sara stopped covering up for her husband and discontinued the constant caretaking that had enabled him to pursue sexual highs without concern for the consequences, he hit bottom and sought help. Several more months passed before Sara was able to trust that her husband was actually making progress and no longer indulging in sexual rituals. At that point, they began couples therapy and their life together improved—at first.

"He said he wanted to be more accountable," Sara recalls. "He wanted to act responsibly, and he really wasn't doing a lot of the things he did before. Even so, he would get off work at five, but a couple of times a week he wouldn't get home until seven or seven-thirty. He said he just didn't want to sit in traffic, so he'd stopped in a coffee shop and read the evening newspaper. Maybe he was doing that, but it sounded an awful lot like the excuses he used to give me when he was drinking and picking up women. I thought I was being overly suspicious, so I let him slide, at first. But then I realized that, whether he was innocently reading the paper or not, he was putting me in the position of worrying about him and not trusting him. I put my foot down. I said, 'That's going to have to stop. You say you want to be accountable, but not getting home at the time you said you would get home is *not* being accountable.' "

Of course, Sara's husband did not *like* what he heard, and he did not immediately nod his head and say, "Yes, dear." In fact, he angrily accused her of being paranoid. "When are you going to learn you can trust me? What do I have to do to prove I really have changed?" he asked.

Sara did not cave in. She recognized—as you must—that she needed time to rebuild her shattered trust and that her husband could not expect her to do that if he were acting irresponsibly. After a lengthy, at times emotional, discussion, they reached an agreement. Unless he called in advance to tell her he would be late—for reasons both agreed were acceptable—he would come directly home from work.

Sara's experience is a clear-cut example of healthy bargaining. The bargaining process was not easy or painless for either person, but in the end, both got something that they wanted. Sara was freed from worrying about her husband's lateness. Her husband got to be more accountable—which was something he had said on several occasions that he wanted. She no longer harbored resentments about his lateness, and he was released from his guilt. Both benefited from no longer arguing about this particular issue.

A NEW ATTITUDE: ASSERTIVENESS

To strike a healthy bargain, you must assert yourself, communicating your feelings and needs to another person, requesting that he or she respect your position, and actually asking for what you need from him or her. The communication skills involved in assertiveness may be unfamiliar to you, and if they are, you can learn them by taking assertiveness training courses or reading any of the excellent books on the subject. However, all the skills in the world will not help you if you do not believe your own needs are important or think you do not have the right to ask for anything from your partner or anyone else.

Recently, during a couples therapy session, one of our co-dependent patients announced that she had decided to become more assertive. She was going to take charge of her own life and do what was best for her own well-being. We couldn't help but notice that the entire time she was speaking, she kept glancing over at her husband to see how he was responding to this revelation. She said all the right words, but it was clear from her tone and behavior that she had not yet broken her habitual pattern of looking to the sex addict and others for approval.

People-pleasers have great difficulty pleasing themselves. And if you are a co-dependent, you are probably a people-pleaser, operating on a belief ingrained during childhood: anyone's, indeed everyone's, needs and happiness are more important than your own. As you did while working through your anger, seek help from your therapist and/or your self-help group to replace this attitude of self-sacrifice with an attitude of healthy self-interest. With their support and feedback, identify your feelings and needs, distinguish reasonable requests from unreasonable ones, and rehearse assertive interactions. Realize, too, that the real thing—asserting yourself with your partner or others in your life—demands the courage to both express yourself honestly and to allow the other person to respond honestly.

And, please, go easy on yourself. Assertiveness and healthy bargaining are new to you. You are bound to make mistakes—at times demanding too much and at others backing down too easily. Keep trying. To get through this stage and get on with your own recovery, you must clearly identify your own feelings, clearly define your own needs, and send clear messages to your partner.

DEPRESSION

When Sara came to us for help, she did not know she was a co-dependent. She did know she was depressed, confused, and down-hearted—so fatigued and lethargic that she could barely handle her homemaking and child-rearing responsibilities. She felt trapped. Sara's depression, like the depression experienced by most co-dependents, resulted from the inability to control her sexually addicted husband's behavior or single-handedly create the sort of relationship and life she imagined she should have. She had assumed responsibility for meeting all of her husband's and children's needs, as well as keeping up a happy-family façade, because she sincerely believed she had no other choice.

But Sara did have other choices—and so do you. You can choose *not* to go on sacrificing yourself and meeting everyone else's needs at the expense of your own health and happiness. Instead of dwelling on your failure to change your partner, you can choose to change yourself.

Sara did make those choices. She admitted she was powerless over the addict in her life and also acknowledged that she was *not* destined to eternally play the victim or the martyr. Once she set ground rules for her relationship and stuck to them, she proved beyond a shadow of a doubt that she had the power to determine how she lived *her* life—even if she could not control the way her husband lived his.

You too can stop feeling sorry for yourself and start taking care of yourself instead. *Anything* you do for yourself confirms your personal power and lets you know that you do *not* have to spend the rest of your life feeling helpless and depressed.

Work through your anger, because the anger you turn inward eats away at your self-esteem and contributes to depression. Free yourself to do things that make *you* feel good. Let back into your life the activities and relationships you neglected while under the influence of co-depen-dency. Add new, positive experiences to your life, getting involved with church or community groups, learning new skills, exercising, or pursuing hobbies. Work your Twelve Steps recovery program, which—with or without the added benefit of professional treatment—helps you disarm other sources of depression: negative self-talk and endless self-criticism.

ACCEPTANCE

Acceptance is the stage of the grieving process which co-dependency never permitted you to reach. Now, in recovery, you finally learn to accept yourself, other people—including your partner—and your rela-tionship *for what they really are,* rather than how you wish or imagine them to be.

ACCEPT THE FACT THAT CO-DEPENDENCY, LIKE SEX ADDICTION, IS A PROGRESSIVE DISEASE

You cannot accept what you do not understand, and therefore, you must obtain factual information about sex addiction and co-dependency in order to pave the way for healthier attitudes about yourself and your partner. According to Sara, "Once I started looking at sex addiction as a disease, a big weight was lifted off my shoulders. For one thing, it helped to know my husband wasn't intentionally trying to hurt me when he went out and did those things. He wasn't being mean, waking up in the morning and thinking, 'Today, I'll do something to make my family miserable and risk losing my job.' He didn't have that kind of control."

Once you realize co-dependency is also a progressive disease, you will understand, as Molly did, that you were doing the best you could, based on the information you had to work with at the time. "In a way I was set up to be a co-dependent," Molly realizes. "I was doing the same things I'd done all my life, the things I'd learned were good things to do. I didn't know they were enabling behaviors. There were a lot of things I didn't know. Now that I do, I can behave differently."

This book and other resources help you understand the true nature of both sex addiction and co-dependency. Self-help groups, therapists, and working the Twelve Steps help you to better understand yourself and your partner. And when it comes to accepting reality, this knowledge goes a long, long way.

ACCEPT YOURSELF

Unfortunately, a good deal of what you find out about yourself and the destructiveness of your past behavior is going to make you feel worse before it helps you feel better. Like the recovering sex addict, you are likely to view yourself and the world in a very dim light and find your confidence and self-esteem at an all-time low. To avoid sinking back into depression or deciding you are too hopeless to recover, you must come to view yourself as a whole person with positive attributes as well as negative ones.

Turn to the acceptance exercise for sex addicts found on page 252 and complete the "I am _____" and "I am a good _____" sentences about yourself. Or every day, write down one thing that you like about yourself. Post it on your mirror, so that you can look at yourself and what you've written at the same time. Read the positive affirmation aloud. Add something new each day, something you celebrate about yourself.

In addition, you can conduct a dialogue between the positive and the negative sides of yourself, affirming your good qualities and resolving to improve the unhealthy aspects of yourself. You can write out a dialogue between the "good me" and the "bad me" or talk through it, moving back and forth between two chairs that face each other—one representing yourself when you feel entirely hopeless and powerless to do anything about your life, and the other representing yourself when you feel powerful, hopeful, and proud of the things you're already doing and the things you can and will do. Have the two parts of you talk to each other—the negative part uttering self-criticism and pessimistic forecasts for the future and the positive part countering with affirmations of your strong points and more optimistic predictions about what you can and will do to make yourself and your life better.

This exercise, if you allow yourself to get into it, helps you see how your negative self-talk keeps you down and how a more positive outlook can push you forward on your road to recovery. You will reaffirm your ability to change the attitudes and behaviors you don't like, as well as come to view and accept yourself as a whole person—as more than a co-dependent.

ACCEPTING YOUR PARTNER

"There just comes a point where you have to say, Gosh, everyone makes mistakes," Cheryl explains. "A point where you have to decide to keep on crucifying someone for what he did in the past or to let go and get on with your life. I do tend to think now that the past is the past and that the future can be better. I could feel differently tomorrow, especially if my husband stopped working on his problems. But for now, I'm trying to move forward instead of always looking backward."

As Cheryl has learned, recovery progresses when you leave the past behind and forgive it, accepting the addict as an imperfect human being who can and did make mistakes. Of course, forgiveness is one of those truly gray areas of life. When we say that until you forgive the past and the addict, you cannot move forward in your own recovery, we are by no means suggesting that you go back to being your partner's doormat, enabling the addict to act out sexually because "I'll forgive you, whatever you do." Forgiving your partner for what he or she did in the past does not give the addict carte blanche to do whatever he or she wants, today or in the future. You are in recovery now. You no longer assume responsibility for the addict and no longer make it easy for your partner to act out without suffering a single consequence.

When we speak of forgiveness, we *do* mean no longer crucifying your partner for the sins of the past, recognizing that the addict is a whole person, too, with positive features as well as flaws, and giving him or her room to change and grow. Healthy forgiveness, intended to leave the past behind and get on with life in recovery, does as much for you as it does for the other person—which is how you distinguish it from the unhealthy kind.

DETACHMENT

Once you reach the acceptance stage of the grieving process, you make two discoveries that are vital to your continued recovery. First, you realize that sex addiction is not all there is to your partner's identity.

RECOVERING FROM SEX ADDICTION

Separating the problem from the person, you take an important stride forward. You can stop taking care of your partner's problems *without* having to stop caring about him or her as a person.

You also come to understand that worrying and compensating for your partner's problems is not all there is to your identity, either. Accepting the fact that you are already more than you once believed—and can be even better—frees you to detach yourself from the problem of sex addiction and take responsibility for *your own* life. Through detachment, you finally stop blaming yourself for the addict's problems and stop blaming the addict for yours. No longer imprisoned by guilt or resentment, you can truly embrace recovery and get on with your life.

You Are Not Responsible for the Sex Addict

"I know I'm making progress, because I don't try to determine what my husband does or doesn't do," Diane says proudly. Since beginning his own recovery—nine months after Diane began hers—Diane's husband has, on several occasions, slipped back into old compulsive sexual rituals of seeking out prostitutes. Diane's recovery has stayed on track in spite of her husband's relapses. "If he wants to stay sober, he'll stay sober," she says. Diane no longer tries to control her husband's behavior. She knows his actions are not her responsibility.

To recover from co-dependency, you will have to stop assuming that your partner's problems are your problems and thinking you are responsible for solving them. You can, however, go right on caring about the person who has those problems. Indeed, because you love or have loved your partner and have shared good times as well as bad with him or her, we encourage you to show those feelings and even try to help your partner pursue recovery, if that is what he or she finally decides to do. To be helpful, however, this time around, you will have to do things differently, effectively serving yourself *and* the addict by clearly stating, *"I will not take responsibility for your behavior anymore."*

Ask yourself, "Do I do things for others that they should do for themselves?" Especially during the early stages of your recovery, your answer to that question is likely to reveal that you do let others off the hook too quickly and easily. For instance, Peggy, a member of our group for co-dependents whose husband was progressing well in recovery as far as his acting out was concerned, tended to treat her husband like a child. Although they had agreed that he would share household chores, including doing the dinner dishes, Peggy's husband invariably left some of those dishes unwashed, and she completed the job for him. Thus, she did something for him that he should have done himself, as if he were a little boy and she was his mother. As another member of the co-dependency group put it, "It was like she was saying, 'Good boy, you did some of the dishes. It would be silly for me to expect you to be grown up enough to finish the job.' "

As we have mentioned time and time again, when you take on all responsibility for making sure that everything around you runs smoothly,

283

you only end up making sure that nothing changes. For your own recovery and to improve your relationship, stop babying the sex addict. You are not your partner's parent, and he or she is no longer a child.

The more you detach yourself from the sex addict's problems, the more obvious to you your partner's addictive behavior will become. You may be tempted to point out every mistake, to berate your partner endlessly. Don't do it. You are not a judge, jury, or jailer. Persecuting your partner, like parenting him or her, is counterproductive not only to the addict's recovery, but to your own as well. When you have truly detached yourself from the problem, you will recognize that making the addict pay serves no positive purpose. You will come to believe, as Cheryl did, that "unless you're in somebody's shoes, you just can't know what the person feels or what's behind the decisions he or she makes. Trying to get my husband to think and do things my way only made *me* crazy. Now, I try not to let things affect me as much."

When you recognize that you are not responsible for or capable of controlling the addict's disease, you can finally stop blaming yourself for your partner's behavior. Convinced of her own unattractiveness, Diane used to believe that her husband sought out prostitutes because Diane herself was not good enough to please or satisfy him. Now, she understands that "He could have been living with Miss America, and it wouldn't have made a difference. What he did had nothing to do with the person he was living with or a sexual problem between us."

In accepting that you are neither the cause nor the cure for your partner's addiction, you spare yourself from the constant anxiety you once felt—and might still feel if you are misguided enough to think you have any more control over the addict's recovery than you did over his or her disease. Tanya, a twenty-nine-year-old homemaker, fell into a trap you would do well to avoid. She was so afraid her husband would have a relapse that, during the first months of their recovery, she didn't want to let him out of her sight. Not only did she convince him not to go back to work even though he was perfectly capable of resuming his career, but, until she stopped trying to oversee her husband's recovery, she became extremely anxious and agitated every time he left the house—her pulse raced and her heart pounded.

Other co-dependents try to direct their partners' recovery from behind the scenes, attempting to manipulate the sex addict's therapist by calling before an individual session with the partner and saying, "Don't mention that I called, but I wanted to make sure you knew that the sex addict did this and this and this." This has happened to us many times, and we gently remind such callers that if we keep secrets from our patients, we become part of the problem. Just as you would detach yourself from the problem if your partner was not seeking help, when your partner is also in recovery, concentrate on your own progress instead of trying to control the addict's.

You Are Responsible for Yourself

You have a problem that needs treatment and you have your work cut out for you. The road ahead involves identifying patterns of thought and behavior that keep you stuck in co-dependency, understanding your need to control, recognizing your tendency to isolate yourself from others and lose sight of yourself by focusing on your partner. Other people—your therapist, your sponsor, members of your self-help group—can help you spot your destructive habits and steer you in the direction you want to go. They can suggest new approaches and teach you new skills, boost your confidence, and give you emotional support. But the real work of recovery—actually thinking and acting in new ways—is left to you. *You* are responsible for yourself and your life.

You used to react automatically to each and every problem, playing and replaying the same old scenes with your partner. Now, having gained detached objectivity and a clearer sense of what is and is not your responsibility, you think through and plan your responses more carefully. You no longer protect your partner from the consequences of compulsive behavior. You waste no more emotion or energy trying to make life wonderful and trouble-free.

Although your partner probably won't like it much, letting the addict take care of himself or herself instead of catering to every whim allows you to respect yourself again. Kowtowing, covering up, and keeping secrets whittled away at your self-esteem. You do not have to do that anymore, and you won't if you truly take responsibility for your own recovery. As they say at Twelve Steps meetings, "You're as sick as your secrets," and if you want to get well, you will stop keeping so many of them. Admit that you cannot handle the problem alone; share your story at a recovery meeting; call in a member of the clergy, a therapist, a doctor, a psychologist, any expert whose confidentiality you can trust and who might have the ability to help you. Talking about your problems is not an act of betrayal. It is a step toward recovery.

Detaching yourself from the problem, you become more objective about what you can expect from yourself. You realize that taking responsibility for yourself is not the same as taking responsibility for solving the problem yourself. It is okay *not* to know exactly how to handle every situation you encounter. It is okay *not* to be in control all the time, and instead, to turn to your Higher Power and to other people to get you through rough times. And most important, it is okay to make mistakes. As you will no doubt hear again and again at self-help meetings, the goal of recovery is not to achieve perfection but to make progress. By working to take charge of the only person you can change—yourself—you will most certainly reach that goal.

You Deserve the New Life That Recovery Offers You

- What do you hope to gain by recovering from co-dependency?
- How would you like to live your life?
- What do you want to do for yourself now that you have avoided doing for yourself in the past?
- How can your life be better *for you* than it was before?

In attempting to answer these questions, do you feel compelled to respond the way someone else would want you to? Is your first reaction to wonder what your spouse, parents, children, friends, or even your therapist or the members of your self-help group want to hear you say? Are you tempted to frame your answers to meet their approval first and meet your own needs and desires second?

Most co-dependents find it extremely difficult to define what they want out of life and even more difficult to believe they deserve those things. There are several reasons for this difficulty, including the fact that co-dependents are trained from childhood to put other people's needs before their own. In addition, family rules—both during childhood and in their own adult homes—discouraged any kind of independent thinking, preventing co-dependents from learning to trust their own judgment. It seems safer to do what other people want than to risk making the wrong choices for themselves. In addition, romantic illusions of love or marriage frequently lead co-dependents to believe that two people become one in an intimate relationship, that their needs and desires *should* be the same as their partners'. And finally, many co-dependents have had their self-esteem so badly battered by life with sex addicts that they have trouble believing they are worthy of a better life.

Diane, for example, has "trouble accepting it when people are nice to me. When good things happen to me, if my husband does something kind or loving, even when I make something good happen myself, I feel like I don't deserve it. I guess things have been so bad for so long, and I've been hurt so many times, that I think that's the way my life is supposed to be."

Recovery promises you a new way of living, based on what is best for *you,* what you personally want your new life to be. But, you will not be able to accept what recovery offers until you get to know what you want for yourself and believe you deserve to have it. To do this, you must once again detach yourself from other people's problems, recognizing that their lives are not yours, that their needs and desires may be (and probably are) different from yours. Take time to examine your personal value system and to decide what is important to you, what you need to be healthy and happy. Ask yourself over and over again, "Do I want this for myself or to please someone else? Am I doing this to improve my life or to somehow manipulate or manage someone else's life?"

For Cheryl, giving herself permission to want a better life and coming to believe that she deserved it enabled her to take steps to actually improve her life. "I do things for myself, and I don't put up with what I used to put up with," she says. "I'm more assertive, willing to ask for things that I never would have asked for before. And I get what I ask for more than I ever thought I would. I always feared people would say no, thought I didn't deserve to even ask. Now, I have more self-respect, more self-confidence."

Cheryl has created a positive cycle—and so can you. By defining and taking steps to get what you want for yourself, you build self-esteem. In turn, this greater self-respect and self-confidence helps you ask for and get more of what you personally want from your life.

Set this positive cycle in motion by taking steps to connect with others, develop outside interests, and get involved in activities that you think are fun. Create a more active lifestyle—developing friendships, exercising, finding a job if you want one and don't already have one, and joining church or community organizations. All of these action steps should be taken because *you* want to take them, and pursued whether or not your partner chooses to participate in them with you. In this way, you will be able to put some distance between yourself and your problems, reduce stress, and improve the quality of your own life. For the first time in years, you will meet some of your needs outside of the relationship, instead of using only the sex addict's behavior to gauge your own happiness and sense of self-worth.

Set Realistic Goals for Your Own Recovery

Through recovery, you become aware of many needs and desires you previously denied. For perhaps the first time in your life, you recognize how much better you *could* be. Unlike the romantic illusions of the past, you see a life you not only want but may actually be able to attain. Yet, even in recovery, you can fall prey to your old idealistic—and unrealistic—ways of thinking, setting unreasonable, unattainable goals for yourself. Like many co-dependents who have traveled the road to recovery before you, you may find yourself thinking, "All right, now that I finally see where I want to go, I want to get there right now." But that is not how recovery works. Wanting too much too soon, expecting yourself to recover quickly and perfectly, leads to feelings of frustration, bringing on the negative self-talk that can sabotage your recovery efforts.

"You have to work hard today and probably for the rest of your life," Jenny now realizes. "You don't walk into a meeting or therapy one day and walk out cured the next." Recovery takes time. How much time? is a question asked by virtually every sex addict and co-dependent who comes to us for treatment. We have found that a patient who is determined to recover and works hard generally needs two to three months of intensive treatment, followed by about a year of ongoing treatments, to make significant and lasting changes. We do not want to scare you off, but we would be remiss if we did not tell you that many of our patients—particularly the ones who are court committed or pressured into treatment—need a good deal more time than that. And, as we have stressed again and again, sustaining the gains made during the first year or so of recovery requires a lifelong commitment to continue changing and growing.

In addition, recovery demands patience and perseverance. You will encounter many rough spots and difficult choices. In fact, during the early stages of recovery, when you are stirring up long-buried emotions and trying to live day to day without your old defense mechanisms, you may actually feel worse instead of better. Tough times do pass, although they are likely to return from time to time during your recovery. For your own sake, don't give up. Remember that even the worst moments of recovery are not as bad as your entire life once was, and will be again if you return to living it as a co-dependent.

In addition, unrealistic expectations of a recovering sex addict can undermine your progress and the addict's. Reality is going to fall on you like a ton of bricks if you expect your partner to be a new person overnight and stay that way forevermore. The truth is that if your partner is like most sex addicts, he or she will have at least one relapse at some point during recovery, and you are going to feel hurt and angry about each and every slip. Remember that you are not responsible for the addict's sobriety any more than you were responsible for his or her addiction. However, you *are* responsible for your reaction to the addict's relapses.

For instance, Sara recalls, "One time, after I came back from taking the kids to visit my parents, I found a lot of 900 numbers on our phone bill, the same numbers my husband used to call before he stopped acting out. When I asked him about it, he admitted what he had been doing, but I didn't get really crazy about it. I took it for what it was, a slip. I called a good friend of his from SA, so he would have to be accountable to more than just me, and we slept in separate bedrooms again, until I was sure he wasn't acting out anymore."

As you can tell from Sara's story, you do not have to suffer a relapse in your own recovery just because the sex addict has. Decide how you will handle your partner's slips *before* they happen. Take into consideration how you will deal with your own feelings, as well as what you will do in response to the addict's renewed pursuit of sexual highs. Let your partner know what you plan to do, keeping in mind that empty ultimatums—like the ones you failed to follow through on in the past—are interpreted by the sex addict as permission to continue acting out.

Thinking that your relationship will immediately improve once your partner stops acting out is yet another common but unrealistic expectation, as is believing the changes you make in yourself will automatically have a positive effect on the relationship. In fact, especially at first, the new you may not be welcomed with open arms—as Cheryl quickly discovered. "To tell you the truth, we had more fights about my new attitudes than we ever had about his problems while he was acting out," she admits. "I wouldn't respond to him in the old co-dependent way, and sometimes he'd get furious about it."

The changes one or both of you make during the course of your recovery will not be enough to change the relationship. That is something you will have to work on together, often over a long period of time. However, through your own and/or your partner's ongoing recovery, you will be able to better understand and communicate about the relationship. As you will learn from the next chapter, you *can* face and work through the difficult issue of whether to end the relationship or continue it in a new and more intimate fashion.

14

FACING HARD CHOICES: Recovery and Your Family

"Separating from Hank was a really difficult thing to do," Molly acknowledges. "Almost as difficult as finally deciding to get help for my own problems. I did that first, and if I hadn't, I probably wouldn't have known my life could be different. I wouldn't have had the strength to go through with the separation, even though my marriage, the way it was then, was just wearing me down to nothing."

Admitting that your relationship is not working and choosing to separate temporarily or to officially end the marriage through divorce is indeed as difficult as, and sometimes more difficult than, facing your addiction or co-dependency. In fact, these decisions go hand in hand. In some cases, the dissolution of the relationship forces you to hit bottom and seek help. Or, as it did for Molly, the awareness gained through personal recovery may convince you that the relationship cannot continue.

As you may recall, when Molly found her two sons going through Hank's stash of porno magazines, she realized matters had gotten out of control. "That hit me really hard," Molly recalls. "Because the only satisfaction I was getting out of life was coming from the idea that I was making a good home life for my kids. No matter how bad things got with Hank, I'd always been able to convince myself it wasn't affecting the kids. The kids were what kept me going. But I guess, for the most part, I was afraid of what would happen if Hank and I split up because—let's face it—it's not an easy life being a single parent.''

Realizing that Hank's sex addiction *was* affecting the children, and that her own efforts to protect them and control Hank had failed, Molly reached out for help—entering therapy and eventually becoming active in S-Anon as well as in our group for co-dependents. As her recovery progressed, Molly's world expanded, and her confidence grew. "I had been wrapped up in Hank's problem and my co-dependency for so long that I hadn't ever really been exposed to the outside world. I didn't know I had choices at all," she admits. "But as time went on—I felt that if I had to, I could go out and take care of myself. Financially, I would still need help, but I got a job and that helped me see that there were things I could do, ways I could change myself that I hadn't considered before.''

Molly followed almost all of the suggestions we shared with you in the preceding chapter, detaching herself from Hank's problem, taking responsibility for herself, working through the stages of grief, and setting ground rules for her relationship. A year and a half after she began her own recovery, Hank still had made no move to seek help for his addiction or even admit he had one. According to Molly, "It just got to the point where I really didn't want to deal with it anymore. Hank wasn't getting better. The marriage wasn't getting better. It finally dawned on me that if I really wanted to get better, I would have to get out of the relationship for a while." With support from us and the members of her recovery groups, Molly legally separated from Hank.

Like Molly, at some point in your personal recovery from addiction or co-dependency, you will have to consider objectively whether or not your relationship has a future. Sometimes, this honest, fearless examination reveals that the relationship must end—for your own sake, your partner's, and if you have children, for their sake as well. You may be more likely to reach that conclusion if you, like Molly, are in recovery and your partner is not. However, even when both you and your partner seek help and improve individually, there is no guarantee that the relationship can be salvaged. Of course, it certainly might improve, and often does, if both of you work together to rebuild it. But just as often, one or both recovering partners look hard for a reason to stay together, find none, and decide to separate or divorce.

RECOVERY ALONE CANNOT SAVE A RELATIONSHIP

"I left the door open for us to get back together if Hank ever got his act together," Molly explains. "Our splitting up did make him see that he needed help and I was glad, even if that wasn't the reason I did it. He's a lot better now, and he wants us to get back together. But I'm not sure that's realistic anymore. He is in recovery and doing pretty well, and we're in counseling together, working on the relationship, but I still might decide not to go back. I don't know, maybe there's just too much water over the dam, too much damage to the foundation to build a new life.''

Although it is never too late to restore your own life through recovery, the same cannot be said for your marriage or relationship. By the time you and/or your partner hit bottom and seek help, the fallout from years of addiction and co-dependency may have done irreparable damage, inflicting wounds no amount of therapy or Twelve Steps work can heal. To use Molly's metaphor, sometimes, there really isn't enough of a foundation left to make rebuilding the relationship a viable option. In other instances, so much pain, resentment, and anger have accumulated over the years that the relationship bottoms out *before* you do. And often, particularly if you are the co-dependent partner, in order to recover at all, you may have to distance yourself from the relationship completely, separating from your partner, at least temporarily.

''I figured that if we separated for a while, and he couldn't say I was putting too much pressure on him all the time, maybe then, he would deal with his problems,'' says Diane, whose husband finally did make a commitment to recovery and stopped slipping back into his old habits after she left him. Their temporary breakup was more than a ploy to make him change, however. ''It was probably as important for me as for him,'' Diane admits. ''I just couldn't handle the situation anymore. I needed time for myself, to cool off and get *my* act together.''

Cheryl, too, decided neither she nor her husband could grow while staying together. ''After a year or two of Al-Anon and S-Anon meetings, I finally got to the point where I knew I had to leave him,'' she explains. ''I came to the realization that I was not helping him or myself by staying with him. He was so bad off that he couldn't function at all. He wasn't working, just out drinking and acting out, or in bed being sick. It was a nightmare, and it didn't get better until I left. I wasn't around to take care of him, and that was the best thing for him and the best thing for me.''

As it was for Cheryl and Diane, a trial separation or even a divorce often proves to be the healthiest option for everyone involved. In fact, your own recovery and the honest self-examination it demands may even reveal that you and your partner have been staying together only out of habit or mutual co-dependency, instead of love and mutual affection. That is certainly true of Janet, whose loveless marriage has lasted for nearly two decades in spite of the fact that she and her husband rarely talk and never make love. Long aware of the relationship's deficiencies, Janet sought solace through a compulsive sex-only affair that lasted for five years. After months of intensive therapy, she is just beginning to face the possibility of ending her marriage. ''One of us ought to go,'' she declares. ''I don't think it's fair for either of us to live this sort of a life. I should have somebody I care for, and he should have somebody he cares for.''

Such an awareness simply was not possible for Janet while her life revolved around compulsive sexual rituals. And you, too, may see your relationship clearly for the first time only after you begin to deal with your addiction or co-dependency. Hiding a large part of yourself in order to keep your addiction hidden, or hiding from yourself by focusing all your attention on the addict, you may not have noticed that your serious communication problems or the inability to solve regular, everyday problems has also driven a wedge between you and your partner. Once the fog of addiction or co-dependency lifts, you may discover that whatever feelings there had once been between you have disappeared. You may even realize that the bond you once believed existed between you was never more than an illusion, part of the romantic vision or happy-family façade you fought so hard to maintain. Indeed, you may find you don't even like each other very much, that you seem to be inherently incompatible.

"We just weren't a good match," Jenny realizes now, although she still thinks there must have been some logical reason behind her attraction to the handsome young artist she lived with long after she became aware of his compulsion to have sex with as many women as possible as often as possible. "Our personalities weren't compatible," she continues. "He is so impatient and has a really hot temper. I kind of hang back, take my time, and keep my feelings inside. We probably would have driven each other crazy eventually, even if he didn't have this problem."

Jenny ultimately ended the relationship. "After a while, I realized splitting up was the only option that made sense," she explains. "But even though I knew that it was the best thing for both of us, and I had a lot of recovery behind me, it still wasn't easy to do." Deciding to separate or divorce is never easy and, in our opinion, it shouldn't be. Because choosing to end a relationship is a serious matter, the decision should not be made impulsively. You are well advised to think carefully about whether you really want to separate, and if you do, what will be the best way to go about it.

BUT WHAT IF YOU DON'T BELIEVE IN DIVORCE?

Many of our patients, addicts and co-dependents alike, recognize that there is nothing of value left in their marriages, and that there is no way to rebuild the relationships, yet they cannot bring themselves to accept separation or divorce as an option. They do not believe in divorce under any circumstances, they tell us. More often than not, this disbelief is connected to their religious convictions. As destructive and unsatisfying as their relationships have been and continue to be, these patients believe that the pain caused by their marriages pales in comparison to the anguish they would feel if they went against their religious persuasion that divorce is a sin God will not forgive.

Long before we met her, Lynn went through this gut-wrenching struggle. A fundamentalist Christian, who was devoted to her religion and grateful for the solace it had provided for her over the years, Lynn strongly believed that getting a divorce was going against God's will. Yet, Lynn desperately wanted to escape her alcoholic husband's physical abuse and, having tried everything else, realized that the only solution was to get out of the marriage altogether. Torn between her physical and emotional needs for safety and self-respect and her spiritual need to follow the tenets of her religion, Lynn felt trapped in a no-win situation.

"I thought, God hates divorce, period," Lynn explains. "Everything I was raised to believe, everything I heard at church and Bible study, told me that. My mother was an example of that. But when she died, I began to wonder what God thought about the kind of marriage she had and the kind I had. Did God want us to be abused and hate ourselves and suffer right up until the day we died? Did he approve of people who lived a lie the way I did? I didn't love my husband. There was no bond between us. He was beating me. I was lying every day, covering up when he went on drinking binges, telling everyone we had this great marriage, all the time hoping they wouldn't see the bruises or question what I told them about my broken arm or cracked ribs. It was my childhood all over again. And it didn't make sense. I struggled with it for a long time, but finally decided that God couldn't really want me to go on suffering, and I got out of the marriage."

Although you may not come to the same conclusion, or choose the same course of action that Lynn did, if you find yourself in a relationship that's destroying you, you may want to reexamine some of your religious beliefs—perhaps consulting a member of the clergy, a respected individual from your church or synagogue, your therapist, or someone from your recovery group who has gone through a similar struggle. No matter how much authority any of these people have or how much you look up to them, do not expect them to settle the issue for you. However you come to terms with the concept of God's will, you should be the one who ultimately decides whether to stay in your relationship or get out of it.

THINKING THROUGH A DIFFICULT CHOICE

"I wanted to leave my husband long before I actually did," says Sara. "About two months after I started counseling, when I really started to understand what had been going on for the past ten years, I just wanted to walk away from my marriage and never look back. I didn't want to be indecisive anymore. I wanted to get it over with, to know that at least I'd finally made a decision. But a lot of people told me not to be impulsive about it, and they were right. We did end up getting divorced, but the whole thing went more smoothly and was a lot less painful because we waited and worked it out like responsible adults."

Like Sara, you may feel impatient to get it over with and want to make a decision about the relationship immediately, once and for all. Early in recovery, especially, when long-buried anger is rising to the surface, you may be tempted to rush into a decision that you may later regret. Because jumping into a divorce can be just as damaging as jumping into a marriage, we advise you to wait until you have worked through some of the pain or anger and are thinking clearly again before making your final judgment on the matter.

As family therapists, we want our patients to take as much time as they need to consider objectively their options and responsibly select the course of action that is best for them. This preference has nothing to do with a moral judgment about whether divorce is good or bad. We never tell our patients that they *should* get a divorce or *should* stay together. That is their decision. Even where incest is involved, although we strongly advise both separation of the sex addict from his or her family during treatment and intensive counseling for every family member, our patients must ultimately make the choice about whether or not to divorce. However, we have learned through years of experience that a reasonable, well-thought-out decision can rarely be made while individual lives and relationships are still being dictated by addiction and co-dependency. Therefore, we encourage our patients to continue their own growth and recovery, using the Twelve Steps, therapy, and the support found in self-help groups to help them work through pain and anger, and to learn new ways of communicating with each other and rebuilding shattered trust.

"We both were in individual therapy and went to a couples communication course. And I was getting group therapy and attending AA and SA meetings," says Don, whose wife began living with him again after he was discharged from an alcoholism treatment program. "But everything was still bent out of shape between us," he says. "I think we both found out our differences were so great that we were better off just ending things completely. We were too far apart, and nothing could bring us close enough together again to save the marriage."

Like Don, you may find that individual recovery and couples therapy confirm the fact that the relationship cannot be saved. However, you are just as likely to see improvement in a relationship that previously seemed beyond repair. Whatever the outcome, by first dealing with addiction and co-dependency and then giving the relationship a chance to improve, you will be able to make a truly healthy choice rather than an impulsive or self-destructive one.

But remember, that choice is always *yours* to make. You can and probably should call on others for support, but no one—not a therapist, a clergy member, a friend in your support group, a parent, or your partner—can make the decision for you. Some of these people can help you view yourself and your life realistically and reinforce the idea that you must function as an adult who behaves and makes decisions responsibly. In the end, however, it is up to you alone to make a choice that takes into account what you want out of life, what you hope to find in a relationship, how you want to rear your children—in short, your entire value system.

HELPING YOUR CHILDREN RECOVER

That choice becomes even more complicated, of course, if you have children. As Molly finally realized, her children had not escaped unscathed from growing up in a sex-addicted family. Although she and Hank had sincerely believed that they were good parents who always put their children first, in fact, they had allowed Hank's sex addiction and Molly's co-dependency to rule and ravage the family. Years of living in such a household had taken their toll on the kids, paving the way for them to become addicts of some kind or co-dependents themselves.

Like Molly's children, yours need to begin their own recovery *immediately*. But they can't do it on their own. They need your aid desperately, even though they may resist it at first. And that means that no matter where you or your spouse or partner are in your own recoveries, or whether you plan to split up or stay together, you need to turn your attention to your children and get them help fast. Otherwise, you will find that your children will carry on the horrible legacy of addiction and co-dependency, as Lynn did.

Lynn grew up in a home ruled by sex addiction and co-dependency. All of her beliefs—about herself, other people, work, play, love, marriage, how to behave in any situation, and how to survive in general— were molded during a childhood marked by her father's physical and sexual abuse, as well as her mother's total lack of support. Lynn's mother has been dead for five years. Lynn has not lived in her parents' home for ten. She has been married and divorced, lived with a sex addict and left him, graduated from college, and advanced in her chosen career. Yet, she still bears scars from the wounds inflicted during her childhood.

"I want to confront my father directly," Lynn admits. "Not necessarily to hurt him or punish him, but to finally get things out in the open, to be able to say 'You did some pretty rotten things to me when I was a kid. You shouldn't have treated me the way that you did. I didn't deserve it, and I'm not going to let what happened affect me for the rest of my life.' I think if I could say that, I could stop being so scared of him. I could maybe get rid of all this anger and stop being so hard on myself, too. But I haven't done it yet. In fact, I haven't really talked to him at all in almost a year. I don't want to see him. Of course, I think about him every day. He's always there. What he did is always there."

As pressing as is her need to get her feelings toward her father out in the open, perhaps more distressing are the questions Lynn would like to ask her mother, questions that will remain unanswered because her mother is no longer alive. "I want to know how much she knew about what was going on," Lynn continues. "I want to look her in the eye and ask, 'Where were you? Couldn't you see what he was doing? Why did you have to pretend everything was okay when it wasn't? Why didn't you do *something?*' All my life, I wanted to ask her about those things. But we weren't allowed to talk about anything like that. And by the time I figured out I *could* talk about it, she was gone. Now, I'll never know. I'll always wonder why."

The impact of being parented by a sex addict and a co-dependent goes beyond unanswered questions and unresolved conflicts about compulsive and co-dependent behaviors. Lynn also struggles to fill in the gaps left by an inadequate and inconsistent upbringing.

"No one ever talked to me about sex," Lynn explains. "I had no sex education whatsoever. Everything I know, I learned after I got married, and my husband wasn't exactly the world's greatest teacher. My boyfriend was really sick sexually, but I didn't know that until after I'd convinced myself that I was the one who was messed up, inhibited, or frigid or something. There were a lot of things I didn't understand until recently. And I'm still not really sure I can ever have a normal sex life. I hope I can, but I just don't know."

Like other children of sex addicts, by the time Lynn reached adulthood, she had developed certain quirks—fears and anxieties—that made no sense to her or the people around her. "I always dressed or undressed in the bathroom with the door locked," Lynn continues. "I wouldn't even let my husband in to get a towel, even if I was just brushing my teeth or combing my hair. I won't use the restroom at work unless I'm sure no one else is in there, and if someone comes in, I just sit there holding my breath, waiting for them to leave. That's just how I am. I never knew why, until my therapist helped me remember how my father wouldn't let us close the bathroom door, how he would burst into the bathroom while I was taking a shower, and watch me get undressed at night."

In addition, Lynn absorbed both her mother's co-dependent tendencies and her father's addictive ones, marrying an alcoholic and putting up with his brutal physical abuse for more than five years, then getting involved in a live-in relationship with a sex addict. Her enjoyment of life has been diminished by her workaholism, and she has gotten into serious financial difficulties because of her compulsive spending. As you can see, Lynn, like anyone raised in an addictive environment, has paid a high price for something she had no control over—being born to sexually addicted and co-dependent parents. And, if she had not sought help to overcome the devastating effects of her upbringing, Lynn might have gone right on paying—and passed the painful, self-destructive lessons she learned as a child on to any children she might ever have.

The Lessons of Addiction and Co-Dependency: What You Taught Your Children in the Past

Like Lynn's parents, because of your sex addiction and co-dependency, you have inadvertently taught your children lessons that could last for the rest of their lives. Your attitudes, your actions toward them and toward each other, and the "don't talk, don't feel, don't trust" rules governing all family interactions helped shape their personalities. They absorbed your attitudes, adopted your behaviors, and laid the groundwork for adult lives tainted by anxiety and confusion and, more often than not, addiction or co-dependency problems of their own.

- The secretiveness and the lack of communication in your home taught your children not to speak openly about their own thoughts or feelings.
- The unpredictable, seemingly unprovoked emotional outbursts of one or both parents, as well as constant criticism and disregard for any of their own displays of emotion, led your children to believe that having feelings is dangerous and expressing them is a cardinal sin.

- The half-truths and outright lies they heard, the mixed messages they received—and the baffling mood swings and erratic behavior they observed—convinced your children not to trust you, themselves, or anyone else.
- The restrictive or confusing sex education—or none at all—they received, and the little or no physical or emotional intimacy they witnessed in their home, gave your children inaccurate information or inappropriate social skills for healthy sexual relationships.

Fortunately, none of these lessons is irreversible. Your children can learn new attitudes and behaviors. Just as you have through your own recovery, they can embrace a new way of living. They can work through the pain and heartache they have already experienced, leaving the past behind them and leading fuller, healthier lives. Lynn is living proof of this. After a year of intensive therapy and participation in self-help groups, she says with honesty and delight:

"Today, I feel really alive. I still have work to do, of course. But I feel more confident than I ever thought I could and know that I do a lot of things really well. I can look in the mirror now and think that I am a good person, that I have value, that I have something to offer other people. I used to think I was doomed, that my fate in life was to suffer and fail. But now, I not only know I can be happy and at peace with myself, but I can also help other people recover and be happy."

Lynn was almost thirty when she began to recover from the effects of her parents' sex addiction and co-dependency. By then, the damage done during her childhood had already caused many problems in her adult life. Your children, however, need not wait to seek help. No matter how young they are, your children can begin to recover from the effects of this family disease—if you are willing to give them, and get them, the help they need. Until recently, resources for children of sex addicts and co-dependents were few, and understanding of the impact of addictive diseases on children was limited. Fortunately, today, you and the professional therapy community are armed with a great deal more knowledge and skill for helping children recover *before* they develop addictions, co-dependencies, or other problems of their own.

The Lessons of Recovery: What You Can Teach Your Children Now

During their childhoods, Lynn and other adult children of sex addicts who come to us for help firmly believed that they could not turn to their parents for help—and their perception was probably quite accurate. Trapped in their addiction and co-dependency, those parents were too consumed by their own obsessions, compulsions, and ever more desperate attempts to deny the existence of a problem to be of much help or support to their children. They did not know they were sexually addicted or co-dependent, and they made no real effort to recover themselves.

You, however, if only from reading this book, know enough about sex addiction and co-dependency to realize that the lessons your children have learned from you thus far have had a powerful impact on them, and can go on affecting them for years to come. If you have not already figured it out for yourself, let us inform you—in no uncertain terms—that you must now do everything you possibly can to rectify the situation. At the very least, you must seek help for yourself and become a role model of recovery for your children rather than continue to be a role model of addiction or co-dependency. Setting a positive example and modeling a different style of living and communicating is the very best way to teach your children that people can change and that facing problems—talking, feeling, and trusting—are healthy and healing, not dangerous and destructive.

You can become a positive role model for your children even if your partner is not pursuing his or her own recovery. In fact, your example of healthy communication and other behaviors is even more critical if your spouse is still pursuing compulsive sexual rituals or still behaving co-dependently. But this does not mean that you must compensate for your partner's behavior or make amends for his or her wrongs. No matter how much you wish you could, you cannot make everything "all better." You can, however, demonstrate appropriate responses to unacceptable behavior and be available to support your children as they struggle with their own reactions to the situation.

As you now know, both co-dependency and addictions—including sex addiction—tend to get handed down from generation to generation. While heredity may or may not play a part in passing on this family disease, the environment of an addictive household definitely does. Therefore, you must do everything in your power to make your home environment one that promotes recovery rather than one that perpetuates the cycle of addiction.

Just as the first step in your own recovery program required you to admit your problem and your inability to manage your own life because of it, the first step to take in helping your children recover is to talk with them frankly and openly—acknowledging that a problem exists and verifying that the troubles they observed in the past did in fact happen, that they were not imagining things or making mountains out of molehills.

And you must make sure that your actions do not contradict your words, as they did so often in the past. If you tell your children that you will no longer pretend that problems have not happened, stand by your words. The next time you are upset, own up to your feelings instead of saying, "I'm fine." The next time you and your spouse argue, do not brush reality under the rug or minimize it. Do not try to convince your kids that you weren't arguing, when they have seen and heard for themselves that you were. Sending mixed messages was what you *used to do*. Now you must say what you really mean and behave accordingly. Your honesty, and the other changes you make in the course of your own recovery, teach your children that they *can talk about their thoughts and feelings* without being punished or rejected.

Everything you do to create a safer, more secure environment—and all the progress you make in your own recovery—helps counteract the harmful lessons you have conveyed in the past. For instance, admitting your own wrongs and making amends as part of your Twelve Steps work will teach your children that *nobody is perfect, not even a mother or father*. Learning that *everybody makes mistakes* gives children permission to make their own. They will be able to push through their old fears about being anything less than perfect, take risks, and partake in new intellectual, physical, and emotional experiences. Of course, after keeping your children on such a tight rein for so long, you'll want to be careful not to go to the other extreme by giving them license to act any way they please. Simply ease up a bit on your overprotectiveness and make house rules less restrictive, giving your children opportunities to make more of their decisions and to experience both the positive and negative consequences of their choices.

By improving your social skills, you show children how to improve theirs. Your new ability to communicate openly and express feelings honestly not only gives children permission for similar self-expression but models how to communicate effectively. In addition, your use of resources like therapy and self-help groups teaches children to *get help for themselves whenever they need it*. Because your children will need help in their recovery—just as you need help in yours—it is critical for them to understand that *it is okay to talk about personal problems* with other family members, as well as with people outside the immediate family. Encourage children to seek advice, rather than keep secrets.

If you are a recovering co-dependent whose spouse is *not* making an attempt to recover from sex addiction, you are probably going to discover that your spouse is vehemently opposed to the idea of obtaining outside help for the children. Assert yourself, insisting that not only you but also your kids will get the help needed, whether your partner does or not. Your children's recovery is worth fighting for. Their present and future well-being is at stake, and you simply cannot take no for an answer—no matter how adamantly your partner vows to change, or how scary it is for you to stand up to him or her. You cannot afford to cop out where your kids are concerned.

You may also feel reluctant to get outsiders involved in helping your children and try to convince yourself that you can give your children all the love and support that they need. Please remember that trying to fix everything by yourself is what got you into this mess in the first place. Although you can do a great many things to help your children, you cannot act as a therapist to your own family. You are too close to your children, and too intricately involved in their lives, to view their problems objectively. In addition, your tendency to blame yourself, minimize the magnitude of problems, and apply quick fixes hampers your ability to be as helpful as a more detached outsider can be. And no matter how committed to recovery you are, or how much you have learned about your own and your partner's diseases, you are not equipped to undo the damage done by the more subtle aspects of sex addiction and co-dependency—denial, attempts to control, hiding feelings, sending confusing mixed messages, and inconsistency.

Until a few months ago, Cheryl resisted our suggestions to get her children involved in therapy. Although she kept telling us that "the impact sex addiction has had on my kids really concerns me, because everything I read says they are affected by it and that addictions are passed on to the kids," every time we asked her what she was doing to help them, she replied, "I guess I'll just trust God. Somehow, they'll get through it." Cheryl's attitude is healthier than one that ignores the effect of sex addiction and co-dependency on children, and she is on the right track when she turns to her Higher Power for help. But Cheryl—and you—must go further, accepting your responsibility to do what *you* can, which includes making sure your kids get the outside help they need.

If your children are incest victims, they need professional help—no ifs, ands, or buts about it. If you allow your own denial or disbelief to prevent you from seeking help for them, you are victimizing your children as much as the sexual abuser is. No matter how hurt, frightened, or shocked you feel when your children tell you they have been sexually molested by your spouse or anyone else, you *must* put your feelings aside and believe them. Kids almost never fabricate stories about incest. In fact, more often than not, they are too scared or ashamed to mention it at all. If your children give you even the slightest hint that they are being sexually abused, take them seriously and investigate the matter thoroughly.

Begin today to ease your children's embarrassment about discussing sexual topics—especially sexual abuse of any kind, by anyone. Teach them at an early age that their genitals are private parts, and that nobody should touch them there without their permission. Let them know that giving in because someone threatens them, tricks them, or tries to assure them it is okay is *not* the same as giving their permission. Encourage them to tell you if anyone does anything that makes them feel uncomfortable, explaining that if anybody—in or out of the family—does molest them and warns them not to tell, they should tell you anyway. Also, make sure that they understand that when someone touches them without their permission, *that* person is the one who has done something wrong, not the child.

And please remember that incest is *definitely* a problem you cannot handle on your own. You need outside help *right away.* Sexually abusing children is a serious crime and should be reported to the proper authorities. Child protective services and, in some instances, the police must be notified. Immediate professional help for everyone in the family must be obtained. And to prevent further abuse, either the children or the abuser will have to leave the home, at least until the addict receives professional treatment. We cannot stress strongly enough that when incest has occurred, protecting your children *must* take priority over your desire to deny the problem, spare the addict's feelings, or maintain the family image.

Reestablishing Boundaries: Recognizing That Your Children Have Their Own Needs

For as long as sex addiction ruled your household, each individual's interests, needs, and desires were sacrificed in order to maintain the status quo, to keep the addiction a secret within and outside the family, and to avoid making any waves that might shatter the family's delicate balance. Family members played roles instead of developing separate and distinct personalities, and the boundary lines between one person's needs and another's became blurred to the point where no one in the family seemed to have an identity of his or her own. Also, in the past, you insisted that your children behave more maturely than their age warranted—expecting them to control their own emotions, for example, or to assume adult responsibilities. You may have even turned to them to meet your emotional needs, letting them take care of you, when you should have been taking care of them.

To advance your own, your partner's, and your children's recovery, you must re-draw the boundary lines between individual family members and stop acting as if your needs and your children's are one and the same. First and foremost, you must free your children to be children again, to think and feel and act the way children do—reminding yourself over and over again that your kids *are* children, not adults.

This will not be easy for you—or your children. They have already experienced as much trauma and handled as much responsibility as some people do in a lifetime. They are accustomed to the roles they have played for all these years, and are likely to need a great deal of help to change their habitual ways of dealing with things. You are going to have to take a close, fearless look at your children, both the rebellious ones who act out at home and at school and the "little adults" who behave hyperresponsibly. You will have to look beyond the behavior to the reasons for it, asking yourself why your children are acting in certain ways. Long after you and your spouse have stopped acting compulsively or co-dependently, your children may continue or return to their old patterns. If they do, you must ask yourself: What family problems are they trying to solve by taking on these roles? Who is taking care of whom here? Who is taking the heat off other family members? Has there been a reversal of the parent/child relationship? Obviously, these are complicated questions that you will have trouble answering yourself, which is why we recommend that our patients get family therapy to help them find the answers and redefine the boundaries between family members.

From here on in, you must also make a concerted effort not to meet your own needs at your children's expense. Resist the temptation to use your children as sounding boards, for example, selfishly venting your anger or bitterness on them, and especially sharing resentments and detailed lists about their other parent's faults or failures. If you want to build a healthier parent/child relationship, you can no longer use children as confidants, either. Resist the temptation to reveal intimate personal information to children who do not need to know those details and usually are too young to fully understand them. Do not look to your children for the support and intimacy you may not be getting from your partner. Your children need *your* emotional support and nurturing, not the other way around. Develop other resources to meet your needs. Turning to a self-help group, friends, or your therapist instead of your kids when you want emotional support enables you to fulfill your own needs *and* your children's.

NO MORE PRETENDING: LIVING BY A NEW SET OF RULES

Once you get serious about recovery for the whole family, you, your spouse, and your children begin a new life, one without secrets, lies, or buried feelings. In the past, each of you and all of your interactions were governed by rules that told you not to talk, not to feel, and not to trust. The rules for a family in recovery are a complete reversal of the rules of the past. In word and deed, you must reinforce these new rules—setting a positive example and actively encouraging your children to talk, feel, and trust.

Talk

Your children need to know that a problem does exist. They need to be reassured that they aren't crazy people imagining the tension they feel. They need to hear that what they have observed in the past did in fact happen, and they are literally owed explanations for why you told them nothing was wrong. The first step toward abolishing the old "don't talk" rule is to openly acknowledge the family's real problems, discussing what has happened in the past and exploring the children's thoughts and feelings about it. As often and as honestly as possible, explain that the behaviors and attitudes of the past were *not* okay, that everyone in the family got hurt because of them, and that you have made a commitment to act differently now and in the future.

The problems of the past are not all you will talk about with your children. They need to hear what you have to say about your relationship with them and with your spouse—especially when a separation or divorce occurs. If you and your partner still feel something for each other and the separation is intended to be temporary, reassure your children that you both still care about each other, perhaps explaining the situation the way Hank and Molly did. "We love each other, but we are still having some problems being together," they told them. "They are our problems. They are not your fault. We know you feel unhappy about our separation, but we have to work out our problems before we try living together again."

Even if you are certain that your marriage is over, let your children know that you both still care about *them*. Although your affection for your children may never have wavered, they may not know it. Your own problems have prevented you from expressing affection, and your actions may have even convinced your children that you did not really care for them at all. They need to hear you *actually say* that you love them and will continue to love them.

Just as you cannot assume that your children know how you feel about them, you cannot assume that they are doing well and recovering just because they look okay on the outside. Instead of superficially observing that your children *seem* fine, take the time to find out how they really *are*. Encourage them to talk about what they think and what they feel, and respond by talking openly about your own thoughts and feelings.

Unquestionably, the most difficult topic to talk about is sex addiction itself. "We still haven't figured out how to explain it in a way the kids will understand," says Peggy, whose husband, Ray, used to run up enormous bills calling phone sex services and turned over substantial chunks of his salary to prostitutes, whom he had sex with at least daily and sometimes several times a day. The family's financial situation became even more unstable as Ray's compulsive gambling raged out of control. "Our kids know about the gambling, because my husband talks so openly and freely about it," Peggy explains. "He came right out and told them that gambling was not the way to go out and make money, that gambling's not an acceptable behavior. Because it got to the point where the kids were saying, 'Well, just go up to Las Vegas, Dad, and get some money.' We both knew we had to deal with it directly."

If, like Peggy and Ray, you and/or your spouse are recovering from other addictions or compulsive behaviors, you can help your children understand the nature of the family's problems by thoroughly discussing those behaviors. However, if sex addiction is the only addiction that has affected the family or the one that your children heard you and your spouse arguing about on various occasions, you are going to have to say *something* about it. What details and how much to share with your children is a truly tricky question, and you must trust your instincts to arrive at the best answer. The ninth step of recovery advises you to admit your wrongs and make amends ". . . except when to do so would injure them or others." With these words in mind, you must decide if a full account of every detail is really necessary. Edit out any details that might harm children who are not mature enough to comprehend them—taking particular care not to give children the impression that all sexual behavior is dirty, disgusting, or something that causes only pain and shame.

Of course, you may not be at all reluctant to talk about sex addiction. Co-dependents in particular may want to get everything out in the open once and for all and may feel tempted to use information about sex addiction as a weapon against their partners or as a new technique to humiliate addicts into abandoning compulsive sexual behavior. Before *you* act on such an impulse, stop to examine your motives. Ask yourself whose needs you would meet by sharing every gory detail with your kids. Certainly, not the children's. If you find that you are too angry, bitter, resentful, or confused to rely on your own discretion, turn to objective outsiders—therapists and self-help group members—to help you decide how much to tell your children. A family therapist can also provide valuable assistance, as you come to what is always a highly individualized decision that takes into account your specific situation, including how much children already know and how much information children of various ages can actually handle.

While circumstances vary greatly and there is no blanket rule about how much to tell your children about sex addiction, it is our opinion that they may not need to be told any specifics at all

> *If* compulsive sexual behaviors have not directly involved them—through incest or any sort of encouragement to try inappropriate sexual practices,
>
> and
>
> *If* neither parent has previously mentioned the topic directly to or within earshot of the children—arguing about the addict's sexual activity while the children were nearby, or saying something to them like "I don't ever want you to grow up to be like your father, running around to prostitutes and having affairs," for instance.

While we discourage you from providing details they do not need to know (to young children especially), we do feel that when children get older—when they are going off to work, or to college, or embarking upon intimate relationships of their own—then the full picture should be revealed to them, simply to alert them to the possibility of a problem in their own lives.

In addition, if your children have seen or heard something about the sex addict's behavior, and especially if they bring up the subject themselves, it is essential that you sit them down immediately, find out what they know, and confirm or correct their impressions. Even if you previously decided that the information was inappropriate for children of their age, *do not deny* any facts that they are aware of already.

Naturally, you want to protect children from truths that might upset them and, fearing that you will lose your children's love and respect, you may want to protect yourself, as well. But you actually open yourself to more dire consequences when you respond to children who have already begun to piece clues together, by saying, "No, you're wrong. That never happened. It couldn't have happened. You're just imagining things." Refuting children's real observations leaves them feeling more confused, even crazy. Unless you are honest with your children and deal openly with whatever they already know about the situation, they will never learn to trust themselves or you. Indeed, if their suspicions are later confirmed in other ways, they *will* lose respect for you, and you will have a crisis on your hands instead of what could have been a calm, healing discussion.

Even if your children do not indicate that they have any idea of what has gone on, if you choose not to tell them anything at all about sex addiction, you may one day have to deal with the fallout of their accidental discoveries about it. All too often, information about sex addiction comes to children's attention because of a sex addict's indiscretion or a co-dependent's anger. Children may pick up the telephone extension and hear a parent conversing with a phone sex service employee, or see a parent leaving a motel with his or her lover, or read in the newspaper that a parent has been arrested for voyeurism, exhibitionism, or in a police raid on a massage parlor. And children certainly know plenty of details about sex addiction if they have been victims of it directly. Moreover, children in all kinds of families overhear arguments between their parents every day. And in your home, during a heated argument, details about sex addiction are liable to come out into the open.

If children find out about a parent's sex addiction in one of these ways, you may have to explain the disease in detail, as well as make sure your kids have ample opportunity to deal with their feelings of betrayal, embarrassment, or shame. Especially when sexual behavior becomes public knowledge because of the addict's arrest or some other sort of scandal, children are likely to be ridiculed by their peers and playmates, overhear adults' whispered disapproval, or, in the case of incest, go through numerous in-depth interviews and perhaps even have to move out of their home. You cannot completely shield children from these harsh realities. But you can prepare them for any ordeals they may have to go through, discussing what they can reasonably expect and trying to explain why people might treat them cruelly even though they have done nothing wrong themselves. You might even point out that this public exposure could actually have positive results, that sometimes the bad things that happen help people start to get better.

In most cases, helping children cope after sex addiction has been publicly exposed, like helping them recover from incest, is more than any parent can handle alone. You are reeling from the crisis yourself and can barely cope with your own feelings, much less help your children work through theirs. For your own sake and your family's, we strongly suggest that you seek professional help to get you through the crisis. And even after the crisis has passed, or if you are lucky enough not to experience one at all, we recommend self-help support groups like Alateen, teen youth groups, or professional therapy for children whose parents are sexually addicted or co-dependent. Children need an opportunity to work through their pain, frustration, anger, and shame away from their home and their parents. Your children's tendencies to try to please you, and to try not to upset you, often prevent them from feeling free to tell you everything they need to get out of their systems. You must still do everything you can to help them work through their problems with you, but you must also give them the chance to work out certain issues without you.

Feel

How do you undo the damage caused by the "don't feel" rule, which encouraged all family members to deny or bury their true feelings? Begin by permitting children to express their emotions openly, to say what they really feel. You must know what your children are feeling before you can help them work through those feelings.

Model emotional expression, setting a positive example by articulating your own anger, hurt, and pain as well as your joy, excitement, and affection. Talk about what your feelings mean and what they don't mean.

"Our kids have always been able to see when we were tense or irritated with each other," Peggy admits. "Just like they knew about Ray's gambling, they knew when things were not all right between us. But we never talked to them about our feelings or let out other feelings. Tension and anger were all they knew. Now, they also see us make up. When we're grouchy or worried, we tell them why. When something good happens and we feel pleased, we show that, too. And when we do fight, we explain that being angry with someone sometimes doesn't mean you stop loving that person, that we still love each other and still love them—even when we don't feel happy."

Children also need to know that feelings are not permanent, that no one can be happy all of the time, and that anger or sadness will go away if you—and they—talk about it, try to understand why you feel it, and then release it. And of course, actually observing you handle emotions in this way carries much more weight than mere words can.

With your encouragement and role modeling, your children will discover that it is okay for them to feel unhappy or angry or hurt, too, and that they will not be punished or discounted when they voice their feelings—whether those feelings are positive or negative. They can even say, "This family stinks," if that is what they feel at the moment. You may not want to hear that, and the truth is it will always be difficult to hear negative emotions being expressed by your children—who you wish could always be happy in general and happy with you in particular. But, like you and your partner, children need to *verbalize* their feelings in order to recognize them and eventually get beyond them.

When the entire family is in recovery, individual members no longer have to pretend to feel what they do not really feel. There is no more putting on a happy face, to convince each other and everyone else that you are a perfect, problem-free family. In the past, you denied reality by shutting off all unpleasant feelings, convincing yourself that you and your family were safe and secure. Unfortunately, by encouraging your children to deal with their feelings in that same way, you ensured that the events children blocked out of their memories and the feelings they buried would one day come back to haunt them.

The adult children of sex addicts whom we treat literally cannot remember large portions of their childhoods. To keep from feeling their pain, anger, or fear, they simply forgot that the events that caused those feelings ever happened. Not only do they sense that part of their identities are missing, but—because they are unable to grieve over pain from the past or work through old feelings that still have an effect on them—they have trouble moving forward in their adult lives.

Your children need not suffer these consequences. By encouraging children to recognize, express, and release their feelings about both pleasant and unpleasant events, and showing them how to do it by doing it yourself, you prevent future problems and enable them to begin living full, healthy lives immediately.

Like you, children will need to do more than talk about their feelings in order to work through them. In fact, children are prone to act out their feelings rather than merely discuss them. Try to provide children various nondestructive outlets for acting out their feelings—punching a pillow when they are angry, crying when they are sad, drawing pictures or putting on puppet shows to work through their fears, and so on.

Perhaps the most difficult feelings for both you and your children to deal with will be your children's feelings toward you. No matter how much you encourage them to openly and honestly express their real emotions, children may continue to fear that you will reject or ridicule them if they tell you how they really feel about you. From time to time, they may even have such strong feelings of hostility toward you that they do not want to give you the satisfaction of knowing you hurt them. One way or another, you must clear the air between you, and you may need a family therapist to help you do that. It can also help to suggest to your children how you might feel if you were in their shoes. Verbalizing their possible feelings for them in this way often opens the door for them to say "Yes, that's how I feel," and elaborate, or "No, that's not how I feel," and explain their points of view.

Whether your children are expressing feelings about you or someone or something else that matters to them, you must be willing to listen to their points of view, no matter how much that might hurt or scare you. Do not get defensive. Do not angrily label children ingrates or spoiled brats and bombard them with a full account of all the things you've ever done for them. Do not lay on the guilt or inform them that they should not feel the way they do. They, like you, are entitled to feel what they feel. Giving children permission to express their emotions *and* responding supportively is what promotes recovery for the entire family.

Trust

The accumulated effects of the "don't trust" rule are the most difficult and will take the most time to overcome. We probably do not need to remind you that you have given your kids ample reason not to trust you. When your all-consuming obsession with either sex or the sex addict dictated your every move, your children simply could not depend on you to do what you said you would do. As a result, you can't just talk about the things that have happened in the past, promise that things will be different, and expect your children to trust you again. You have already broken too many promises, for them to take you at your word now. You must earn back their trust by consistently and repeatedly acting trustworthy. You must *show* your children that you will no longer neglect them and their needs as you did in the past. You must prove that they can count on you. And you cannot begin to do this until you stop behaving compulsively and co-dependently, until you pursue your own recovery.

And even then, you must give your children time to observe and feel confident that you have *really* changed.

Lies, deception, and denial destroyed any trust your children ever had in you. Honesty will help rebuild it. Acknowledge the problems of the past honestly, especially the times you betrayed your children's trust by breaking promises to them, acting irresponsibly, or ignoring them when they needed you to take care of them. Be honest about the problems that still exist, especially if your sexually addicted partner is not in recovery. *Never encourage your children to trust an active sex addict.* The addiction makes him or her inherently untrustworthy, and you do more harm than good by assuring your kids that Daddy or Mommy can be trusted when you know that isn't true.

Your children also lost their trust in you because they could not predict your reactions from one moment to the next. To earn back their trust, when you are angry at your spouse or frustrated by life in general, don't take it out on your children. Making children scapegoats not only destroys their ability to trust but also damages their self-esteem. If you must punish your children for misbehavior, be consistent about it. Letting things slide one day and then blowing your top about them the next prevents children from trusting you and keeps them from trusting their own judgment, as well. These and other habitual ways of venting frustration and losing control when interacting with your children will be difficult to change, and you should once again turn to self-help groups or therapists for help. And because your children have probably learned how to push your buttons, or even imitate your outbursts by throwing tantrums of their own, family therapy is particularly useful for teaching all family members new ways of interacting with each other.

As a result of their upbringing thus far, your children probably have trouble trusting themselves and others, as well as you and your partner. Here again, you have an opportunity to serve as a positive role model for your children. Your involvement with self-help groups and therapy demonstrates how to trust others to help you. New friendships formed through involvement in church and community organizations prove to children that they, like you, can trust people enough to let them get to know you. In addition, you teach children to trust themselves by demonstrating that you trust them to make certain decisions for themselves. Co-dependents in particular can become so obsessed with keeping their children safe and secure that they will not even let children go outside to play on their own or permit anyone outside the family to baby-sit for their children. You must guard against such overprotectiveness. Even young children must be given room to make, and learn from, their own mistakes, and it is absolutely essential for teenagers to make their own choices and accept both the positive and negative consequences of those choices.

Although the consequences of not trusting are truly devastating, rebuilding trust presents a valuable opportunity for your children to learn what trust really is. All children must eventually learn that their parents are not perfect, that parents as well as others will sometimes disappoint them, be dishonest, or betray their trust. Your children have learned those lessons painfully and repeatedly at a very early age, but as you work together to recover, they also learn how to realistically trust people and what constitutes truly trustworthy behavior.

Your children will discover that they can never have blind faith in another person, but they need not become cynics, walking through life with their "dukes up," waiting for people to hurt them. Through your own recovery, you demonstrate trustworthy behavior. You show children that although you are not perfect, more often than not they can depend on you to do what you say and to deliver on the commitments you make. If, through your own recovery, you can truly be trustworthy, you will teach your children enough about trust to convince them they can risk making themselves vulnerable with other people, too. Indeed, if you take advantage of it, recovery offers you and your children a rare opportunity to understand the nature of trust, intimacy, and relationships.

Sex Education

Along with the harmful messages about communication, emotions, and trust, while caught up in your own sex addiction and co-dependency, you unwittingly sent children unhealthy and inaccurate messages about sex and sexuality. You may think that your kids weren't old enough to understand such things, but the truth is that your children learned a great deal from observing the relationship between you and your partner. Moreover, most of the impressions they have already formed are not the ones you really want them to carry with them into relationships of their own. Fortunately, it is not too late to change things by beginning immediately to provide your children with a good, complete sex education.

You can:

- help your children develop the social skills they will need in order to achieve intimacy—encouraging them to build friendships and get involved in group activities that interest them.
- counteract any negative impressions of sex that they formed in the past, explaining that sex is not dirty or disgusting, but more often than not a loving, pleasurable act between two people who love each other.
- create a safe, open home environment in which children can feel free to frankly discuss sexual matters and bring up questions about sex and sexuality.
- take advantage of opportunities to candidly discuss the wide variety of sexual stimuli that exist in the world, including masturbation, pornography, prostitution, and intimate sexual relationships.
- and, of course, provide accurate, age-appropriate information about human sexuality and sexual behavior.

As children mature and not only accumulate more information about sex but also begin to explore their own sexual feelings, you must help them put sex into perspective and define what is appropriate for them to

LONELY ALL THE TIME

do and what is not. They need to know that it's perfectly normal and healthy to feel sexually excited, but that sex in itself is not the most important thing in the world. Tell your children—and show them as well—what a healthy, intimate sexual relationship is. Without discounting that sex sometimes happens in the absence of an emotionally intimate relationship, let them know that ideally it occurs within the context of a caring relationship, one in which both partners value themselves and each other.

A complete and useful sex education always broaches the topic of responsible sexual behavior and includes information about pregnancy, birth control, and sexually transmitted diseases. It is important as well to reinforce the idea that children have the right to say no and should not succumb to pressure from anyone to do things they do not want to do.

Naturally, if you still feel uncomfortable about your own sexuality, you will have tremendous difficulty helping your children feel comfortable about theirs. In addition, if you are just beginning to develop your own social skills or intimate relationship, you will not yet be equipped to pass these lessons on to your children. Children, teenagers in particular, cannot afford to wait for you to change before learning about intimacy and sexuality, so once again we encourage you to seek outside help, consulting both books and trained professionals. Supplement school sex education programs—which unfortunately are often less than comprehensive—with other resources that teach appropriate social and sexual behavior, programs offered by your church or synagogue, for instance. As in recovery itself, where your children's sex education is concerned, you must be willing to go to any lengths to make sure they get the information they need and that they overcome any attitudinal damage that might one day lead to their own sex addiction or co-dependency.

Every child who has ever been touched by sex addiction and co-dependency needs to work through the tasks of recovery mentioned in this chapter. To overcome the damage they have already sustained, and prevent difficulties during their adult lives, children must learn—by observing parental role models and through direct communication—how to talk openly, how to recognize and express their emotions, how to trust themselves and others, and how to feel comfortable with their sexuality. This holds true when both parents are in recovery, when only one parent is, and even when parents separate or divorce.

In helping children accomplish these tasks, single parents face the greatest challenge. In addition, single parents who are recovering co-dependents are most likely to think that since the sexually addicted parent is no longer present in the home, children no longer need help and treatment. That is patently untrue. Neither your problems nor your children's will disappear just because the sex addict has. Because all of the effects produced by years of tension, secrecy, and dishonesty still linger, both you and your children will need to continue actively pursuing recovery.

Whether or not your family stays together, as things start to get better, be careful not to turn the page of sex addiction too quickly, deciding that that episode has ended once and for all and you've all recovered completely. The deep-seated pain each family member experiences does not go away completely—ever. Long after the addict's sexual rituals have stopped and the co-dependent's behavior has changed, you will all have to go on doing whatever you can to make your situation and your family better. There will always be individual issues and relationship problems to resolve and, as each individual grows and changes, every other family member will be called upon to adapt and change, as well.

Recovery is a lifetime undertaking. There will be times when you will curse recovery and the demands it makes of you. But as time goes on, you will also celebrate recovery and feel grateful for each and every change that has led to a new openness in your home and a new life for you and your family. Whether you are cursing or celebrating, hanging onto recovery by a thread during a down time or dancing on air during a good time, you still have the knowledge, skill, and resources to continue to get better. Recognizing that all of you are traveling the road to recovery together, you also know that you can support one another every step of the way.

Appendixes

APPENDIX A
Recommended
Reading

Many of our patients, both sex addicts and co-dependents, have found the following books helpful in recognizing, coping with, and recovering from the family diseases of sex addiction and co-dependency:

Beattie, Melody. *Codependent No More*. Center City, Minnesota: Hazelden, 1987.

Carnes, Patrick. *Out of the Shadows: Understanding Sexual Addiction*. Minneapolis, Minnesota: CompCare Publications, 1985.

Dobson, James. *Love Must Be Tough*. Waco, Texas: Word Books, 1986.

Forward, Susan & Torres, Joan. *Men Who Hate Women and the Women Who Love Them*. New York: Bantam Books, 1987.

Larsen, Earnie. *Stage II Relationships: Love Beyond Addiction*. New York: Harper & Row, 1987.

Marlin, Emily. *Hope: New Choices and Recovery Strategies for Adult Children of Alcoholics*. New York: Harper & Row, 1987.

Norwood, Robin. *Women Who Love Too Much*. New York: Simon & Schuster (Pocket Books), 1986.

Peck, M. Scott. *The Road Less Traveled*. New York: Simon & Schuster (Touchstone Books), 1978.

Seamands, David. *Healing for Damaged Emotions*. New York: Walker & Company, 1987.

The 12 Steps: A Way Out. Recovery Publications, 1987.

Wegscheider-Cruse, Sharon. *Another Chance: Hope and Health for the Alcoholic Family*. Palo Alto, California: Science & Behavior Books, 1981.

Wegscheider-Cruse, Sharon. *Choicemaking*. Pompano Beach, Florida: Health Communications, 1985.

Woititz, Janet G. *Adult Children of Alcoholics*. Pompano Beach, Florida: Health Communications, 1985.

APPENDIX B
Resource
Organizations

If you are a sex addict or a co-dependent, you will find it helpful to seek out one or more of the following resources and self-help organizations in your community that will aid you in your recovery from sex addiction, co-dependency, and the many other problems that often accompany them:

Sex Addiction and the Family

Sex Addicts Anonymous (SAA)
P.O. Box 3038
Minneapolis, Minnesota 55403
612-871-1520

Codependents of Sexual Addicts (COSA)
P.O. Box 14537
Minneapolis, Minnesota 55414

Sexaholics Anonymous (SA)
P.O. Box 300
Simi Valley, California 93062
818-704-9854

S-Anon
P.O. Box 5117
Sherman Oaks, California 91413
818-990-6910

Sex and Love Addicts Anonymous (SLAA)
Augustine Fellowship
P.O. Box 119
New Town Branch
Boston, Massachusetts 02258

National Association on Sex Addiction Problems
800-622-9494

Sexually Transmitted Diseases

VD National Hotline
1-800-227-8922
1-800-982-5883 (in California)

Herpes Resource Center
415-328-7710

American Social Health Association
260 Sheridan Avenue, Suite 307
Palo Alto, California 94306

National AIDS Hotline
800-342-AIDS (800-342-2437)

Child Abuse (physical and sexual)

Adults Molested as Children United (AMACU)
P.O. Box 952
San Jose, California 95108
408-280-5055

Incest Survivors Anonymous
P.O. Box 5613
Long Beach, California 90805
213-422-1632

Incest Survivors Resource Network, International, Inc.
P.O. Box 911
Hicksville, New York 11802
516-935-3031

National Child Abuse Hotline
Childhelp USA
P.O. Box 630
Hollywood, California 90028
800-4-A-CHILD (800-422-4453)

APPENDIX B

Parents Anonymous–National Office
6733 South Sepulveda Boulevard, Suite 270
Los Angeles, California 90045
800-421-0353

Survivors of Incest Gaining Health (SIGH)
20 West Adams, Suite 2015
Chicago, Illinois 60606

Victims Anonymous (VA)
9514-9 Roseda Boulevard, #607
Northridge, California 91324
818-993-1139

Victims of Incest Can Emerge Survivors (V.O.I.C.E.S.) in Action
P.O. Box 148309
Chicago, Illinois 60614
312-327-1500

Alcoholism and the Family

Alcoholics Anonymous World Services (AA)
P.O. Box 459, Grand Central Station
New York, New York 10163
212-686-1100

Alcoholics Anonymous–General Services Office (AA)
468 Park Avenue South
New York, New York 10016
212-686-1100

Al-Anon Family Group Headquarters
1372 Broadway (at 38th Street)
7th Floor
New York, New York 10018
800-245-4656
212-302-7240 (in New York area)

Alateen
Call Al-Anon (cited above).

National Association of Children of Alcoholics (NACOA)
31706 Coast Highway
South Laguna, California 92677
714-499-3889

Children of Alcoholics Foundation
200 Park Avenue
31st Floor
New York, New York 10166
212-949-1404

Drug Addiction

American Atheist Addiction Recovery Groups (AAARG)
2344 South Broadway
Denver, Colorado 80210
303-722-1525

Cocaine Anonymous–National Office
P.O. Box 1367
Culver City, California 90232
213-559-5833

Drugs Anonymous
Look for groups in your area.

Narcotics Anonymous–World Services Office (NA)
P.O. Box 9999
Van Nuys, California 91409
818-780-3951

Nar-Anon
Check local listings.

National Cocaine Abuse Hotline
800-COCAINE (800-262-2463)

National Institute of Drug Abuse (NIDA)
Parklawn Building, 5600 Fishers Lane
Rockville, Maryland 20852
Information Office: 301-443-6245
For Help: 800-662-HELP (800-662-4357)
For Employers: 800-843-4971
For Literature: National Clearinghouse for Information
                P.O. Box 416
                Kensington, Maryland 20895

Eating Disorders

American Anorexia/Bulimia Association, Inc.
133 Cedar Lane
Teaneck, New Jersey 07666
201-836-1800

Overeaters Anonymous–National Office
4025 Spencer Street, Suite 203
Torrance, California 90504
213-542-8363

O-Anon
Check local listings.

APPENDIX B

Compulsive Gambling

Gamblers Anonymous
National Council on Compulsive Gambling
444 West 56th Street, Room 3207S
New York, New York 10019
212-765-3833

Gam-Anon
Check local listings.

Compulsive Spending

Debtors Anonymous
Check local area for groups, or for Shopaholic groups.

Spender Menders
Check local listings.

If You Can't Find It Listed Here

National Self-Help Clearinghouse
33 West 42nd Street
New York, New York 10036
212-840-1259

Index

Index

problem solving and, 155
progressive disease of, 281
recovery and, 271–88
rituals and, 167–70
roles of, 173–78
romantic illusions of, 286
secrets of, 130, 163–65
self-esteem of, 130, 133, 145, 153,
    158–60, 177, 185–86
self-help groups for, 141, 214
self-talk and, 157–60
sense of responsibility in, 165
STDs and, 223
superficiality and, 166
traits of, 134
traumatic events and, 141–44
world view of, 274
See also Relationship, primary
Codependents of Sexual Addicts
    (COSA), 214, 317
Communication
with children, 302–5
about discovery of addiction, 140
group therapy and, 217
sexual, 265
Community help, recovery and, 221–
    22
Compassion, 255–56
Compulsions
absences from home and, 135
in addition to sex, 137
and adrenaline, 33
choice of, 31
co-dependents and, 153–54
denial and, 109
dependence on, 263
of family members, 70
HALT feelings and, 102
individual therapy and, 218
sex as, 17
stress and, 17, 71
triggers for, 30
See also Obsession; Ritual
Conditional love, 75
Conferences, 220
Confidantes, children as, 195, 301
Confrontation, family intervention
    and, 272–73

Consistency, trust and, 199
Control
binges and, 106–7
bullying and, 175
childhood learning of, 154
co-dependents, need for, 154
drive to, 100–106
family and, 92
illusion of, 97–114
intimacy and, 106
lack of, over family situations, 73
need for, 24–25, 44
rituals and, 35, 105
of sexual needs, 105–6
See also Willpower
Coping skills
of co-dependents, 154
role models and, 152
Core beliefs, 19
COSA (Codependents of Sexual Ad-
    dicts), 214, 317
Costs, of therapy, 223
Couples, therapy for, 157, 219–20
Crisis
denial and, 108
reaction to, 143, 152
Criticism
of children, 69, 74
scars from, 72
Culture
co-dependency and, 156
coping skills and, 152
denial and, 146–47
exhibitionism and, 58
pornography and, 50

Dating, 85–86, 265
Death, of parent, 21, 78
Debtors Anonymous, 215, 321
Deception. *See* Lying
Defense mechanisms. *See* Denial
Denial, 18, 37–38, 97–114, 140, 178
anger and, 108–9, 179–81
childhood traumas and, 79
co-dependents and, 142–46, 160–65
culture and, 146–47
family therapy and, 219

forms of, 108–9
learned from parents, 81
lying to others, 112–14
lying to self, 109–12
motives for, 146–47, 161
of need for change, 179
of risky behavior, 117–18
progression of, 111
refusing to accept responsibility
    and, 119
self-talk and, 110–11
Twelve Steps and, 238
Dependence
healthy, 263–64
Twelve Steps and, 237
Depression
co-dependents and, 184–86, 280
grieving process and, 280
hitting bottom and, 211
individual therapy and, 218
progressive, 120
repressed anger and, 163
self-talk and, 107
Despair, 36–37, 169–70
Detachment, co-dependents and, 272,
    282–88
Disappearances, as sign of addiction,
    135
Disease(s). *See* Sexually transmitted
    diseases (STDs)
Diseased thinking, 20–22
Diversion, 108
Divorce, 71
co-dependents and, 144
disbelief in, 292–93
trauma of, 78
Drug, sex as, 4, 15
Drug addiction, self-help groups for,
    320
Drugs Anonymous, 320

Eating disorders, self-help groups for,
    320
Efficiency lapses, as sign of addiction,
    135–36
Emotions
after addictive behavior, 36

children's expression of, 195–99,
    305–7
constructive expression of, 275–76
listening to, 255
need to escape, 18
Employment
efficiency lapses in, 135–36
hitting bottom and, 210
lying and, 113
risk to, 119
stress from, 260
Enabling behaviors
of co-dependents, 165–66
of family, 129–30
of therapists, 224
Encouragement, 69
Ethical beliefs
contradictions of, 45
Judeo-Christian, 155, 234
See also Morality
Euphoria. *See* High
Evil, sex as, 86–87
Exercise
recovery period and, 222
stress release and, 222
Exhibitionism, 3, 54, 56, 57–59
voyeurism and, 62

Family
addictive patterns in, 70, 90
alienation from, 91–92
child molesters and, 59
chronic illness in, 70, 72–73
as co-dependents, 5
of co-dependents, 133
control and, 92
as enablers, 129–30
living with sex addicts and, 120–47
obsessive/compulsive behavior in,
    70
recovery and, 289–311
religious, 46, 70, 86–87
risk to, 119
secrecy in, 91, 145–46, 190–95, 296
self-help groups for, 213–16, 317–18
self-talk and, 93
therapy for, 2, 219–20

trust and, 69, 93
unpredictability in, 77–78
unrealistic images of, 147
See also Children; Co-dependents;
    Parents
Family histories
    of co-dependents, 152–55
    questionnaire for, 90–95
    of sex addicts, 90–95, 137–38
Family intervention therapy, 272–73
Family-of-origin therapy, 219–20
Fantasies
    state of mind and, 22
    strength of, 33
    of superiority, 118–19
    time in thinking about, 31
Fears, of children, 92–93
Fetishism, 45, 51–52
Films. *See* Movies
Financial problems
    family and, 91
    hitting bottom and, 210
    as sign of addiction, 135–36
Fixation, on memories, 31–33
Flashers. *See* Exhibitionism
Forgiveness, recovery and, 257, 282
Friends
    affairs with, 49
    for co-dependents, 287
    network of, 222
Frotteurism. *See* Inappropriate touch
Functional families, 6

Gam-Anon, 215, 321
Gamblers Anonymous, 215, 321
Gambling, self-help groups for, 321
Gardnerella, 123–24
Genital warts (condyloma), 122–23
Gonorrhea, 123
Grieving process
    acceptance, 280–82
    anger and, 274–76
    bargaining, 277–79
    co-dependents and, 178–86, 272,
        273–74
    depression and, 178

stages of, 178
stress and, 259
Group. *See* Support group
Group therapy
    professional, 216–18
    Twelve Steps and, 227
Guilt
    bargaining and, 182
    after binge, 36
    of co-dependents, 185
    facing mistakes and, 244–245
    incest and, 95, 203
    lashing out from, 159
    learned in childhood, 88

HALT (Hungry, Angry, Lonely,
    Tired), 102
Hangovers, 14, 36–37, 106–7
Help, admission of need for, 232–36.
    See also Treatment
Hemophilus influenza, 124
Heroes
    children as, 198
    parents as, 196–97
Herpes, 122, 123
Herpes Resource Center, 318
High
    dependence on, 252, 262–67
    risking everything for, 116, 117–20
    search for, 30–37
Higher Power
    admission of wrongs and, 240–41
    letting go and, 236–38
    as part of daily life, 248–49
    reliance on, 232–36
    removal of shortcomings and, 243–
        44
    removing defects of character, 241–
        43
Hitting bottom
    co-dependents and, 209
    sex addicts and, 120–21, 209–11
Hobbies, 262
Honesty
    problems with, 29
    recovery and, 298
    teaching children, 308
    See also Denial

Martyrs
  co-dependents as, 155, 176–77
  sexual, 183–84
Martyrdom, and religion, 155–56
Mascot, children's role of, 198
Masochism. *See* Sadomasochism
Masters, William, 86
Masturbation, 45, 49–50
  control and, 105
  phone sex services and, 62
  pornography and, 62
Memories, fixation on, 31
Men, exhibitionism and, 58
Mental health professionals, 6. *See
  also* Therapy
Minimizing, 108
Mirroring, and addiction, 157–60
Mistakes, facing, 244–45
Monogamy, recovery and, 266–67
Mood swings
  of co-dependents, 162–63
  effect on children, 200, 296–97
  as symptom of addiction, 136
Moral inventory, 238–40
Morality
  cultural, 49
  learned, 84–89
  religion and, 67
  See also Ethical beliefs
Movies, sex education and, 50

NACOA (National Association of Chil-
  dren of Alcoholics), 319
Nar-Anon, 215, 320
Narcissism, 57
Narcotics Anonymous, 215, 320
National AIDS Hotline, 318
National Association of Children of
  Alcoholics (NACOA), 319
National Association on Sex Addiction
  Problems, 318
National Child Abuse Hotline, 318
National Cocaine Abuse Hotline, 320
National Institute of Drug Abuse
  (NIDA), 320
National Self-Help Clearinghouse, 321
Neglect, 20

NIDA (National Institute of Drug
  Abuse), 320
Nonspecific urethritis, 122

O-Anon, 215, 320
Obedience, conditional love for, 83
Objects
  attributing sexual meaning to, 22
  fetishism for, 51–52
Obscene phone calls, 54, 55–56
Obsession
  co-dependents and, 176–80
  defined, 3–4
  of family members, 70
  recovery as, 269
  religious, 70
  trigger for, 17
  See also Compulsions; Ritual
On Death and Dying (Kübler-Ross),
  178
One-night stands, 44–45, 48–49
Opportunities, turning negative conse-
  quences into, 120
Orgasm, buildup to, 36
Out of the Shadows (Carnes), 19, 220
Overeaters Anonymous, 215, 320

Pain
  avoidance of, 38
  co-dependents and, 167
  denial and, 108
Parent(s)
  abuse from, 79–80
  addictions of, 68, 90
  attention from, 74
  coping skills of, 18
  covering up, 91
  domineering, 75–76
  early death of, 21
  in family therapy, 219
  as heroes/villains, 196–197
  loss of, 78–79
  love from, 79
  negative feelings about, 196
  perfectionist, 72–73
  as role models, 71, 298

seductive, 83–84
separation from, 78–79
sexual relationship of, 85, 95
single, 310
treatment of each other, 68
uncommunicative, 69
See also Family
Parents Anonymous, 319
Parent surrogates, co-dependents as, 150
Partners. *See* Relationship, primary
Patience, recovery and, 265
Peeping. *See* Voyeurism
Pelvic inflammatory disease, 122
Perfectionism, 70, 72–73, 104, 254
Performance anxiety, 104–5
Phone sex services, 45, 50–51, 62
Physical evidence, of sex addiction, 139
Physical examination, 223
Pleasing behaviors, 74
Pornography, 45, 50, 62
Power
  need for, 44
  sex as, 3, 24–25
  See also Control
Powerlessness
  admission of, 231–32
  co-dependents and, 169–70
Pregnancy
  education about, 310
  sexually transmitted diseases and, 122, 123
Problem, admission of, 231–32
Problem solving, co-dependents and, 155
Professional help, combined with self-help, 212. *See also* Therapy
Projection, 108
Prostitution, 45, 52–53, 122
Public awareness, 5, 6
Punishment, emotional expression and, 69, 197. *See also* Sadomasochism

Rape, 54, 60–61
Rationalizations, 20, 108

insight and, 69
morality and, 49
Twelve Steps and, 238
Reaching out, need for, 207–28
Reading, treatment and, 220–21, 315–16
Reality
  interpretations of, 23
  turning lies into, 194
  war between ideals and, 144–47
  See also Denial
Recovery
  binges and, 269
  children and, 294–302
  co-dependents and, 271–88
  helping others and, 249–50
  lessons of, 297–301
  as lifelong process, 247
  monogamy and, 266–67
  as obsession, 269
  patience and, 265
  primary relationship and, 290–92
  realistic goals for, 287–88
  self-help groups for, 213–16
  sex education and, 264
  single parents and, 310
  slip-ups and, 267–70
  social skills and, 265, 269
  sticking with, 251–70
  talking to others and, 262
  time needed for, 212–13
  See also Treatment
Rejection, fear of, 29, 30, 78–79, 92
Relationship, primary
  addictive behaviors in, 47
  affairs and, 44
  crisis in, 38–39
  ground rules for, 277–79
  group therapy and, 2
  hitting bottom and, 210–11
  ideal, 43
  improving skills in, 261, 265
  need for change in, 179
  recovery and, 290–92
  separating from, 273, 277–78, 289–94
  sexual demands on, 138–39

SLAA (Sex and Love Addicts Anonymous), 213, 318
Slip-ups, dealing with, 247–48, 267–70
Small talk, proficiency in, 29
Sobriety
    concept of, 235–36
    defined, 266
    length of, 268
Social skills
    child molesters and, 59
    children and, 81–84, 297, 309
    group activities and, 221
    group therapy and, 217
    incest and, 60
    lack of, 18, 19, 26, 67
    recovery and, 265, 299
    stress and, 28–29
Sociopaths, sex crimes and, 55, 61
Spender Menders, 215
Spending, self-help groups for, 321
Sponsors, self-help groups and, 214
Spouses. See Relationship, primary
STDs. See Sexually transmitted diseases
Strep throat, 124
Stress
    catalyst of, 4, 27–30
    caused by relationships, 85–86
    changes in routine and, 100
    compulsions and, 27, 71
    coping with, 251, 259–62
    deception as cause of, 28
    domino effect of, 102–3
    from employment, 260
    exercise and, 262
    genital warts and, 123
    grief and, 259
    inability to cope with, 18
    inconsistent behavior and, 77
    lack of social skills and, 28–29
    physical symptoms of, 124
    recognizing, 259–60
    See also Anxiety
Superficial relationships, 82–83, 166
Support group
    choice of, 225–28
    friends as, 222
    as Higher Power, 234

self-help, 212
using Twelve Steps, 6
See also Group therapy
Survivors of Incest Gaining Health (SIGH), 216, 319
Syphillis, 123

Telephone. See Obscene phone calls; Phone sex services
Television shows, as pornography, 45
Therapist
    choice of, 141, 223–25
    discomfort with, 225
Therapy
    family, 2, 219–20
    group, 2, 216–18, 227
    individual, 218–19
    masturbation and, 49
    movies and, 50
    sex surrogates and, 52
Thinking
    diseased, 20–22
    repetitive. See Compulsions
Threat, as bargaining tool, 182
Time lapses, as sign of addiction, 135
Trance state, 32
Trauma, childhood, 68, 69, 78–79
Treatment
    bibliotherapy, 220–21, 315–16
    caring for body and, 222–23
    choice of, 223–27
    church involvement, 221–22
    community involvement, 221–22
    couples and, 38, 219–20
    family intervention and, 272–73
    family/sexual history and, 67
    forms of, 211–12
    opportunity to seek, 144
    reaching out and, 207–28
    separation from partner and, 293–94
    Twelve Steps and, 229–50
    workshops, 220
Treatment See also Recovery; Therapy
Trichomonas, 122, 123–24
Trust
    building, 258–59, 278

children and, 199–201, 297, 307–9
family and, 69, 93
fear of, 92
from others, 114
Higher Power and, 238
incest and, 203
individual therapy and, 219
lack of, in others, 79–80
Tuberculosis, 124
Twelve Steps, 213, 227, 229–50
The 12 Steps: A Way Out, 221

Unpredictable behavior, 77
Urethritis, nonspecific, 122

VA (Victims Anonymous), 319
Vaginitis, 123–24
Values
betrayal of, 53
of co-dependents, 152
VD National Hotline, 318
Venereal diseases. *See* Sexually trans-
mitted diseases
Victimizing behaviors, 54–61
Victimless behaviors, 44–45
Victims Anonymous (VA), 319

Viral gastric infections, 124
Visualization, 218
Voyeurism, 54, 56–57, 62

Weapon, sex as, 180–81
Wegscheider-Cruse, Sharon, *Another
Chance: Hope and Health for
the Alcoholic Family*, 198
Willpower
addiction and, 13, 16, 232
of co-dependents, 154
delusions of, 110
Higher Power and, 237
Women
double standard for, 49
masturbation and, 49
support groups for, 226
Workbooks, 221
Workshops, 220
World view
childhood lessons and, 67, 77–80
of co-dependents, 274
Writing exercises, 218
Wrongs, admission of, 240–41

Yeast infections, 124

p 69 – 90   Lessons ao children.
               Particular 80 – 81 – Silence